THE HANDBOOK OF ANCIENT WISDOM

The Handbook of Ancient Wisdom

Cassandra Eason

Sterling Publishing Co., Inc.
New York

Library of Congress
Cataloging-in-Publication Data Available

10 9 8 7 6 5 4 3 2 1

Published in 1997 by Sterling Publishing Company, Inc
387 Park Avenue South, New York, N.Y. 10016

Originally published in Great Britain in 1997
by Robinson Publishing Ltd

Distributed in Canada by Sterling Publishing
c/o Canadian Manda Group, One Atlantic Avenue, Suite 105
Toronto, Ontario, Canada M6K 3E7

Printed and bound in Great Britain

Sterling ISBN 0-8069-1353-3

CONTENTS

PREFACE

This book describes popular magical systems spanning 3,000 years and many cultures. It provides practical examples of 40 different forms of divination which have been adapted for use in the modern world so that readers can explore their own destinies, using easily obtained objects.

Although the systems come from places as far apart as Europe, the United States, China, Australia and Africa, there are remarkable similarities in both the symbols and the methods of divination. For popular magic is rooted in the lives of ordinary people, using animals, birds, flowers, trees and the natural world to focus their inherent powers.

Use Mayan Magic to discover whether your day sign is an alligator or flower and whether you are a natural home maker or an idealist in love and life. Create a Native American Medicine Wheel in your own back yard. Roll a ring in a form of Eskimo drum divination to discover whether the Moon Man in the Igloo or Nanook the Bear offers the strength and wisdom that you need right now. Try plant divination to see whether you should marry Tom or Harry, Joanne or Jane, or perhaps wait for an unknown stranger. Use Gypsy Love Cards to mend a quarrel in a relationship. Cast shells like the Maoris to uncover whether the power of Maui, the Inventor, or Ruau-Moki, God of Earthquakes, will best help you make necessary positive change in your life.

Each section of the book describes the land and times that shaped the magic, whether mountain or rocky shore, Celtic grove or African bush. Myths recall the ancient deities and heroes who controlled the moon, stars and sun, caused rain and thunder and created lands out of fire and ice or fished up islands from the bottom of the ocean. Learn how the Rainbow Snake of the Aborigines created the water-holes, rivers and trails of Australia as he pursued the All-Father's dog, Djaringin, in order to obtain the secrets of law, ritual and ceremony for the people.

The book recounts the magical festivals of ordinary people such as that of the Chinese Oxherd and the Weaving Maidens, held on the seventh day of the seventh moon. This ancient festival was based on a legend in which two star-crossed lovers, an oxherd and maiden, plunged into the fast-flowing waters that divided them and were drowned. The Gods transformed them into two stars, shining on either side of the Milky Way, and the lovers were reunited each year on the seventh night of the seventh moon.

Although the natives called on ancient deities for aid when they cast bone, shells and crystals to decide on future action, the wisdom behind all the magical systems in this book came from deep within the practitioners and from the natural energies of the earth. Those same powers of intuition and foreknowledge can help people in modern cities to focus on a goal, as once they did for dwellers on the open plains or in dense forest.

All you need to try out any of these magical forms are ordinary household items from any supermarket or hardware store or plants you may find growing in the garden or park. Nor do you need to go to exotic locations to discover your own natural magical powers. Your home or garden, an ancient site, a beach, a local beauty spot or even a piece of waste land can act as the backcloth, not for strange rites but for simple rituals and divination.

The natural energies of magic are common to all ages and cultures: water, fire, flowers, trees, herbs and candles. The divinatory forms do not involve expensive Tarot cards or dark ouija boards but tea leaves, light and shadow on water, dried herbs, fruits and candle wax. The moon and the sun and their time cycles have always guided the lives of people.

Although shamans, wise men and women, and in modern times, clairvoyants have interpreted and practised magic on behalf of others, men and women have always carried out personal magical rituals and divination on the old festivals. At Hallowe'en, young girls would sit in front of a mirror eating an apple, the old Celtic symbol of love, and their future love's vision would appear in the glass. Many families have a grandma who reads the tea leaves, relying not on a hundred set meanings but on her own timeless wisdom. Women at night, sitting by a sick child, in the state between sleep and waking, see visions of the past and sometimes of the future. We all have these powers, the same instincts that prompt you to telephone your mother only to find the phone is busy because at that same moment she is trying to contact you.

In the modern world, it is much harder to trust these instincts and to accept that we do not need a psychic expert to use magic. The issues for which we need magic – love, money and happiness – are those that concern people in all places and times and so the methods of bone casting, flower divination and the Celtic tree staves are equally relevant in New York, Tokyo, Auckland and Birmingham.

Within the book there may be one or two cultures or lands to which you are especially attracted. Perhaps in some past life you had a link to them. But if something feels wrong, change it. Magic is not set in stone but was created by people for people and unless it evolves, it loses its relevance. The forms of magic and ritual in this book express the spirit and not the letter of the magic, so that you can experience the rituals from the inside and not follow a 'psychic recipe book'.

Trust yourself and your instincts and remember that you are special. The real power lies in you, not the tools. You may never be incredibly rich and famous; on the other hand you might be. Magic cannot give you the pretty woman, the handsome film star or the pot of gold, at least not without paying a very high price. But it can help you to do whatever it is you really want. If you use magic to achieve your own unique destiny, whether to be an explorer, a top executive or to grow the biggest tomatoes in town, to say I love you or to say goodbye, then the book has achieved its purpose.

Cassandra Eason
March 1997

1

ABORIGINAL MAGIC

ITS ROOTS

The magic of the Aborigines was shaped by the size, geological and historical stability and emptiness of Australia. Before European settlers arrived 200 years ago, probably no more than 300,000 Aborigines inhabited Australia's 7,686,884 square kilometres (2,967,909 square miles), nine-tenths of which is flat. Originally they lived mainly in coastal areas, but were forced inland to the semi-arid or desert interior when European settlements were established.

The Aborigines arrived from South-East Asia in two migrations at least 40,000 years ago and lived in unique unbroken isolation and in harmony with nature. Because of their intimacy with natural forces, even something as seemingly insignificant as the blooming of a particular flower became a sign for them that certain animals were about to enter their territory. When yellow flowers bloomed on the wattle it indicated that the magpie geese would be flying along their annual route from swamp to swamp and so could be trapped.

To the Aborigines, magic was indivisible from this natural world and life was a continuing ritual. Their tradition is oral, carried through myth and ritual, and ideographic, depicted on cave walls and in natural rock formations. The rock engravings especially illustrated the Aboriginal belief in the Dream Time when their hero gods made human beings from plants, animals and natural features, that became their totem or guardian spirits.

Particularly important were the songs which had magical powers. In the following legends you will find examples of gods changing men by singing and people singing themselves to death.

Their myths say that when the two original Sky Beings (the Numbakulla) saw Inapwerta (embryo creatures with neither limbs nor senses), they took pity on them and transformed them into men. Even after humans were created, the Aborigines believed that they were still rooted in the matter from which they had been formed, animal, vegetable or mineral. Therefore the totem affirms what the Aborigine was and still is at the time of the Dreaming.

DREAMING

'Dreaming' is the root and purpose of Aboriginal life. It is a formless state from which various Sky Beings emerged to shape the land and bring culture, law, ritual and religion to the Aborigines. Where the concept of Dreaming differs from other idealized creation myths is that it is timeless and still exists in ritual and art at sacred sites. All Aborigines and not just their *mekigars* (magic men) contact the Other-World. By performing sacred rites the Aborigines made sure that rain and fine weather came and drought and disease did not afflict the people.

Each Aborigine believed he or she came from the Dreaming to take human form. Therefore, the Aboriginal lifestyle was bound to specific regions where tribal ancestors had established sacred places during the 'Dreamtime'. Members of each group believed that spirits existed in that territory until they were incarnated and after death would return to the same territory.

They believed that the spirit child enters the mother at conception, fully-formed. Conception follows a visit by the biological mother to a totem area or when a mother feels the baby move for the first time after a visit to a particular totem. A child who is conceived on a visit to distant relatives would feel alienated from his family until he was able to claim his totem.

The Creation

Many Aboriginal tribes subscribed to the belief in a Sky Father (Ungud was one of his names), a formless, invisible, all-embracing power that is manifest in every plant, rock, animal and human.

The Rainbow Snake Jarapiri was the *visible* manifest form of the formless First Cause or All-Father (his *invisible* counterpart was called Ekarlarwan). Jarapiri came, according to different myths, from the sea or underground and gave form to the land. He still slumbers in sacred waterholes, under waterfalls or in caves and re-enacts through the tribespeople various annual sacred rites for making rain.

The formation of the land was not planned but resulted from the conflicts of the Sky Beings. Jarapiri or Kunukban, the Rainbow Snake, came ashore, wanting to capture Ekarlarwan, the invisible First Cause, to obtain from him the secrets of the people, law, ritual and ceremony. Instead Jarapiri found himself chasing after Ekarlarwan's dog, Djaringin, who acted as a decoy. The dog made a winding track all over the country and the snake's slitherings and turnings as he followed created landmarks, rivers and waterholes.

Ekarlarwan was angry when the Rainbow Snake finally obtained the secrets and then travelled throughout the continent, teaching the law and creating landmarks as he went. So Ekarlarwan sent the Butcher Bird, Jolpol, after the Rainbow Snake. By trickery, Jolpol managed to push Jarapiri's head into the camp fire to try to burn him to death. However, the Storm Bird, Kurukura, who was Jarapiri's protector, attacked the Butcher Bird and drove him away.

Evil and suffering had now entered the world for the Storm Bird was burnt all over by the fire, Jolpol was partially burnt and the Rainbow Snake received burns to his head. Because of this, the Aborigines believe, the Storm Bird is black, the Butcher Bird is black and white and there is a black-headed python.

The Sacred Land

The land is regarded as a living entity. Uluru (Ayers Rock), the vast mass of red rock in the Northern Territory and the largest monolith in the world, is regarded as the navel of the Earth.

The Aborigines talk of *djang*, supernatural Earth wisdom. The rocks and stones are living expressions of the spirit world, the Dreaming, and embodiments of the Sky Heroes can be seen in the rock formations.

Myths account for the formation of sacred sites, such as Ayers Rock. Originally, say the legends, the plain was dominated by Uluru waterhole and Mutitjilda Spring, one of the sites where the Rainbow Snake was said to reside. Two groups of Sky Heroes lived there: the Mala or Hare Wallaby people on the sunny side and the Kunia or Carpet Snake people on the shady side. At the time of the Dreaming they lived in harmony.

Far to the west lived another tribe of Sky Heroes, the Windulka or Mulga Seed People. The Mulga Seed people asked the Bell Bird, Panpanpalana, to invite the Hare Wallaby and Carpet Snake people to attend the initiation of their youths. The Carpet Snake people agreed but the Hare Wallaby people were in the middle of their own initiation ceremonies and declined. The Hare Wallaby people also refused to give their much-prized eagle chick, Kedrun, to the Mulga Seed people who wanted its down for their body paintings.

The Carpet Snake people set off, camping the first night at Uluru waterhole. Here was the camp of the Sleepy Lizard Women and the Carpet Snake people decided to stay with them at Mutitjilda Springs rather than continue the journey. In spite of a further visitation by the Bell Bird, neither the Hare Wallaby nor the Carpet Snake people would come to the celebrations. The Mulga Seed people were angry and their clever men created a devil dingo dog, Kulpunia. This creature attacked the Hare Wallaby people and those who were not killed escaped to the south-west, never to return.

The Mulga Seed People then asked their friends the Liru or Poisonous Snake people to destroy the Carpet Snake people. After the ensuing battle at Mutitjilda Spring, the Carpet Snake people, dispirited by the death of their leader, Ungata, and the burning of the Sleepy Lizard Women's camp, 'sang' themselves to death, using the destructive form of the magical power of song.

The resounding of so much suffering in the earth caused Uluru, Ayers Rock, to rise from the ashes of the Sleepy Lizard Women's camp. Three rock holes, high on Uluru, depict where Ungata bled to death. The rainwater that fills them and flows down Uluru's slope into Wanambi's pool is regarded as Ungata's ever-flowing blood changed into the coppery water.

Natural Phenomena

Natural phenomena such as storms are not only portrayed in a mythological way, but hold in them and their seasonal renewal the continuing link between the world of spirit and the natural world, confirming the eternal presence of the time of Dreaming. For example, before the rainy season the Lightning Brothers are said to fight over a wife. Their struggles bring lightning and rain which is vital for the world's renewal. These Sky Heroes form the focus of great ceremonial rituals prior to the end of each dry season.

Rituals and Ceremonies

The Aborigines calculate time in sleeps and fix their festivals by the Moon. Most ceremonies are linked with the passage of human, animal and plant life, the fertility of the Earth, birth, initiation, marriage and death. Initiation at puberty is one of the most central ceremonies and the initiates recreate the journeys of the ancient heroes.

One of the most famous sacred rites is that of Kunapipi and the Rainbow Snake in northern Australia. The Rainbow Snake manifests itself in the ritual as the Aboriginal male and Kunapipi, the Earth Mother, is represented by the female Aborigine. They were considered necessary to bring the annual monsoons. Kunapipi is the symbol of the reproductive qualities of the Earth, the eternal replenisher of human, animal and plant life. Sometimes she appears as two sisters or as her own two daughters.

Totems

Totemism is the most important element in the man-nature relationship. All members of a tribe are said to be descendants of a particular kind of plant or animal from which the Ancestors formed humanity and which was recognized as their totem. All the various totems had sacred places which were also the home of the ancestral beings of that group.

When a woman who had married into a particular group became pregnant, the conception of her child was linked with a particular spirit from the local totem which had entered her body. The child was seen as a complete spiritual being on conception and therefore tied forever to that area.

Totemic ceremonies were held at the time of the year when the totem species bore fruit or gave birth to its young. These secret rituals were believed to ensure the continuity of the totem species. The secrets of these rites and the myths of the Dreamtime were passed on by the Tribal Elders to the younger generations at the totem initiation rites. Although a totem is usually an animal or plant, it can also be a natural phenomenon, such as water, the sun, cloud or wind.

Churingas

The churinga is a tangible symbol of the Dreamtime and especially symbolizes the totemic heritage. It is usually made of wood, a narrow oval in shape with the markings and symbols of the totem etched on it.

It is said to embody a man's totem. Carved by the paternal grandfather with wood cut from the totem area, it is presented upon initiation at puberty, along with the sacred laws and symbols of the totem. A stone churinga is also presented to the initiate representing the totemic Sky Hero.

The totemic centre of a community was the storehouse where the totem symbols were kept. The spirits of the whole group, including those of the ancestors, reside in these objects. Some had a hole near the end and could be attached to twine and whirled in the air. They were known as bullroarers.

Clever Men

Becoming a *mekigar, karadji* or clever man, involves complex and prolonged initiation rites whereby the initiate meets the All-Father by flying to the place of Dreaming and may undergo a ritual death in which his internal organs are replaced.

Crystal quartz used in the creation of a mekigar is especially sacred and is seen as frozen light, the embodiment of the Living Spirit. The All-Father's throne is said to be made of crystal quartz.

Ungud or Balame, the All-Father, uses the magical power of song to sing a piece of quartz crystal into the initiate's head, giving him X-ray vision. Balame removes a sacred fire from his own body and sings it into the initiate's body. Finally he sings into the initiate a thick sinew cord that enables the newly-created mekigar to ascend to the Dreaming at will.

In some tribes the initiation is carried out by other clever men who press crystals into the initiate's body beginning at his legs and working up to his head. Crystals are forced under the nails of one finger and his tongue is cut and a crystal inserted.

It is said that only clever men can ascend the aerial ladder to the spirit world, although all men can on their initiation into their totem learn the sacred language that enables them to conduct a dialogue with the Dreaming.

THE DIVINATION SYSTEM

The Aborigines did not foretell the future, certainly not a personal one. Rather they created it in their rites. So this divination system, adapted from their myths and beliefs, offers not a glimpse into the future but a chance to explore seemingly opposing forces to create harmony in our lives.

There are eight 'wild' stones', as the empowering quartz of the mekigar is called, representing 16 forms of the manifest spirit. The ninth stone is left blank for the All-Father.

You need either clear crystal quartz about the size of a large coin or round white pebbles.

Draw on both sides with red paint or permanent pen for the creature's Sunny Side of the Stone and black and yellow for the Shady. In this way you can distinguish between sunny and shady creatures who may have similar shape. The illustrations are given later together with the meanings of the stones. Do not worry about the standard of your artwork but try to capture the fluid, primitive but beautifully expressive feeling of Aboriginal art. However simple your artwork, try to capture what the legends mean to you.

The Sunny Aspect is listed first.

Stone 1: The Rainbow Snake is the alter-ego of the Black-Headed Python.

Stone 2: The Dingo dog is the alter-ego of the Black Dog.

Stone 3: The Hare Wallaby is the alter-ego of the Lizard Woman.
Stone 4: The Poisonous Snake is the alter-ego of the Carpet Snake.
Stone 5: The Black-throated Butcher Bird is the alter-ego of the Storm Bird.
Stone 6: The Lightning Brothers are the alter-ego of the Earth Sisters.
Stone 7: The Sacred Rock is the alter-ego of the Cave.
Stone 8: The Rain is the alter-ego of the Cloud.
Stone 9: The All-Father is left blank.

The Sunny Principle is transformed into the Shady Principle and back again in the constant cycle of day/night, creation/destruction. Neither is intrinsically good or bad, merely the two poles of existence as one becomes the other in the cycle of life. The Sunny or Active Force can sometimes be the destroyer and instrument of necessary change.

You can cast the stones in any open flat place. Sand or red earth are especially evocative of the landscape from which the tradition comes. Try to find an empty place, perhaps in the early morning, to capture the Aboriginal sense of vast isolation. Draw a circle sunwise or clockwise to represent the Dreaming. Place your stones in a plain bag of cloth or light-coloured straw. Think of a question and take a stone without looking. As you cast it, see the power of the quartz or white pebble connecting you with the land and the spiritual realms.

The first stone you pick and cast will tell you which guardian spirit can answer your present outer needs. See whether it falls on the sunny or shady side. If the sunny side is foremost, then you know that the guardian spirit offers the strength to initiate change, whether creative or destructive. The shady side offers the patience to wait, respond, mend and relieve what already exists rather than the force to push for new beginnings or endings.

Pick a second stone and cast it. This one shows the guardian who can answer your inner needs.

If both stones are sunny or shady, your inner and outer worlds are at one over this issue. If there is one of each, you need to modify your outer action to recognize your inner needs.

Read the meanings for each stone and see how they apply to your own life.

Stone One

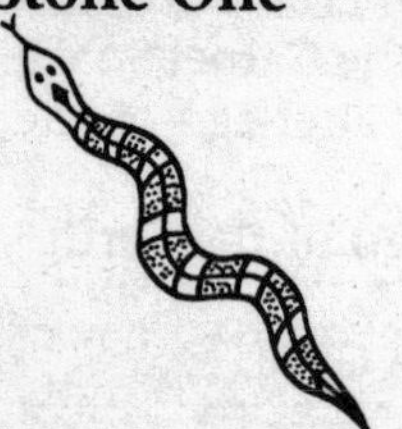

Sunny: The Rainbow Snake

The Rainbow Snake is the male creative force and represents action, energy, single-mindedness and pure ideas and idealism, untempered by thoughts of consequences. The Snake single-mindedly chased after the invisible All-Father's dog to obtain the secrets of culture for the Aborigines and created the waterholes by accident.

Shady: The Black-headed Python

The Black-headed Python represents the Rainbow Snake after he was held in the fire by the Butcher Bird. He represents ideas modified by reality. He is aware of the need for compromise, to recognize the consequences of action and that there can be a price for change.

Stone Two

Sunny: The Dingo Dog

Maletji or dingo dogs were said to have swum across the Indian Ocean bringing knowledge of Aboriginal law and customs as well as creating trails and waterholes used by the Aborigines in their nomadic journeys. The Dingo Dog is the law-giver and keeper, representing the beneficial effects of following the conventional path and conventional wisdom, of staying with the pack rather than going it alone. He is the instigator of lawful action.

Shady: The Black Dog

The Black Dog, Kulpunya, was the instrument of the Mulga Seed people, created by the mekigars to avenge the indifference of the Hare Wallaby people. He therefore represents our being driven along a path we may not have chosen. This is not bad in itself but bears the message that if we go along with the rules and norms of others, we may cause destruction not of our choosing or find ourselves at enmity with others for quarrels we did not begin.

Stone 3

Sunny: The Hare-Wallaby

This symbolizes the innocence of the first race, the untried untested happiness that represents human love and childhood. The active force of the Hare Wallaby lies in using that positivity for the good of others, in giving freely of one's talents and possessions and not keeping happiness for oneself. The Hare Wallaby tribe refused to share Kedrun, the eagle chick, with the Mulga Seed people who needed it and so were destroyed.

Shady: The Sleepy Lizard Woman

The Lizard Woman is the temptress who diverted the Carpet Snake people from their mission. She represents relationships, the love that comes from experience and the sacrifices that are necessary in demanding and receiving love. The Lizard Woman says that sometimes it is important to accept limitations and pain as the price for not being alone.

Stone 4

Sunny: The Carpet Snake

The Carpet Snake people, though in myth living on the Shady side of Uluru, nevertheless fought courageously against the Poisonous Snake people and at the end, when their leader Ungata was killed, sang themselves to death rather than live without their leader and the women they loved. The Carpet Snake represents sacrifice, the need to stand for beliefs and, if necessary, suffer for them. It represents loyalty and altruism.

Shady: The Poisonous Snake

The Poisonous Snake, the Liru people, represents the lesson that we have to shed the redundant to move on, just as a snake sheds its useless skin. They were acting as emissaries for their wronged friends, the Mulga Seed people, when they attacked the Carpet Snake people and as a result of the battle, Ayers Rock was formed and the early innocent existence of the Carpet Snake people was tempered by the venom necessary for a complete world of light and darkness.

Stone 5

Sunny: The Black-throated Butcher Bird
The Black-throated Butcher Bird represents achievement through words. He tricked the Rainbow Snake to try to preserve the secret knowledge of the All-Father for his master. Sometimes progress has to be made by a roundabout method, seeking a way round obstacles and at others being ruthless and suffering achieves what seems the right end.

Shady: The Black Cuckoo or Storm Bird
The Storm Bird is the helper who saved the Rainbow Snake from the fire. He represents a different kind of sacrifice, an endurance and willingness to put others first whether in a single act of courage or a longer commitment. He symbolizes friendship and altruism in helping out those in need.

Stone 6

Sunny: The Lightning Brothers
The Lightning Brothers, Jagbagjula and Jabarringa, continue to fight over one of their wives to create storms and rains. They represent anger and resentment as a positive force of change and renewal, a challenge to the status quo and a determination to persist even when results are slow to come.

Shady: The Earth Sisters
The Waugeluk sisters emerged from the sea with their mother, Kunapipi, at the time of Dreaming. They then travelled north, carrying the knowledge of ritual and fertility with them. They were eaten by the Rainbow Snake and henceforward he spoke with their voice. They represent the inner voice of instinct and intuition that is often swallowed up by logic. It is important to be guided by this inner wisdom, especially when it urges caution.

Stone 7

Sunny: The Sacred Rock
The Sacred Rock is the upward connection with the Spirit. Rocky outcrops were regarded as manifestations of the Sky Heroes and often their forms are etched in the rock. For example, three huge gashes in the eastern rock face of Uluru are said to be those inflicted by Ungarta on Kulikitjeri, leader of the Poisonous Snake people. Therefore rocks symbolized the higher spiritual self, expressed in the real world but nevertheless aspiring to loftier ambitions, above daily concerns.

Shady: The Cave
The Cave is associated with the womb of Kunapipi, the Earth Mother. Caves often contain many fine paintings of the Sky Heroes, such as the Great Snake at Ngama that was believed to have been formed by the Great Snake himself entering the cave wall. Such sites have sacred guardians and represent the secret inner world of dreams where even the active principle, such as the Snake, still resides. It represents inner stillness and harmony, an acceptance of self and of dreams and inner wisdom.

Stone 8

Sunny: The Rain
The Rain is the ultimate life-giving power that comes from the ultimate union between the male and female, Snake and Earth Mother. It is a seasonal concept, offering assurance that if the right time is chosen and a person is prepared to merge totally with natural forces, then success is promised.

Shady: The Cloud
The cloud talks of waiting for this right moment, of accepting that action is dependent upon circumstance. The cloud, the womb of the rain, says that patience and being prepared for change are sometimes the only options.

Stone 9

The All-Father
This stone is left blank as it is the stone of pure spirit, of your destiny, the rest of your life that stretches before you. When the blank crystal

appears, the question, or perhaps the question that remains unvoiced, is central to your essential self. Take time; do not attempt to answer the question now.

If it appears as the second stone in your reading, let the first stone act as a guide and let the wisdom of the All-Father unfold gradually. If the blank stone is first to appear, do not cast a second but try to spend time alone in a quiet, open space and let what you see, hear and feel guide you. Sleep with the blank stone under your pillow and the answer will come in your dreams.

A SAMPLE WILD STONE READING

Tom, who is in his thirties, needed to decide whether to move a vast distance for career promotion or to stay in the area where he had lived since childhood, which he loved deeply.

Tom's first stone was the Hare Wallaby, representing innocent untried happiness. The message of the stone was that to preserve happiness, Tom must adopt the sunny principle and move forward. The Hare Wallaby people were destroyed because they refused to go into the world.

The second stone was the Dingo Dog, the law-bringer who swam across the Indian Ocean with the laws necessary for the Aborigines to survive. A second sunny stone said that inwardly there was a whole, powerful, authoritative, seeking side that Tom had never developed. It was as if the adult potential was still waiting.

Tom took the job and, although lonely at first, made a successful and happy life, returning to his old home for holidays and bringing his new wife.

CRYSTAL MAGIC

Initiates of the mekigars or clever men were able to visit the Dreaming by growing feathers from the sacred water of liquified crystal poured on them by the All-Father. Mekigars could ascend the aerial cord to the Other World at will.

Using clear quartz crystals and visualization, it is possible to travel astrally beyond our conscious world. Twenty-four hours before you hope to travel astrally, place your crystal in water and leave it through a sun and moon cycle. You can sprinkle this water over your arms to let your soft feathery unseen wings grow.

Like the mekigar initiates, place a clear quartz crystal on your feet to allow them to loosen their hold on the earth. Put the crystal next to your heart where the All-Father placed the sacred flame, and feel the crystal stirring the desire to move beyond the immediate. Let your crystal touch your tongue to allow your inner voice to speak. Finally place it on your brow just above and between your eyes. This is regarded as the seat of the third eye. Let its clear vision take you to unseen realms.

Lie quietly outside under the stars if it is warm or on a bed or couch where you can see the sky. The full moon is a potent period for astral travel. Hold your crystal in your clasped hands and close your eyes. See the crystal in your mind's eye growing larger and larger until you are within it and its rainbow brilliance fills every fibre of your being. See a door in one corner and walk through it into the night, spread your white wings and fly wherever you will.

When you wish to come home, head for the dawn and you will see the scarlet light on the door back into the crystal. Let the crystal enclose you in its soft benign clouds and sleep until the sun wakes you.

2

AIR MAGIC

GODS IN THE SKY

From earliest times the sky has been the home of the deities. The Greek Pantheon, led by Zeus, passed their days on Mount Olympus. Sacred offerings and prayers were sent heavenwards in many traditions and the flames of the sacred fires rose upwards, carrying the essence of the sacrifice or tribute to the waiting sky gods (see also *Fire Magic*, page 211). The All-Father Odin in the Norse tradition lived in Asgard, the land near the top of Yggdrasil, the World Tree.

In China, the sky represented pure yang, the great dragon in the sky. In oriental tradition coloured streamers and kites were released bearing entreaties skywards (see also *Chinese Magic*, page 63).

Air or sky magic is therefore directed towards success, achievement in the external world, personal endeavours and ambition, the acquisition of wisdom and all matters concerned with career, the law and justice. It is also the magic of personal joy and talks not only of success in the world's terms, but of what makes you happy.

Sky Myths

The Sky Father was originally the supreme force of nature, espoused to the Earth Mother. Together they brought into being the natural world and its inhabitants. For example, in Maori myth, Rangi the Sky Father and Papa the Earth Mother were locked in perpetual embrace. One of their sons, Tane-Mahuta, God of the Forests, became a tree and forced the sky upwards. He clothed his father with Kohu the God of Mist, Ika-Roa, the Milky Way and the shining stars. Maoris believe they are descended directly from Rani and Papa (see *Maori Magic*, page 300).

Occasionally the sky is seen as a mother. In Ancient Egyptian lore, the goddess Nut formed the vault of the heavens by arching her body over the earth. She rested the weight on her hands and feet over the recumbent body of her husband, Seb, who represented the Earth. Her arms and legs formed the four pillars of the sky and over her body were scattered the countless constellations of stars. Nut is called 'Lady of Heaven' and was always painted blue in Egyptian art and sculpture.

Gradually the Sky Father took on the role of Creator God, Father of All and so became a warlike figure who presided over justice and wisdom. Jupiter was the supreme deity of the Romans and controlled the affairs of men, making known his future intent through heavenly signs and omens.

Sylphs

Sylphs are beautiful female elemental air spirits said to protect young innocent maidens. They are the souls of chaste maidens who in life flirted but never gave their favours. Sometimes they appear as butterflies, especially around fragrant white flowers. They inhabit hilltops and open plains and can be seen in the rising mist.

Zephyrs

These guardians of the winds are named after Zephyrus, the West Wind in Greek mythology, son of Astraeus and Aurora, Goddess of the Dawn. Zephyrus was the lover of Flora, Goddess of Flowers, and so blew gently, bringing rain that her flowers might grow. Zephyrs are often pictured blowing trumpets from which the winds emanated.

RAISING THE WIND

Raising the wind is a very old folk version of Air Magic, originally used when winds were vital for sailing and also for turning windmills to grind corn and wheat. One belief was that if a sailor threw a coin he found on deck towards the wind, it would buy a fair wind for the day.

Witches were reputed to sell winds in the form of a knotted cord to sailors. The first knot was untied for a light breeze, the second for a strong wind and the third for a gale. When the King of Sweden was fighting the Danes in 1563, he took four witches to sea with him to manipulate the weather in his favour. Swedish seafarers also built stone labyrinths on the shore, believing that these would ensure fair winds to aid their voyages. If the winds died down during their journey, seafarers would row to the nearest island or rocky outcrop and create a new labyrinth.

In other parts of the Northern world, offerings of milk, money, ale and coins were made in dobbie stones (naturally hollowed stones) to give a good breeze to turn the mill or offer local sailors a swift passage.

Magical power over the winds was a double-edged sword. It was popularly feared that angry witches might whistle up storms, hence the rhyme:

A whistling woman and a crowing hen
Are neither good for God nor men.

In modern magic, raising winds through knot tying provides a powerful symbolic focus for releasing magical energies. Knots are no longer regarded as the province of witches, but the power of the wind can clear stagnation in your life, blow you in a new direction or carry you forward to success.

A HILLTOP KNOT RITUAL

Use an old, brightly coloured scarf or ribbon with happy associations and made of material sufficiently light to catch the breeze. On a windy day, take the scarf to the top of a hill or an open plain and, as you walk, tie a large loose knot in the centre to represent a problem that must be resolved or an obstacle that must be surmounted to put you on the road to success or happiness. As you tie the knot, visualize power rising through your body from earth and sky, like glorious rainbow liquids rising in a crystal phial. When you reach the top of the hill or the centre of the plain where the wind is strongest, hold your scarf by one end and feel the power tugging to escape.

Turn round clockwise nine times, holding the scarf and saying,

Blow free,
Blow me,
Wind untie,
Knot fly,
Fly free.

On the ninth chanting, untie your knot and run fast, letting the scarf or ribbon fly away. Recite again and again, *The power is free*, until your scarf is carried far away on the breeze. The scarf may be found by someone, perhaps a child to whom it will also bring happiness.

Open your arms and feel the power of the wind, carrying you like the scarf above all the petty restrictions and problems that are holding you back. Run as you did when a child and feel again the possibilities of the open sky as you, too, tug free from the cords. You can now fly free anywhere you wish.

BALLOON MAGIC

The principle behind balloon magic is to free your wishes or decisions from their earthly bounds in a magical rush of energy. Of course, you still have to put in the hard work as well, but balloon magic provides the impetus if you have any doubts and inertia.

You can use a string of coloured balloons tied together or a single silver helium-filled balloon, decorated with a symbol of your need or wish; for example hearts for love, flowers for fertility, boats or planes for travel, golden scales or keys for a court case or a matter of justice, toys for children and family concerns and golden circles for money. There are a vast range of decorated helium balloons on sale, so you can be very creative in your choice of wishes. Walking along with a silver helium balloon or a bunch of balloons tugging at the string is a joyful experience, no matter how old you are.

Take your balloons to an open space or a hillside on a windy day. Write on a long piece of paper your secret dream or need. Tie this to the balloon strings. Wait for a strong gust of wind and let your balloons fly free. If your balloons fly directly upwards, then your wish should be fulfilled within a short time. If they fly diagonally for a while before ascending, you know that you may need to put some extra effort into the venture and be patient (see also *Bird Magic*, page 35).

SKY DIVINATION

This form of divination traditionally involves studying cloud formations and rising morning mists for visions. In Maori myth, it was said that morning mists were caused by the tears of the parted Rani and Papa rising from the earth and falling from heaven as rain.

One of the earliest forms of Air Scrying (looking for recognizable images) involved interpreting pictures made by the grey and white trails of mist as the early sun suddenly broke through. Lakes have always evoked mysterious scenes when viewed through the early morning haar, as mist is called in Scotland, revealing drowned villages whose bells can dimly be heard and ghostly hands rising from the waters.

Dozmary pool on Bodmin Moor in Cornwall, England is just one of the locations where Excalibur, King Arthur's Sword, is said to be held by the Lady of the Lake. It is said that the sword and outstretched arm can be seen momentarily as the mists part. Glastonbury is another suggested location for the mythical Isle of Avalon in whose waters the dying Arthur cast his sword.

Mist magic is a much gentler form of Sky Magic than knot rituals or balloon magic and is potent in divining personal happiness, especially where happiness lies in finding or acknowledging love. You may be by a lake or riverside when mists rise and see your visions of future joy arise quite spontaneously. However, you can also use this old form of magic at home.

Steam and Mirror Divination

Use a kettle or a hot tap to steam up a mirror. If you carry out the divination in your bathroom or washroom, the whole atmosphere of swirling mist will create images beyond as well as in the mirror.

Use soft lighting or early morning natural light and add a few drops of a heady fragrant oil such as jasmine or ylang-ylang to the bath water or a bowl in the kitchen if you are using a kettle. Half-close your eyes and breathe in the scent of exotic flowers. Slowly, as the mist clears, touch the wisps of steam with your fingers to create moving forms that change quite slowly into other shapes before evaporating. If you are feeling emotionally or physically exhausted or are worried that your efforts are getting nowhere, use eucalyptus oil for stimulating visions and renewed energies.

MARILYN'S STEAM DIVINATION

Marilyn, a struggling actress, lives in the middle of a city in cramped accommodation. Her older sister, whose husband is very wealthy, has invited her to move in with them at their lakeside home in Canada and help with the children. However, Marilyn does not get on with her sister who is ten years older. The children are very boisterous and used to having their own way. But money is tight and Marilyn hates the crowded city streets, especially in summer.

Marilyn heats the kettle in her tiny kitchen and soon the mirror on the wall is misted over. She uses rose oil and a wonderful fragrance of rose gardens floods her senses. As the mirror begins to clear she sees a stage by a lake that slowly changes into a train that winds through pine forests.

At first, her vision does not make sense, except that Marilyn feels sudden confidence in her present lifestyle. She goes out to buy some roses, a wild extravagance, and on the way stops impulsively to buy a theatrical magazine that she had given up ordering because of her straitened finances. As she sits at the table with the rose fragrance uplifting her, she sees an advertisement in the magazine for a job as a stage assistant with a travelling theatre group who take Shakespeare to remote parts of Canada and the United States, performing in the open air. She applies for the job and gets it with a promise of walk-on parts at first and perhaps chances for bigger roles if she does well. The first location is a lakeside resort. The second, after a journey on a train through dense pine forests, is in a huge natural park, the stage surrounded by wild rose bushes.

Coincidence? Magic? Perhaps it was a combination of both. Trusting psychic insights can open many doors in the real world.

Cloud Divination

This was used by the Druids whose magic relied very heavily on intuitive processes (see *Celtic Magic*, page 50). Look for large single dark clouds in a clear sky or a dense cumulus cloud formation at sunrise or sunset when the clouds are touched with gold. My son Jack and his sister Miranda created a whole mythology about an iceman who lived in the clouds.

The key to cloud divination is not to try to identify and name specific pictures in the sky, but let the shapes, whether a single image or a series, suggest an idea or picture quite spontaneously to you. Others will see the same cloud entirely differently because we all have a different world view.

AN EXAMPLE OF CLOUD DIVINATION

Peter and Suzy had been friends for years. They were standing in Suzy's garden one evening when a long, dark cloud appeared in an otherwise blue sky. Peter saw it as a dragon with a fiery tail, Suzy as a long peninsula extending into the sea. The cloud offered both of them an answer to questions they had separately been turning over in their minds, while talking of other things.

Peter was unhappy at work because of a bullying boss who delighted in making him the target of sarcastic remarks. As Peter was quiet and peace-loving, he had become depressed and his work was suffering. He identified the dragon at once, not as his boss, but as his own fear of conflict that so many times had left him suffering in silence. The next time his boss criticized him unfairly, to everyone's amazement, he retaliated firmly but politely, pointing out a few of the mistakes that his superior had made. Peter continued to respond firmly, but not with hostility, to his boss, gently drawing to light errors and miscalculations that previously he would have corrected without comment. His boss became more cautious, especially as he discovered that the rest of the workers in the office supported Peter. Gradually Peter became more confident, the bullying ceased and within a few months he was promoted.

Suzy's problem was less clear cut. Her peninsula in the clouds represented her own feelings of isolation from her world and her increasing dissatisfaction with the frantic social life she was pursuing. She decided that at heart she was a loner, bought a house miles from anywhere and after work she began to explore her talents as a writer.

Cloud divination is more fragile than many forms of air magic, but it can address profound issues and provoke major life-changes with its slow-moving images that can penetrate a very deep level of unconscious wisdom, perhaps the knowledge accumulated by the human race.

AIR FRAGRANCES

Fragrances can awaken deep magical impulses within us. Burning oils in a special burner or lighting incense cones or sticks provides easy access to magical visions. Whether you meditate or just enjoy sitting quietly while your favourite incense or oil releases its fragrance into the air, the spontaneous impressions can offer insight beyond visual or aural senses.

Incense and the Planets

Certain scents are linked with the properties of different planets and these can evoke the intuitive energies symbolized by them. Each incense or oil is associated with a different day of the week. If you light your oil burner or incense cone or warm the oil on a saucer over a radiator on the appropriate day of the week, you can tap into a subtle but powerful energy source, whether for energy, wisdom or healing.

A second oil is listed below, and you can add a few drops of this to the first oil if you wish. If you need the strength of a particular planet on another day of the week – for example, energy for a job interview or to meet a deadline – you could burn a frankincense stick or oil to give you a sudden burst of energy or inspiration.

Sunday, Day of the Sun: Frankincense the Energizer

Burn frankincense, oil and incense of the Sun, for visions of golden, sunny days and exotic places, of deserts and nomads with rich tents, fire and summer festivals.

Frankincense oil comes from Africa and the Middle East and was highly prized in ancient civilizations, being given by one of the wise men to the infant Jesus. It can be mixed with chamomile, another oil of the Sun.

Monday, Day of the Moon: Jasmine the Dreamer

Burn jasmine, oil and incense of the moon, for visions of fairy-tale castles in the moonlight, unicorns and fairy folk.

Jasmine oil is one of the most expensive to produce, taking many hundreds of flowers, which must be picked by night when they give up their fragrance, to make even a tiny quantity of oil. It comes from India and Mediterranean countries and can be mixed with lemon oil, another fragrance of the Moon.

Tuesday, Day of Mars: Pine the Invigorator

Burn a pine oil or incense, the fragrance of Mars, the planet of courage, for visions of forests, mountains and scenes of nature at its most turbulent and magnificent. There may be tall trees blown by the wind or winter celebrations with pines decorated with candles.

Pine oil was used by the Ancient Greeks and Romans to help with breathing problems and today is produced commercially in the parts of the United States and Northern Europe where pine forests abound. Mix it with just one or two drops of Australian eucalyptus, another life-enhancing fragrance of Mars.

Wednesday, Day of Mercury: Lavender the Uplifter

Burn lavender, the oil and incense of Mercury, the planet of communication, for far-off sounds of music and glimpses of distant exotic places with fragrant spices, silks and brilliant domes touched with gold.

Lavender oil was used by the Ancient Romans for soothing mind and body. Although it was originally produced in Mediterranean regions, it is now available almost everywhere in the world. Mix lavender with geranium, another oil of Mercury.

Thursday, Day of Jupiter: Sandalwood the Wise Healer

Burn sandalwood, the oil and incense of the Jupiter, for scenes of ornamental temples, shrines, processions, pageants and slow rituals that go back to the beginning of time. There may also be old, wise souls to offer advice.

Sandalwood oil comes from India, where the fragrant wood is used in carvings, and was also used as an incense by the Ancient Egyptians and Chinese. The oil can also be mixed with neroli, another oil of Jupiter.

Friday, Day of Venus: Rose the Peacemaker
Burn rose, the oil and incense of Venus, for visions of present and future lovers, scenes of passion and also pictures of family scenes and tender romance.

Rose oils have been associated with love in all cultures. The oil mainly comes from flowers grown in India, China, Morocco and France. Mix rose with ylang-ylang, another oil of Venus.

Saturday, Day of Saturn: Cypress the Assimilator
Burn cypress, the oil and incense of Saturn, the planet of restriction, for small cameos of work and home life, tool-shops, factories, schools and houses full of industry, wash day, cooking and cleaning.

Cypress oils were a symbol of immortality, being used by the Ancient Egyptians for preserving the body in the tomb. Mix cypress with patchouli from the Far East, another oil of Saturn.

Using Oils

Oils need a great deal of care in combining and diluting when used for massage or inhalation. You can use the first or second oil separately. The magical mixtures listed above are for a standard oil burner, warmed by a candle or in a dish heated over a radiator. The oil combinations listed appeal to me, but add the second oil drop by drop until you get the right fragrance for you. If you do not like a suggested combination, add another oil that harmonizes with your oil of the day. Rose and lavender will mix with any other essential oils. Citrus oils, such as orange and lemon, do not mix well. Chamomile, frankincense, geranium, jasmine, neroli, rose, sandalwood and ylang-ylang, tend to be good-tempered mixers.

If you are going to use any oil for inhalation or massage, consult an aromatherapy expert for advice. Frankincense, for example, can be an irritant to the skin and some oils should not be used by pregnant women or people with specific medical conditions.

You can use sandalwood, lavender and pine during the daytime, especially on a sunny day when sunbeams dance on the walls. I find rose, jasmine and cypress more effective at night.

Your Astrological Incense and Oils

You can burn these during your Sun Sign month or whenever you need to summon your personal strength or remind yourself of your unique talents.

Aries (21 March–20 April): cedarwood or chamomile
Taurus (21 April–21 May): patchouli or rose
Gemini (22 May–21 June): lavender or lemongrass
Cancer (22 June–22 July): eucalyptus or jasmine
Leo (23 July–23 August): frankincense or cinnamon
Virgo (24 August–22 September): rosemary or mimosa
Libra (23 September–23 October): geranium or spearmint
Scorpio (24 October–22 November): myrrh or ginger
Sagittarius (23 November–21 December): sandalwood or orange
Capricorn (22 December–20 January): cypress or neroli
Aquarius (21 January–18 February): lemon or juniper
Pisces (19 February–March 20): rosemary or pine

ANIMAL MAGIC

BRINGING OUT THE ANIMAL IN YOU

It is common enough to say of someone that he has the heart of a lion or she has the cunning of a fox, but for Native American Indians and Australian Aborigines this is more than just a figure of speech. They believe that we all have kinship with certain animals who can endow us with their qualities (see also *Aboriginal Magic*, (page 1, and *Native North American Magic*, page 348).

Modern men and women, too, can draw upon the universal qualities of various creatures, using them as a 'totem' to help steer a path through life. For example, if you are seeking independence, you may sense affinity with the cat. You may find that if you are faced with a difficult dilemma and conflicting opinions, the elephant can offer wisdom and stability. The tiger can offer strength to endure difficulties and the knowledge that, given courage, the future can be changed for the better.

Each of the animals listed here has a magical quality that by association can be harnessed in times of need. You might like to choose one of these animals, whether or not it is native to your land, as a symbol of a particular quality that would be helpful at a certain point in your life. Choose a symbol or picture of the animal or visit it in an animal park.

Bears: Protection and Sacrifice

Use the bear when you need to protect those you love or temporarily give up a pleasure for long-term gain.

Bear shrines and bear skulls and bones were buried with human remains by Neanderthal Man. In Ancient Greece and Rome, bears were sacred to the moon goddesses Artemis and Diana. In the cult of Artemis, maidens in yellow robes imitated bears at the festival of Brauronia. The expression 'licked into shape', comes from the ancient belief that bears were born without form and were licked into shape by their mothers.

Traditionally bears are companions of dwarfs and guard their treasure, although as in the fairy story *Snow White and Rose Red,* the bear was actually an enchanted prince.

Bees: Clear Communication

Use the bee when it is important to convey your views or feelings or overcome prejudice in others.

Bees, like birds, are traditionally messengers of the gods. If you have a bee hive, you should keep the bees informed of the family news. For example, if someone in the family gives birth, marries or dies, you are supposed to tell the local bees or they will stop making honey. It is said that if you listen outside a bee hive on Christmas Eve, you will hear the bees humming the twenty-third Psalm (see also *Christmas Magic*, page 75).

If a bee flies into your house, a stranger will call before nightfall and if it flies straight out again, luck will follow. Therefore, it is as well to keep some flowers rich in pollen indoors so that bees will circle them before leaving.

Fishermen believe that if a bee is flying in the same direction as their boat it will mean a good catch.

Cats: Independence

Use the cat when you need to assert your own identity and to escape from petty restrictions or possessiveness in others.

Cats are the most magical of animals, although traditions vary as to whether they are fortunate or unfortunate omens. They were worshipped in Ancient Egypt and were sacred to Bast, the cat-headed goddess and protector of pregnant women. In Ancient Rome, the cat was the symbol of freedom and the Goddess of Liberty was depicted with a cat at her feet.

Black cats are said to be the familiar spirits of witches. This association may have come about because Freyja, the Norse fertility goddess, had a chariot pulled by black cats. When Christianity reached Scandinavia in the eleventh century, the female pagan deities were regarded as witches and the cats became their familiars. It was said that after seven years a cat became a witch.

Black cats are usually regarded as lucky in Britain, especially if seen at weddings or seen walking towards you. In North America, it is considered a misfortune should one cross your path. However, the Japanese believe that a black cat crossing your path will bring good fortune.

Sailors like black cats and their wives keep them to ensure that their husbands return home safely. It is said that if you keep a black cat, you'll never lack for lovers. A restless cat means a storm is coming.

Cows: Caring for Others

Use the cow for patience when family responsibilities seem very heavy or you are concerned with the health of another.

The cow is a sacred creature to the Hindus and milk is offered to the gods in temples to represent both the nourishing Earth Mother and the Lunar Goddess. Hathor, the Ancient Egyptian Goddess of Women and Love, was represented as a cow and later as a goddess with the head of a cow, her horns being the crescent moon. The link between the cow and the moon lies in the link between the moon and fertility and the Earth Mother and fertility. The moon was also associated with the weather, growth and fruitfulness. In Scandinavian legend, Audumla the Cow sprang from the melting ice at the Creation and licked a block of salt to create the first Hero God, Buri. The Zulus believe that the human race was belched up by a cow.

There are numerous legends of the properties of the milk of magical cows, not least the famous Dun Cow in Shropshire, England. Said to belong to a giant, she gladly gave milk to all who asked. But one day a greedy woman filled her pail and then demanded that the cow give milk for her sieve as well. Enraged by such ingratitude, the Dun Cow ran amok until she reached nearby Dunsmore Heath where she was killed by Guy of Warwick. An object said to be her giant horn can be seen at Warwick Castle today.

Dogs: Fidelity and Friendship

Use the dog when friends need your support or when your loyalties are divided.

Dogs have been 'man's best friend' for thousands of years, certainly from about 7500 BC in early Egypt. Hermes or Mercury, the messenger of the Greek and Roman gods was accompanied by his faithful dog. One of the most famous dogs was Odysseus's faithful hound, Argos, described in Homer's *Odyssey*. Argos waited faithfully for Odysseus to return from the Trojan War and was the only one to recognize his heavily disguised master after many years' absence, but the joy was too much for his old heart and he died.

Dogs are said to sense evil or death approaching and to howl a warning. This is an Ancient Greek belief but prevails throughout the world.

Elephants: Wisdom and Stability

Use the elephant when others are offering conflicting advice or trying to force you down a path that you feel is unwise.

It was once believed that the elephant had no joints in its legs and so had to sleep standing up. The Ancient Roman scholar Pliny believed that the elephant had religious feelings and worshipped the ancient deities of the moon and stars. The Greek philosopher Aristotle credited the elephant with great wisdom and intelligence, a trait echoed in Hinduism where elephant-headed Ganesh is God of Wisdom and is always invoked at the beginning of any journey or before any important enterprise (see also *Travelling Magic*, page 450).

White Elephants are sacred to Buddha since one announced his birth to his mother, Queen Maya. Because of this and their rarity, they are not allowed to work. A white elephant came to represent an expensive unwanted gift because a certain King of Siam would present a white elephant to courtiers he wished to ruin financially. The unlucky recipient would have to feed, house and cherish this costly and useless gift.

Horses: Swift Action

Use the horse when you must respond to a sudden challenge or crisis or need to make a swift decision.

The horse, which was first domesticated in about 1750 BC, is a magical symbol of swiftness and power who can bear heroes and gods not only across the earth at incredible speeds, but can also carry them through the skies, across the waves and even through the Underworld in safety. According to classical myth, Poseidon (Neptune in Roman myth) first created the horse Arion (meaning warlike) by striking the earth with his trident. Its right feet were those of a man, it had a human voice and ran as fast as the wind. At first it was given to Adrastus, King of Argos, who led the Seven Heroes against Thebes. The horse eventually passed to Hercules. Pegasus, the winged horse of classical myth, was ridden by the hero Bellerophon who performed many hazardous task with its help, including slaying the Chimaera, a hideous monster with the head of a lion, the body of a goat and a dragon's tail.

When a horse dies, it is said to be lucky to keep its hoof. An ass's right forefoot is said to be good for easing the pains of childbirth. If you find the back tooth of a horse, carry it always and you will never lack money. The charm works only if the tooth is found by chance. Nine hairs plucked from a stallion's tail will cure warts, but you must not say thank you or pay for them. Plait them and wear them in a bag near the afflicted spot. If two lovers encounter a white horse, they are promised eternal happiness. You should always take off your hat to a donkey. A pregnant woman who meets a donkey will have a very clever and good baby because the donkey is associated with Jesus.

Lions: Courage and Nobility

Use the lion when principles are at stake or you are cornered by those who have no scruples.

In Western mythology, the lion is the King of the Beasts. He represents the power of the sun and was associated with the sun gods and later with kings. The lioness is a symbol of the Moon Goddesses and often pulled their chariots. Juno, wife of Jupiter, had a chariot drawn by lions. The lion was sacred to the Egyptians who decorated their doors with gaping lions' mouths because the Nile, source of water and prosperity, began to rise when the sun was in Leo. A lion guarded the tunnel through which Ra the Sun God passed at night. In China, stone lions protected the courts of justice and were believed to come to life at night.

It was originally thought that lion cubs were born dead and that after three days the lion breathed life into them and the lioness howled over them to call down power into their limbs. Lions were said to sleep with their eyes open and, when moving, destroy their tracks with their tail.

The story best known as 'Androcles and the lion', in which a lion is helped by a human and later repays its helper, takes many forms. The medieval version recounts how the gallant crusader Sir Geoffrey de Latour saved a lion from serpents. Months later, Sir Geoffrey was knocked from his horse during a raging battle. As he lay waiting for the death blow, he heard a roar. It was his friend the lion who tossed aside the enemy and saved Sir Geoffrey. Thereafter man and lion fought side by side. Once the battles were over, the lion tried to board the ship carrying his master Sir Geoffrey back to England, but it fell into the water and drowned.

Tigers: Strength and Permanence

Use the tiger when faced with a long-standing problem or when making a permanent commitment to maintain your resolve.

The tiger is the King of Beasts in Eastern mythology. In China, it is given the title of Lord of the Land Animals. Coloured tigers are used to represent the seasons and different directions. The White Tiger represents the Earth, the West, the Autumn and the region of death because the West is the direction of the setting sun. The Blue Tiger is the East, Spring and Plant Life. The Red Tiger is the South, Summer and Fire. The Black Tiger is the North, Winter and Water. The Yellow tiger in the centre is the Sun. In Japan, the tiger is believed to live for a thousand years. Malaysian legend tells that tigers contain the soul of sorcerers and therefore their name must be used with care for fear of attracting bad magic.

ASTROLOGICAL ASSOCIATIONS

Astrological Animals represent more permanent qualities in our nature. Whereas you may temporarily need to seek the loyalty of the dog when friends are under stress, astrological associations are linked to an underlying trait that you perhaps noticed in yourself when you were a child, but which you may have forgotten. In this case your Astrological or Power Animal may be a source of untapped strength.

A combination of your Astrological Animal with a symbol of a temporary animal strength from the list above at a time of major crisis or when making a big decision can put you in control of any situation. When you discover your suggested Totem or Power Animal in the section on *Native North American Magic* (see page 348), you may find it echoes your Astrological Animal under this system.

Your Personal Animal Collection

You can find Astrological Animals in many forms: paper butterflies for Gemini, a brightly painted pottery tortoise for Cancer or photographs of lions or tigers for Leo. Astrological Animals make a lovely collection as a reminder of your core strengths and qualities. You can also buy a symbol of the appropriate astrological animal as a gift on the birthday of a friend or family member. Children may value additions to a personal astrological collection year by year, as a way of affirming their special place in the world.

Best of all is a visit to 'your own power animal', either in the wild or a well-tended animal park where you can watch it quietly and make a psychic connection. Observe how the animal moves and its natural dignity and strength and as you go to sleep in the evening, let the last picture in your mind be of 'your animal'.

Your Animal Signs

Aries (21 March–20 April): Rams, sheep. The virtue of the ram and a sheep with young is its determination to overcome any opposition.
Taurus (21 April–21 May): Cattle, bulls. Their virtue is quiet strength unless angered.
Gemini (22 May–21 June): Parrots and brightly coloured birds, monkeys and butterflies. Their virtue is swift movement and versatility.
Cancer (22 June–22 July): Creatures with a shell, including tortoises, turtles, crabs and lobsters. Their virtue is protectiveness towards the vulnerable.

Leo (23 July–23 August): Lions, tigers and other big cats. Their virtue is courage and nobility.
Virgo (24 August–22 September): All domestic pets, especially cats and bees. Their virtue is loyalty to those who deserve it.
Libra (23 September–23 October): Lizards and small reptiles. Their virtue is survival in any situation by adapting to the environment.
Scorpio (24 October–22 November): Snakes, invertebrates (animals without backbones) and insects. Their virtue is to live happily and successfully within the limits circumstances impose.
Sagittarius (23 November–21 December): Horses and hunted animals such as deer. Their virtue is to be constantly alert to the changing situations.
Capricorn (22 December–20 January): Goats and all cloven-hoofed animals. Their virtue is to cling and be loyal to what is of value in their lives.
Aquarius (21 January–18 February): Large birds, capable of sustained flight, such as the eagle, heron and albatross. Their virtue is to exist free of material concerns and the burdens of convention.
Pisces (19 February–19 March): Mammals that love water, such as seals, whales and dolphins and all fish. Their virtue is to immerse themselves in life and move intuitively through it, rather than being stifled by it.

PETS AND TELEPATHY

All animals are psychic but pets develop particular bonds with their owners. For example, Pauline, who is in her fifties, told me that when she lived in Liverpool, England as a child, the family cat and dog would go into the hall about five minutes before her father came home and sit by the door expectantly. Her father worked as a steward on the ships that went to Ireland and it was never known in advance what time his shifts would end or how many days he would be away, as rotas would be changed at the last minute and the family had no telephone. However, he always brought titbits home for the animals and they 'knew' he was coming. This experience is very common among pet owners.

USING THE TELEPATHIC LINK WITH YOUR PET

If you are going to be late home and are worried that your dog or cat may be missing you, try to contact it telepathically. In your mind's eye, visualize your animal, the colour and texture of its coat and any distinctive markings or mannerisms, such as putting its head to one side when listening. Let your mind focus on this picture until you can feel the soft fur. Then, with your left hand, gently stroke your dog or cat as though it was with you in the room. Feel the gentle nuzzle and hear a soft purr or a welcoming bark. If you are in a crowded or public place, you can caress the animal in your mind. Explain that you will be late but that you are coming back soon and bringing a special treat. Stop to buy one as the animal will be expecting it.

When you return home, you will find your pet waiting quietly by the door. No matter how busy or tired you are, spend a few extra minutes with the animal. If you doubt your ability, get a neighbour or friend to observe the dog from a distance at the time you are mentally stroking it. Experiments have shown that an animal responds to an owner stroking it psychically in another room, especially if the animal has grown up with the owner or is still very young. Whether the owner uses the astral body to travel to the animal or this is a telepathic process based on love and emotion is a mystery that has not yet been unravelled. Perhaps it is both. But do not worry about the technicalities. Trust your loving instincts and let them do the work.

PET DIVINATION

As with birds, you can use a pet for a 'yes' or 'no' decision or even to select numbers for a lottery or other 'game of chance'.

A Yes/No, Go/Stay Decision

Because your pet is so close to you intuitively it can express your hidden inner knowledge without the barriers of language or analysis that block natural spontaneous wisdom.

If you have a decision to make, mark two or more large circles of paper with the choices. You can have up to four options. Before your pet enters the room, place a single identical pet chew, chocolate drop or other small treat in the centre of each circle and arrange them at equal distances from the door, making sure that none of the circles is close to a favourite place or usual feeding area as this would bias the response. Feed your pet or offer it a small treat before the experiment so that it is not influenced by hunger or the novelty of a treat.

Open the door. Your dog or cat may go directly to one circle and eat the treat or uncharacteristically circle all of them before choosing. If the pet chooses one immediately, the decision is clear-cut. A more deliberate choice or hesitation may mean that each option has pros and cons, so the decision may involve certain regrets in rejecting one course of action. If the pet approaches one circle and then goes to another, it may mean that the first option is instantly more attractive although it may prove unfulfilling in the long run, so stay with the final decision. A pet may leave one treat uneaten or half-eaten. This can indicate that the person or option indicated may need careful handling. If a pet eats the treats in rapid succession, you may find that the decision chosen first is likely to provide a good short-term solution or option, but that you may have to adapt your plans if they are to succeed in the long term. If, as occasionally happens, the pet refuses the treats, you may need to rethink the whole question as none of the options may be viable or right. Remember to stroke your pet and thank it after it has performed for you

Selecting Lucky Numbers

This time use very small treats, one placed on a circle of relevant numbers. In the case of the British Lottery, for example, you would write out the numbers one to 49 in random order. Feed the animal a small amount first and offer a treat.

Place the animal in the centre of the circle and gently turn it round anti-clockwise. You will find that your pet does not begin at the first number and progress regularly, but darts around. Note down however many numbers you need and disregard any others. Let your pet eat a few more treats, then clear them away, so that it does not associate the experiment with indiscriminate eating. Thank your pet for its help and if it is a dog, take it for a walk, or take time to stroke a cat. You could try this experiment on a large scale with a friendly family horse, using slices of carrot or apple.

FINDING A LOST PET

If a cat does not come home or a dog breaks free from the lead, try not to panic. Animal radar defies science and technology. Pets lost in house moves have travelled across lands as vast as the United States or Australia to a home they have never seen. Nevertheless, after you have notified relevant authorities and searched an animal's customary hiding places, you can feel very helpless.

Lighting the Way Home

Sit quietly by a window as darkness falls and light a purple candle or small lamp to guide your pet home. See your animal guided by the soft beam of light and send your own loving calm thought to add to the homing power. If you have a picture of your pet, put it by the light and leave the lamp or candle burning (if you have no picture of your pet then use one of the same breed or colour or even a pottery cat or dog). Even if you are on the fifth floor of an apartment block, your light will guide your lost pet.

Pendulum Power

By morning, your pet may have returned demanding breakfast. If not, make a pendulum from a key on a chain, a favourite charm on a cord or use a crystal pendulum obtainable from any New Age shop and increasingly from department stores.

Place your pet's picture or an image of a similar animal in your pocket and leave home by your pet's customary route, pausing where it usually stops. Your pendulum will be swinging, whether clockwise or anti-clockwise to indicate a positive response. If it suddenly stops or moves in a different way, pause and change direction. Where there are bushes or an outbuilding at the place the action ceases, call your pet's name softly but clearly and you may get a response. If not, continue in the new direction with your pendulum swinging its 'go on' response until it again stops or indicates a change.

If you feel a strong pulling, then stop and investigate. If your pet does not reply to your call, it may be asleep or weak. If the pendulum's pull is near a building, seek permission to search there. If you are stopped by an area of undergrowth, search thoroughly and, above all, trust your instincts. I once rescued my white cat Haegl from a summer house that the owners insisted had not been opened for several weeks. However, the pendulum and my own instincts insisted otherwise and Haegl was found hiding in the summer house behind a work bench.

If you have other pets, ask them. I once rescued my old black and white cat Simba from a very unfriendly neighbour's shed. Although the other cats usually spat at her, they circled the shed and sat on top meowing to alert me to her plight.

PSYCHIC PROTECTION

Pets are very sensitive to unfriendly atmospheres and the presence of unwelcoming psychic presences, although they will happily co-exist with a friendly family ghost. If you are thinking of buying or renting a new home, you cannot turn up to view with your dog or cat, but before finalizing any deal, take your pet and show it the front garden or front of the building. If a dog's hackles rise or a cat hisses and its fur stands on end, you should seriously consider whether the home is a happy one psychically, however smart the paintwork.

If there are certain areas in your home where pets will not go or where they appear distressed, burn a purifying oil, such as eucalyptus or rosemary, in that place or burn a pure white candle to shed light and joy in a gloomy area.

TRADITIONAL ANIMAL CURES

It is now accepted scientifically that a relationship with a pet can lower your blood pressure, slow your heart rate and have many beneficial effects on your health and psychological well-being. However, animals have always been involved with healing. An Irish cure for mumps was to wear a donkey's bridle or blinkers while drinking at a well or river. If the patient was a child, his or her head would be rubbed against the back of a pig with the words, *Pig, pig, here are your mumps*. The pig would then have mumps instead.

A donkey was also used to cure whooping cough. The child would be passed three times over and under the animal's back and stomach, as the cross on its back was thought to have healing powers. Donkeys are often kept with cows to ensure their health. Sleeping in a cow shed is supposed to cure colds and coughs.

Finally an old wives' cure, not to be recommended, was to insert a live duck's beak in your mouth or carry a bag of caterpillars round your neck to cure a sore throat.

BIRD MAGIC

4

ORIGINS OF BIRD MAGIC

Birds were regarded as magical in every culture because they could fly. They were seen as messengers of the gods or even a god in disguise and because they were in harmony with the elements, their behaviour has been used from early times for predicting changes in the weather and for foretelling the success of ventures.

FABULOUS BIRDS

The Bestiaries, books of ancient lore on mythical as well as real birds and beasts from many cultures, gained great popularity in the Middle Ages in Europe. These are some of the birds which were said by the Bestiaries to link Earth with the Heavens.

Bird of Paradise

Real birds of paradise are now under conservation in New Guinea and its neighbouring islands. The female birds are dull but the males have brilliant plumage.

It may have been these birds or a similarly rainbow-plumed creature that inspired stories of the legendary Bird of Paradise, who perched in the Tree of Life in various cultures, especially in the Far East. Also called the Bird of God, the mythical Bird of Paradise was said to have brilliantly coloured plumage but no wings nor feet. It used its slender tail feathers to hang from trees and according to Far Eastern legend, its eggs were dropped from the tree on to the ground where full-grown birds emerged.

Phoenix

The Phoenix is of Egyptian origin, being the Sun Bird of Ra, the Sun God, and a sign of resurrection. To the Chinese, it is one of the Sacred Creatures, like the dragon. In China and Japan its appearance foretold the coming of a great emperor or sage and images of the Phoenix were carried or worn to ensure long life and health.

In the Western world, the Phoenix became associated with medieval alchemy and the 'glorious Phoenix' was a symbol of alchemy's ultimate aim of turning base metal into gold. This symbolism stemmed from the ancient legend that the Phoenix was made up of the elements of the cosmos. It burned itself on a funeral pyre every five hundred years but rose again golden from the ashes.

The Roc

The Roc, a huge white bird described in the Arabian Nights, was, according to myth, so strong it that it could carry elephants to its nest in its claws. It was a storm bird. Its wings controlled the winds and lightning flashed from its eyes as it flew. The Roc lands only on Mount Qaf, the Axis Mundi (World Axis). Its huge egg shone so brilliantly that it represented the sun.

The Thunderbird

Thunderbirds, a magical form of the eagle, are most usually associated with Amerindian tradition (see *Native North American Magic*, page 348). To many tribes, it is the bringer of rain which spills from a lake on its back as it flies, while its flashing eyes create lightning and its vast eagle-like wings cause the thunder.

Japan also has a Thunderbird that resembles a giant rook, like the eagle a solar bird. It creates thunder and lightning and guards the approaches to the Heavens.

THE LORE OF BIRDS

Real birds also have magical and mythical associations. In bird divination, known as auspicy, bird flight is an important source of information, particularly its direction and height.

The kind of bird seen can add significance to the divination, not as in former days when birds were seen as harbingers of good or bad luck or even warnings of death, but as a focus for a particular quality or area of life. The system is described later but listed below are some birds that represent money, health, love and other concerns.

Such birds can be used as a focus for magic as well as for divination. Even if a bird is not native to your part of the world, you can carry a talisman of it. A rough outline etched on a piece of crystal quartz or stone from the sea or marshes will serve; or you might prefer to buy a china ornament or silver charm. Alternatively, find a bird in your region with similar qualities to one listed below and find its likely habitat if you need its particular strengths. For example, if mothering or health are issues in your life, a long-legged bird, such as the heron or flamingo, will replace the stork or the crane. Any small flying birds, such as swifts or sparrows who are natural augurs of love, will replace the magical swallows or wagtails for bird flight divination.

Bird gardens and parks often have species from different parts of the world where you can see the bird that represents your particular need. Equally, any song bird can be used in bird song divination.

Albatross: Bearing Burdens

A legendary weather prophet, forecasting winds and bad weather, the albatross is said to care for its eggs on a floating raft and sleep motionless on the wing.

Killing one brings a curse (the English poet Coleridge based his *Rime of the Ancient Mariner* on the legend of a sailor who brought disaster to the ship by killing one and was condemned to carry its corpse around his neck).

The albatross is a sacred bird in Japanese folk lore. It is the servant of the chief god of the sea and seeing one is a good omen. In New Zealand, ancestors sometimes appear as giant cormorants, birds with similar oracular properties.

Cockerel: Protection

The cockerel was a sacrificial animal in many cultures and was also buried under the foundations of buildings as a guardian.

There are two cockerels in Norse myth. Vithafmir, the golden cockerel, perched at the top of Yggdrasil, the World Tree, as a guardian against evil. Fralar, Cockerel of the Underworld, lived in Valhalla, abode of slain warriors, to waken the heroes for the final battle.

It is said that if a cock crows in the afternoon, an unexpected visitor will arrive, while crowing at sunset foretells a wet sunrise. For a girl to hear a cock crowing while she is thinking of her sweetheart is a good omen. However, if a bride or groom on the way to church hears a cockerel crowing, this portends bickering.

Crane: Health

The crane is a sacred bird in Japan, symbol of health and long life. It is called the 'Honourable Lord Crane' and according to both Japanese and Chinese myth lives for a thousand years or more. In China, the Crane is the Patriarch of the Feathered Tribe. White cranes are especially sacred and live on the Islands of the Blest, the Chinese earthly paradise.

The Roman author Pliny tells that cranes post sentries while they sleep. The sentry holds a stone in its claw. Should it fall asleep, it will drop the stone and the noise will alert the other birds.

Crow: Change

Crows are the birds of Apollo, the Greek Sun God, who took the form of a crow when fleeing from Typhon, the hundred-headed monster. They were also sacred to Athena, although she would not allow them to perch on the Acropolis in Athens since this was regarded as a bad omen.

Like many black birds, the crow was traditionally regarded as inauspicious, but in more modern terms they represent the need to move on.

In Celtic myth, the white crow is associated with Bronwen, sister of Bran, the Celtic God-King. It is also a Totem (power) creature in Native North American lore where it is seen as a messenger to the spirit world, a guardian of sacred laws and a sign of coming change. As with magpies, a single crow should be greeted by your removing your hat, bowing and wishing the crow good day. Then he will grant you a pleasant day.

Cuckoo: Prosperity

The cuckoo is herald of spring and in southern England an old woman traditionally lets a cuckoo out of her basket at Heathfield Fair, known as the Heffle Cuckoo Fair, on 14 April to mark the beginning of spring.

When you first hear the cuckoo turn your money over and you'll have money in your purse till he comes again. Cuckoos heard on the right-hand side are a sign of imminent prosperity. If the call is heard from the left, the prosperity will be slower in coming.

Dove or Pigeon: Reconciliation and Love

The dove is called the happiest of birds and symbolizes love, happiness and wedded bliss. In classical days, it was the emblem of Venus and so especially fortunate for lovers.

It features in the Flood stories of the Babylonians, Hebrews, Chaldeans and Greeks, as a symbol of peace and reconciliation. The dove bearing the olive branch back to Noah's Ark has become an international sign of peace. Therefore, a talisman made in its shape is said to be powerful in healing quarrels.

If a single white pigeon or dove flies around a home or perches on the roof, a love match or marriage of a member of the household is to be expected in the near future. The cooing of sacred pigeons or doves in the oracular groves dedicated to Zeus at Dodona in north-west Greece, were used for prophecy. Only in Japan is the dove sacred to the war-god Hachiman.

Duck: Consolation

A quacking duck, especially away from water, indicates coming prosperity. Flying ducks, especially in the direction of the sun, promise happier times for those who are sad or worried.

Eagles: Vision and Courage

The eagle, the true King of Birds and a symbol of courage and power in many cultures, is central to Native North American magic. In Amerindian lore, its feathers carry the prayers of the people to the Father Sun. It was said that the eagle could fly closest to the sun and not be burned and could look into the noonday sun without flinching and not be blinded. The white-headed American eagle with wings outstretched is the emblem of the United States.

In Ancient Egypt, it was believed that the eagle flew into the fires of hell every ten years, soared upwards aflame and plunged into the ocean where life is renewed.

In India, the eagle Garuda was the bearer of the God Vishnu and carried him to his victories over the powers of darkness.

In Ancient Greece when Zeus was preparing for his battle with the Titans, a race of giants, the eagle brought him thunderbolts and was adopted as the emblem of Zeus and later of the Roman god Jupiter. Because of its close connection with Jupiter, the eagle became a symbol of earthly power and in Ancient Rome it became part of the insignia of the Republic.

In the Christian Church, the eagle is the symbol of St John the Evangelist and appears on church lecterns, while a less orthodox legend suggests that Adam and Eve did not die but were turned into eagles and flew to Ireland, which became the Blessed Isle.

In China and Japan, tiny eagle mascots made of stone or metal were carried by warriors.

Falcon or Kestrel: Vigilance

Like many smaller birds of prey, the falcon was traditionally regarded as an omen, warning of sudden disaster, especially if it was seen swooping down from the left. However, modern interpretation takes a more positive view of it as heralding sudden unexpected change or perhaps opposition and cautions vigilance.

The Bush Falcon, found in the Antipodes, was regarded as a messenger from the Earth to the Heavens and was used in establishing whether a location for a new Maori ceremonial house was favourable to the gods and ancestors. It was imprisoned by its flight feathers on the ridge pole which was then put in its position on the front post of the new building. If the falcon flew free, it was seen as returning to the gods and ancestors who had sent it. However, if it remained trapped, the ceremonial house would not be used.

Goose: the Home and Domestic Happiness

In Ancient Egypt, the goose, like the swan in other cultures, laid the great cosmic egg. Ra, the Sun God, emerged from this egg and so brought light into the world.

In the classical world the goose was also linked with Hera and Juno in their roles as wife and mother and became the symbol of domestic happiness and the good housewifery. Cackling geese alerted the Romans when the Gauls were making a silent raid on the Capitol and geese were kept on the hill thereafter to warn of danger. The cackling of geese became a sign of hidden enemies and anyone who hears them, especially in the early morning, should be alert for the following few days against possible spite and malice.

Hawk: Enlightenment

In Egyptian mythology, the hawk, like the eagle, was a bird of the sun and could also soar towards the sun and look into its brilliant face without being blinded. Sacred to Horus, God of Learning, the hawk was a symbol of the return of light after darkness and so of joy after sorrow. Ra, the Sun God and Horus were both pictured with the head of a hawk or falcon.

In the classical world, the hawk was special emissary of Apollo, God of the Sun. Gayatri, the hawk of Indian legend, brought *soma* from the heavens, a juice that induced sleep and prophetic visions. In Polynesia, the hawk was both prophet and healer, while among the Australian Aborigines, the hawk was a powerful Totem Creature.

Hummingbird: Truth and Joy

The Hummingbird was one of the birds who helped to carry back fire to the North American Indians, according to the legends of the Wintu tribe. He always speaks the truth. Bird of the gods, he is a bringer of harmony and happiness to all who see or hear him. Because the hummingbird was skilled in hovering and flying backwards, his feathers were used as charms.

The hummingbird was the creature of the Feathered Serpent, Quetzalcoatl, the Sky and Sun God of the Mayans and Aztecs, who wore the feathers of the hummingbird.

Ibis: Wisdom

The white and black ibis was sacred to the Ancient Egyptians, and was worshipped as the incarnation of Thoth, God of Wisdom and Learning. Thoth was usually depicted as having the head of an ibis.

The ibis was also associated with Hermes, Greek God of Wisdom, Learning and the Written Arts. Hermes assumed the shape of an ibis in his flight from Thyphon, the hundred-headed monster who was killed by Zeus's thunderbolt

Kingfisher: Harmony

A kingfisher or any bright blue bird promises a tranquil period for 14 days after it has been seen. It is often called the 'halcyon bird' and gave the expression 'halcyon days'. The origin of these halcyon days comes from Greek myth. Alcyone, daughter of Aeolus, King of the Winds, threw herself into the sea, overcome with grief at the death of her husband. The gods transformed her into a kingfisher and Aeolus said that henceforward the winds would not stir up the sea during the 'halcyon days'. These 14 calm days, often located around the Mid-Winter Solstice, last from the hatching of eggs to when the young birds are able to fly.

Magpie: Good News

Magpies are divinatory birds. One magpie alone is traditionally considered a bad omen and unless a second follows rapidly, you should take off your hat and bow, saying 'Good morning (or afternoon or evening), Mr Magpie, and how are you today?' This ensures any news you receive that day will be good. There are several versions of the children's rhyme referring to the prophetic nature of the magpie. I quote two:

One for sorrow,
Two for mirth,
Three for a letter,
Four for a birth,
Five for silver,
Six for gold
And seven for a secret never to be told.

Another version says:

One's sorrow,
Two's mirth,
Three's a wedding,
Four's a birth,
Five's a christening,

Six a dearth,
Seven's heaven,
Eight is hell
And nine the Devil's self as well.

Modern interpretation would see the rhyme as foretelling the kind of news to be received or the form it will take, with one as a delay rather than bad news and eight and nine as suggesting that gossip may be heard that should be ignored.

In the Far East, the magpie's arrival is one to be welcomed wholeheartedly for the bird is a symbol of happiness and prosperity and its chattering, according to modern usage, heralds unexpected but very welcome visitors, bringing good news.

Ostrich: Justice

Although it does not fly, the ostrich, like the emu and rhea, can be used in divination according to the direction in which it runs. In Ancient Egypt, an ostrich feather was worn by Maat, Goddess of Wisdom and Justice and used to balance the heart of a dead person on the Scales of Justice.

The ostrich is also important in African magic. It is a symbol of perpetual light and motion and its eggs have great magical significance as symbols of fertility and new life.

Owl: Learning

Traditionally, owls have a dual role as symbols of wisdom and learning and harbingers of bad tidings. In modern magic, the positive aspect is emphasized.

In the classical world, the owl was the special bird of Minerva, Roman Goddess of Wisdom and in her earlier form as the Greek Athena. Owl charms or talismans were worn from early times to bring success in study.

The darker aspect of the owl originated in Rome where the deaths of several Roman Emperors were signalled by an owl landing on the roof and hooting. The association with death also came from Celtic lore where the owl was the bird of darkness and the 'night hag' of the Underworld. It was one of the forms taken by Gwynn, God of the Underworld, who ruled the souls of slain warriors.

In Japanese folklore, the omens varied according to the kind of owl. The eagle owl as messenger of gods symbolized wisdom and favour from the gods. The screech owl was friend to the hunter. Only the call of the Horned Owl heralded misfortune.

Although some Native North American tribes associated the owl with sorcery and ghosts, others emphasized the protective aspect.

To them the Owl was Father of the Night and could give warriors, especially those of his Totem, power to see in the dark, as well as offering protection to all who must travel by night.

In New Zealand, owls, especially white ones, are seen as guardian spirits and noble ancestors in Maori tradition.

Peacock: Lasting Happiness and Older People

The peacock is the bird of the Roman goddess Juno and it is said that if a peacock spreads its tail feathers before your eyes, happiness and prosperity will follow. Because its flesh was said never to decay and it was associated with the deities, it became a symbol of immortality in Rome and was adopted by both emperor and empress.

However, as the old pagan gods and goddesses became discredited with the spread of Christianity, the eyes on the tail feathers were regarded as the 'evil eye'. Therefore, it is considered unlucky to bring peacock feathers indoors. The peacock is a weather prophet, its dance foretelling rain and storms. Straw peacocks are traditionally placed on the roofs of thatched houses to protect them against storms.

Pelican: Motherhood and Nurturing

The pelican is famed for her maternal instinct. She is said to love her young so much she smothers them but revives them by feeding them with the blood from her own breast, a myth that arose because the female has red breast feathers.

In Winchester Cathedral, England, the pelican is displayed along the top of stone pillars, with stone eggs placed in its nest by medieval craftsmen. The eggs cannot be seen from the ground but the important point to the medieval craftsmen was that God could look down on them.

Quail: Fertility

The quail is associated with passion and fertility for it is a bird of fire. To see a quail or hear one calling, whether from the right or left, is a sign of fertility. Its eggs were eaten at the time of the full moon to ensure fertility.

It is associated with the coming of spring or summer depending on the country where it lives. It also symbolized victory and valour in battle for the Romans. The author Pliny reported that on migration quails displayed great intelligence and organizational powers, dropping stones as they flew to tell whether they were over water.

In Russian tradition, the quail lived in the sun and the hare in the moon.

Raven: Lost Objects or Hidden Potential

Although the raven, like other dark-plumed birds, is sometimes seen as a prophet of disaster, it has a strong tradition as a guardian, especially in battle or times of danger.

The Raven is the sacred bird of Bran, the Celtic God-King, whose head is said to be buried at the White Mount in what is now the Tower of London. Ravens are still kept at the Tower of London because legend says that if they should leave their sacred place, the Tower and London itself would be destroyed. It is also believed that if ravens leave an area, then hard times are ahead.

Ravens are also the birds of Odin, the Norse All-Father. His two ravens, Hugin and Mugin (Mind and Memory), sat on his shoulders and the Vikings carried Odin's Raven Banners into battle. These banners could be made only by the virgin daughters of Norse hero-warriors.

The protective role has spread to domestic property. Ravens bring great luck to the house where they nest and, unlike the thieving jackdaw, the raven is a finder of lost property, a role called the Raven's Knowledge. If you lose something, ask a raven for its location and a picture will form in your mind of its whereabouts.

Robin: Compassion

Several legends explain why the robin has a red breast. One says that he burned it in the fires of hell bringing water to lost souls. Others claim it was stained with the blood of Christ as the robin pulled the thorns from Christ's Crown. A third version says that the robin covered the dead with leaves and as he was covering Christ, was touched by His blood.

In Native North American tradition, the raven, who was sometimes called the Big Grandfather in his Creator role, made the robin to bring joy with his warbling.

The robin is so loved that he is protected by various prohibitions. One old rhyme says:

If a robin you dare kill,
Your right hand will lose it all its skill.

The robin can also grant wishes, especially the first robin of spring. It is said that robins near a house or in a garden promise good luck to all who live there.

Seagull: Travel

Seagulls are said to be the souls of dead sailors and so should never be shot. Stormy petrels, known as Mother Carey's chickens, are especially protected by sailors. If a gull settles on any part of a ship in which a person is travelling, it is said the voyage will be a happy one.

Stork: Babies and Children

Storks are said to carry the unborn babies from the salt marshes where they grow to waiting parents. The strong association with birth came about because the stork represented woman as the bringer of life in the form of the Mother Goddesses Hera and Juno.

Because the stork is also sacred to Venus the Goddess of Love, a nesting pair of storks on or near a home was considered a blessing from her and a promise of enduring love.

In many countries the stork is encouraged to nest on the housetops. The stork got its name, according to Scandinavian myth, at the Crucifixion. A stork flew round the cross, uttering cries of distress, 'styrka, styrka', which means 'strengthen'.

Swallow and Martin: Revival and Consolation

The swallow has been a symbol of awakening after winter and the renewal of life since early times. To see a swallow in early spring is a promise of a happy summer. If swallows build in the eaves of a house, success, happiness and good fortune are promised to all who live there.

The swallow was sacred to Isis, the Egyptian Mother Goddess and also to Venus and Aphrodite, the classical Goddesses of Love. In Swedish tradition the swallow, like the stork, flew over the cross, calling '*svala, svala*', which means 'console'.

Swan: Creativity

In India, the swan, like the Egyptian goose, laid the golden cosmic egg from which Brahma, Hindu Creator of the Universe, emerged. A swan was said to carry Saraswati, Hindu Goddess of Wisdom and Music and the wife of Brahma.

In Native North American tradition, the great White Swan calls up the four winds. The Black Swans of Australia are, in some areas, the manifestation of the Mother/Sister female counterpart of Balame, the All-Father.

Swans are said to contain the souls of great poets, writers and musicians, since Apollo's soul also took the form of a swan. Hence Shakespeare is sometimes called the Swan of Avon, the river that runs through his birthplace Stratford-upon-Avon. Outside the Royal Shakespeare Theatre many swans congregate.

Turkey: Self-sacrifice and Altruism

Turkeys, known as the 'jewelled fowl', were sacrificial creatures in Mesoamerican society and so on the American continent became a symbol of self-sacrifice in the noblest sense. The turkey was central to the tribal new fire ceremonies and became the focus of Thanksgiving Day in North America on the fourth Thursday in November. This festival commemorates the first Harvest Feast of the Pilgrim Fathers in 1621 when four wild turkeys were eaten. When introduced into Britain, it became a feature of the Christmas dinner table, ousting the more traditional goose.

Wagtail: Love

In Japanese folk tradition, the wagtail assisted with the Creation of the Earth. The Earth in its original form was a huge marsh. The Creator sent wagtails to beat the land with their wings and tails. At last hills were formed so that the water could drain away and mankind could till the land. The water-wagtail is also a love bird in Japanese myth and its feathers are highly prized as love tokens.

In Indian, the wagtail is the chief divinatory bird. Predictions were made by the direction of its flight and where it landed. For example if it perched near a lotus, elephant or the sacred cow, good fortune was promised to any who saw it.

The Wren: Ingenuity

The wren wrested the title of King of the Birds from the eagle by an ingenious plan. According to Norse myth there was a contest between all the birds. Whoever flew nearest the sun would be King. The eagle soared highest, but the wren hid in his feathers and as the eagle approached the sun, the wren perched on his head.

The wren was also the Celtic King of the Birds and was used for prophecy. This role lies behind the strange symbolic Killing the Wren ceremony that occurs on 26 December in Wales, parts of northern and western England and remote parts of Brittany.

The wren is said to be blessed because it carried moss to the stable on Christmas Eve to line Baby Jesus's manger. In Japanese folklore, the bird is greeted as the small god which brought fire from heaven to mankind. It is considered especially lucky to see a wren while hunting.

BIRD DIVINATION

Bird Flight and Song

Bird divination was one of the most important forms of auspicy (messages coming from the sky) practised in cultures throughout the world. Omens were gathered either through the singing, crowing or croaking of birds or through the pattern and direction of their flight. The term auspice for a prediction comes from the Latin for an observer of birds. In Ancient Rome special augurs (trained philosophers) would interpret the auspicy which was seen as a message from Jupiter. In Rome, flight auspicy took place within a sacred space, called a templum that was not a building but imaginary divisions marked off in the sky or on the ground by an augur.

Interpreting Bird Flight

You can use a flock of birds or a single one. Ask a question or think of a decision that involves a course of action and watch the behaviour of the bird. I have given the modern interpretations of the old auguries. If you are in a place where a variety of birds fly and perch, you might like to use the bird meanings given above to interpret areas of strength or concern. If you are in no hurry, sit and wait for the first birds to arrive. A bag of corn may hasten the process.

Dark and Light

As a rule of thumb, where there is more than one species of bird, a light or bright-coloured bird indicates immediate action while darker ones indicate a delay. If the question involves options, the arrival or movement of a light-coloured bird would tell you to act, a darker one to wait. Sometimes you can find darker and lighter birds among the same flock of pigeons and can observe which arrives or departs first.

Direction

Birds flying from the right indicate a smooth passage in any venture and that confident action should be taken. Birds flying from the left indicate delays and perhaps counsel waiting or remaining silent for a while. Birds flying straight towards the questioner indicate that happier times are coming. Those flying directly away suggest that the next few days are a time for tact and caution and for making plans rather than embarking on new ventures.

Height

The higher the flight, the more favourable the omen. If a bird flies directly upwards, then the venture should achieve swift success with little effort needed on your part. If the flight is horizontal or veers up and down with the bird landing and flying off then landing again, you may need to apply more effort and not be deterred by initial obstacles.

Changing Course

If a bird suddenly changes direction, there may be sudden changes of heart or inconstancy from those close to you or sudden doubts of your own that you need to examine.

Hovering

If a bird hovers directly overhead, beware of hidden criticism or new friends who may be less than direct.

Bird Song

If a song bird sings or utters a cry as it takes flight, it is a good sign for going ahead at once with any matter. A bird that calls as it lands may indicate caution is needed. If a dark bird or a bird of prey screams as it circles, unless it is near its nest there may be unexpected opposition to overcome.

Interpreting Song

Dawn is a good time for listening to bird song. Go where there are a number of birds, such as doves or blackbirds. Ask a question and close your eyes. Let the chorus form pictures and words in your mind. Your answer will come with the flow of the song.

Divination by Selection

A third method of divination traditionally involved sacred chickens and birds pecking corn in areas marked with letters or special signs. The areas where the chickens pecked first indicated the answer. This method was used by Roman legions on military expeditions who carried the caged sacred birds.

In India, omens are still studied according to the behaviour of birds such as parrots that will select a 'yes' or 'no' answer or pick letters to indicate the name of a future lover. Although in some cases the street vendors have trained the birds to make set responses and so have destroyed natural divination, the method is one that can be used at home with pet birds or in an open space with wild ones.

Yes/No/Go/Stay

The method works best with a straight choice between two options. You can also use the method to choose between two people.

With wild birds, go to an open space where birds regularly gather early in the morning. Designate one distinct area as the affirmative and one the negative. Scatter an equal amount of corn in each and wait. See where the first birds land for your yes/no. Observe also which area of corn disappears first or the one where most is eaten. This can indicate the longer-term results. It may be that 'yes' will bring an instant response or happiness (the first bird to land) but that the other option or person will prove more lasting or satisfying in the long run (the area where the corn is cleared first). I have met people who interpret the area first clear as the least enduring and if this seems to work better for you, follow your own interpretations.

With a pet bird, wait until its usual time of feeding and flying free. Place two small dishes of food next to the other. Do not use a regular feeding dish as this may bias the results. Under each dish write on a piece of paper your options or the names of two people. See which dish the bird approaches first and which is ultimately left empty. You can use fowl to carry out the same method.

Add more options or dishes or place letters of the alphabet in a circle with a few grains on each and allow your pet to choose the order. This can give you the initials of someone important or a future love. Do not try to train your pet bird to pick certain letters as this spoils the natural selection process.

A Calendar

Time lapse can also be judged by placing 12 numbered cards in a circle. Designate one as January or the current month. Ask when an important event will occur and see which number the bird first pecks. If it goes to a second number, that may indicate when the matter will be completed. Count only the first two numbers selected as any intelligent bird will finish the meal.

Finally if your pet bird takes an instant dislike to a stranger or new acquaintance, take your bird's warning seriously. Birds can tap different levels of awareness.

CELTIC MAGIC

CELTIC MYTHOLOGY

Because the Celtic tradition was almost entirely oral, much of its ancient wisdom has been lost. The poems and legends were written down no earlier than the eighth century in Ireland and not long before the early Middle Ages in Wales. Because almost all were set down by monks, much of the richness of myth may have been lost, diluted or Christianized and the knights and kings of Wales probably referred to the earlier gods.

Many of the Celtic crosses in Britain were created by the Celtic Christian Church as an attempt to Christianize the original ancient standing stones that were once places of great mystical power. If you listen to Welsh or Irish harp music and the stirring lyrics of a solitary unaccompanied singer, especially in Gaelic, you will feel something of that early magic of the Celtic world. The best way to understand the Celts is to go to a region that has the characteristics of Wales, Brittany and Ireland, the last strongholds of Celtic lore; green, wet places, with mist, hills, mountains, wild seas, rushing streams, still deep lakes, craggy brooding rocks and ancient standing stones.

What is known of the Celtic world? During the last half of the first millennium BC, these Iron Age peoples occupied huge tracts of western and central Europe, extending at their height of power from the British Isles to Turkey. They were famed for their metalwork, road building, chariot-making and their agricultural and rich cultural life. They were the fierce Gauls of Caesar's Gallic Wars and indeed the 'barbari' sacked Rome in 290 BC. However, the systematic extension of the Roman Empire and the Anglo-Saxon and Norse invasions gradually destroyed the separate identity of the Celts, whose influence nevertheless has pervaded many aspects of religious, cultural and magical life throughout the Western world.

The Celts were not united either politically or linguistically, but shared the same mythology and very strong religious beliefs. Both mother and warrior goddesses were of great importance in the Celtic world as women had high status, for example Boadicea or Boudicca, Chief of the Iceni who stood against the Roman invaders. The triple-headed Goddess was also a feature of Celtic mythology, representing the different stages of life and linking with the phases of the moon.

THE CELTIC DEITIES

Irish Celtic deities have been taken here as representative of the Celtic world. There are many similarities between Welsh and Irish myths and the differences are largely those of name.

In the *Mythological Cycles*, recorded by the early monastic scribes, the main tale is of the Battle of Moytura (Cath Maig Tuired). This is the final conflict between the Tuatha de Danaan, the People of the Goddess Danu, and their enemies the Formoiri. The Tuatha de Danaan used their superior magical powers to gain victory.

There are various interpretations of this decisive battle in which all the Irish deities took part, one version seeing it as the decisive struggle of good against evil. The Tuatha de Danaan were beautiful and wise, while the Formoiri were half-monsters. Another interpretation sees the battle as the struggle between the old order of gods and the new, between Blar or Balor and a new god Lug Samildanach. A third view has the battle of the priest and warrior classes (the Tuatha de Danaan) and the farmers, the providers.

Danu

Danu, or Don in the British tradition, was the Earth Goddess, the great Mother of the Gods. She stands at the head of the tribe, superior to the male chief deity. She is not seen as the physical mother of all the gods but some kind of early creator. Each year Danu ritually mates with the god of tribe to ensure the fertility of the soil as well as that of the tribe. This forms the basis of many of the Western fertility and corn rituals that have echoes in our own festivals, such as May Day and Harvest Home.

Brigit

Brigit, the Triple-Goddess, is daughter of Dagda and has inherited many of the attributes of Danu. She is patron of smiths, poets and healers and has the longest enduring cult in Ireland which merged into that of St Brigit of Kildar. Her name means 'high one' and she is sometimes seen as three sisters, daughters of the god Dagda, the Divine Father, or as the three-generation maiden, mother and crone Triple Goddess.

Dagda, the Good Father

In the Celtic tradition, Dagda was also called Eochaid Ollathair (Father of All) and Ruadh Rofessa (the Red One of Knowledge).

He was King of the Tuatha de Danaan, 'for it was he who performed miracles and saw to the weather and the harvest'. He was not Father of all the Gods, nor did he have the importance of Danu. Nevertheless, he was Lord of Life and Death and the Fertility God. With his huge club, he made the bones of his people's enemies 'fall like hail beneath the horses'. With one end of the club he could kill nine men with a single blow and with the other instantly restore them to life.

His great cauldron was handed on to his daughter Brigit (in the Welsh tradition it passed to the Mother Goddess Cerridwen). He could feed everyone without the cauldron ever emptying and transform anything within it. The cauldron also had great healing powers.

In some legends, Dagda is associated with Balor of the Formoiri who was slain by the young solar God Lug at the Battle of Moytura, thus representing the ascent of the new sun. Dagda is God of the Druids.

Lug, The Young God

Lug the shining one, who gives his name to Lughnasadh, Celtic festival of the first harvest, was the young solar deity who ultimately replaced the Dagda as supreme King.

When Lug arrived to join the Tuatha de Danaan, he went to the palace of Tara and asked for a place. He said he was a carpenter, but was told that the company of gods already had one. Lug then declared he was a smith, but again was told that the company had one. He then declared that he was a poet, warrior, historian, hero and sorcerer. The court already had members who performed each function. Lug demanded whether anyone could perform all these tasks as he could. He was then admitted to the Tuatha de Danaan.

Unlike the crude Dagda with his club, Lug was skilled with spear and sling; he killed Balor at the final battle against the Formoiri with this sling. Balor was their champion and his single eye represented the solar power of the old order. Now the radiant Lug was the hero of the Tuatha de Danaan and eventually became their leader.

Callieach, the Old or Veiled One

Also called Gyre Carlin or the Grey Hag of Winter, she is the legendary old woman of experience, the Dark Woman of wisdom who with her cauldron heals the hero of myth and gives him wisdom to complete his task.

The Morrigan is a version of Callieach with whom Dagda mates on 1 November, the first day of the Celtic winter and the Celtic New Year, on the banks of the River Unnius in Connacht.

Callieach is associated with death and life and prophesies the ultimate doom of the world because of mankind's own folly:

I shall not long see the world I love
But Summer without flowers,
Cattle without milk . . .
Seas where no fish flash.

Sometimes the Triple Goddess, the maiden, mother and crone, are seen as Brigit, Danu and Callieach or the waxing, full and waning moons.

CELTIC DRAGONS

In Celtic legend, the dragon had healing power. Herbs that grew on scorched earth where these dragons landed had magical properties. This idea has similarities to Chinese mythology. The Welsh flag today bears the Welsh Dragon.

TWO MAJOR CELTIC FESTIVALS

The influence of the eight-festival year has remained in the Western magical tradition and forms the basis of popular celebrations, such as Easter, Christmas and May Day. *Christmas Magic* (page 75), *Seasonal Magic* (page 398), *Sun Magic* (page 410) and *Hallowe'en Magic* (page 260) demonstrate ways that the old festivals have been transformed. Two that have been almost lost in modern times, Oimlec and Lammas, still have powerful energies with much to offer if we rekindle the occasions and use them as a focus for rituals to give us the impetus for change in the everyday world.

Oimelc or Brigantia

This celebrates the coming of spring and is the Celtic Festival of New Beginnings. Imbolc, Oimelc or Brigantia, the festival of Ewe's Milk, was held from sunset on 31 January until sunset on 2 February. It was one of the moon festivals that were celebrated between the equinoxes and solstices; the Celtic year was divided into six-week periods, beginning with Hallowe'en or Samhain, the Celtic New

Year (see *Hallowe'en Magic*, page 260, and also *Seasonal Magic*, page 398, for the full list of ancient festivals).

Oimelc was the first festival of the Celtic spring when the early lambs were born and so fresh milk was available after the long winter. The original Brigit or Brigid, the maiden Goddess after whom the festival takes one of its names, was the daughter of Dagda, the Celtic Father God who had a cauldron that always gave nourishment. His daughter became the symbol of fertility and replenishment.

On Bride's Eve, 31 January, a Bride's Bed with straw was made in front of the fire and the inhabitants would shout: 'Bride, come in, your bed is ready.' The symbolic Bride maiden would leave her cows and a cauldron at the door, bringing in peace and plenty. This custom survived especially in remote parts when a Bride Bed of a sheaf of corn, sometimes with corn preserved from the last corn cut down at the first harvest at Lammas (end of July), would be decorated with ribbons to represent the Earth Goddess. It would also be decorated with any early spring flowers.

Milk and honey were poured over the Bride Bed by the women of the household. Originally the bed was laid in the home of the chief of the village, but later it was made in the main farm of an area. The menfolk were summoned and, having paid either a coin, a flower posy or a kiss, would enter the circle of firelight and ask for help with their craft or agriculture and make a wish on the Bride Bed. Household candles were blessed, for the end of the long winter nights was at hand. This rural festival faded with the Industrial Revolution but continued in rural areas until the middle of the twentieth century.

Christians took over the festival of Candlemas which is celebrated on 2 February, the third day of the old Celtic festival. It was said to be the day that the Virgin Mary was cleansed, 40 days after the birth of Christ and He was taken to the Temple and was hailed as the light of the world.

In the old tradition, the Celtic Bride was deflowered by her mate, a tribal chieftain, on the Bride Bed and customarily became pregnant at the Spring Equinox, close to the Christian Annunciation of the Virgin Mary, to give birth to the Son, the Sun, at the Mid-winter Solstice. The Celts would choose a maiden to act as Bride and either a suitable male as the representative of the God or the chief. Their fertility was believed to ensure the fertility of the earth and that spring would follow.

In the Celtic tradition, Brigantia was the time when the Maiden Goddess replaced the old Hag of Winter. In Roman tradition, an early February candle feast, when torches were carried down to rivers, was linked to the Goddess Februs. On 2 February, children played a board game with the figure of a hag on one side and a maiden on the other. The hag was defended by a dragon, the maiden by a lamb. The lamb won. Pope Boniface was told that the Sibyl, a pagan prophetess, had taught the boys the game and so he banned it as pagan heresy.

In popular tradition, the Celtic was gradually replaced by St Bride, the Abbess of Kilbride who died in 525. She was made a saint because she performed miracles, including making her cows give milk three times a day and causing food to increase. Once she threw straw into the water during a famine and fish leaped up. She is also credited with being the midwife of Christ, presumably in an earlier incarnation.

There are old wells formerly dedicated to Brigid where flowers were thrown at Candlemas to represent her deflowering. Well-dressing continues at St Bride's Wells as they are now called.

Brigantia Magic for New Beginnings

Brigantia naturally represents a time for new beginnings, the first flowers, the first lambs. Wherever you live in the world, you can focus on new beginnings by using symbols of the old festival.

Make a circle of eight pink and pale green candles as close to the eight compass directions (north, north-east, east, south-east, south, south-west, west, north-west) as you can manage and put a dish of fresh milk in the centre. Amethysts, garnets and bloodstones are crystals associated with this festival and can be placed between the candles to amplify the natural energies. Burn an incense or oil of the festival, such as basil, lavender or myrrh. Place any budding flowers or leaves next to the milk in the centre of your candles.

Light the candles one at a time, beginning with the one in the north-east, the traditional position of Brigantia. After you have lighted the first candle, take a dish of seeds, such sunflower, poppy or sesame and dip a seed into the milk while visualizing the first step towards a new beginning in whatever area of your life you would like change. Eat the seed. In old magical beliefs, as you ate a wish or need, you were actually taking in the magical energies (see also *Food Magic*, page 233).

Continue to light the candles, dipping a seed in the milk each time, making a wish or visualizing a step towards your future and eating the seed. When all the candles are lit, enjoy your Brigantia meal and then blow out your candles one by one, sending your wishes and new determination into the cosmos. Foods for this festival include seed breads and cakes, milk, honey, seeds of all kinds and all dairy products.

The evening of 31 January is the most powerful time for Brigantia magic but you can carry out new beginning rituals at any time of the year when you need a new beginning.

Lammas or Lughnassadh

This is the festival of the Harvest and the time of Justice and Completion. In Celtic times it was held from sunset on the eve of 31 August until sunset on 2 September. It is a lunar festival and powerful for magic concerning justice, rights and partnerships, both personal and legal.

'As ye sow, so shall ye reap,' is the sentiment that lies behind Lammas. This festival marked the beginning of autumn and was a celebration of the Celtic God of Wisdom and Light, Lug or Lugh. As well as the harvesting of the corn, it involved the baking of the first loaf, hence the name Loaf-Mass. Like many pagan festivals, it was taken over as Lammastide in the Church calendar.

It was considered unlucky to cut down the last sheaf of corn as this was thought to represent the Corn God. Harvesters would all hurl their sickles at the last sheaf so no one knew who had killed the Corn God. This last sheaf was made into a corn dolly, symbol of the Earth Mother, and decorated with the scarlet ribbons of Cerridwen, the Celtic Mother Goddess. It would be hung over the hearth throughout winter.

As Lammas was a time for feasting and meeting distant members of the tribe, it was a natural occasion for arranging marriages. Trial marriages for a year and a day were frequently set up at Lammas. The young couple would thrust their hands through a holed stone and agree to part after the designated period if either became disenchanted. Contracts were fixed at this time and the old name for the month was Claim-time. Roads were sufficiently dry for travelling during this period and courts of justice would travel round settling disputes and ordering the payment of debts.

Lammas Completion Magic

Lammas naturally represents a time for magic for settling old quarrels and resolving outstanding problems. Completion Magic is very different from Banishing Magic since you are creating a magical barrier to mark the end of a phase, whether a dispute or the completion of a period of sustained effort towards a goal. You are either consigning your work to the elements to bear fruit, or casting aside ill feeling so that an issue may become positively resolved in the fullness of time.

Use a straw object as your focus, such as a corn dolly, a corn knot, a straw hat, perhaps decorated with poppies or cornflowers, or a container of mixed cereals. Circle this with crystals of Lammas, which include tiger's eye, fossilized woods, amber and rutilated quartz, or with dark yellow and brown stones. Light a thick brown or dark yellow candle and burn incense or oil of Lammas, such as cedarwood, cinnamon, frankincense, ginger and heather. Have a Lammas meal alone or with a friend. Lammas foods include cereals, nuts, berries, rice, ale and elderberry wine.

Power from the Earth
Take a handful of cereals and plant them in the garden or a pot of soil with some fast-growing seeds of a yellow or brown flower so that your efforts will grow and come to fruition.

Power from Fire
Write down the quarrel to be mended or your project that you need to succeed on a slip of paper and burn it in the candle flame.

Power from Air
Pass the incense stick over the ashes of your message or carefully pour a little of the hot fragrant oil over it. Bury your ashes on a compost heap.

Power from Water
Scratch the name of the person with whom you wish to become reconciled or details of the matter you wish to be resolved on a stone and cast it into running water. Finally, place your corn dolly, corn knot or straw hat on a nail on the wall and leave it in place until matters have been resolved or your venture has borne fruit.

THE DRUIDS

The Druids were the Celtic priesthood who held the secrets of magic and healing. Being a Druid took a lifelong training which began when a boy was selected for his spiritual nature or early wisdom. It took 12 years or more to reach the first level, that of a Bard. The Bards were said to be the memory of the tribe. They preserved its history by learning hundreds of poems, stories and the secret tree alphabet and creating new songs and poetry to record current events.

One of their methods of training involved sensory deprivation. The novice would lie in a dark stone hut with a heavy stone on his chest for 24 hours or more until inspiration came deep from within him. Periods without food and in darkness could last for several days. This method was also employed by the Native American Indians at times of initiation so that their guardian spirits would come to them.

The next stage in the training was that of the Ovate which took a further ten years or more. The Ovate studied natural medicine, divination and prophesy and passed between the dimensions. It was he who contacted the Otherworld, especially at Samhain (see *Hallowe'en Magic*, page 260) and travelled to the Realm of the Ancestors to seek their wisdom. The souls of men were believed to reside in this Otherworld until after many years they might choose to be reborn, taking their accumulated wisdom with them. The Ovate divined with water, cloud shapes, fire and using haruspicy, the study of the entrails and flowing blood of a dying victim. This was also practised by the Romans.

After a further ten years of study the novice became a Druid, adviser to kings, judge, philosopher and high priest of the tribe. After the formal Druidic religion was wiped out in Wales by Julius Caesar during his conquest of Britain, the wisdom went underground. Many minstrels travelled round passing it on to secret converts as they sang the old songs for entertainment. Others fled to Ireland where the tradition lasted much longer.

Mistletoe

Mistletoe was the sacred plant of the Druids. It was cut from the sacred oak with a golden sickle by the Druids at the Midwinter Solstice, caught in a white sheet by young virgins, and known as the All-Healer for its magical powers.

Bardic Inspiration

If you have a problem that needs inspiration to solve or you are feeling overwhelmed by the world, lie in a quiet darkened room. Light a gentle fragrance of inspiration, such as lavender or pine, and close your eyes or place a silk scarf lightly over them. Place an unshaded lamp with a very bright light next to your bed, but do not switch it on.

Do not seek answers consciously but move quite deliberately into the darkness, seeing it as a gentle tunnel of dark water along which you are floating. You may sleep and dream or you may just drift in and out of different states. When you are ready, sit up and switch on the lamp. Stare into the brightness, switch it off and on the darkness you will see after-images of light that may form pictures or trigger words that will provide the answer that you need.

THE TREE ALPHABET

The Celtic Tree Alphabet carried the ancient secrets of the Celts through times of persecution. It consisted of angular markings, signed out using different joints of the fingers, and incorporated a complex grammar for transmitting secret wisdom and lore. It was not used in formal writing.

The Ogham Staves

The Tree Alphabet was also used for magical purposes and for divination. It consisted of 25 symbols, etched on pieces of wood and cast, much as the runes were, on to the ground or a white cloth. Each tree represented had a magical meaning, like the Norse runes (see also *Norse Magic*, page 375).

These symbols were known as the Ogham Staves after Ogma, warrior god, deity of wisdom and champion of the gods at the Battle of Moytura. He is said to have invented Ogham writing in the fourth century. The full Ogham system is quite complex, but you can use seven of the Ogham signs to represent the seven sacred trees of the Celts, etched on the appropriate wood to represent the energies of the different days of the week (see also *Tree Magic*, page 460). You can also scratch or paint your seven daily Ogham signs on seven stones, preferably small ones with natural holes, so that you can hang your symbol around your neck on a cord. It does not matter at all if your stones are of different shapes or substances.

You can also use crystals, bound on a clasp or seven crystal pendants (these can be bought quite cheaply if they are mounted on an alloy), threaded on a special silver or gold chain. Paint your Ogham sign on the appropriate stone or suggested crystal named below.

The best material of all for the Ogham talismans is a small piece from the seven trees or any strong wood with the symbol etched or burned into the bark. You do not need to wear or carry your Ogham talisman every day, only when you feel that you need the special strength, wisdom or the courage of Ogma, creator of the staves.

The Sacred Trees of the Celts

To the Celts, trees were especially magical and seven were known as the sacred trees. The seven sacred trees were birch, willow, holly, hazel, oak, apple and alder. They are dedicated to various days of the week.

Birch: Sunday

The birch is the symbol of rebirth and purification, so your Sunday tree represents new beginnings, new hopes for another week. It marks the leaving behind of last week's failures and regrets. If you can find some birch wood, etch your Ogham sign on it. Make your symbol small enough to carry or wear on Sundays when you feel that you have a heavy load to shed from the previous week.

Willow: Monday

This is the tree of intuition, of listening to your inner voice and wisdom. Carry or wear your willow symbol on Mondays if you feel that other people are influencing you with their expertise and pushing you along paths you do not wish to travel. It can also protect you against double-dealing.

Holly: Tuesday

The holly was regarded as the King of the Waning Year and sacred to the Celtic God Taranis, God of Lightning and a Protector God with his mighty club. The Tuesday tree represents concern for domestic issues and protection of any family members or close friends who may be vulnerable. Wear or carry your holly symbol on Tuesdays when those you love are under threat or you feel the need to draw strength from hearth and home.

Hazel: Wednesday

This is the tree of official wisdom and justice, of following the conventional path and paying attention to detail. Carry it or wear it on Wednesdays if you have contact with officialdom, finance or the law or you need assistance with any kind of formal learning or testing.

Oak: Thursday

This was regarded as the king of the waxing year ruling from the Winter to the Summer Solstice. The Thursday tree is the symbol of nobility of purpose and independence. Wear or carry your oak symbol on Thursdays when you need to assert your principles, assert your independence or make a stand against injustice.

Apple: Friday

To the Celts the apple was the symbol of fertility and immortality. Your Friday tree represents the effort you need to put into your life so that it will bear fruit. Wear your apple symbol to expand your horizons and find new approaches to old problems and for love or fertility matters.

Alder: Saturday

This was traditionally used for bridges and foundations. For example the foundations of Amsterdam, Holland, in later times were made of alder. Your Saturday tree represents firm foundations, security and a bridge between different opinions. Carry or wear your alder symbol on Saturdays when you experience doubt in yourself or your achievements. It says that you are on the right path and that your unique talents make you special and of worth.

Ogham Divination

Use any of your daily symbols when you need them, not only on the actual day that they represent. You can also etch the seven symbols on wood or stone and place them in a bag. Draw one to tell you the best day of the week to act and your best approach to a problem or issue of concern.

AN EXAMPLE OF OGHAM DIVINATION

Jack was working for his final exams at college when his girlfriend Anna told him that their relationship had been a sham. Anna demolished his world, telling him that he was not only inadequate as a lover, but also as a person and that everybody laughed at him behind his back. Jack wondered whether it was worth continuing with his exams or whether he should leave college.

He picked the alder. That says that if you are wavering from your path or feeling insecure, wear or carry your alder as a reminder of your own ability and value. By chance – or was it something more? – the willow fell out of the bag on to the floor. Jack confided in a friend who told him that Anna was afraid that Jack might do better than her in the forthcoming exams and for weeks had been ridiculing him behind his back.

Jack decided to listen to his inner voice and took his examinations, which he passed with honours. He began his exams on a Monday, the willow day but made his decision to continue on the previous Saturday (alder).

Ogham Crystals

These can be carried on the appropriate day to inspire you in the same way as your Ogham symbols.

Sunday: clear quartz, cornelian or any yellow or orange crystals.
Monday: moonstone, mother-of-pearl or any silvery or pale crystal.
Tuesday: red jasper, tiger's eye or any red or brown crystals.
Wednesday: dyed blue howzite, sodalite or any blue crystal.
Thursday: citrine, yellow jasper or any yellow crystals or stones.
Friday: rose quartz, jade or any green or pink crystals.
Saturday: amethyst, smoky quartz or any purple or black crystal.

6

CHINESE MAGIC

CREATION MYTHS

There are several Chinese creation myths. The most common one relates that at the beginning of time there were two oceans, one in the south and one in the north, with land in the centre. Shu was Lord of the Southern Ocean, Hu was Lord of the Northern Ocean and the unformed land was under the Lordship of Hwun-Tun (Chaos).

Shu and Hu met often on the land and because Hwun-Tun was so gracious towards them they decided to reward him for his kindness. He was blind, deaf and dumb since his eyes, ears and mouth were sealed, so each day Hu and Shu went to the central land to release him. On the seventh day, Chaos was freed. However, although he could now breathe, eat and use all his senses, he could not survive because he had been transformed into the Cosmos.

After countless ages, the Cosmos divided into two parts, male and female, later called the Greater Yang and Yin. These also divided to make the Lesser Yang and Yin. Eventually from the interaction of these four was born the first giant or world God, P'au Ku. Another version of the myth says that P'au Ku was hatched from the cosmic egg by the primaeval goose.

P'au Ku was given a hammer and chisel and travelled throughout the universe as Divine Artisan, shaping mountains and hammering out the sky. He was accompanied by the Primaeval Tortoise, the Phoenix and a Dragon. In Confucianism, Ch'ien the Great Father God of Heaven and Kun, the Great Mother, the Goddess of Earth, were the creators of P'au Ku, the ancestor of three families, the rulers of Heaven, Earth and mankind.

Of P'au Ku's legendary descendants, Fu Hsai was the first great ruler of China, his dynasty extending from 2953 BC to 2838 BC. He was said to be the product of a miraculous conception and to have instructed the Chinese how to live civilized lives, make fishing nets, cultivate the land, obey laws and create dwellings. He began formalized religion and kept six kinds of animals, which he sacrificed on the solstices each year, marking these as sacred days.

THE DEITIES

The Chinese pantheon operates on several levels and is influenced by an amalgamation of the three main religions: Taoism, Buddhism and Confucianism. It also includes nature spirits, such as the dragons, and ancestor worship. A family had its household gods and venerated its ancestors. Within a neighbourhood, local gods responsible for these areas were worshipped. In early China, the State Gods, who were venerated mainly by the ruling classes, included Tien (Heaven), Ti (Earth) and the Royal Ancestors. Gradually the State Gods filtered into popular worship.

The Jade Emperor

Yu-Huang, the Jade Emperor, was the ruler of the heavenly court and became the principal deity in popular religion. The idea of an Emperor controlling public life was so central to Chinese philosophy that it was applied to the heavenly realms. The Jade Emperor officially assumed eminence in heaven around AD 1017 when a state cult was set up for the Great Heavenly Emperor of Jade Purity. However, the cult of the Jade Emperor began much earlier, during the Tang dynasty (618–906). In the Jade Emperor's court were various ranks of deities responsible for the specific ministries, such as epidemics, fire, healing, sacred mountains, thunder and wind. Tsao Chun was the God of the Stove who oversaw domestic matters. Chang Huang was God of Cities, Fu Shen God of Happiness and Tsai Chen the God of Wealth. The Jade Emperor's festival was held on the ninth day of the first lunar month.

Ancestor Worship

The veneration of ancestors is an enduring focus of Chinese life, despite attempts during the Cultural Revolution of the 1960s and 1970s to destroy it. Ancestor worship dates back to the early Shang dynasty that began about 1500 BC and is seen as mutually enriching, not only for the living whose ancestors offer protection, but for the ancestor's soul that is nurtured by offerings from his descendants. The soul is said to reside at the burial place and can become angry if not offered due respect.

The Dragons

The Dragons, divinities of water and rain, can assume different forms: a youth or old person, a lovely maiden or a hideous crone, a rat, a snake or tree. Whatever its shape, the Dragon is also the Thunder God who causes rain to fall.

In the season of drought, the dragons are supposed to sleep in their pools or wells until they begin to stir in the spring and fight each other. The Chinese rejoice as the first dragon wakes after the winter for then storms break out and rain pours down in torrents, bringing the land to life. They say that pearls and fireballs fall to the ground, the pearls giving promise of continuing fruitfulness.

The Chinese Dragon of the East is blue. He is the predominant spirit of rain and rules the spring. In the South were two dragon gods, the red and the yellow. The Red God ruled all the summer season except for the last month when the yellow Dragon held sway. In the West was the White Dragon of Autumn. The Northern Dragon was black, presiding over the Winter.

The Dragons were also healers, offering cures for diseases. The Red Cloud herb and other healing plants were found by the dragon pools after a thunderstorm. They were associated with light, the sun, moon, day and night. On the fifteenth day of the first month, a dragon made of paper, linen and bamboo with a red ball in front of it was carried through the streets. This was the Azure Dragon, on whose head rose the star that heralded spring.

THE FESTIVALS

Chinese festivals were linked to the ancient lunar calendar. They also reflected the agricultural year, especially the times of sowing and reaping. New and full moon festivals were celebrated outdoors in a garden or pavilion. The most important was the Harvest Moon Festival, held on the fifteenth day of the eighth month. The whole night was spent watching the moon, while listening to poems and songs composed in praise of its beauty.

The first and most significant festival in the Chinese calendar is Yuan Tan, the Chinese New Year, which is held at the first full moon in February. Houses are spring-cleaned, debts settled and the paper gods of the door are renewed. Streamers of red paper decorated with Chinese characters wishing long life, wealth, health and happiness on all who enter, are draped on doorposts and all around the house. Offerings are made to the gods and the ancestors. Drums and cymbals are banged loudly and fireworks are ignited to drive off the evil powers that linger at the turn of the year. The New Year ends with the three-day Feast of Lanterns (see also *New Year Magic*, page 362). Lanterns of many sizes and colours, except white, the colour of death, are lit in front of homes and official buildings. Huge paper dragons and papier mâché lions parade through the streets.

The Dragon Boat Festival

This ancient summer sun festival is still celebrated in Southern China, Hong Kong and Malaysia on the fifth day of the fifth moon. Its aim is to procure a rich harvest from the dragon gods. It also remembers the death of a famous poet and politician Chu Yuan who lived around 343–279 BC. He was disillusioned by the warring lords of China and drowned himself to bring about reform. Boats decorated with dragons take to the water and offerings are cast into the rivers.

The Festival of Oxherd and the Weaving Maidens

This was celebrated on the seventh day of the seventh month and commemorates two star-crossed lovers of ancient myth who perished in a fast-flowing river so that they would be together in death. The gods made them into two stars, shining on either side of the Milky Way. They were reunited each year on the seventh night of the seventh moon. At this festival, women would take silver or gold needles with seven holes to thread melon seeds and would pray to the two star lovers for skill in weaving and sewing. The festival was also celebrated in Japan.

Chung Yuan, the Festival of Hungry Souls

From the fifteenth day of the seventh lunar month until the end of the month, offerings were made to those who had died unprepared or homeless or who had no descendants to venerate them. The festival also commemorated those without a grave because they had drowned. Offerings included paper houses, money, clothes and food to give them succour in the spirit world. The paper objects were thrown into fires and rivers.

Chung Yeung, another festival of the dead, occurred on the ninth day of the ninth moon. It was celebrated by going to high places and flying kites in the form of dragons, butterflies, birds and centipedes. Graves were visited and gifts taken for the departed. Paper effigies of goods were burned to send them to the next world. The dead were also sent objects they had desired but had not possessed while they were alive.

YANG AND YIN

Chinese and oriental divination is very different from that of the Western world. Chinese philosophy is based not on the concept of a linear path towards perfect love, success and happiness, but on a constantly changing state. When an extreme, whether joy or sorrow, is reached, it changes into its opposite and both darkness and light, good and evil are an integral part of existence. These energies, Yang and Yin and their interrelation, represent the natural laws of the universe and the constantly changing patterns of existence. Natural law is a central element of divination. In traditional Chinese divination, patterns in natural forces were symbols of immediate conditions in the wider eternal flow of events in time.

The I Ching

The *I Ching*, the *Book of Changes*, is based on a system of trigrams and hexagrams, patterns made of broken and unbroken lines representing Yang and Yin. Fu Hsai, the father of Chinese civilization, is credited with creating the eight trigrams, based on eight natural forces, that became the basis for the system.

He discovered the first eight trigrams by studying the patterns of a tortoise shell. The Primaeval Tortoise was regarded as sacred since it accompanied the Divine Artisan as he created the world. The long life of the tortoise has made it a magical creature. Legends abound throughout the Eastern world of giant tortoises holding up the world and the Islands of the Blest, the earthly equivalent of paradise where immortality was assured to those who resided there. In the Far East there is said to be a tortoise that lives in the middle of the ocean and has one eye in the middle of its forehead. Once every three thousand years it rises to the surface and rolls over on its back to see the sun. This accounts for land movements and tidal waves. The tortoise became sacred as a symbol of permanence and high-ranking officials would wear tortoiseshell girdles.

In ancient China, tortoise shells were heated in a fire until they cracked and the pattern of cracks was then interpreted by a diviner. In creating the trigrams, Fu Hsai brought order to the random recurring patterns. His trigrams, which are used as the basis for the divinatory method described in this book, emphasized the fluid, constantly changing quality of eight natural forces: the sky, the water of lakes and marshes, fire, lightning and the sun, thunder, wind, tree and wood, mountain or hill and the earth.

The formal *Book of Changes* or *I Ching*, was first set down by King Wen who founded the Chou dynasty, around 1143 BC. He created an order for the 64 hexagrams, six lines of Yangs and Yin from the earlier trigrams, gave them names and made the first written commentaries. His son the Duke of Chou added to these.

Confucius who lived from 551 BC to 479 BC was not, as is often thought, the founder of the *I Ching*. He came to it quite late in life but added ten major commentaries, interpreting the texts in terms of 'superior man', his idealized Chinese male, who was devoted to social order and justice and put social development before personal advancement. Confucian scholars added to the commentaries and it is hard to ascertain what actually was original Confucius. The *I Ching* is still used by Chinese and Japanese businessmen when making decisions.

Yang and Yin in Ancient and Modern Thought

The ancient meaning of Yin was the 'shaded north side' of a hill while Yang meant the 'sunny south side'. Yang controls heaven and all things positive, active, light, masculine, unyielding, moving and living. Yin controls the Earth and all negative, passive, dark, soft, still and non-living entities.

Traditionally Yang is written as a single unbroken line and Yin as a broken line. External changes are attributed to the waxing and waning of the relative qualities of Yang and Yin (see sections on *Earth Magic*, page 153, and *Feng Shui*, page 135). Any particular situation at a given moment contains a specific balance of these qualities.

The seasons reflect the Yang-Yin balance. In winter, Yin is at its greatest power and Yang is at its least. In spring, Yang and Yin are equal, as Yang waxes and Yin wanes. In the summer, Yang reaches its height and by autumn, the balance of Yang and Yin has returned, but with Yin waxing and Yang waning. The cycle continues into the next year and in an unbroken circle.

Yang and Yin in Action

Yang, shown by an unbroken line, –, represents the creative, logical and assertive element in our lives and is an essential part of both male and female make-up if we are to achieve our potential and not be swamped by the needs of others. It stands for action, determination, strength and light. In the Westernized system of the four elements, Yang is fire and air, representing in Jungian terms creativity and logic, the mind functions, the conscious world.

Yin, shown by a broken line, – –, is the receptive, accepting, intuitive side that is integral to being a woman, but it is also important for a man to acknowledge his gentler, intuitive nature. Yin stands for patience, endurance, emotion, dreams, intuition, empathy, fluidity, darkness and the world of the unconscious. In the Westernized system Yin belongs to earth and water, Jung's practical and feeling functions.

USING CHINESE MAGIC

Making I Ching Stones

One of the easiest and most spiritual ways of using Yang and Yin magic is to make your own set of Yang/Yin stones and marking a Yang (single unbroken line) and Yin (two smaller broken lines) on the side of each stone with paint or permanent ink.

You can make these from white or light-coloured stones, but jade crystals are a particularly beautiful and magical material for Yang and Yin stones. Inexpensive jade crystals about the size of a large coin are available from mineral or New Age shops. The colour ranges from the palest transparent green to a deep, almost opaque hue.

According to myth, the Mother Goddess created jade from her soul substance. It is a stone linked both with vegetation and the moon. From early in China's civilization, jade was carved into beautiful objects. There is an old Chinese saying that 'he who swallows jade will exist as long as jade'. Gold and jade were traditionally placed in the apertures of a corpse to prevent decay.

The Yes/No/Yang/Yin Oracle

In the earliest form of Chinese magic, single Yangs and Yins were used to make decisions or decide between options. Use your six stones or coins (heads for Yang or yes and tails for Yin or no). You cannot use the oracle even on this basic level to predict the future, asking such questions as 'Will I meet the girl/man of my dreams?' or 'Will I win the lottery?' The answer to both questions may well be negative and preclude more likely ways of meeting someone you will be happy with or possible ways of making money that involve earthly input. But for 'Should I – ' questions where an instant response is required or where you've been arguing round in circles in your head, the yes/no method is valuable. It is helpful for both a simple question or as part of a series of questions.

If you get an even number of Yangs and Yins or yes and no answers, you need to try another one. If an answer is predominantly yes or no, that can be taken as the degree of certainty and the need for immediate action. Six Yangs and no Yins and you should apply for that job, book that travel ticket or propose immediately!

Choosing between options

You can also use the yes/no oracle to choose between people or places. If the stones are equally balanced, three Yangs and three Yins, neither option is right and you should seek a third way. Try phrasing your query in a different way or look for alternatives.

The Method

Think of a question involving two alternatives. Place your six stones, each marked Yang on one side and Yin on the other, into a bag or purse. Take each one without looking, throw it on to a table or the floor and count the number of Yangs and number of Yins to see how the question has been answered.

Throw the stones again if the Yangs and Yins were even, using a different way of asking the question. If it still remains unclear, try again another day as your inner psyche needs longer to work on the issue. Even if an answer is straightforward, you may like to ask another related question. You can ask as many questions as you wish. It may be that the final question has moved quite a way from the original one but will help you to understand the wider issues.

THE EIGHT FORCES OF NATURE

Using the Trigrams to Plan your Daily Strategy

The trigrams can be created by choosing at random three Yin or Yang stones. The Chinese fashion is to work from the bottom to the top. The first stone that you choose will be the bottom line of your trigram. Mark it on a piece of paper. The second will be the second line and so on. So if you chose at random Yin, Yang, Yang, your trigram would look like this:

Each trigram is made up of a mixture of Yangs and Yin that reflects the quality of the natural force it represents. One of these natural forces is the predominant energy of the day that can guide you through the challenges and hazards. Each person will pick a different trigram, because Yang/Yin Magic taps into the personal intuitive and psychic source of the person who throws the stones.

If there is a decision you have to make, you can throw a trigram to see what is the best path ahead for you.

The Trigrams

Sky or Heaven

Made up of three Yangs, this is the Father or pure energy trigram. It comes to tell you that you can succeed if you just believe in yourself and your abilities. It is the trigram of ideas, independence and new beginnings. Use the logic or air and the limitless potential of the sky to assert what it is you want and go for it alone if necessary.

Tessa threw the trigram Sky when she was offered a job after ten years at home bringing up the children. She was scared that she would fail as the office was full of young, confident girls. Sky told her to believe in herself and to seize any opportunity with both hands. After a few anxious weeks of adjustment, Tessa discovered that her experience of life gave her the ability to stay ahead of the youngsters.

Earth

Made up of three Yins, this is the Mother or pure nurturing, accepting trigram. It says that it is important to let any ventures and relationships blossom in their own time and to offer love and acceptance to others rather than criticism. Fulfilment comes through others and through waiting rather than acting.

Paul threw the Earth trigram when he had been offered the chance to travel to France for a few days with friends from work. But his grandma was seriously ill and had asked her favourite grandson to come to her birthday party. Paul followed Earth's advice and stayed. When his grandmother died the day after the party, Paul was glad he had made her last birthday a happy occasion.

Fire Lightning or the Sun

This is the trigram of inspiration and creativity. Lightning reveals hidden corners of darkness, fire consumes all in its path, while the sun offers clarity and drives away doubt. The trigram talks of sudden illumination, an answer that suddenly comes to an old problem, of optimism and the stirring of happiness perhaps after a dark period. Use your imagination and enthusiasm to make your ideas happen.

John made the Fire trigram when he was contemplating selling his car, his only asset, to pay his mortgage arrears and avoid repossession of his home. But, that meant he would be unable to continue with his car hire business and so he would ultimately lose his house anyway. He suddenly realized that with his experience he could obtain a job as a live-in chauffeur. He signed on with an agency and was able to let his home at a profit, while he worked for an oil magnate who needed a chauffeur/personal assistant as he travelled around Europe.

Water

This is the trigram of fluid movement. It advises moving forward wherever opportunity arises, however unlikely. It tells you to tune into people's feelings, especially those beneath the surface and be adaptable to the current situation. Water always finds a way and although it may begin as a tiny stream, it gathers momentum and always reaches the ultimate goal, however many diversions life puts in the way.

Pam threw the Water trigram after she was made redundant. Her divorced boyfriend Ken had suggested that she move in with him and take care of his children. Her only alternative was a retraining course a long way away in a bleak industrial town. Water advised her to move forward, however bad the way seemed. Pam decided to turn down the safe option since she did not get on with Ken's children and realized that he just wanted an unpaid housekeeper. Instead she accepted the course and is really enjoying it, especially since she discovered that the town is surrounded by beautiful countryside.

Thunder

This is the trigram of sudden, dramatic movement, shaking the status quo and heralding change. In the Chinese tradition, thunder slept within the womb of Earth during the winter and burst forth in the spring, scattering the seeds of new life. Therefore it is important to let any resentments and frustration be known. Make decisive change and use the sudden thrust of energy to make life more as you want it and to make your unique identity and strengths felt.

Margaret got Thunder when she discovered her husband Tim was having yet another affair. She drew out a large sum from their joint savings which she had built up and went on an extended holiday with a girlfriend to Australia and New Zealand. She enjoyed herself so much she realized that she did not need Tim any more.

Wind, wood or tree

This is the trigram of more gradual, gentle change, for the wind is a gentle but penetrating breeze rather than a hurricane and the tree had firm roots but grows slowly, linking earth with sky. This trigram says that the way forward is through gentle persistence, a step at a time towards the fulfilment of any goal, whether large or small. Your dreams may seem an age away from reality, but as long as you keep going and resist pressures to give up, you will get there in the end.

Gillian threw the Wind trigram when the plans she and her husband had made to retire to Majorca were frustrated by her elderly mother's increasing dependence. Wind told her that rather than abandon everything because her dream could not be achieved immediately, she should persevere in slow, small stages. Rather than give up the idea of living abroad, she and her husband decided to buy a holiday apartment to use when they could arrange respite care for the old lady.

Mountain or hill

This is the trigram of stillness, of looking beyond the immediate to a long-term aim. The mountain that has grown from the earth touches the sky and so speaks of limitations of time and space within the human spirit. From the peak of the mountain the spirit can touch the sky and so Mountain is a symbol of spiritual as well as worldly yearnings for something beyond the immediate and material. Do not settle for second best or be weighed down by the concerns of mundane existence.

David threw the Mountain trigram at a key point in his life. He was a successful businessman, travelling the world. But as the years went by and one relationship after another failed, he was increasingly aware that his life was materially rich but that it had no real meaning. The Mountain trigram reminded him of old dreams. Quite suddenly he quit his job to run a vineyard in France with an old friend and although he has not yet broken even, feels for the first time a real satisfaction in his life.

Lake

This holds water that is very different from the free-flowing water of the earlier trigram. It is contained and therefore the movement is downwards rather than forward. Lake talks of inner joy and tranquillity from looking inward and concentrating on dreams, on the world of the psychic and spiritual. It is the Mountain reversed. This trigram says that you may be feeling exhausted or out of touch with the world. If so, withdraw for a while and listen to your own counsel rather than that of others.

Peter threw the Lake trigram when he lost his temper at work over a minor incident and realized that he had become increasingly impatient and unable to relax. He had been spending every evening either at the sports centre or out with friends and at weekends was studying for a business qualification. After contemplating lake's message of calm, he decided to cut down on the sports and spend three or four nights a week at home until his joy in life and energy returned.

Making Your Trigrams

Try casting a trigram in the morning to discover whether it is a Sky day when you strike out alone, a Lake day to withdraw as far as possible and so on. Alternatively, you can ask a question and let the trigram guide you as to the meaning.

7

CHRISTMAS MAGIC

THE ORIGINS

Christmas draws its name from Christes Mass which originated in the angels' song in Bethlehem, but the idea of a mid-winter festival goes back to early times when men and women feared that the sun would die on the shortest day of the year (around 21 December in the Northern hemisphere). So they lit fires to persuade the sun to rise once more and hung evergreen boughs to encourage the other trees to grow leaves once more.

Because it was a time when light was restored into the world, many cultures recognised the mid-winter solstice as the festival of spiritual and religious rebirth. The Persians had a mid-winter feast at which they kindled great fires for the birth of Mithras, the Sun God. In many ancient traditions, corn and vegetation gods, such as Osiris in Ancient Egypt and Tammuz of the Babylonians, died on this day and were restored to life by their Queen Consorts or mothers. The solstice was the Feast of the Unconquerable Sun when the Queen of Heaven or Earth Mother gave birth to the Sun God in a cave. The Ancient Egyptian priests would emerge from underground caves to pronounce that the Virgin had brought forth the sun.

The Mexicans and Peruvians celebrated the birth of the son of the Celestial Queen. In Northern Europe Odin or Woden, the original Father Christmas, rode through the sky in his chariot pulled by Sleipnir, his eight-legged horse. He dropped gifts for the blessed or sometimes left them at the foot of his sacred pine.

The Romans observed Saturnalia, beginning on 19 December for seven days, centred around a debauched version of Saturn or Old Father Time, another Father Christmas figure. A slave was picked as the Lord of Misrule.

In 353 Pope Julius I changed the celebration of the birth of Christ from 6 January to 25 December. However in many parts of Europe the old date for festivities persisted until the introduction of the Gregorian Calendar.

The Feast of Epiphany is still a focus of Christmas celebrations in Spain and Italy. On 6 January children leave grass or hay for the Three Kings who bring them gifts. In folk tradition Befena, the benevolent witch, flies down the chimney and leaves sweets and tiny toys in the stockings of good children. According to legend, Befena was too busy with household affairs to attend to the Kings when they passed her home on their way to visit the Christ Child. She said she would care for them on the way back but they went another way. Therefore every Twelfth Night, Befena, also known as Epiphania, watches for the Kings but she always misses them.

The Eve of St Nicholas's Day, 6 December, is still the occasion for the Saint (whose name has changed into Santa Claus) to visit the homes of children in Holland, Germany and Austria, promising presents for good children and writing the name in his book of children who have been bad. Children leave out their shoes for him to fill. He is accompanied by Knight Rupert or Black Peter, a Christianized version of Odin.

A Swedish celebration, the Festival of St Lucy, occurs on 13 December, commemorating Saint Lucia or Lucy who went down into the catacombs to take food for Christians who were hiding from persecution. She wore a wreath of candles so both her hands were free. One of the daughters of the family wears a battery-powered wreath and serves the family spicy buns for breakfast at first light, singing a traditional St Lucy song. The festival, like the mid-winter solstice, commemorates the return of light to the world.

MODERN RESEARCH

Television has been blamed for making children more cynical but that is not the full story, according to Dr Maire Messenger Davies who addressed the British Psychological Society in December 1995. In her survey of young American television watchers, all the six-year-olds she questioned believed in Santa Claus but three-quarters of them knew that Superman could not really fly. Ninety per cent of 11-year-olds knew the truth about Santa as well. Dr Davies concluded that although television challenges children to think about reality, 'there are other things it cannot alter, like believing in Santa Claus. Younger children still do live in a world where there is magic and fantasy.'

Santa Claus has become big business. A Santa Claus School in Beverley Hills trains 3,000 Santas a year for the festive season and at the town of Santa Claus in Indiana the college offers a BSc in Santa Clausery. Would-be Santa Clauses risk turning into fireballs unless they have the necessary magic to defy science. Scientists at the Massachusetts Institute of Technology have calculated that, with an estimated 92 million homes to visit around the world each Christmas Eve (1,064 visits per second), Santa's sleigh would have to move at 650 miles per second, 3,000 times the speed of sound. Even if his reindeer were 10 times as strong as ordinary deer, he would still need 214,000 of them to pull 353,430 tons of presents. The scientists concluded that this weight travelling at mach 3,000 would mean Santa would burst into a fireball on contact with the Earth's atmosphere.

For techno-children, Santa Claus can now be contacted on E-Mail at Santa@northpole.net. In 1994, he received 500 requests a day, mostly for Power Rangers and Barbie Dolls.

CHRISTMAS LEGENDS

Santa Claus

Saint Nicholas was a fourth-century bishop of Myra in Asia Minor. He was patron saint of children and in his lifetime frequently gave tiny presents to all he met. According to legend, one mid-December, St Nicholas was passing a house when he saw three young women sitting by the fireside, weeping. Their father, a nobleman, had lost his fortune and so they had no dowries to wed the men they loved. St Nicholas dropped three bags of gold down the chimney. One went into each of their stockings which were drying by the fire. To this day three golden balls in memory of St Nicholas' gift may be seen outside pawnbrokers' shops, for he is also patron saint to them as well as unmarried women, children, perfumiers, sailors and Russia.

From this legend grew our Santa. Dutch settlers took it to New Amsterdam, now New York, where he was called Sinter Klaus (Saint Nicholas), then Santa Claus. The image of St Nicholas, the forerunner of Santa Claus, as a whiskery Dutch settler continued in the United States where there would be annual parades through the street on his day. These St Nicholas parades became enshrined in the 1800s. Dr Clement C Moore's poem, *A Visit from St Nicholas*, written in 1822, developed the image of Santa landing on rooftops in his sleigh and climbing down chimneys to bring presents. The poem was illustrated some years later in 1863 by Thomas Nast in *Harper's Illustrated Weekly*, giving him the red regalia which has reinforced the present image of Father Christmas.

Legends of the Talking Animals

On Christmas Eve animals have the power to talk because they were present in the stable when Jesus was born. Cows fall to their knees and turn to the East at midnight, cockerels crow, 'Christus natus est,' (Christ is born), Oxen ask 'Ubi?' (where) and the sheep reply 'Be – ee-thlehem'.

Bees traditionally hum the Twenty-third Psalm on Christmas Eve. It was also believed that all the trees in the forest bloom briefly and are covered with fruit at midnight on Christmas Eve. If you could eat one of the fruits you would gain immortality, but they always disappeared on touch.

CHRISTMAS CUSTOMS

Some old customs translate well into modern life in any country, such as Stir Pudding Day or the Festival of Candles on St Lucy's Day (13 December).

Christmas Crib

The crib was introduced by St Francis of Assisi in 1224 who was trying to remind people of the religious meaning of Christmas. He led the local people up the hills to a cave where he had created a scene complete with animals. In part of France *santons*, clay figures, are made for the nativity scene that include models of local village characters and dignitaries.

Christmas Fare

Mince pies were originally brought to Europe from the Holy Land by the Crusaders and were savoury, made from meat with spices to preserve them. They were in the shape of a crib with a pastry baby on top. One was eaten on each of the Twelve Days of Christmas.

Christmas Pudding

Christmas pudding was until the sixteenth century a semi-liquid porridge, containing the fruits, grains and metals (silver coins and charms) of the earth, representing the Earth Mother. In the Northern tradition, the sprig of holly was the World Tree.

The pudding was cooked on Stir Pudding Day, the last Sunday before Advent. The mix was traditionally enough for thirteen puddings, the last of which would be given away to someone in need. Thirteen ingredients were used and each member of the family, ending with the youngest, would stir the pudding nine times clockwise and make a wish that would come true only if it was kept a secret.

Christmas Trees

These date back to early tribes who adorned the trees with blazing brands at the mid-winter solstice to persuade the sun to shine again. Lights, ornaments and offerings were hung on the trees in the groves, sacred to the Mother Goddesses who gave birth to the new sun and to pagan solar gods, such as Dionysius, who were reborn at this time. The Druids hung golden apples on trees.

The first Christmas decorations were made of pastry and were suns, moons and stars to represent the rebirth of the sun. The Romans trimmed trees with gifts and trinkets during Saturnalia.

On 21 December at the pagan Mid-winter Solstice, St Boniface, who in the eighth century travelled from England to convert the Bavarians, encountered some Druids about to tie a young boy to a sacred oak and sacrifice him. Boniface chopped down the tree and behind it was a tiny evergreen. The Druids fell to their knees and hung their lanterns on the little tree.

The decorated Christmas tree gained popularity in Germany at the time of Martin Luther who hung candles on a tree to show his family the wonders of the stars in the firmament. Prince Albert, the Consort of Queen Victoria, made the Christmas tree a tradition in Britain by introducing one at Windsor Castle in 1841. British families, eager to emulate the royal family, took up the custom.

The pine tree was the symbol of Attis, the Phrygian God of Death and Resurrection. He was killed under a pine tree, then reborn on 25 December. Sacred offerings were placed at the base of a pine tree and it was decorated with gold and silver ornaments.

Holly and Mistletoe

The Holly and the Ivy,
Now they are both full grown,
Of all the trees that are in the wood,
The holly bears the crown.

So runs the Christian carol, but its words look back to the earlier pagan festival when the holly was the King of the Waning Year and the ivy the female principle.

Holly wreaths offer shelter to tree spirits and so are hung on doors at Christmas to provide protection for them and all who lived within the house, for no evil could pass the door. In pre-Christian times holly was sacred to Saturn and used to decorate his temples at the feast of Saturnalia. The ivy crown was worn by the Lord of Misrule.

Christianity associated holly berries with the blood of Christ. Popular myth recounted that the berries were stained red by the blood of a little lamb at the first Nativity who caught himself on holly thorns. Mistletoe, the Golden Bough and All-Healer of the Druids, is an ancient fertility symbol. It was harvested by unspoilt maidens with golden sickles from an oak tree at the Mid-winter Solstice. Another legend says that the Norse Goddess Frigg, the mother of Baldur the Sun God, who was slain by a mistletoe twig, wept at his death and her tears turned to pearls on the plant. Mistletoe means 'give me a kiss' in the language of flowers and lovers should continue kissing until they have plucked all the berries, one for each kiss.

Tinsel

When Mary and Joseph were fleeing from Herod to Egypt with the baby Jesus they hid in a cave. Popular myth says that a spider wove a beautiful web over the entrance to keep them warm. When Herod's soldiers came by, they saw the entrance to the cave covered with webs and thought no one could be inside. So it is said to be unlucky to kill a spider and we put tinsel on our trees to remember how it saved the Christ Child.

Poinsettia Plants

A Mexican legends says that a little boy was too poor to put a gift in the charity box on Christmas Eve. He cried because he so much wanted to give something. At that moment a beautiful scarlet flower bloomed where his tears fell. He took it into the church and placed it before the crib. So the plant is known as *Flor de la Noche Buene,* Flower of the Holy Night, and is ever after a reminder that Christmas is about love, not material offerings.

Yule Logs

Yule means the yoke of the year, the point of balance across the lowest point of sunlight. The Yule Log was usually made of oak, King of the new Waxing Year, and was sacrificed to give life to the sun. It was kindled from wood saved from the previous year's log and the Yule fire was kept burning from the Solstice Eve to Twelfth Night,

6 January. As the log was ignited, a sacred charge was made such as: 'I charge this log to burn bright and to give light, health and wealth to this house and all who dwell therein.'

A small piece of the log was preserved for the following year and the ashes scattered on fields and gardens to make them fruitful. The burning of the Yule log was common throughout Europe and Scandinavia, although the pine or birch, symbol of regeneration, was used in Scandinavia, with an ash faggot in the centre, to represent the World Tree.

In modern celebrations the Yule Log is usually replaced by scarlet candles, one for each day of the Twelve Days of Christmas from Christmas Eve to Twelfth Night.

CHRISTMAS DIVINATION AND RITUALS

Christmas is another popular time for love rituals and divination. You may like to try some, either on the eve of the Shortest Day or Christmas Eve or Night.

Sew nine holly leaves to your night clothes and place a gold-coloured ring on your heart or wedding finger before going to bed. You will dream of your future wedding day and see your true love standing beside you.

Tie a sprig of holly to each of the legs of your bed and eat a baked apple before going to sleep. Your true love will speak to you in your dreams.

Three or more unmarried people can make a chain of holly, mistletoe and juniper and between each strand tie an acorn or hazel nuts. At midnight they must lock the door and hang the key over the mantelpiece. They should wrap the chain around a log, sprinkle it with oil, salt and earth and burn it on the fire. Each sits around the fire with a prayer book opened at the wedding service. Once the chain is burned, each will see his or her future wife or husband crossing the room.

Dumb Cakes, made of oats, barley and water were made in silence by young girls on Christmas Eve and placed in the oven late in the evening. However, in more liberated times, men who wish a glimpse of their true love can also make dumb cakes. At midnight the kitchen door will open and your true love will come and turn the cakes. If not, you can have your pick of the local fire brigade.

Walk upstairs backwards eating a piece of Christmas cake and place the crumbs beneath your pillow. You will dream of your true love.

ANGELS AND FATHER CHRISTMAS

Angels are much in evidence at Christmas in school nativity plays and on Christmas cards around the crib. However, during my own research into angels, I have discovered that children do see what are to them real angels. Quite frequently, they are traditional ones with golden wings, halos and beautiful white robes.

My favourite angel is the one who visited five-year-old Julie just before Christmas. I met Julie's mother Angela, whom I know slightly, in a local supermarket. I mentioned a radio broadcast I was going to do about Christmas angels in Ireland the next day. When I said that a lot of people were sceptical about the existence of angels she told me that her young daughter had seen one, complete with glittering wings, just before Christmas the previous year. Angela explained: 'My own mother had died suddenly at the beginning of December and though I was making the best of Christmas for the children, my heart was not in it and even the children were not excited. Then one morning Julie came thundering downstairs and told me, "I have just seen a beautiful angel, all silver with huge wings. She told me that Nanny is in heaven and is perfectly happy and says we're to have a good Christmas or else."

'So we did have a good Christmas after all and I felt my mother around the whole time, which was very comforting.'

THE CHRISTMAS CANDLE

In Ireland, Brittany and among American families who have Celtic connections, the Christmas Eve custom still survives of leaving a lighted candle in the window to help the Virgin Mary on her way. Food and drink are left in the kitchen in case she is hungry or thirsty.

I heard of the experience of a woman called Mary, who lives in Eire. She was 18 years old and spending her last Christmas at home before she married. On Christmas Eve she and her mother were in the kitchen waiting to attend Midnight Mass when they heard footsteps in the hall and the soft sighing of a woman who sounded very tired. Thinking that her aunt had arrived early and used her key, Mary went into the hall. All the doors were locked and every room undisturbed as she entered. Her aunt arrived some time later. Mary believes that on her last Christmas at home, the Virgin Mary had seen the Christmas candle in the window and had stopped on her journey to rest.

A CHRISTMAS NEAR DEATH EXPERIENCE

Some people who have technically died on the operating table have described 'near death experiences' in which they float out of their bodies and look down on the people trying to save them. Often they describe meeting relatives or angels. Children's near death experiences tend to be very vivid and usually it is the voice of a living rather than deceased relative that calls them back. My favourite near death experience is that of a 12-year-old girl, Megan, who nearly died at Christmas. I found her experience among some old archives in Oxford.

'I had a big operation on my shoulder for a useless arm damaged at birth,' she said. 'My mother had died giving birth to me. I was told later I nearly died during the operation. I had the Last Rites although I do not remember this. I had been looking forward to Christmas even though I was in hospital. What I saw was the most lovely bright light.

'Then I saw Father Christmas going through that lovely ray of light. I could see him going up and up. Before he got to the top, I heard someone call my name, "Meg, Meg," which people called me in those days. The bright light seemed to fade away from me. Father Christmas was gone when I felt someone holding my hand, saying, "Don't die, Meggie".

'I opened my eyes to see my father crying and then I began to recover. I will never forget that wonderful light, a light I have never seen again.'

MODERN MID-WINTER CELEBRATIONS

It is very easy to idealize the past. However, the emphasis of traditional Christmas was on the whole family doing and making, rather than the adults becoming over-burdened and the children left out and irritable. The preparations were as important as the actual celebration. Problems often arise because the entire celebration is crammed into a single day. It can be more enjoyable to combine the traditions in a series of mini-celebrations.

Alternative Festivities

Begin with Stir Pudding Day at the end of November, followed by a St Nicholas Eve meal of goose, red cabbage and stollen cake on 5/6 December. The children can leave shoes or slippers on St Nicholas Eve to be filled with tiny toys or sweets.

The next celebration could be on the Festival of Lights on 13 December, with a special candlelight breakfast of spicy buns and perhaps presents of torches for children.

The Mid-winter Solstice celebrations on 21 December can provide an alternative focus if families cannot spend Christmas Day together, perhaps because of work, access arrangements or the need to spend Christmas with one set of in-laws rather than another.

On Christmas Eve, make *santons* out of clay for your crib, moulding images of all the local characters as well as the angels, wise men, shepherds and the Holy Family. At dusk, light a Christmas candle in the window to guide Mary on her way to Bethlehem. Try some of the old Christmas rituals and love divination by the light of a candle as midnight draws near. Before bedtime, children and adults alike can leave food for Santa and his reindeer and hang up red felt stockings. Older children can be given a small amount of money to choose surprises for adults and fill their stockings in secrecy.

On Christmas Day, let all the family, even the youngest, join in assembling a meal of their favourite foods. You may end up with maple syrup pancakes, rice pudding and veggie burgers trimmed with holly for Christmas dinner, but the meal will be a real Christmas feast.

Sing carols as you prepare the food. While it is simmering, play old-fashioned games such as Hunt the Thimble and make home-made crackers with tiny charms. After lunch go for a long walk through the woods or park or to the beach in a warm climate. In the evening sit round the fire or by candlelight, telling stories of Christmases past, triumphs and disasters and old Christmas stories. Best of all, children love the story of Mary and Joseph and baby Jesus, the talking animals and the Christmas tinsel.

St Stephen's or Boxing Day, 26 December, was the day when apprentices and servants would be allowed to visit their own homes. They would take boxes made up by employers of left-over Christmas fare, clothes and little trinkets, while each apprentice or servant would have a clay box in which tips were collected throughout the year and broken open on Boxing Day.

In places with Celtic connections this was when a wren was paraded in a cage. The wren was the divinatory bird of the Druids and in earlier times was sacrificed on this day. In modern times, 26 December is a good time to go to a nature reserve, a bird or animal park or to join in sporting activities to get the energies of the new light and life stirring.

The season can end with the feast of Befena, the benevolent witch who fills children's stockings with tiny toys on the Eve of Twelfth

Night, 5 January. Remember to leave out nourishment for the Kings and their camels and to burn frankincense and myrrh either as oils or incense.

Have a final hour of fun as you put the decorations away for another year on Twelfth Night, scatter any ashes from the fire on the garden and blow out your final Yule candle, sending love and light into the world and especially to absent or estranged members of the family.

The Mid-winter Solstice

The Shortest Day offers the chance to celebrate the beginning of new life and the promise of longer, warmer days. Check your calendar for yearly variations in the date.

Foods of the Mid-winter Solstice

Goose, turkey, cakes and puddings made with dried fruits, fruits that represent the new-born sun, such as tangerines or oranges, lentils, dried peas, barley and root vegetables, cider and mulled wines, are all appropriate. The herbs, oils and incenses of the Mid-winter Solstice are bay, cedar, cinnamon, frankincense, mistletoe, myrrh, juniper and rosemary.

Mid-winter Candle Colours

As well as the scarlet of the yule, burn golden and green candles set in a circle of evergreens. Place a golden candle in the centre to represent the new sun on the eve of the Mid-winter Solstice.

Mid-winter Crystals

Use garnets, red and green jaspers, bloodstones and a golden sparkling stone such as a citrine or a clear crystal quartz to represent the reborn sun. Put them in a ring around your candles.

Magic for the Shortest Day

Rise before the light breaks on the Solstice Day and light a golden candle to greet the dawn. Let it burn itself out. Have a breakfast of spicy buns or fruit bread, flavoured with cinnamon and try to spend the day as a family or with close friends. If it is not too cold, go outdoors to watch the sun rise and gather evergreens to decorate your home for Christmas.

This should be the time you create and put up your Christmas decorations, plan surprises and make a huge pot of vegetable and lentil soup, flavoured with bay and rosemary for lunch. The children can paint fir cones gold and tie ribbons to evergreens.

In the afternoon, collect dead wood or suitable rubbish for a bonfire and, as dusk falls, watch the sky darken. Return home and in the early evening light your bonfire or a scarlet candle. Scratch your wishes on wood or write them on paper, then throw them into the flame. Burn juniper oil or berries to cleanse your home of all negative influences and regrets. Go to bed early and lie in the dark, welcoming not fearing it, and for once let tomorrow take care of itself.

COLOUR MAGIC

THE SIGNIFICANCE OF COLOURS

Colour has played a part in many magical systems from the Babylonians and Ancient Egyptians onwards. In India and China, colour magic extends back thousands of years and colour energies have been a feature of healing work. The symbolic energy centres of the human body, known as Chakras in Hindu and Buddhist literature, are said to be ruled by colours from red of the Root or Base physical red to the purple of the Third Eye and the white at the Crown.

In the Hebrew tradition, the mystical realms or sefirot of the Kabbala are also linked with colours and, as with the Chakras, Kether, the Crown or topmost realm is white. Colours are also associated with different planets: orange or gold for the sun, silver or white for the moon, yellow for Mercury, red for Mars, blue for Jupiter, green for Venus and black for Saturn.

These ancient beliefs have been found to have psychological and physical validity. For example, blue helps to lower blood pressure and steadies respiration, while red raises the metabolic rate and orange stimulates the appetite and aids digestion. Pink is sometimes used to create soothing environments in prisons and hospitals as it seems to reduce aggressiveness or anxiety, although this effect can be counter-productive after prolonged exposure. However, the effects of colour seem to extend even beyond the psychological to a deeper psychic level.

Wear the following colours or carry crystals or talismans of the appropriate colour to call on these inherent energies and amplify your own inner powers, whether for achievement or harmony. The list also includes shades and tints, which although not primary colours, have distinct magical meanings.

White

This is the colour of Divinity and the life force. The Greek philosopher Pythagoras believed that white contained all sound as well as colour. In magic, white represents light, vitality and boundless energy and so is helpful where a new beginning is needed. Wear white for clear vision and original ideas and as you step into the unknown.

Black

This is the colour not only of death, but also of regeneration. In Ancient Egypt the black silt of the Nile brought new life each year and black cats were especially sacred. In magic, black is the colour of endings that carry within them seeds of new beginnings. Wear black for marking the boundaries of the past and moving towards the future.

Red

This is a magical colour in many traditions, representing blood or the essence of life. The runes of the Norsemen were marked in red, while in China the pigtails of sages would be interwoven with red threads to keep away evil influences. In magic, red is the colour of power, physical energy and determination. Wear red for courage when facing opposition and for change under difficult circumstances.

Orange

This is the colour of the sun and the abundant fruits of the Earth. An orange tree yields a vast crop each year and its white blossoms are traditionally worn as a fertility symbol by brides. Orange is therefore the colour of fertility, health and joy. Use orange in magic for fertility, whether personal or to bring a project to fruition and to find personal happiness.

Yellow

Traditionally the colour of the mind and communication, yellow has sometimes been associated with jealousy and treachery. Judas is seen in medieval paintings wearing yellow, and so, too, is the Devil. Yellow ochre is painted on the bodies of Australian Aborigines at burial ceremonies. In magic, yellow is the colour for intellectual achievement, learning and by association with Mercury, travel. Wear yellow when facing a mental challenge or when it is important to express yourself clearly or to change location.

Green

This is the colour of Venus and so of the heart, love and emotions. Unlucky connotations of green stem from its association with fairy folk. However, if you blow gently on a dandelion clock or thistledown to help fairies on their way, you can wear the colour with impunity. In magic, it is the colour for finding new love and developing affairs of the heart.

Blue

This is the 'healing colour' and the colour of the spirit. The Hindu God Vishnu was blue. Blue in magic is the colour of conventional wisdom and limitless possibilities, worn by Odin and other Northern Father/Sky Gods. In magic, blue can expand the boundaries of possibility and create confidence. Wear blue for idealism, when dealing with officialdom and when seeking justice.

Purple

This is the royal colour, worn by deities, emperors, kings and priests. It is especially sacred to Osiris and Jupiter. In magic it provides a link with higher dimensions, nobility of spirit and inspiration. Wear purple when you need to trust your inner voice and for psychic insights and spiritual strength.

Brown

This is the colour of the Earth and Earth elementals. Rich vibrant brown represents rooted power and instinctive wisdom. In magic, it is the colour of affinity with the natural world and acts as a protective force. Wear brown when others would mislead you and you need to keep your feet firmly on the ground.

Pink

This is another of Venus's colours. It represents the gentler aspects of love and kindness. In magic, it is the colour of reconciliation and harmony and can induce quiet sleep. Wear pink when you need to mend quarrels or to restore your own inner harmony.

Grey

This is the shade of compromise and adaptability. In magic it is the colour of invisibility and protection against psychic attack. Wear grey when you wish to avoid confrontation and need to keep secrets.

Gold

This is the colour of the sun and its deities, such as the Egyptians' Ra and the Greeks' Apollo. Gold is the height of worldly achievement, wealth and recognition. In magic, it represents money, long life and great ambitions. Wear gold for the confidence to aim high and achieve your dreams.

Silver

This is the colour of the moon and the lunar Goddesses, Isis and Diana. It represents dreams, visions and a desire for fulfilment beyond the material world. Silver in magic represents intuition and sudden insights, especially in your dreams. Wear silver to bring to the fore your hidden potential.

ASTROLOGICAL COLOURS

Wear your astrological colour or carry a talisman of the colour to affirm your core identity and unique qualities. The power is especially potent during your sun sign period, but is also effective when you feel under threat or lack confidence. As well as their inherent meanings, the colours amplify your zodiacal strengths. The birth sign's key quality is listed after the colour

Aries (21 March–20 April): red, especially scarlet, determination
Taurus (21 April–21 May): pink, patience
Gemini (22 May–21 June): yellow, versatility
Cancer (22 June–22 July): silver, hidden potential
Leo (23 July–23 August): gold, ambition
Virgo (24 August–22 September): brown, attention to detail
Libra (23 September–23 October): blue, balance
Scorpio (24 October–22 November): burgundy or indigo, penetrating vision
Sagittarius (23 November–21 December): orange, clear direction
Capricorn (22 December–20 January): black/dark grey, perseverance
Aquarius (21 January–18 February): white, independence
Pisces (19 February–20 March): violet/purple, hidden awareness

COLOUR DIVINATION

You can use coloured ribbons, buttons, crystals, coloured pencils or pens. Rather than answering 'yes' or 'no' or making a choice between two options, colour magic is more subtle and can suggest a strategy for success.

The Method

Take 12 ribbons, crystals, buttons or coloured pencils and place them in a box or bag. Without looking, take out a single colour. Replace it and take out a second. Put that back and take out a third. The first colour, the key issue, tells you the real area of concern, which may not be the surface one. The second colour talks about conflicting issues or opposition. The third colour suggests the best strategy for success or happiness.

White

Issue: You or someone close is feeling restless and wants to change an important aspect of his or her life.
Opposition: Change would threaten the status quo or may be making people close to you feel insecure.
Strategy: Initiate the change regardless, although you may have to begin slowly.

Black

Issue: There is a lot of unresolved business around you.
Opposition: Your own fears and doubts may be holding you in a negative situation.
Strategy: Counteract any negativity with positive actions, however small.

Grey

Issue: You may feel in limbo and vacillate between moving forward and hesitating.
Opposition: The indecisiveness or conflicting opinions of others may be holding you back.
Strategy: Accept that issues are rarely clear cut and adapt your plans so that you can achieve at least some of your aims.

Red

Issue: You may feel angry or resentful about a matter or are concerned with a survival issue.
Opposition: Because feelings may be running high, you could be involved in unnecessary confrontations.
Strategy: Direct any anger, whether your own or that of others, into positive action, rather than responding on a personal level.

Orange

Issue: Your identity and core beliefs may be at stake or you may feel that your personal happiness has been buried beneath the needs of others.

Opposition: A person may be trying to dominate you, perhaps in the nicest way.
Strategy: Resist any erosion of your personal space without damaging the egos of others.

Yellow

Issue: You may feel that your talents and mind are being spread over too many fields.
Opposition: Jealousy and even treachery are undermining your efforts.
Strategy: Be logical about priorities and be aware of what others are saying, especially when they think they are out of your hearing.

Green

Issue: Should you follow your heart or commit your emotional well-being to another?
Opposition: Others may be playing on your kind heart and even exercising subtle emotional blackmail.
Strategy: Trust your emotions and, if it feels right, move forward or closer. However, if instincts tell you otherwise, listen to them and not the words of others.

Blue

Issue: You may be involved with officialdom or are contemplating an unconventional approach or move.
Opposition: An official or even someone close may be hindering your progress by arguing over minor details or attempting to hide behind rules.
Strategy: Follow the conventional approach for now but use ingenuity to get things moving and do not compromise your high ideals.

Purple

Issue: You may be undecided whether to accept short-term material advantage or deeper satisfaction that may be a long way off.
Opposition: Unrealistic dreams and hopes, whether your own or those of others, may be holding you back.
Strategy: Use your intuition and listen to your inner voice rather than conventional wisdom.

Brown

Issue: You may be feeling overwhelmed by responsibility or the demands and opinions of others.
Opposition: The people who are making demands or offering advice may be suggesting that your ideas are ill-informed or selfish.
Strategy: Trust the evidence of your five senses and above all your common sense and off-load unfair obligations.

Pink

Issue: You may be feeling less than harmonious in your attempts to keep the peace in your personal or work life.
Opposition: The quarrels of others may be forcing you into choices you do not wish to make.
Strategy: Withdraw from the conflict of others and concentrate on restoring harmony to your personal sphere.

Gold

Issue: Should you aim high or accept the limitations of present circumstances?
Opposition: Others tell you that you have reached your limits of potential.
Strategy: Believe in yourself and your own abilities and make your own targets.

SUSAN'S RIBBON COLOUR DIVINATION

Susan was very concerned about her 18-year-old daughter Sarah who had dropped out of college to take seasonal work at the local holiday camp and was talking about applying for tourist work abroad with her new boyfriend.

Susan picked first a white ribbon, then an orange one and finally a second white ribbon. The white ribbon, the Issue, reflected Sarah's restlessness. This was her first real boyfriend. She had gone to the local college straight from school to take a secretarial and business studies course and was still living at home. The course had seemed a compromise since Sarah had been uncertain about a career. Once Susan could see the reasons behind Sarah's sudden actions, they seemed less threatening.

The second ribbon, orange the Opposition, Susan recognized

reluctantly was her own attempt to organize her daughter's life, albeit for the best motives. Since Susan was divorced, she relied heavily on Sarah for company and Sarah had gone through none of the usual teenage rebellions. Sarah's actions were partly a late rebellion.

The third ribbon, another white, suggested that Susan should help Sarah to steer her desire for change along a positive path, since change was inevitable. However, Susan was aware that it was important for Sarah to create a new path slowly so that it would be a positive move and not just change for the sake of it.

Together Susan and Sarah explored openings and training in the leisure industry. Sarah is planning to spend six months working as a nanny in the United States before deciding on a more permanent career. Sarah's new boyfriend was not an issue, once Sarah realized that Susan was not opposed to her future plans and gradually the affair faded.

AURA MAGIC

The most exciting aspect of colour magic lies in reading your own and other people's colour auras, a technique that is remarkably easy to learn.

What is an Aura?

Plants emanate light round their forms that can be detected in Kirlian photography. Plant auras fade when they are cut or deprived of water. Humans, too, have auras. Saints have auras of gold or pure white light. This golden or white glow can be seen around their heads in medieval icons. But around the heads and bodies of quite ordinary people can be perceived a white energy source, several inches from and following our outlines. This white field of light is diffused into rainbow colours of varying brightness and intensity. The colours and clarity change according to the state of our health, our inner harmony and our current preoccupations.

In Your True Colours

Auras can be seen in the mind's eye, although some people see them physically. Neither method is better and absolutely everyone can tune into their own and other people's auric energies. Non-verbal signals are a useful clue in any interaction, but auras show the deeper emotions that can be masked even on a non-verbal level by someone who is very controlled.

Generally there are one or two predominant colours in the aura at any given time and if these are clear and bright, you know communication is going to be easy and you can be open. If the aura of a person you are with is dark or murky, you know it is not a time for confrontation or making demands. What is more, the predominant colour/colours can tell you his or her dominant concerns or hidden insecurities.

Studying Your Own Aura

Look in the mirror in sunlight or with a candle or soft lighting behind you. You cannot see anything? Close your eyes and let the picture of the rainbow emerge around your head, the easiest place to see it. Now open your eyes and see what colours are left in the after-image. That is your predominant aura at present.

Try at regular intervals, after a quarrel, after making love, after a success at work or home and when you are sad, tired and sleepy. Note down the colours. Try this for two or three weeks to get a representative pattern.

The most important study of auras will always be your own as a key to what is going on inside you. If you keep an aura diary, you may find that certain situations evoke the same auric pattern, perhaps before visiting a difficult relation or even going along to an activity you feel you ought to enjoy but do not any more. We all tend to have a root aura that reflects our predominant mode of operating in the everyday world, especially at times when not much is happening. For example, pink might suggest that you are naturally a peacemaker; green a person ruled by emotions; blue primarily logical. The aura colour meanings are listed in detail below.

Usually you will find that you have a secondary colour that is closely related. Two entirely opposing auric strands, for example, blue for mind and green for the heart would, if the colours are clear, suggest a balanced approach. If they are muddy, it may be that you are having problems integrating the different strands. If you always present the same two auric colours regardless of the situation or person, you may need to become more adaptable. Equally, if you have no predominant auric pattern, you may be influenced too much by people and situations.

Strengthening Your Aura

The easiest method of strengthening or changing your aura is to use crystals to give you the colour you need for a particular encounter or venture, whether at work or in your personal life. A list of easily obtainable crystals in each colour is at the end of the Chapter. You can also use the yellow of the sun, colours from flowers, trees, the ribbons from your colour divination, even the clothes that you wear to draw into yourself the colour you need.

Hold the crystal or focus on the flower or garment of the colour you need before you put it on. See the colour rising up and flowing around your outline, permeating every pose until your whole body vibrates with it. Now let the colour rise so it forms a halo round your head. You can carry the crystal or wear the flower or garment of the appropriate colour to strengthen you through the day.

Studying the Auras of Others

Other people also have one or two main identifiable strands in their aura. If these never vary you need to be aware of a certain fixed nature that can make interactions difficult. Equally, if an aura changes at every encounter, you may be dealing with someone who tries to please whoever he or she is with and who may, therefore, be unreliable.

The next step is to begin to monitor patterns of important people in your world. Once you have the idea, you can go on to tackling strangers and authority figures. You may see the aura best framed against a window on a sunny day or in subdued lighting. If it is difficult to see the colours physically, let your mind's eye intervene and note down the first impression or picture before your rational processes block the information.

Select someone close in your personal world and a second person with whom you have a more formal but regular relationship and monitor the first aura you see each day or night with them. You may find regular time patterns if you make the study for at least two months. If there are any particular lows, try to find out by tactful questioning what is happening, even in seemingly unrelated spheres in that person's life.

Taking Control of the Interaction

Once you are confident about reading the auras of people you know well, you can try on strangers. After a few weeks you will not even notice that you are doing it. However, by being aware of the predominant mood colour or attitude of the person with whom you are dealing, you can modify your approach so that your interactions become suddenly far more harmonious.

For example, if you can offer a softer initial aura in a confrontation, perhaps pink for reconciliation or rich brown for practical proposals, you can defuse potential opposition. If you feel emotionally threatened or know that a person will try to override your ideas, a strong identity colour, such as orange, would give you the strength to withstand pressure. If you need to persuade the other person to accept a new idea or cut through formalities, a clear logical blue or bright yellow should get communication going. Practise on your children or nearest and most tolerant until you've got the idea.

Auric Variations

There are different shades of each colour in the aura that are packed with information. By strengthening the right shade in your own aura and recognizing the significance of these variations in other people, you can use colour magic in all areas of your life.

Red

This is a very creative, life-enhancing auric colour and varies from brilliant scarlet to deep ruby. It is also the colour of the instincts for basic survival and when harsh or murky in tone can reflect anger, a desire to dominate or a strong desire to change.

A paler red can suggest buried anger or resentment and guilt at feeling that way and needs a particularly careful response. Pale red can give the lie to a seemingly calm, reasonable exterior and you ignore the underlying negativity at your peril.

Orange

This often appears as the predominant auric colour when a question of identity is at stake. In its clearest shades it represents optimism, joy and good health. However, in a close relationship too much orange can suggest a lack of commitment.

Pale orange over any length of time in your own aura can suggest your identity is perhaps being eroded by your desire to please others and in others it can suggest they rely on you more than they admit.

Yellow

This is the auric colour of communication and when it is a lovely golden yellow, communication is clear and creative. The sun positively shines from every enthusiastic fibre. It can warm and enrich the auras of others. It is also the colour of a sharp intellect, so do not underestimate your opponent.

However, when yellow is dull, there may be something concealed, some less than honest intent.

Green

This is the auric colour of the heart and emotions and is especially dominant when relationships are the main issue. In matters of love, a clear green aura is a good sign of a faithful heart and in friendship it indicates trustworthiness. Often a bright green aura may be the first sign of an emotional commitment and can be encouraging if you are uncertain whether to reveal your own friendly or loving feelings.

A paler green can suggest an emotional dependency. That is fine with children and also in love and friendship as long as it alternates with a stronger shade. A dull, muddy green can conceal conflicting emotions or an emotional leech, so be aware and maybe beware. Yellowy green can be a sign of possessiveness and unwarranted jealousy.

Blue

This is an aura concerned with principles and ideals. Bright blue is altruistic and the person will put principles before personal gain. The softer blues, often associated with healing, soften idealism with compassion. Navy blue has an unworldiness about it which can be infuriating when financial or business matters must be resolved. When the aura is ice blue, it can suggest a touch of heartlessness.

A dull blue can suggest that concern for convention is leading to rigidity.

Purple

This is the auric colour that deals with the spiritual and psychic side of human nature that can so easily get swamped by everyday living. Because it is a colour related to intuition, it can often provide an answer when logic and emotion fail. Deep, rich purple talks of deeply spiritual areas and a strong intuitive nature.

Paler purple relates to the inner world and suggests that its wearer considers inner happiness more vital than material success. Only when the auric purple is muddy or blurred does it imply that its owner is spending too long on daydreams and illusions.

Pink

In an aura pink is a good sign as it means that you are a natural peacemaker or that the other person is in a reconciliatory mood. If the pink is bright and clear, you know that whether you are in a work, social or emotional situation, the other person will be receptive to your suggestions, fears and feelings.

A pale but clear pink reveals inner harmony and means that the person you are dealing with is likely to take a balanced view of whatever is the matter in hand. If the pink is misty, it can mean that you are dealing with someone who sees other people's points of view to such an extent that he or she is unlikely to reach any decisions without firm direction.

Brown

Sometimes this is quite wrongly associated with a disorder of the aura. A clear, shining brown, like ploughed fields in sunlight, is a sign of a strong streak of practicality, reliability, humour and common sense. Pale, clear brown shows that practicality is tinged with enthusiasm and versatility. Problems come only if this brown aura is unvarying. Your auric diary would probably indicate that this aura was too often in evidence if someone close to you operated only in the practical and material sphere and needed a little fun in his or her life. A very dark brown can suggest feeling overloaded by responsibilities that may be masked as a lack of enthusiasm or irritability.

White

This is the synthesis of all the other colours and talks of creativity, energy and focused aims in an everyday context. It is a very exciting aura to develop personally when initiating a new phase. Because white contains all other colours, it can clear stagnation in any area and promote one of those inspirational leaps that take us from an unfulfilling but secure situation to the thrilling unknown.

However, a dirty white aura or one with streaks of black hints that there is a lot of unfinished business to be resolved before moving forward.

Black

This is the ultimate receptive colour of the aura and is not necessarily a negative colour. Black at its clearest and most silvery represents the receptive, nurturing, accepting side of human nature. It is a very stabilizing auric shade to encounter as long as the black is not fuzzy at the edges or so heavy with caring that the person disappears beneath its weight. It has a second aspect; in its softer or denser shades it can represent a natural fluidity in life that does not insist on demarcations and accepts people for what they are and not who they are. A dense, heavy black can mean that unwarranted guilt may be causing depression and that the person whose aura is so dark has a very poor self-image and sense of worth.

CRYSTAL COLOURS

Red for action: garnet, red cornelian, red jasper, red or blood agate
Orange for identity: amber, orange beryl, orange cornelian, orange calcite
Yellow for communication: citrine, topaz, golden tiger's eye, yellow zircon, yellow rutilated quartz
Green for love and emotions: malachite, bloodstone, aventurine, amazonite, jade, moss agate
Blue for logic and conventional wisdom: falcon's Eye (blue tiger's eye), lapis lazuli, turquoise, dyed blue howzite, blue lace agate
Purple for intuition and psychic insight: sodalite, sugilite, amethyst, purple fluorite
White for pure energy and creativity: clear crystal quartz, snow quartz, white mother-of-pearl, white moonstone
Black for acceptance, nurturing and protection: obsidian (apache tear), black onyx, jet
Pink for reconciliation and harmony: rose quartz, pink sugilite, rhodochrosite, strawberry quartz
Brown for the five senses and a practical, pragmatic approach to life: brown tiger's eye, fossilized wood, brown jasper, brown agate, brown rutilated quartz

9

CRYSTALLOMANCY

CRYSTAL BALL AND MIRROR SCRYING

Scrying means seeing magical images in a reflective medium, such as a crystal ball. What you see can shed light on the present and guide future action. The word 'scry' comes from the Anglo-Saxon 'descry', which means to see.

Scrying in shiny surfaces has been practised in every culture and time, not only by mystics and magicians, but by every girl who has gazed into a mirror and performed rituals to see her lover's face, or by any man who has sought wisdom in moonlit water. Crystallomancy differs from other forms of scrying, such as tea leaves, because the images are not formed by the medium itself, but from within your pysche. People sometimes feel that they cannot use a crystal ball or mirror successfully because there are no concrete images on which to work. For this reason, scryers can become anxious and actually block the natural and very vivid images cast on to the glass by the mind's eye.

THE ORIGINS OF CRYSTALLOMANCY

The Maya used the crystal which was sacred to the Sun God Tezcatlipoca and his temple walls were lined with mirrors. Apaches gazed into crystals not only to discover if an expedition would be successful, but to find the location of property and ponies stolen by other tribes.

Crystal ball divination became popular in Europe in the fifteenth century when it was believed that spirits or angels would appear in the glass. Rituals were long and complex. One in a sixteenth-century manuscript included purification rituals as well as invoking protection from God and the good angels: 'First say one Paternoster, one Ave Maria, one Creed, then say Vobiscum Spiritu, God of Abraham, God of Isaac, God Of Jacob, God of Elias . . . who hast given virtues to stones, woods and herbs, consecrate this stone.'

One of the most famous scryers was Sir John Dee (1527–1608) who was astrologer to Queen Elizabeth I. On 21 November 1582, he bought a crystal 'as big as an egg, most bryght, clere and glorious' and through this sphere he communicated with his angels. These not only gave him all kinds of knowledge, but, he believed, protected the Queen and England. He called his crystal his 'shew-stone'. It was not a clear crystal, but an obsidian, a stone through which light can be seen when held to the sun. It is said that this crystal provided forewarning of the Spanish Armada.

Although the crystal ball is the most mystical of all divinatory forms, it is quite accessible. You can use a conventional sphere of deep blue or yellow beryl or clear crystal quartz, a household mirror, a clear glass, a paperweight or even a large spherical glass such as a brandy glass.

Why Crystals and Mirrors are seen as Magical

The circle and sphere are symbols of completeness and it was believed that a crystal sphere was a microcosm (a miniature version) of the wider universe. Therefore information about past, present and future could be captured within it.

Mirrors were believed to reflect the soul. This is why, according to myth, you cannot see the reflection of a bad witch in a mirror. It was considered unlucky to smash a mirror as you were damaging your immortal soul. The Romans believed that it took seven years for the soul to grow again, hence the idea of seven years' bad luck.

CRYSTAL BALLS

Crystal balls are traditionally made of either clear quartz crystal or beryl. The energies of natural crystal are very powerful, especially for healing, but many modern 'crystal' balls are made of glass. If you cannot afford a real crystal ball, a glass one is fine since the psychic energies that create the images come from your own very powerful intuition. You need not buy a very large and expensive crystal sphere. One the size of a small orange provides an excellent focus. You can practise crystallomancy with any small reflective crystal or an ordinary mirror.

Crystal Quartz

Clear crystal quartz is found in most parts of the world and has always provided a link between dimensions. Descriptions of it include: 'frozen light', 'holy water' from on high and the 'essence of the dragon' as the crystal ball was called in Chinese and Japanese tradition; 'visible nothingness' according to the Buddhists; 'clear ice' in the Greek tradition, the crystal truth dropped by Hercules from Mount Olympus that shattered into the millions of smaller crystals we find today; and 'solidified light' which the Australian Aborigines said contained the Great Spirit.

Because crystal is believed to connect heaven and earth, it forms a natural medium for scrying. Quartz is the commonest mineral, making up about 12 per cent of the volume of the earth's crust. The coarse crystalline form is found as clear quartz and with varying impurities as rose quartz and amethyst, both of which provide excellent crystal spheres for gentle visions. Rutilated quartz with its inner angles, smoky quartz and tiger's eye are also powerful for scrying.

Beryl

Beryl, which comes in deep blue and yellow, brilliant green and red, was used for crystal balls even before clear quartz. Mainly the blue and yellow varieties were used, although bright green beryl is a good stone for small stone scrying as a substitute for emeralds.

Beryl was used in fifth-century Ireland for scrying and is called the stone of the seer. Spheres of beryl as well as round, flat beryl mirrors, held in white cloth, were a powerful focus for early Celtic visions. White cloths, rather than the black backing that is traditional beneath clear crystal balls, seem to provide the best surface for beryl spheres.

Beryl scrying is best during the period of the waxing moon and is especially good for finding lost objects. Hold your beryl sphere in your left hand and 'see' the missing object in your right.

How to Read a Crystal Ball

There are several ways of using the focus of the crystal ball for capturing your inner vision. Experiment until you find a way of using your ball that feels right. Do not expect it to act as a goldfish bowl or feel disappointed if, when you look inside, you initially see nothing but reflections.

You are using your crystal ball as a focus for the inner visions in your mind. The image begins in your mind's eye and is then held in the ball so you can study it. If you feel anxious or doubt that the crystal will work for you, close your eyes and let an image form in the darkness, perhaps a bird, a butterfly or a face. You may want to ask a question or let the image dictate the area of your life to which it refers. Open your eyes quickly and project the image on to the surface of the ball. Do this several times, each time casting the image further into the crystal. Next, only half-close your eyes and let an image appear directly either on the surface or inside the crystal. Do not pause or rationalize and if nothing appears, blink rapidly. When you open your eyes, you will see the image.

You will find that the image says something to you. Do not worry about conventional meanings. You may see colours, impressions, single images or whole scenes. Let your own magical insights guide you.

Twilight is said to be the best time of all to read a crystal ball. Some scryers breathe heavily on the ball so that it mists over. When the mists clear, the image is waiting for them. Others see the crystal ball itself as getting larger and larger, enclosing them on all sides until they themselves are inside its world, experiencing the scene or images as a direct observer.

Interpreting Images

- An image moving towards the scryer suggests that the event or person will occur or appear very soon.
- An image moving away suggests that the event or person is either moving away from the scryer's world or that a past issue or relationship may still be exerting undue influence on the scryer.
- Images appearing on the left are actual physical occurrences.
- Images appearing in the centre or to the right tend to be symbolic.
- Pictures near the top of the ball are important and need prompt attention.
- Those at the bottom are less prominent or urgent.
- The relative size of the images can indicate their importance.

The Changing Scene: a Colour Method

You may see the ball get duller, then suddenly become very bright. Initially a white mist may be followed by red or green mists, then by grey or black upon which pinpoints of light are seen dancing. Eventually, a brilliant blue mist may appear against which sharp images may be seen.

For some scryers this is a spontaneous occurrence and if it works for you, it can be a good sequence for reaching images. It is also one you can acquire if you want to use a more formal approach to crystal ball divination. Begin by visualizing the sequence of colours in the centre of the ball. Gradually you will find that the sequence becomes automatic.

A More Formal Crystal Ball Ritual

Unless you are reading for a friend, make your crystal ball a quiet, solitary time. Before you begin, burn a divinatory incense, such as frankincense or cinnamon, that also offers protection. Light a purple candle if it is dark and set it behind you or use a shaded soft light that casts gentle shadows to exclude external visual distractions.

Before you begin to study the crystal ball, close your eyes for a few minutes to exclude disturbing visions on the retina. Hold your crystal ball or sphere in your hands between your fingers and thumbs. Place the sphere on a black or dark background if it is crystal quartz or a white cloth if it is made of beryl. Use the crystal ball for about five minutes at a time when you begin or until you feel that you are becoming restless or tired.

Once you are accustomed to this form of scrying, you can use the crystal ball for ten or 15 minutes. Sit quietly once the pictures have ceased and in your mind let yourself wander through the pathways within the crystal. You may come across some of the images that you saw in the ball along the way and you will understand them better. Do not try to force psychic journeyings or analysis at this stage.

When you are ready, blow out the candle and wrap the crystal ball in its cloth. This is the stage to polish it, ready for the next session. Go for a walk or have a long bath, using a gentle fragrance or oil, such as lavender, and the images you saw will form a sequence in your mind and answer questions you had not consciously formulated.

The Cloud Method

Some people only ever see clouds in their crystal ball and over time this has formed a coherent divination system.

White clouds imply a positive decision or answer and the favourable outcome of any issue under question.

Black clouds suggest a negative response and advise caution in any projected undertakings. If the dark clouds suddenly become lighter, wait for the right moment which is not far away and will bring success or happiness.

Light shades of any colour are a good omen, while darker colours are less auspicious.

Green clouds talk of happiness in love.

Blue clouds promise success in a money or career matter.

Violet clouds herald helpful friends or good advice.

Pink clouds indicate someone new coming into your life or a new beginning.

Brown clouds talk of a home or job move or perhaps a first permanent home.

Silver clouds promise consolation or a new opportunity, but definitely a change for the better.

Gold clouds mean dreams coming true and ambitions fulfilled.

Red clouds warn of anger, violent emotions and quarrels.

Orange clouds indicate separation, someone moving out of your life and perhaps being alone for a while.

Yellow clouds signify malice, envy and jealousy.

Ascending clouds indicate a positive outcome and descending clouds suggest a negative one.

Clouds moving to the right indicate helpful influences while those moving to the left suggest that you should beware of opposition, especially from friends.

The Three Images Method

You can use any of the above methods when reading the crystal ball for a friend. However, the best readings for others come when they are directly involved in the reading and not just passive observers. You and the person you are reading for should sit either side of the crystal ball. Let the other person hold the crystal for a few minutes in the left hand and place the right hand on top of it. Place your hands on top of the ball for a moment so that you cover the seeker's right hand.

Take the hands away and tell the seeker to gaze into the ball and name the first image that comes into his or her mind. Then, without pause, ask for a second image and a third. The images will be a joint projection and you may actually see them in the crystal as the other person speaks. Ask the seeker what the first image suggests to him or her, then the second and finally the third. Then join the images into a continuous story. You can also use this method for your own readings if you have a specific question.

A THREE IMAGE READING

Jenny was concerned because her partner Kevin was unwilling to make a permanent commitment although they had been together for several years. She had reached the age where, if she was going to have a family, she would have to start thinking about having her first child. But Kevin was unwilling to discuss either marriage or a baby.

Jenny's first image was a bird soaring through the sky, the second an upturned cradle and the third an open door. Jenny identified Kevin as the bird, soaring away from her. Recently he had been very remote and had been staying out late. The upturned cradle, she realized, was her hope for having a child with Kevin.

She did not interpret the open door as I would have done: that if she left the door open and gave Kevin his freedom he might return. Instead, Jenny saw the door as an opening for herself to move on. She had the offer of promotion at the bank where she worked, but that would mean moving to a branch at the other end of the country. She was about to turn the chance down, just as she had rejected previous openings in the hope that Kevin would commit himself. Now she acknowledged that Kevin wanted her to live her life through him, but was prepared to offer nothing in return.

The crystal offered no magical solutions or happy-ever-afters, but because Jenny was able to use it to access what she knew on a deep level but could not admit consciously, she was able to move forward, perhaps to a different kind of happiness after the pain.

The Angel in the Glass

Dr John Dee believed that angels and demons appeared in the crystal ball and offered good or bad advice. In modern times this idea is neither acceptable nor desirable. Control by another being, whether from another dimension or an earthly source, denies us the power to make our future. However, to see an inner angelic being or spiritual guide in the crystal can be a positive focus for crystal work.

You may see your 'angel' or 'guide' quite spontaneously if you sit quietly with your crystal in the twilight. It may be a figure who has recurred from your dreams or one you have sensed close to you since childhood, an angel, a nun, a gypsy, a Chinese sage. This may represent a part of yourself, perhaps a past life form or a symbol of wisdom and protection. You may see your 'angel in the glass' whenever you use the crystal or perhaps only when you are tired or anxious. You may hear words of encouragement or reassurance in your head. Listen to the wisdom that comes from deep within and that may be able to tap into the knowledge of other times and places.

Crystal Ball Healing

Quartz crystal balls were also used medicinally to concentrate the rays of the sun upon a diseased or painful area of the body or in the direction of some internal organ. The clear crystal stone has always been associated with energizing powers and with healing. So in its spherical form of completeness it is perhaps the ultimate healing and magical stone.

If you have a pain or feel unwell, wait until sunlight is filtering into the room. Place your crystal ball in the sunlight until it is shining. Let the energy form tiny rainbows and place your crystal ball over the pain or near the area of pressure. Move your crystal ball in gentle circles and let the warm rainbow rays enter your body, visualizing them warming and invigorating you. Gently rub your crystal and, instead of returning it to its cloth, let it absorb the sunlight for a few minutes. Place some yellow flowers or seeds in a pot to return to the cosmos the golden energies you have used.

USING A MAGIC SCRYING MIRROR

Magical mirrors feature in both fairy stories and legends. For example:

Mirror, mirror on the wall,
Who is the fairest of us all?

So asked the wicked Queen in *Snow White*. When the magic mirror told her that Snow White, her step-daughter, was the most beautiful, the Queen ordered Snow White's death. The mirror also told the Queen that Snow White was hidden in the forest with the seven dwarfs. In one version, the Queen is told by the mirror that Snow White has not died from the poisoned apple given to her by her step-mother disguised as an old woman, but has been reunited with her prince. In fury she shatters the mirror into a thousand pieces and because she has bound her soul with the mirror, she dies.

Hathor's Magical Mirror

Hathor, Egyptian Goddess of Love, Music and Dancing, was once entrusted with the sacred eye of Ra, the Sun God, through which she could see all things. She carried a shield that could reflect all things in their true light. From it she fashioned the first magic mirror. One side was endowed with the power of Ra's eye to see everything, no matter how distant or how far into the future. The other side showed the gazer in his or her true light and only a brave person could look at it without flinching.

Mirrors of highly polished metal were consulted in Ancient China to determine what would happen. Merlin, King Arthur's magician, used his magical mirror to warn the King about plots and potential invasions by enemy forces. Vulcan, the Roman God of Fire and Metalworkers, also fashioned a mirror that showed past, present and future. The mirror was given by Cupid to Ulysses' wife Penelope. The Greeks used bronze mirrors to see into the future. In Ancient Rome practitioners were called *specularii*. Black shiny mirrors, often called witches' mirrors, were used in medieaval times, but because of their association with darker practices are now rarely possessed by ordinary scryers.

How to Mirror-Read

It is not necessary to have a 'witch's mirror'. An ordinary small mirror on a stand is ideal. You may wish to keep this exclusively for scrying, covered with a soft cloth when not in use. As with crystal ball reading, the hour before sunset is a good time. Place the mirror on a table of medium height and light a pink or orange candle, Hathor's colours, on either side of the mirror. Use rose incense, the incense of Hathor, on either side. Let the mirror face a plain wall and sit slightly to one side so that you do not see your own face reflected, unless you are, like Hathor, seeking to see yourself in your true light. Let the pictures form either within the mirror or in your mind's eye. When you have finished, blow out the candles and let the light offer protection to all who need it.

Cover your mirror once more and spend some time quietly and alone, letting the images offer their own message.

Shadow Scrying

Unlike crystal ball and mirror scrying, this form uses the shadows cast by the sun or candles.

Agates have been used for scrying for many centuries in Asia. Opaque agate, onyx and marble eggs, especially those of green and yellow, are excellent for shadow scrying and can be bought very cheaply. You do not need a large sphere. Buy one that you can hold comfortably in your hands so you can turn it to catch the reflections of sunshine or candlelight and shadow on its surface.

Like the scryers of Asia, gaze at the markings on the stone while you think of a question or a person. Light green and blue candles for the balance of heart and mind or sit where the light is shining on to the stone. Hold the stone in your left hand and turn it slowly clockwise from the top nine times. As you do so, repeat your question or recite your need nine times. Hold the stone up to the light between your hands and you will see pictures of light and shadow unfolding on the surface. These may be scenes of your own life or symbols that point a way forward. Finally turn your stone again, this time anti-clockwise nine times, and as you do this, the answer to your question will come into your head.

SCRYING WITH SMALL CRYSTALS

Traditionally multi-faceted gems, such as emeralds and rubies, were used for scrying. They were held in the left hand while surrounded by jewel-coloured candles. Any highly reflective, richly coloured crystal will serve for scrying, especially those with recognized divinatory properties: amber, especially for past life visions, polished agate, green beryl, tiger's eye, silvery haematite, jet and obsidian.

Making a Self-stone for Scrying

Unlike your crystal ball or mirror, which should be reserved for scrying alone, use a crystal that has meaning for you and carry it for a full day and night so that it has absorbed your essence. Place it in the bath with you, in the car as you drive and under your pillow, whether you are indulging in quiet sleep or passion, so that your stone is not excluded from any part of your life. Let it absorb your worries as well as your hopes, your tender words as well as your quarrelsome ones for it is the crystal of your whole self, shadows as well as light, negative as well as positive feelings.

When you are ready to scry, sprinkle pure sea salt over the crystals for the practicality of the Earth element, for all your concerns with home and money, for your five senses and common sense. Next pass a lighted incense stick over it or hold your crystal in the fragrance of a burning oil, such as pine or lemon, for the sharpness of the Air element. This will bring logic, courage and determination to overcome any obstacles and the ability to shed illusion. Thirdly, pass your self-stone through a golden or yellow candle for the fire of the sun and your own creativity and inspiration to strengthen your unique gifts and restore optimism and confidence. Finally, invoke the Water element by sprinkling the stone with rose water, made by steeping petals in water for 24 hours. You could also use an essence of peppermint for protection and for heightened intuition.

You can use your self crystals for scrying by day or night. However, if you prefer scrying by night, a moonstone under a full moon can provide a powerful focus not only for your inner world, but of all those factors in your daily life that are hidden from view, especially the intentions of others. By night, hold your stone framed against a candle or moonlight so that a dark ring forms round it. In the daytime, hold your crystal where sunlight sparkles the surface, especially if you can catch the reflections on water. An agate or tiger's eye can be especially potent.

Half-close your eyes and let your visions come, not as pictures in a larger crystal ball, but as dreams, daydreams, inner visions in your mind's eye, filtered from the jewelled light.

When you have finished, wash your crystal gently under running water and leave it for a full 24 hours exposed to sunlight and moonlight so it can rest. Then wrap it in silk and place it in a fragrant drawer until you need it again or for a particularly important occasion when you may wish to carry your self crystal to give you courage or conviction in your daily world.

10

DICE MAGIC

ORIGINS

Dice magic was popularized by travelling people, especially those in fairs and circuses, because it was a very portable method of divination and one that crossed language barriers easily. The same set of dice was frequently used for gaming and for magic.

Dice of ivory, wood, metal and glass have been discovered among the relics of Ancient Egypt, Greece and Rome, marked with dots like modern-day dice. The British author, poet and critic Robert Graves records that the Roman Emperor Claudius felt safe to embark on his invasion of Britain because a dice roll promised success. The Druids used wooden dice, carved with *coelbrenn* (secret letters) on each face. These were cast like conventional dice and were used not only for telling the future, but also for passing secret messages.

In the Far East dice were made of gems or crystals, such as sacred green jade, to add to their potency. In Tibet as recently as the nineteenth century, dice were used purely for foretelling events and not for gambling. Even today Tibetan Buddhist Lamas cast the dice and interpret the oracle for devotees. One system, invoking the Buddhist Protectress Palden Lhamo, uses three dice offering 15 possible answers, with each answer broken down further to relate to different areas of experience, such as money or health. A second system, sacred to the Buddhist Saint of Wisdom Manjushri, uses only one dice. On its six faces are inscribed the last six of the seven syllables of a mantra, the sacred chant of Manjushri. This system requires devotees to visualize Manjushri in the sky while reciting his mantra and asking his blessing. Then the dice is thrown twice and the oracle consulted.

Nineteenth-century Western systems developed a fortune-telling method with sets of 30 or more questions. When each was applied to the different number combinations created by the roll of two dice, such as three and two or four and three, a large number of optional answers were provided. For example in answer to the question, 'Where will I find a missing article?', a roll of one-one might proclaim 'in the closet', while three-three would, in a traditional system, suggest that a child has it. Six-six would indicate it was hidden in a box. Such methods tend to concentrate on specifics.

A combination of the profound spiritualism of Eastern dice-casting and the focused questioning of the Western tradition forms the basis for the two methods described here. Both focus on a personal question that changes with the occasion and relies on an intuitive response to the numbers thrown by the dice to expand and adapt the basic number meanings to a relevant and in some cases profound answer.

NUMBER MEANINGS

Dice, like other number systems (see also *Domino Divination*, page 140), depend on number meanings that can then be adapted to interpret personal situations. Like any form of divination, whether runic markings, Tarot cards, numbers or their representative dots, they offer a basic focus for intuition.

As far back as the sixth century BC, the Greek philosopher and mathematician Pythagoras believed that the universe had a mathematical order and that numbers were its key. The primary numbers 1–9 make up the basis for any numerological system, all other numbers being a combination of them and reducible to them. Although one of the dice methods described uses numbers up to 18, these can be reduced to one of the core primary numbers 1–9, while a very simple method linked with planetary meanings concentrates solely on the nine single numbers.

Basic Primary Number Meanings

Each of the numbers 1–9 is related to one of the planets known to the early astronomers (Uranus was not discovered until 1781, Neptune in 1846 and Pluto in 1930), together with the the sun and moon.

Sun 1 and 4
Moon 2 and 7
Jupiter 3
Mercury 5
Venus 6
Saturn 8
Mars 9

One ruled by the Morning Sun
One is the number of new beginnings, individualism, pure creation and vision. It endows you with its golden energy and confidence to

achieve any aim. If your birthday or birth month contains a one, then throwing a one in a dice reading echoes your energy and enthusiasm for any venture.

Two ruled by the Waxing Moon

Two is the number of duality, partnerships and balance and so endows you with unconscious wisdom, hidden insights and heightened intuition. If your birthday or your birth month contains a two, then throwing a two in a dice reading will reflect the wise counsel offered by your inner voice.

Three ruled by Jupiter

Three is the number of fertility and increase, conscious wisdom and expansion. It endows you with the power to bring ideas to fruition and to increase the possibilities open to you. If your birthday or birth month contains a three, then throwing a three in a dice reading strengthens your understanding of the wider context and deeper significance of any decision.

Four ruled by the Evening Sun

Four is the number of time and space and of achievement and success within the limitations imposed by the environment in which you live. It endows you with the ability to adapt your ideas and dreams to the real world and to compromise. If your birthday or birth month contains a four, then throwing a four in a dice reading echoes your ability to succeed in any circumstances.

Five ruled by Mercury

Five is the number of versatility, communication, restlessness and ingenuity. It endows you with the ability to adapt to changing circumstances and to find alternative approaches if one fails. If your birthday or birth month contains a five, then throwing a five in a dice reading reflects your power to communicate your ideas persuasively.

Six ruled by Venus

Six is the number of emotions and of attaining peace and harmony in relationships and life. It endows you with the ability to sympathize with others and to use your understanding of people to reconcile differences. If your birthday or birth month contains a six, throwing a six in a dice reading reflects your power to spread happiness.

Seven ruled by the Waning Moon
Seven is the number of mystery, dreams and the world of the spirit. It endows you with the power to see beyond the immediate and material gain to what is worthwhile. If your birthday or birth month contains a seven, then throwing a seven in a dice reading strengthens your resolve to trust your dreams and waking visions when decisions are necessary.

Eight ruled by Saturn
Eight is the number of prudence, business acumen and practicality. It endows you with the purpose to create order and stability in your own world and that of others. If your birthday or birth month contains an eight, then throwing an eight in a dice reading enhances your organizational skills in chaotic situations.

Nine ruled by Mars
Nine is the number of completion and perfection. It carries seeds of future regeneration, endowing you with the desire to strive for perfection, to seek the ideal and to regard every ending as a new opportunity. If your birthday or birth month contains a nine, then a nine in a dice reading enables you to give your best in any situation.

Dice Readings

The simplest form of dice divination, planet readings, involves throwing two dice and adding their values. If the numbers on the uppermost faces add up to more than nine, add the two digits to give a single digit. For example, 10 becomes 1 + 0 = 1 and 12 becomes 1 + 2 = 3. The planet number you throw tells you which area of your life will predominate during the coming months and offer you the greatest potential happiness.

Sun (morning): 1 personal happiness
Moon (waxing): 2 fertility of people or plans
Jupiter: 3 career
Sun (evening): 4 new talents or interests
Mercury: 5 travel
Venus: 6 love/marriage/important friendship
Moon (waning): 7 psychic ability/unexpected luck
Saturn: 8 money/business affairs
Mars: 9 A major change in direction or a house move

Planet timings provide a second method. Likely times for the important changes or improvements can be divined by drawing a small chalk circle clockwise about 30 cm (12 inches) in diameter and throwing your two dice towards it. If neither lands in the circle, the event is unlikely to take place during the next 12 months. If one dice falls outside, disregard it and read the other one. If both fall in the circle, add together the number of dots on the uppermost face on each dice. Then count forward from the current month to find the probable date.

This is a good method for a quick reading or to ascertain a general view of the year ahead. However, dice divination can be a very spiritual experience and provide a focus for deep insights.

Preparing for Divination

Although dice divination can be carried out absolutely anywhere, you may wish, like the Tibetans, to prepare your psyche and remove the stresses of the day. Early evening is considered especially propitious for dice divination.

Have a bath using an essential oil such as jasmine (the essence of the moon), rose or orange, which are fragrances that enhance psychic awareness. Put on a loose robe and spread out an Indian rug, a blanket or large soft cushions on which to sit. In front of it draw a white chalk circle, clockwise, this time about 60 cm (2 feet) in diameter, in an unbroken sweep. Light incense, such as frankincense, cinnamon and sandalwood, for both psychic insight and protection during psychic work.

See the four corners of your rug protected by golden pillars of light. As you direct your gaze through half-opened eyes on the empty circle, let it be filled with colours, lights and gentle images as your mind's eye flows outwards.

Cast your dice using one of the following systems and as you do so, let images form and words echo in your mind. These will illuminate the basic meanings and make them personal to your life and world. If, as you throw the dice, you get a definite picture or impression, follow it even if it does not accord with the standard meaning. We are all equal, expert and beginner, in magic. It is a gift that comes through innocence and good faith and not formal learning. If we could forget all we know, we would be natural magicians, as children are.

When you have finished your dice divination, erase the circle moonwise, widdershins or anti-clockwise. Sit quietly for a while and let the words and pictures that have been released flow gently around without attempting to analyze or question them. Silently thank the golden pillars of light and send them to whoever needs light or love.

Once the incense has burned out, fold your rug or blanket and go for a quiet walk or listen to soft music to allow your psychic vibes to subside naturally.

Beginning Dice Divination

In each of the following methods, the dice are rolled twice. The first number gives a course of suggested action and the second a possible outcome. You can obtain additional information under either system by adding the two throws together until you are left with a single digit. This remaining core number, the planetary number, reveals the special strengths necessary to ensure success or a satisfactory resolution of the problem raised. As with the planetary divination system, if the number you receive in an answer is contained in your birthday or birth month, then it reflects an underlying strength in your make-up and its effect will be doubled.

Method One

Use two or three dice and add the numbers to give a maximum of 18. A roll of two and three and four and one would give the same answer. Only dice falling within the circle are counted.

If all the dice fall outside the circle, abandon your dice divination for today. Thank the pillars of light for their protection, leave the circle and the rug ready for the next day, leaving the incense to burn away in its own time. Go for a walk, turn out a cupboard or dig the garden and go to sleep early, seeing in the darkness your white chalk circle filled with soft pink protective images.

Carry out the divination in the early morning light with the windows open so the fragrances and smells of the day replace the heady incense of the evening. Pick some flowers and place them near the circle. The answers should be clear, but if not, rephrase your question or ask the first one that enters your head, however unlikely. This spontaneous question may hold the key to deeper concerns.

Add the numbers of first throw together. This will provide you with a suggested action or help you to decide the right option. Throw the dice a second time and add the two numbers. This will give you the likely outcome of any choice or action. If at this stage the dice do not fall in the circle, the outcome is uncertain for now and you should ask another time. It does not mean that there will be a bad outcome, merely that your psyche needs longer to work.

Finally, add all the numbers from both throws. If the numbers form double figures, add the two digits to form a single number. That is your core number which indicates the strengths needed to help you achieve your aim.

Dice Meanings

One
This number, which can turn up if only one dice falls within the circle, talks of new beginnings and the need to act rather than wait.

As an Outcome, one promises that if you have confidence in yourself and your abilities, success and happiness will follow.

Two
This involves balancing two options or demands and says that it is important to sort out your immediate priorities.

As an Outcome, two promises that if you wait rather than act, listen rather than speak, any partnership or shared enterprise will be successful.

Three
This says that you should expand your horizons and options and seize any opportunities.

As an Outcome, it promises that your plans will be fruitful if you are prepared to give your whole self to the venture.

Four
This emphasizes that it is important to accept any limitations and make your plans to fit in with the real situation.

As an Outcome, four promises that realistic dreams can still come true.

Five
This says that clear communication and versatility can overcome any opposition or obstacles.

As an Outcome, five promises that if you channel any restlessness into positive measures, you can bring flexibility even to a rigid situation.

Six
This says that harmonious relationships and compromise in interactions are the key to happiness.

As an Outcome, six promises peace and emotional stability if peace predominates over principle.

Seven
This urges you to look beyond immediate gain and happiness and trust your inner wisdom rather than the opinions of others.

As an Outcome, seven promises real happiness if you are prepared to take the long-term view.

Eight
This reminds you that caution is the keynote and that it is better to follow the conventional path at the moment.

As an Outcome, eight promises material security and rewards as long as you anticipate your future needs.

Nine
This says that you should strive for perfection and fight for what matters to you.

As an Outcome, nine promises happiness if you do not compromise your high standards.

Ten
This heralds the natural ending of a natural phase or situation and says that it's a time for tying up loose ends.

As an Outcome, ten promises a new beginning once you have resolved unfinished matters.

Eleven
This says that you may have to choose between two conflicting options or people, since you cannot keep everyone happy.

As an Outcome, eleven promises that making a decision puts you back in control of your life.

Twelve
This suggests that you should seek outside advice or expertise in any unresolved issues or major decisions.

As an Outcome, twelve promises that wise counsel will clear any doubts in your mind once and for all.

AN EXAMPLE WITH TWO DICE

David and his wife Maxine have two young children. Maxine would like another baby but David is worried about the financial implications as Maxine was about to return to work after a six-year break and money is short. However, Maxine feels that now is the time to complete their family so that the children will be close in age.

David used the dice with scepticism. He threw a five and a two. This made seven for his suggested plan of action, indicating that David should look beyond the immediate and material situation to what mattered to him on an emotional level. The answer was not immediately obvious, but sometimes even a single dice throw can act as a trigger for a stream of thoughts and feelings that have remain buried. This function can far outweigh any 'fortune-telling' value. David acknowledged that he and Maxine had planned a larger family and that family life was important to him as he had been a lonely only child, brought up by an elderly grandmother. However, the financial and practical realities of life with young children had shattered his dreams.

The second throw for the possible Outcome was a three and a two: the five promised happiness if David channelled his restlessness into positive change. David found this significant and it shed light on the previous dice throw. The real issue was his own desire to change his profession, but he felt this was not possible if the family increased. Suddenly he realized that the two were not incompatible. Rather than resigning and starting a new career with less money, a course of action he had considered just about feasible if Maxine returned to work, David decided to explore the possibilities for going on training courses within the multi-national organization in which he worked. This way he could perhaps change the emphasis of his work so that he spent more time with the general public, rather than behind the scenes. Two issues were hidden in one and had become confused.

The next step was to find his core planetary number. He added the two casts of the dice together and then combined the two digits of the result, 12 which left him with the core number three. Since David was born on 3 March, the number had double significance for him. Three, a number often associated with starting or adding to a family as well as expansion or promotion at work, told David that he should go ahead on both counts. His strength lay in expanding the possibilities before him and the family. To this end, Maxine began a home computer course while waiting for the new baby to be born.

Extending the system

Should you feel this method is too restrictive, add a third dice at each throw, giving an extra six possibilities with each cast. Use your chalk circle as before. The first roll of three dice still represents suggested action and the second roll of three a possible outcome, if the suggested action is pursued. Then add the six dice numbers together and reduce to a single digit to obtain the core number.

Additional Number Meanings

Thirteen

This is often regarded as unlucky, but in this system it says that logic and effort can overcome any portents of ill-luck.

As an Outcome, thirteen assures success and happiness if you ignore irrational fears.

Fourteen

This speaks of the need to be patient and accept any temporary difficulties.

As an Outcome, fourteen assures a happier future if you go along with the present situation.

Fifteen

This emphasizes the importance of paying attention to detail and being aware of viewpoints that may strongly differ from your own.

As an Outcome, fifteen promises achievement if you avoid being too rigid in your aims and attitudes.

Sixteen

This says that it is important to balance the need for independence and self-expression with maintaining harmonious relationships.

As an Outcome, sixteen promises a satisfactory resolution if you can reassure those close to you that they still have a place in your life.

Seventeen

This suggests that creative thinking and imagination will offer insight into what is really going on under the surface of the present situation.

As an Outcome, seventeen says that the confidence of others in you depends on your keeping secrets and respecting confidences.

Eighteen

This talks of using strength and effort to make progress in a long-standing issue or situation.

As an Outcome, eighteen promises that persistence and endurance will pay dividends before too long.

AN EXAMPLE WITH THREE DICE

Margaret was aggrieved because she felt that she was doing more than her fair share of work while her junior colleagues seemed to be treating the office as a social club. Her disapproving manner had no effect and so Margaret was considering complaining to the management and threatening to resign.

Margaret cast three dice, a five, a six and another five. Sixteen suggested that she balanced her own needs, in this case a desire for fair treatment, with the need to preserve harmonious working relationships. Since she had no other job on offer and her age would make job-hunting difficult, Margaret reluctantly decided to talk to one of the more approachable younger women. She discovered that the junior members of the team were being thoughtless rather than unkind and had assumed that Margaret did not trust them to undertake many of the routine tasks. Her disapproving comments seemed to confirm this.

At first Margaret could not accept this, but gradually she realized that she had taken on more and more herself because her younger colleagues were slower and seemed less efficient. It had seemed quicker to carry out the work herself than to have to correct their mistakes and so they had given up asking for work.

Her second cast looked at the possible outcome if she tried to make office relations more harmonious and reduce her own work load. Three fives appeared. As an Outcome, fifteen promises an improvement if a person avoids being too rigid. Margaret began to accept that she had become set in her ways and that some of the ideas put forward by her younger colleagues would actually reduce the overall work load. Her dice reading was not at all what she expected, but it has shown her a way forward so that she can begin to enjoy office life more and, above all, delegate.

Finally, Margaret added together the six dice numbers, a total of 31, which reduced to the core number four, the number of the evening sun. This suggested that happiness lay in accepting that both she and her colleagues were less than perfect but that given good will on both sides, a good working relationship could be established.

Method Two

This is similar to the first method in that two dice are rolled in two casts. However, the interpretation is of the dual number in each cast, in other words, three-four and five-two are interpreted as different answers.

The chalk circle still marks out a magical place, but both dice are counted irrespective of whether they fall inside or outside it. The first falling outside might suggest a delay in action because of circumstances, and the second a delayed outcome of several weeks.

Ask a personal question and as the dice fall, let any half-formed thoughts and images guide your interpretation. For example, according to your question or area of concern, a roll of one-one, which favours independent action and a new beginning, would suggest that the projected change, whether foreign travel, a new business venture, moving house or even beginning a new relationship, would be auspicious in the near future.

The answer does not come out of the sky, but reflects the stirring of energies within you towards a new direction. Your images may guide you to another area from the one that your conscious mind envisaged. For example, if you asked whether it was a good time to look for a new job, a roll of one-one would confirm that it was, but you might also see images of planes or trains which would suggest that a change in location was just as important or perhaps even prompted the desire for a career move. In this case, jobs a distance away or connected with the travel industry might be especially advantageous.

One-two and two-one are interpreted in the same way. If the same dice roll appears twice, the issue is a central one. You can then add up your four dice numbers and reduce them to a core strength, as with the previous method. Again a birthday or birth month number occurring is significant.

One-One

A new beginning or opportunity assures success and happiness if you believe in your own abilities and act now.

One-Two

You may need to weigh up the odds and opposition before embarking on a new venture and wait for the right moment.

One-Three

This is a time to be clear about what you want and the best way to go about it before you embark on any drastic changes.

One-Four

Use your experience of life, the negative aspects as well as the positive ones, to avoid making mistakes in a new venture.

One-Five

A new beginning may involve major changes in more than one area of your life that will set you on a different track.

One-Six
Happiness lies in fulfilling your own dreams rather than those of others.

Two-Two
You may feel that neither choice or option is right, in which case wait until you are more certain.

Two-Three
Share your future plans with those who will be supportive and seek happiness or success through a partnership.

Two-Four
Take the safe option and hold on to what you have, rather than gambling on unsubstantiated hopes of success or happiness.

Two-Five
If there are two choices or options, go for the one that offers happiness and opportunities to spread your wings, rather than security.

Two-Six
Try to find compromise and balance in any relationships, whether at work or home, rather than seeking confrontation.

Three-Three
Now is the time to expand your horizons, either physically or mentally and bring a breath of fresh air into your life.

Three-Four
Your present situation contains potential you have not explored. Develop existing opportunities rather than seeking pastures new.

Three-Five
You may need to make major changes to satisfy your desires for a different way of life. Talk through your plans so that you are clear what you are aiming for.

Three-Six
New horizons and projects are more likely to succeed through co-operation with others. Find those who share your dreams and join forces.

Four-Four
It is time to shed a few illusions and see what you can do to improve your present circumstances.

Four-Five
You should not give up your need for change but must be versatile in finding a way to overcome present restrictions.

Four-Six
You should not rely too much on the help of others to smooth your path. Begin with small steps to fulfil your dreams.

Five-Five
Change is in the air and you need to channel your restlessness into new plans rather than ignoring it.

Five-Six
Clear communication is necessary to resolve any conflict, but at the end of the day, you cannot sacrifice yourself or your independence for others.

Six-Six
Harmony depends on considering every possible option, not forgetting your own needs and viewpoint.

AN EXAMPLE OF DUAL DICE ROLLING

Bill could not decide whether to go abroad with his friends and get a summer job or go home as usual for the month-long summer gathering at the family seaside cottage. His parents were pressing him to spend what might be the last summer before he graduated with them at the cottage and offered to support him financially during the holiday.

Bill threw one-five, a new beginning involving major changes in more than one area of his life that would set him on a new track. He realized that the previous summer he had been bored and restless on the family holiday, but still felt guilty that he was, in his mother's words, 'spoiling the family summer' for his parents and his teenage sister.

He made a second dice roll for the outcome. One-six told him that harmony lay in finding his own happiness. Bill went abroad with his friends and found that in spite of his guilt, it was his first taste of real independence. His sister, following his lead, went to work at the local riding stables for the holidays and his parents went away alone for the first time in 20 years. Often the action of one member can act as a catalyst for the others. Bill has found that his parents could survive without him and he is contemplating a career abroad when he graduates.

His core number, reached by adding together the two rolls of the dice was 6 + 7 = 13 = 4. He realized that he could not achieve independence without a certain amount of guilt (loving families can be very hard to leave), but that it was a price worth paying and in the long run it freed his family from a routine that was stopping them all moving forward.

Domestic Magic

MAGIC IN THE HOME

Domestic Magic is often disregarded in the modern world in favour of more exotic versions. Yet it is perhaps one of the most powerful and safest forms of magic. Real magic has always been practised by ordinary people, especially women, who saw pictures in the suds of the wash tub or watched visions form in the light of a solitary candle as they sat at the bedside of a sick child through the long hours of the night.

Wicca and other types of formal witchcraft have divorced magic from its roots as a natural expression of the intuitive side of human nature. They have also taken away the inbuilt protection of magical rituals that use everyday artefacts to achieve aims in the real world.

Domestic Deities

The Chinese Kitchen God, Tsao-wang, the God of the Stove or Hearth, is represented by a picture on paper, rather than a statue. This image is placed in a small wooden temple over the hearth, facing south. Tsao wang nai-nai, his wife who is pictured next to him, carries the sayings of the women of the household to the Jade Emperor. Each morning three incense sticks are burned in the domestic shrine.

The God of the Kitchen goes to the heavens each year on the eve of the Chinese New Year in late January or early February. Here he or she reports to the Jade Emperor on the activities of the family during the past 12 months. On the eve of the New Year the lips of the image of the Kitchen God are sealed with sweets or honey so that he will not reveal family quarrels or dark secrets. His picture is taken down and burned over a little fire of pine twigs to the accompaniment of fire crackers. The next morning a new picture is placed in the shrine and offerings are made to it. Doors are closed for the night, then opened at dawn by the head of the household to bring in good fortune.

In Ancient Rome the Lares and Penates presided over the dwellings and affairs of the Roman households. The Lares were the deified ancestors or heroes and the *lar familiaris*, the spirit of the founder of the house who never left it. The Penates were chiefly the gods of the storeroom and guardians of the home who protected it from outside danger. Their statues had a corner of honour in each house and wine, incense, cakes and honey were offered to them at family festivities.

The hearth was the central place of the home and on a spiritual level the meeting place for the upper and lower worlds. At festivals of the dead (see *Hallowe'en Magic*, page 260), food and drink would be left on the hearth for deceased family members to return to the warmth of the family fire. The Latin word for hearth is *focus* because in the days before central heating and microwaves, cooking and heating centred around the hearth and so it was the natural gathering place.

In Hinduism too, the domestic hearth took on religious as well as family significance, since Agni, God of Fire, was also God of domestic fire (see also *Fire Magic*, page 211).

DOMESTIC FESTIVALS

Mothering Sunday

Many people believe that Mothering Sunday is relatively modern invention, but its roots go back much further than the modern festival launched by an American woman at the turn of the century. Anna Jarvis had devoted her life to caring for her mother and decided that it was important to have a special occasion each year to acknowledge how precious mothers are. The first Mother's Day Service and celebrations in the United States were held in West Virginia in 1908 and five years later Mother's Day became an official holiday throughout America on the second Sunday in May.

However, the European mid-Lenten celebration dates back to the Middle Ages when in Catholic Britain it was the custom for servants to visit their Mother Church (where they had been baptized) on mid-Lent Sunday to make offerings at the high altar. In the *Gentleman's Magazine* for February 1784, Nichols, an English writer, notes that when he was an apprentice the custom was to visit his mother, a native of Nottingham, on mid-Lent Sunday.

Another writer in the same volume says: 'I happened to reside near Chepstow and heard for the first time of Mothering Sunday. The practice was for servants and apprentices on mid-Lent Sunday to visit their parents and make them a present of money or a trinket or some nice eatable.' Indentured servants and apprentices would sometimes travel many miles to present their mothers with gloves, a traditional gift, or even a posy of early spring flowers from the fields through which they trudged, if they had no money to spare from their meagre wages. There would be a special meal which broke the monotony of the Lenten fast and a Simnel cake was baked (see *Food Magic*, page 233).

In Leckford, near Stockbridge in Hampshire, England, Mothering Sunday was called Wafering Sunday from the wafer cake impressed with a seal that young people offered to their mothers on this occasion. A special iron used to impress the cakes had two stamps, one of which had three locked hearts surmounted by a cross enclosed within a circle. The other had foliate ornaments on either side. They were made red hot and the wafer was branded with them by someone employed especially for this job.

MAGICAL PROTECTION OF THE HOME

Because people at home are at their most open and therefore vulnerable, domestic protection has always been of great importance. Rosemary was hung from Romany caravan roofs to protect the living space from negative influences.

Iron fences were erected round more permanent dwellings to halt the flow of evil influences into the home. Nails would also be driven into the walls of houses to protect the inhabitants against illness, for iron had special magical significance. Discovered first in meteorites, it was considered the metal of the gods. This domestic protection was used in Ancient Rome where nails in a building were considered effective against plagues (see also *Metal Magic*, page 323).

Brass objects, such as horse brasses and brass plates, are still seen in traditional rooms, although their magical function has been forgotten. Long-handled brass warming pans, which were filled with hot coals and placed in beds in winter, often hang in hallways, their shiny surfaces reflecting back any hostile influences that seek to enter. Brass door stops and brass-edged steps to houses served the same purpose, as did polished white steps, all sensing sunlight (brass is the metal of the sun), to drive away dark forces.

House-building

It is believed in some parts of the world that only smooth trees should be used for building a house. In the Sudan, to use a thorn-bearing tree in house building would mean that the inhabitants would have a troublesome stay in the home.

Among certain tribes in South Africa, once the site of a new village has been established and the houses are being built, no couple may have conjugal relations until the village is finished to keep the site pure.

Because it was believed that a tree spirit might still be dwelling in the timbers, offerings were made when a house was completed – perhaps this was the origin of house-warming parties. Great care was taken that timber, especially for door posts, was not put in upside down. In houses built in the Middle Ages in Europe, the corpse of a mouse or cat would be placed in the foundations. Human remains have been discovered in the foundations of building from earlier times. They were put there to drive away dark spirits and appease the spirits of the land on which the house was erected. More recently symbols, such as clay pipes or even shoes, have been used in new buildings.

MODERN DOMESTIC PSYCHIC PROTECTION

Protective Light

People no longer believe that malevolent spirits are waiting to enter the home, but after a bad day, most of us come home carrying more than our fair share of negativity and that can sour the sunniest domestic atmosphere.

A mirror facing the front door will deflect any feelings of gloom. Shiny saucepans or a wok hanging up facing the kitchen door will also reflect any darkness out of the back door. Tiny quartz crystals on thread or sun-catchers, popular in the United States, can be hung at windows and over glass doors to catch any sun and spread rainbows throughout the darkest rooms. For protection day and night, place small pieces of iron in each room of the house or bury them at the four corners of the property.

Protective Herbs and Fragrances

You can use pots of herbs, jars of dried herbs or oils in burners (now sold in many large supermarkets) or gently heated on a saucer over a radiator. Protective herbs and fragrances include basil, bay, cedarwood, cinnamon, eucalyptus, lavender, peppermint and rose. All of these can be bought as oils (see also *Herb Magic*, page 268).

Protective Crystals

You may wish to place protective crystals in strategic places around your home, especially in your bedroom and near entrances and windows. Protective crystals include agates of all colours, amber, calcite of all colours, obsidian (apache tear), jade, jasper, jet, malachite, serpentine and tiger's eye of all colours.

A Protective Domestic Crystal Ritual

If you feel afraid when you are at home alone or you are encountering external hostility that is hard to shed at the front door, sit as near as you can to the centre of your home and hold your favourite protective crystal. Gaze into it and let its soft colour enfold you in a protective cocoon. When you feel safe, open doors or windows as you move clockwise round the house towards the main exit. This would be the back door or in an apartment a back or side-facing window. Shake your crystal out of the back door and let any negativity fly upwards in a long black thread until it becomes a dark cloud, which will then disperse into shimmering sunbeams. Close the door and reward your chosen crystal with a soak in pure still mineral water for 12 hours.

KITCHEN MAGIC

You may no longer cook at the magical hearth but the kitchen is still the centre for domestic magic.

Domestic Magic for Money

In parts of the United States, copper coins are kept in a copper pitcher in the kitchen to attract money to the household. Another popular US money ritual involves placing a large stone either on the hearth or near your stove and leaving it for exactly a year to ensure money will flow in.

A variation which can be adapted to the smallest kitchens involves placing a flat stone on a metallic dish near the stove or microwave. Each week, put a small coin to form a circle around the stone. As you do so, light a small, flat, scented candle on top of the stone in a small holder. Choose yellow or orange for money, scented with one of the money fragrances, such as cedarwood, cinnamon or orange. See the smoke and flame of the candle warming and incubating your money and let the candle burn out naturally.

Every time you use your stove or microwave, visualize the heat expanding your money. Tell family and friends not to borrow the coins. Each time you light the candle or stove, see your financial prospects improving and your efforts bearing fruit.

Once the circle is complete, use the money to buy a present for someone who is sad or if there is no one, put it in a charity collecting box. Money should flow in naturally, providing you do not wait for magic to solve your problems. You may find a new source of income or a money-spinning idea comes as soon as you have spent your magical money. Place the stone where someone else may find and use it.

Scrying at the Sink

The most natural place for magical inspirations is gazing into water. However, for every woman (or man) who sought inspiration for poetry or romantic encounters by moonlight lakes, a hundred turned over domestic and family concerns in their minds and often saw pictures and visions in the shapes of the bubbles as they washed the dishes or scoured the pans.

The aim is to make three separate images: your present situation, helpful factors or unexpected considerations and a suggested course of action. Run cold water into a bowl or sink and squeeze in a concentrated green or other dark-coloured liquid detergent. Pour it sparingly and very slowly in widening circles until it forms a moving shape or image. It will not make bubbles, but swirl round and round in a series of shapes, as a kaleidoscope forms. You may want to practise reading pictures in the moving liquid before you use it for a specific question. The key is to pluck the image as soon as it forms and then let it re-form naturally.

If the image has formed a clump of colour, you will not get a second image out of it, so rinse out your bowl in cold water, make sure it is entirely bubble-free and add a second small quantity of liquid. If you are sparing you can always add more.

Sometimes you will find that the first image changes into another and then you do not need to change the water. Only rarely will you get three pictures from the original liquid. It makes no difference how many times you change the water and if one image seems blurred or clumped, tip it away and try again.

When you have three images you are happy with, sketch them and sit quietly at the kitchen table with tea, coffee or juice and let the original ideas expand. You can, if you wish, read your tea leaves or coffee grounds (see *Tea Leaf Reading*, page 425) and you may find the images remarkably similar.

SAM'S READING

Sam was a rising TV presenter who got involved in a demonstration I was doing and rather sceptically decided to try kitchen sink magic.

The first image Sam saw, the present situation, was a knight in shining armour, which seemed to reflect his own life, dashing from one job to another and never seeing his family. He said that he had not been home for seven weeks and was missing his children. The second image, helpful influences, Sam took to be the outline of Ireland, which he saw as a haven of rest and slower times and so he wondered whether he should take a holiday, perhaps in Ireland. The third image was an owl, which Sam interpreted as wisdom and an indication that he should learn, now that he was becoming more successful, not to accept absolutely every commission offered but take a long-term view.

BEDTIME MAGIC

Several bedtime superstitions reflect a very old form of Westernised Earth energies: beds should be parallel with floorboards and a double bed not divided by a beam or there will be quarrels. The foot of the bed should never be turned towards the door and should preferably follow a north/south direction to harness the energies of the Earth's pole. You should always get out of bed on the right side as bad spirits and influences are believed to lurk on the left.

A Bedtime Ritual

Light a soft green or pink candle for love and peace and place it near the window. In its flame see the faces of those you love and for a moment be close to them. You might get absent friends or family members to light a candle at the same time each night, allowing for time differences around the world and link in love. Blow out the candle and send loving light to every corner of the room to protect you while you sleep.

HARMONY IN THE HOME: WESTERN-STYLE

Getting the Elemental Balance Right

The ancient Western and Northern elements of Earth, Air, Fire and Water combine together, according to the Alchemists, to form a fifth element, ether (see *Seasonal Magic*, page 398). To create this magical balance ensure that all the elements are represented in a room, either in the four main compass points or in the four corners, using the top left corner as North, the top right corner as East, the bottom right corner as South and the bottom left corner as West. Choose one of the following for each element or adapt your own ideas.

Examples of Earth Elements

Pot pourri, salt, a dish of peppermint, flowers, dried flowers, an arrangement of leaves or a pottery dish, can represent the Earth in the North.

Examples of Air Elements

A fragrant oil burner, an incense stick, a silver knife, a box of pins or pair of scissors for the penetration of air, a fresh air deodorizer, an arrangement of feathers or feathery grasses, a wind chime, a paper butterfly or bird mobile can represent Air in the East.

Examples of Fire Elements

A clear or golden mirror placed strategically, crystals threaded on cord or a sun-catcher, sun symbols and ornaments, golden candles and bright metallic trays can represent Fire in the East.

Examples of Water Elements

A dish of rose water, a fish tank, a coffee machine, a bowl of water with coloured stones or crystals or a small vase of water coloured with blue or green oils can represent Water in the West.

Obtaining Different Elemental Mixes

You should always keep one example of each element in a room. However, rooms can benefit from additional elements according to their use. You may find it easier to make a larger and more elaborate corner for the required additional element power or spread the extra energies throughout the room.

Bedroom Elements

The bedroom would benefit from an extra water element for quiet sleep and abandonment of conscious worries, as would a living area where you relax. Make your water corner larger and more elaborate in your bedroom and relaxing area, perhaps a large fish tank with glinting tiny fish or a large bowl filled with floating scented candles or flower petals. You can even make a tiny indoor water garden, surrounded by watery coloured crystals, such as jade and green calcite.

Study or Home-Office Elements

If your work is creative, add some extra fire, perhaps crystals or sun-catchers at the windows, tiny mirrors hung on threads or a table lamp with sun motifs traced on it on your desk. If your world involves logic, air will be helpful to you so keep a lively oil, such as lemon or orange, burning or make a picture of pins and shiny nails to hang on the wall. If your thoughts are slow, an environmentally friendly air freshener or throwing open the windows will keep the air circulating.

Kitchen and Dining Areas

Here a good additional mix of earth and fire will make for lively, creative but friendly domestic interaction – and even a sharing of chores. In the kitchen, onions or garlic hanging from hooks on the ceiling are also good for protection. Racks of vegetables in the kitchen and a bowl of fruit in the dining area help to relax the family even after a difficult day (see also *Food Magic*, page 233). Shiny metals bowls, saucepans and utensils will get the creative fires burning. However, make sure that Earth is in predominance, so that accidents in the kitchen will be less likely to occur through carelessness.

HARMONY IN THE HOME: EASTERN-STYLE

The Feng Shui (Wind and Water) practised by ordinary people does not rely so much on precise measurements by experts, but is a more instinctive approach especially to domestic harmony. Ch'i is the invisible life force, the flow of positive energy that pulsates through everything: people, animals, nature and also homes.

When this positive energy becomes blocked, problems can occur, whether physical or a general feeling of malaise or 'dis-ease'. Certain homes seem dark and unfriendly and those who live there may quarrel or lack energy. Feng Shui goes back 5,000 years in China and there are two formal systems: the Form School and the Compass School that involve precise measurement and learning many principles of harmony. However, the folk system of Feng Shui has co-existed alongside them quite cheerfully and without mastering the accumulated rules of five millennia, it is possible to use basic principles to make your home happy and harmonious.

The Flow of Ch'i in the Home

Having entered a home through the main doorway, ch'i should be encouraged to flow in gentle wavy lines through each room before leaving it, entering the next and finally leaving the house. The exit should be different, such as a window, and finally the back door if there is one.

The level and intensity of flow should vary according to the purpose for which the room is used. In work, kitchen or living rooms, ch'i which travels can be encouraged to circulate freely by using mirrors, crystals, wind chimes and other minor modifications, a concept not dissimilar from Western elemental balances.

Bedrooms need less stimulation if they are to promote quiet sleep and happy dreams. Where there are en suite showers and washbasins, doors should be closed and any water exits covered so that ch'i does not vanish down the nearest watercourse. A tall upwards flowing plant in any washroom gives energy to the room and directs the flow of ch'i upwards and onwards.

Creating Harmony

Beds, as in Westernised elemental magic, should not be facing or in line with the door, but rest diagonally. If your bed and especially your feet must face the door, hang a crystal or wind-chime between the bed and the doorway. Mirrors in bedrooms can create too lively a flow of ch'i for restful nights and should be avoided, except by ardent lovers.

Since the forces affecting marriage are said to be in the far right of a room from the front door of a house looking in, this is a good position for a marital bed. If you are trying to conceive a baby, Feng Shui puts the children's position in the central right of a room, so a change in bed position might do wonders for fertility.

Children's beds placed at the centre right of a bedroom, again working from the viewpoint of staring in the front door, can promote happy bedtimes and prevent night terrors.

Because the wealth area is in the top left of any room (seen from the front door looking in) this is a good place for a computer or for a desk in a study or home office used for financial affairs or money-spinning ideas. You can also place a symbol of money in this corner or in a living room. Goldfish in a tank (eight gold and one black) are especially auspicious in a money area.

If money seems to flow out of your home very fast, something heavy in the money corner of a room where you balance the domestic budget, such as a statue or a heavy plant pot, should help to keep money in the home.

Negative Energies

Sha, negative energies, operate in straight lines and around sharp edges or protruding furniture, so break up straight paths and corridors or walk through living areas with plants and seating with rounded edges, using throws and drapes where necessary. Corridors that run from front to back of the house in a straight line or through a series of doors can be broken up with crystals and wind-chimes over the doors or mirrors on the walls.

Welcoming Ch'i

Because ch'i enters through the front door, the door and entrance areas are especially important. They should be light, bright, well-lit and with mirrors, wind-chimes and a picture of whatever guardian you favour or a powerful animal, such as a tiger, horse or dragon, especially if the stairs are straight ahead of the door. If stairs do face the entrance, crystals hung above doors leading off even a tiny hallway can help to spread light and positive energies.

The Right Colours

Light colours, such as white and cream, are ideal for an entrance hall, with bright colours in working areas. Red and green are good for attracting wealth, so you might like to have something red and green in your main money corner. Pastels are ideal for bedrooms. You can decorate a study bedroom in different shades, with brighter ones for work areas and lots of soft pastels in the sleep area. Cuddly toys on beds serve this purpose beautifully.

Going with the Flow

You do not need to be a Feng Shui expert to tune in naturally to the ch'i, sense the blockages and, most importantly, clear them. Overflowing drawers, broken gadgets you will never mend, crammed cupboards and piles of newspapers or heaps of children's toys are irritants as well as blocking the ch'i. It is surprising how much we hoard that we never use: clothes and mementos that should live in our minds and hearts, not on our shelves.

First remove any clutter from your home at least once a month. Families can join in a ch'i releasing day. Children enjoy collecting ch'i blockers in plastic or wicker baskets and as a bonus you get a tidy home. Children's possessions can be stacked in laundry baskets and put away in a softly curtained corner or in toy chests that can be purchased very cheaply from used good stores.

Once 50 per cent of your possessions have been consigned to yesterday, the rest fits easily and you can feel the ch'i flowing.

Finding the Right Place

Often the harmony of a room is wrong because its purpose has been overridden. Formal feng shui relies on identifying different areas of influence on a grid, but even without rearranging your entire house you can make each room resonate with its own vibrations. For example, work papers, computers and files of financial matters can make a bedroom unnecessarily sharp and lead to bad dreams and insomnia. Many children and students have study bedrooms, so it is important to separate the work and sleeping areas, perhaps with a screen or by low room dividers, with plants on top and compartments to hide away computer monitors and televisions at bedtime.

Identifying Blockages

Use a pendulum – a key or a favourite charm on a chain or cord will do (see also *Earth Magic*, page 53, for other uses of pendulums and Dragon Lines). Begin at the entrance to your property, whether a front gate or door. If you have an apartment with a shared hallway, your personal control of ch'i begins at your front door, although a plant or two outside might deflect other people's sha.

Now follow the natural progression of rooms as though you were showing a visitor round your house. Follow a path around each room, around the furniture and back to an different exit, perhaps a window. You do not want to follow the chi's natural exit, so retrace your steps to the door, leaving by another direction. If you have a room without a window, place a chair or plant near the entrance. You can go in by its right side and exit via its left side.

The pendulum will swing regularly as you walk and you can take this as its positive response, even if it is an anti-clockwise swing as occasionally happens. If the pendulum stops, pulls down or swings around in an irregular movement as though encountering resistance, you know you have a blockage. You may feel a sense of stagnation or irritability at the place or suddenly tired. Make a note on a rough sketch of any negative feelings and then continue until you have covered the whole house. If you have a back door, leave by it and use a back entrance from your property if there is one, or go the reverse way round the house to the front entrance.

See where the blockages are and whether there are either sharp angles of furniture or a straight passage where the sha is passing in and the ch'i going straight out or a cluttered area that is slowing down the flow. Traditionally seats should be against walls and not with their backs to windows – for fear of attack – unless facing a mirror. However, in small modern houses and apartments, a strategically placed chair, especially one with soft cushions, can distribute the path of ch'i around the room as long as it does not block an entrance or protrude too much.

Experiment room by room, moving furniture, adding a windchime, a mirror, sun-catcher or some greenery. Living plants and flowers will create a gentle but powerful positive energy flow. Artificial flowers do not have the same energies. Let your pendulum and your own feelings guide you. To get things moving in a stagnant area, burn some eucalyptus oil or lavender. Polishing furniture in living and working rooms and hanging shining saucepans and woks on the kitchen walls also keeps the energies flowing, although you need to avoid leaving around too many jagged steel objects, such as knives, to keep accidents to the minimum.

12

DOMINO DIVINATION

ORIGINS OF DOMINO DIVINATION

A set of dominoes consists of 28 oblong blocks made of ivory, bone, wood or plastic. The game originated in China in ancient times, as dice markings were transferred to pieces of wood called *chims*. This was supposed to prevent the trickery that could occur with dice divination.

One offshoot of these early dominoes were the Mah Jong pieces, also originally a powerful tool of prophecy. But the basic dominoes retained popularity with ordinary people who could use the finely carved ivory or roughly hewn wooden pieces to plan their lives and futures. Dominoes became very popular in the Middle East, probably when they were carried via the trade routes with China and Japan. Dominoes were not introduced in Europe until the middle of the eighteenth century. Gradually they took their place as a form of family divination along with tea cup reading and dice casting.

Because of their ancient beginnings, it is uncertain whether dominoes were first used for games or for divination. But they remain a simple and yet powerful divinatory tool, although often consigned to the children's toy box until after dark.

The first European dominoes had ivory faces, backed with ebony and engraved with ebony dots. They were probably called dominoes because of their resemblance to a hooded cloak, called a domino. Each domino, also called a piece or a man, is divided in half by a line or ridge, with a combination of spots or pips, on each half. One piece is entirely blank. The remainder are numbered downward from double six, that is, 6–6, 6–5, 6–4, 6–3, 6–2, 6–1, 6–0; 5–5, 5–4, 5–3, 5–2, 5–1, 5–0, and so on through all the other numbers.

DOMINO DIVINATION

Because two numbers are joined on a single domino, the divinatory meaning revolves not only around the individual number meanings, but also whether the domino is waxing or waning, that is, whether when read from left to right the number value increases or decreases on the individual domino. So three-four is waxing while four-three is waning. As a rule of thumb, dominoes with increasing numbers tend to be positive and reflect the creative meaning of the number. Waning numbers reflect a more negative, destructive aspect. However, even a more negatively aspected domino does not prophesy doom and gloom, for endings are necessary to lead to new beginnings and a negative emotion can be a powerful impetus for positive change.

No domino is intrinsically good or bad. Whether its positive or negative aspect predominates, depends entirely on which way up the domino lies when it is turned over by the questioner. For example, a domino that presented itself as one-two would talk of increase in happiness or prosperity or planning a partnership and two-one would presage a decrease in unity between two people or perhaps a separation.

Personal Interpretation of Dominoes

Rather than asking a specific question, you may prefer to focus on a particular relationship or issue that is currently occupying your thoughts or worrying you.

As well as the waxing and waning aspects of the dominoes, meanings can also be deduced according to whether the difference between the two numbers on an individual domino is large or small. For example, one-six involves a great deal of action and change but three-four represents a more stable state of affairs. Whether the domino numbers are odd or even also provides information. Even numbers tend to refer to stability, steady relationships, caution and partnerships, whereas odd numbers are faster-moving and linked with individual action, independence and change. A domino with two odd numbers is full of movement, whereas a domino with two even numbers may represent a period of waiting or a time of calm.

An odd and even number on the domino reflect either a firm foundation for a venture or stagnation and frustration, according to whether the positive or negative aspect predominates. So too, a move from an even to an odd number on an individual domino can herald either welcome progress or restlessness according to whether the domino is in its positive or negative phase.

A repeated number on a domino, such as double three, strengthens the core meaning of the number and is always balanced. A double number indicates that a situation has reached a peak or plateau of calm depending on the number itself. Zero is regarded as lower in number value than one and always represents the unknown.

Domino Answers

If the answer seems obscure, even after applying more specific meanings to your initial intuitive response, hold the domino in front of you and let the black and white wood or ivory grow in your mind's eye until it becomes a screen. Watch the dots become silhouette figures, moving and speaking on a stage. Sleep with your domino under your pillow, either wrapped in a black and white scarf or cloth or flanked by a black crystal such as an obsidian (apache tear) and clear white crystal quartz. Black and white pebbles chosen from your garden, local park or the shore are equally effective.

Your domino oracle will be further peopled in your dream. You may find the promised event highlighted by the domino, of which you were only dimly aware on an unconscious level, lies just around the corner.

THE KEY NUMBERS

You will use only the first six numbers for domino divination, plus a zero. This system fits well with an alternative method of numerology that links numbers to the days of the week and the planets in a different order from that used in dice divination.

Think of the numbers zero to six in a circle, just as weeks begin with Sunday which follows Saturday and precedes Monday in an unending cycle. In domino divination, this system begins with number one (Sunday) and ends with the zero (Saturday) of Saturn, God of Fate, leading directly on to the new beginning of one again. For calculating waxing and waning aspects in domino divination, a zero is counted as the lowest number.

You may wonder why this system differs slightly from the planetary attributions used in the section on dice divination. This is because there is no consensus in magic and there are several alternatives in many magical correspondences. You can adopt the one that fits most with your own ideas and intuitions or use different connections according to the method of divination you are using.

One

Ruled here by the sun and Sunday, one is seen as the number of the individual, the I of self that brings everything into creation. It is the initiator, creator and destroyer. Therefore any domino with a waxing one that rises to a higher number value on the chosen domino, such as one-three, represents a surge of individual power and energy that fuels determination and action. If the domino falls so that the one is waning, for example 4–1 or 1-blank, you may be a experiencing a sudden lack of confidence, an uncertainty as to the rightness of your actions or even a feeling of alienation from those around you.

Two

Ruled by the moon and Monday, here the one divides into two, good and bad, light and darkness, positive and negative, male and female. Therefore any domino that contains a waxing two represents duality and partnership in its most positive creative sense, whether an emotional or business partnership, and a balancing of any incongruous factors. A waning two suggests a division or disagreement and perhaps some kind of separation.

Three

Mars and Tuesday rule three in this system. Past efforts bear fruit, horizons expand and ideas and ideals are unrestricted by harsh reality. Any domino with a waxing three represents increasing optimism, confidence and awareness of limitless possibilities. A waning three can represent frustration and pessimism and sometimes unreasonable anger turned against yourself or others.

Four

Mercury and Wednesday rule four. Mercury is often associated with movement (its metal is quicksilver). However, this number represents Mercury's role as the mathematician, alchemist (as the legendary Hermes Trismegistus, father of alchemy) and communicator. Four gives form and structure to vague ideas and brings together the higher and lower worlds in time and space. So four represents stability and order and, as recognition of Mercury's role as messenger, all travel matters. In its waxing aspect, four allows progress to be made in a tangible form, encourages clear, focused communication and favours financial gain and speculation (Mercury is god of moneylenders as well as thieves). Thus order can be created out of chaos. In its waning aspect, four has the negative elements of trickery, false words, restlessness and instability (quicksilver at its most destructive).

Five

Ruled by Jupiter and Thursday, five represents conventional wisdom and learning, success in a career and the power of the mind. As a waxing number, five heralds success in worldly matters, wise counsel, justice and authority. As a waning number five can suggest an intolerance of weakness in others, an over-critical approach, emotional detachment and falling out of favour with authority or the law.

Six

Ruled by Venus and by Friday, six represents love, peace, harmony, friendship and the home. As a waxing number, six promises an increase of love, of harmonious relationships and a happy home and love life. As a waning number, it warns that possessiveness, emotional blackmail and stifling relationships may sour domestic harmony and friendship.

Zero

Ruled by Saturn and Saturday zero represents unformed matter and undeveloped potential, a step into the unknown. The web of fate is woven from personal strengths and failings and intervention from outside forces, whether unexpected good luck or sorrow. Any domino with a zero will represent uncertainty but also unexpected opportunities. This can include people who may come into your life unexpectedly and remain to play an important part in your future. The blank casts a question mark whether at the beginning or end of a domino.

PREPARING FOR DOMINO DIVINATION

Although traditionally Monday and Friday are not considered propitious for domino reading, you can safely ignore the old superstitions and harness the energies of a particular planet on its special day to give your reading added power.

Sunday

The day of the sun is a good day for a reading if the main issues are personal ones, concerned with your identity and independent ventures. As gold is the colour of the sun and Sunday, you can cast your dominoes on either a yellow or gold disc of paper or foil or a brilliant yellow cloth.

Monday

The day of the moon is a propitious day for domino divination if you are concerned with partnership issues or need to make a choice. Silver is the colour of the moon and so you could use a circle of silver paper or foil or a white cloth on which to cast your dominoes.

Tuesday
The day of Mars is a positive day for domino divination if you are concerned with expansion in any field, face opposition or feel strongly about an issue. Red is the colour of Tuesday and Mars and so you can carry out your reading on a circle of red paper or on a red cloth.

Wednesday
The day of Mercury is a good day if you are concerned with travel, communication of any kind, money or business matters. Yellow is the colour of Wednesday and Mercury and so a circle of yellow paper or a pale yellow cloth would be appropriate on which to cast your dominoes.

Thursday
The day of Jupiter is a good day for divination on career matters, for examinations, learning and the law. Blue is the colour of Jupiter and Thursday. Use a blue circle of paper or a blue cloth for readings today.

Friday
The day of Venus is a harmonious day for readings concerning love, relationships and friendship. Lilac or pink are the colours of Venus so use a circle of pink or pale purple paper or a lilac or pink cloth.

Saturday
The day of Saturn is concerned with endings and with the unexpected. So if you feel you are a hostage of fate or need to end a phase in your life, this is the day to try domino divination. Pale grey or deep purple are the colours of Saturn. Use either a circle of paper or a grey or purple cloth for your reading (see also *Colour Magic*, page 87).

Begin your reading as the sun begins to set and if you need light, use a candle of the colour of the day on which you are carrying out your reading or pure white for inspiration and energy.

METHODS OF DOMINO DIVINATION

When used as divinatory tools, dominoes are placed face down and mixed on a flat surface before one is chosen. Some diviners choose the most distant domino, but you may find you are instinctively drawn to a particular one. Other people hold a pendulum or a key on a chain over the dominoes. If you want to try this, pass the pendulum slowly over the dominoes until you feel it pulling towards one particular domino. Turn over the selected domino carefully. Remember to note which way up the domino lies and the order of the numbers as it faces you.

After reading the domino, replace it face down and mix the set again. Close your eyes as you mix the dominoes, so the order is not known to you on an unconscious level. You may decide to select a second domino if the message of the first is not clear. If the two dominoes seem to be giving contradictory messages, they may be reflecting your own deep-rooted uncertainty as to the right course of action or perhaps contradictory messages that you are being given by different people. You may wish to select a third after returning the previous domino and remixing. For most occasions, however, one domino will provide sufficient information.

According to tradition, dominoes should not be consulted more than once a week, but if you have a particularly important or difficult week, you may wish to use this form of oracle more than once. Rules are created by people often in accordance with old superstitions that have no place in the modern world of magic.

Three dominoes are probably the most that will be of use at any one time in divination, unless the same domino is chosen twice. A domino duplicate emphasizes the importance of the original meaning and suggests that results will follow almost immediately.

The meanings given below are only suggested ones and as you use the system regularly, you may find that others fit your own life better. Insert your personal meanings in the book or a special journal and if in doubt, let your intuition guide you to the answer.

Double Blank

This domino is traditionally regarded as the least auspicious, suggesting that caution is needed in money matters and care with possessions since this is a time when belongings are easily lost.

Blank-One

A stranger may offer unexpected help or information that may set you on a new course of action or perhaps to learn a new skill.

One-Blank

Fear of the unknown may be holding you back unnecessarily from a new venture or from striking out alone.

Double One

Believe in yourself and act now. Happiness and success are within your grasp.

Blank-Two
An unexpected friendship or offer of co-operation may prove helpful and redress the balance in your life.

Two-Blank
There may be an unexpected temporary parting, either your own or that of a close relation or friend. Use the time for personal growth.

One-Two
A new partnership deepens, perhaps in a permanent way, whether personal or connected with work.

Two-One
Independence and a clash in priorities may become an issue in a relationship, so make any decisions carefully.

Double Two
A double success in work and home life, with partnerships of any kind bringing special joy.

Blank-Three
An unexpected bonus or opportunity enables you to expand your horizons and lifestyle.

Three-Blank
Avoid jealousy and controversial subjects as there are unsettled feelings flying.

One-Three
A startling revelation or discovery may open a whole new field to you or completely change your perspective.

Three-One
Check any too-good-to-be-true offers as they may be just that.

Two-Three
An additional responsibility or challenge will bring joy and new opportunities in the near future, especially where younger people are concerned.

Three-Two
Beware backbiting or malice by a third party who may try to come between partners or close friends.

Double Three
Now is the time to ask for promotion, more money or for recognition, as reward for your efforts is long overdue.

Blank-Four
Take any unexpected opportunities to travel or to make contact overseas. Contacts now may bear fruit at a later date.

Four-Blank
A time to keep secrets and to mend any quarrels that are still unresolved.

One-Four
A chance for personal financial gain or to achieve tangible recognition or reward for an original idea.

Four-One
A time to settle any debts and to plan future finances carefully, especially if expenditure is likely to rise.

Two-Four
A partnership or joint venture bears fruit and offers long-term security.

Four-Two
A financial or material crisis can be avoided if you let others know in advance of any problems and put your finances in order.

Three-Four
A good time to consolidate any business deals and to put temporary arrangements on a more secure footing.

Four-Three
Share your fears and insecurities about a particular venture rather than giving up, as they may prove to be unfounded.

Double-Four
Travel and financial bonuses should become reality before long, if you continue to be meticulous about planning.

Blank Five
Wise counsel from an unexpected source may solve a long-standing problem or legal dispute.

Five-Blank

Beware taking short cuts or chances, especially from untried sources, as you may fall foul of authority or lose the approval of those whom you respect.

One-Five

You can achieve success whether in your career, learning or exams if you concentrate single-mindedly on your goal.

Five-One

You may find you are standing alone if you cross an authority figure without checking your facts.

Two-Five

It is a good time to formalize any partnerships or co-operative ventures and to resolve any legal problems that may stand in the way.

Five-Two

A power struggle can threaten a partnership so you need to use your mind rather than your heart to avoid a permanent rift.

Three-Five

If you follow the conventional path, you may improve your status and public image.

Five-Three

Seek wise counsel rather than giving vent to anger, however justifiable, because you may regret it later.

Four-Five

You may benefit from legal or professional advice in business or financial matters to make the most of your resources.

Five-Four

Think carefully before making any financial promises or new commitments as you may overstretch yourself at this time.

Five-Five

Trust your own wisdom as you are in a very strong position and your judgement is sound.

Blank-Six
Love at first sight or friendship that comes out of the blue offers great future happiness.

Six-Blank
Your peace of mind is disturbed by factors you cannot understand or an unknown adversary. Wait and things will become clearer.

One-Six
There may be a new or sudden addition to your family circle, that heralds happiness if you accept him or her without reservations.

Six-One
Independence is in the air. A friend or family member may seek to flee the nest. If you respond positively, then the parting will be amicable.

Two-Six
Harmony and stability will be restored in family or social life or partnership, after a period of disruption or isolation.

Six-Two
A close relationship needs attention as a partner or close family member may be feeling neglected.

Three-Six
Relationships will enter a fertile and happy period. It is an excellent time for anyone wanting to start a family or join a ready-made one to put plans into action.

Six-Three
Harmony may be threatened by hidden resentments that need to be recognized and handled with tact.

Four-Six
There is a right time for everything and it is important to accept the natural progress of love rather than trying to force the pace.

Six-Four
Harmony may be threatened by restlessness or apathy in a younger family member who may need to be encouraged to make definite plans for the future.

Five-Six

A firm stand on a family or relationship matter especially concerning an older person will ensure long-term peace.

Six-Five

A family member may feel that he or she has been unjustly treated. Try not to be rigid in your response as there may be a genuine grievance.

Double-Six

Trust your feelings and if necessary reveal them. Happiness and peace of mind are found in family or love relationships or in a close friendship rather than on a solitary path.

A SAMPLE DOMINO READING

Janice has been offered promotion as head of the high school where she had worked for ten years. Six months ago she met Doug on holiday and it was love at first sight. Her feelings grew stronger the better she knew Doug.

For the first time since her divorce three years previously, Janice felt that here was a man with whom she wanted to share her life. Doug followed Janice back to Britain and asked her to marry him. He suggested they should live abroad and that she should help him manage a leisure complex he owned in Italy. Janice's heart urged her to go with Doug but her head reminded her of past disappointments.

She chose a domino at random. It was a Blank followed by a Six, promising that love at first sight would bring permanent happiness. Doubtful, Janice carefully mixed the dominoes with her eyes closed and picked a second, a double six. This advised Janice to trust her feelings, for future joy lay in a close relationship. Still feeling that she was manipulating the dominoes unconsciously (which was precisely what her unconscious was doing by a form of telekinesis that underlies all good divination), Janice chose a third domino. Again it was the blank followed by a six.

When a domino appears twice, it underlines the original message, in this case that love at first sight could bring lasting contentment. However, she exercised the option to pick a substitute domino and this time chose Four-Three. The final domino suggested that she should communicate her fears and doubts as they might prove to be unfounded. Janice talked to Doug for the first time about the insecurities left by the failure of her previous marriage and he was able to reassure her that he would never be unfaithful or take away her independence. Janice went with Doug to Italy.

Random chance? Whatever form of divination is used, the appropriate cards, stones or numbers do appear time after time. Telekinesis or a dip into the collective unconscious of mankind to extract the relevant information? Greg, a US computer executive, to whom I gave a runes reading in a plane above the Atlantic, said that the runes he had selected reflected his current dilemma perfectly. Nevertheless he insisted on throwing the runes again to eliminate the possibility of chance. The chance of the same three runes appearing out of a bag of 30, he equated with the probability of the plane being struck by lightning. The same three runes did appear, but the plane landed safely.

13

EARTH MAGIC

FINDING THE EARTH

Earth is the primaeval source of power, pulsating from earth through the feet and the physical frame. Although Earth Magic belongs to the popular tradition, it has gradually become the province of experts, both in the East and West.

Because the subject of Earth energies is so extensive and Feng Shui has been introduced in *Domestic Magic* (see page 135), this section concentrates mainly on Westernized Earth energies. In particular, we will look at dowsing as a way of tapping the natural energies that run through the Earth. In the West 'expert dowsers' use different weights and lengths of cord on pendulums to detect different substances. Even without such expertise, ordinary men and women can harness the natural energies of the Earth. The best dowsers are those who need to find water or are driven by a desire to uncover historical remains.

ARCHAEOLOGICAL DOWSING

The most successful archaeologists are those who are guided by an instinctive love and understanding of the Earth. A fine example of this craft is Brian Slade, President of the Sheppey Archaeological Society in Britain, an archaeologist, astronomer, historian, author and broadcaster with more than 20 published books on archaeology, history and associated subjects to his name. Brian has lived under the sentence of a terminal illness for several years and is often in pain, but he has a quest that sees him scribbling notes and looking up references in the early hours when he cannot sleep.

He is an incomer to the Isle of Sheppey, which lies off the Kent coast in South-East Britain, often referred to scathingly as London's backyard. Indeed if you look only at the chalets, campers and caravans, the name may seem justifiable, but its history goes back to the Bronze Age and Brian has worked tirelessly to uncover buried archaeological treasures and discover the truth behind the legends. His aim is to inspire modern generations who know nothing of England's 'Second Glastonbury', as he calls it, and to put the island on the map for pilgrimages and historical exploration. Brian has the uncanny and yet quite natural ability to dowse the location of archaeological treasures with unerring accuracy.

At first, like other dowser-archaeologists who wanted to keep their ability secret so that their discoveries would be taken seriously, Brian invented an ancient map of the projected complete Norman Minster and Anglo-Saxon Monasterium Sexburgha complex (the Abbey of St Sexburgha), to explain his uncannily accurate finds to officials and expert bodies. However, when he was very ill in hospital, he realized that it was important to acknowledge openly this ability. He told me: 'I began dowsing back in the 1960s with GEC [General Electricity Company] when looking for cables on old sites. The problem was that 60 or 70 years ago when the cables were first put down, the location of earthing strips would be marked on plans. But once the engineer had left the site, the navvies would, to save time, place the cables via the most direct route and sell any spare copper to a scrap merchant. Therefore many of these early plans were useless. It was not possible to use metal detectors on a site where there were many cables and so much magnetism.'

So Brian resorted to Earth Magic to find the cables and it worked. 'Now I use my dowsing gift to uncover remains. I still use the bent welding rods I used then or old hazel twigs.'

In 1993, Brian carried out a detailed dowsing survey of Minster on the Isle of Sheppey. It convinced him that much of the hilltop where he lived overlaid the remains of a seventh- to ninth-century Anglo-Saxon nunnery, an eleventh- to sixteenth-century Norman Abbey and a cemetery. Brian and his local team have uncovered the remains precisely where he predicted they would be.

'Time and time again,' Brian says, 'it has been shown that if the digging had been even a yard on either side of the spot indicated by the dowsing, nothing of significance would have been found.

'For example, I asked a lady living in Minster village if I might dig up part of her back garden lawn. She agreed with some trepidation and we promptly unearthed seven seventh- and ninth-century Anglo-Saxon bronze dress pins, post hole evidence of seventh- to ninth-century timber buildings, an Anglo-Saxon coin dating back to 737–758, four Henry II long cross silver pennies, examples of Anglo-Saxon glass, ten varieties of Roman pottery and as much Anglo-Saxon Ipswich-type pottery as produced by all the excavations at Canterbury combined. It was a veritable treasure trove.'

PSYCHOMETRY WITH STONES

Few of us may reach Brian's level of expertise. However, it is possible to make a rich and powerful connection with the past by visiting old places, ruined abbeys, castles, standing stones and by touching the stones to gain impressions of bygone ages and perhaps even glimpses of distant times.

Go to less popular places, off the tourist track, or visit tourist attractions early or late in the season either just after opening time or just before closing. Single standing stones (menhirs) with holes in are said to represent the power of the Earth Goddess and to be fertility symbols. To step between them is said to link up with powerful Earth and fertility impulses. Try to be very positive when you step between them so that you can use the powers to bring dreams to fruition.

Stone circles (megaliths or great stones as the larger ones are called) are also places where you can absorb the forces of their ancient creators who aligned them with amazing astronomical accuracy thousands of years ago.

GETTING IN TOUCH WITH THE PAST

Psychometry is a method of dowsing that operates through your fingers. While touching an object, try to receive impressions of all it has absorbed in its lifetime. Gifted psychometrists can produce details of the owners of the object they are holding. While few of us can reach that level, we are all capable of psychometry to a greater or lesser extent and places such as stone circles, which are so rich in impressions, are excellent areas in which to practise this natural ability.

Either touch one of the old stones or hold it, closing your eyes as you run your fingers over it. You may see in your mind's eye scenes from the distant or more recent past, hear voices or receive only vague impressions. Old places, whether stone circles, ruined castles or abandoned abbeys, contain layer upon layer of lives. In a castle or abbey you may find small crumbled pieces of ancient walls that you can pick up and hold.

Trust your visions: you may even find that you can link into a scene that can shed insight on a present dilemma. Follow your instincts as to what to pick up. On the surface, it may not seem anything special; perhaps an old brown stone or a piece of dull clay. Trust yourself. You do not need a Roman coin or Victorian necklace to feel the spirit of the place and hear the feet of passers-by, whose steps may, as you hold the object, walk in unison with your own.

If you feel the desire to move along a particular path, open your eyes and, holding the stone if you have one, follow it. You may see an inscription or exhibit that has special meaning for you. The clues to our destiny are all round if we trust the greatest magician of all, ourselves.

Megaliths: the Great Stones

The oldest and the largest megaliths in the world are at Carnac in Britanny, France. More than 3,000 stones are arranged as avenues, mounds, cromlechs (a chamber of stones either a small circle or single one) and dolmens (a horizontal stone supported by several vertical stones, thought to have been used as a tomb). It is thought that originally there were more than 11,000 stones and the earliest dated mound-covered cromlech dates back to about 4700 BC, predating both the Egyptian Pyramids and Stonehenge.

Stonehenge on Salisbury Plain in Wiltshire, England, was probably started as early as 3500 BC and assumed its present form about 2000 BC. The building of the huge lintel-topped circles of Welsh bluestone has excited the imagination of generations. The stones were transported from the Prescelli Mountains in South Wales by land and sea in a journey that is believed to have taken almost a century. It is said in myth that Merlin the magician carried the stones, which had magical healing powers, from Ireland, using giants to bear the weight.

In 1974, Alexander Thom put forward a theory that Stonehenge was a giant observatory for studying the movement of the moon and stars and other theories have suggested it was a huge Solar Temple. It served as focus for Druidic ceremonies on the Longest Day for thousands of years. However, these are no longer allowed and the stones are fenced off.

A Scientific Study

The Dragon Project Trust, centred around the Rollright Stones in Oxfordshire, England, has studied various ancient stone sites and has detected ultrasonic rays as well as radiation and magnetic energies coming from these stones. According to legend, the stone circle was created when an invading king and his army of nobles were turned to stone by the Old Hag of Rollright (see also *Fertility Magic*, page 199).

The pattern of the recorded energies varies in a way linked with the cycles of the moon and the seasons. Such research into Earth energies may be a way forward, combining the skills of archaeology and physics with dowsing and psychometry, detecting the history of a site by holding objects found there. Photographs from different sources have also identified lights emanating from menhirs.

Magical Standing Stones

Many people detect actual presences near these old stones. Standing stones are said to be doorways to other worlds and people have heard music coming from them, detected lights above them and even seen people within.

According to legend, on the Longest Day and May Day, the Banbury stone on Bredon Hill in Gloucestershire, England, comes down to the river to drink at midnight. Churches, such as that at Godshill on the Isle of Wight, were said to move site during the night several times while they were being constructed until the right place was found (see also *New Year Magic*, page 362).

Creating a Magical Stone Circle in Your Garden

Sadly, close contact with the great stones at Stonehenge is no longer permitted. Years of careless tourists and, in some cases, vandalism has forced English Heritage, the body which cares for the site, to fence them off. However, it is possible to create a stone circle of your own in your garden and let it act as a focus for natural Earth energies. As you use it for positive rituals, the energies accumulate and can give you strength and courage in times of doubt. Your stone circle can be on a far tinier scale than the real thing; the important point is to let it act as a focus.

Take time to create your circle, choosing stones from places close to those of great antiquity; for example the next field to a stone circle where energies will be strong. Bring home stones from places where you have been especially happy. You can mix stones from shore and land and use different colours, for this is your personal circle. Choose sturdy stones no more than 30 cm (12 inches) high for your vertical stones and longer more slender ones for the horizontals.

Choose a place in your garden and with each stone you lay, burn a brown candle. Lay next to it brown dried grasses or ferns for the Earth Mother. You may wish to decorate the centre of your growing circle with small jars of water containing honeysuckle, magnolia, narcissus, vervain (promoter of sleep and calm), cypress or primroses. These are herbs and flowers that are specially sacred to the Earth.

First make the four main compass stones – North, South, East and West – and then the next four – North-East, North-West, South-East and South-West. Once you have the basic outline, you can walk round the circle sunwise or clockwise at dawn, noon or sunset, times of great power.

Each time you place a horizontal stone across two vertical ones to make an arch, leave flowers or golden leaves in a small jar of water or a favourite crystal on top of it for a few days to give energy to the stones.

Consecrating your Circle

When your circle is complete, circle it nine times sunwise (clockwise), beginning in the North or 12 o'clock position, then nine times moonwise (anti-clockwise), just before the sun rises, touching each stone with a living branch.

Light a golden candle in the centre and circle it with your favourite brown, yellow, red or orange crystals. You may wish to invite a few friends to circle dance your mini-Stonehenge. Circle dancing, like many psychic arts, has become regimented with complex steps. Follow your feet, not the manual. A simple step and tread and perhaps a chant of a few words, 'We are one, bless the Earth' or whatever comes spontaneously is more powerful than any set ritual. You are activating the spiralling Earth energies, like the circle dancers who danced the stones on the old festivals.

As dawn breaks blow out your candle and sit quietly for a while in your circle, listening to the early morning sounds.

As the Moon rises, return to your circle and light a purple candle in the centre. Circle it nine times moonwise or anti-clockwise, then nine times sunwise or clockwise. This time, sit close to your circle, letting the candle burn its course. Bury either your earth ritual stone or a favourite brown, orange, red or yellow crystal in the centre of the circle to energize it.

Try to spend a few moments each day with your circle, making sure there are always flowers or leaves and circling it at least once each way to rouse the earth energies. Replace any stones that fall or get broken. Over time your quiet place will grow more powerful so that if you are unhappy or anxious, your circle will offer you healing and strength if you sit in its centre or touch the stones with a branch.

LEY LINES

Ley lines are energy lines running beneath the earth in a regular grid pattern that are reflected in straight, often very ancient tracks above ground. Whether ley energies are psychic, physical or both is uncertain, but because so many people have trodden these old ways, they are naturally endowed with psychic energy and so offer an instant source of energy.

The tradition for these energy lines is very ancient and they have been identified throughout Europe, India and the United States. For example, the Cree Indian trails invariably followed straight tracks. In Chaco Canyon in New Mexico, long straight tracks were laid down by the Anasazi peoples.

In Ancient Egypt cairns were set up on hilltops as markers for the caravan trails. In Central Peru from the Sun Temple that was built in the middle of the city of Cuzco, 41 lines radiate into the surrounding countryside. Along them shrines, temples, graves, sacred hills, bridges and even battlefields lie.

In the late nineteenth century, an Englishman, Alfred Watkins, first put forward the idea that the straight traders' tracks that seemed to stretch back through antiquity were built on natural lines of energy. In 1925 he published his research in a book, *The Old Straight Track*, in which he described how holy sites and ancient places were aligned along the leys.

One theory suggests that the siting of stone circles, cairns on hills and so on are a way of balancing Yang and Yin, the positive and negative energies, and that clumps of hawthorns would often be placed at regular intervals on a plain, perhaps to mark some ancient track. Until recently it was believed that each village had secret guardians who would ensure the maintenance of such natural markers (see also *Fairy Magic*, page 187).

In England the most famous leys run from St Michael's Mount in Cornwall to Bury St Edmunds in East Anglia and these are dotted with ancient sites, burial mounds, hill forts, stone circles and churches. The most significant feature of the St Michael line, as it is called, is that there are many churches dedicated to St Michael and St George, the saints who replaced the pagan sun gods, and to St Mary who replaced the female goddesses.

Sixty churches or more can be found on the line that runs via Glastonbury and Avebury to Hopton on the East coast of England. All these holy places are linked by the line of sunrise at the beginning of May. If a beacon fire is lit on each high point, the sun would be seen to rise behind it when viewed from the next place on the line.

Crossroads

Ley energies are especially strong at crossroads or in certain places where stone circles, standing stones or even churches lie. Witches were traditionally buried at crossroads as recognition that it was a place of pagan power. Many of the Celtic crosses at crossroads are Christianized versions of the more pagan standing stones, once found at such places (see also *Celtic Magic*, page 50).

Finding Ley Lines

To discover ley lines, go to an open rural place where there are low hills and plains. Look at the hills and try to identify a straight track across their tops, marked by boulders or clumps of trees. Look on the plain for intersecting tracks, perhaps with a church, often built on the site of an old pagan temple, trees, tall stones and ponds. These straight tracks may mark the old leys.

Sometimes Roman roads are built along the old ways, so if you find the name of a Roman road, it may be a pointer to a ley. In towns, leys may be harder to follow unless you live in a town or city with a grid road system. Begin at a crossroads near a church or civic building. If you look on a map, you may find that market crosses, chapels and civic buildings are all aligned. Use road or street names to help. Market Way was probably the old route taken by countless travellers and traders. Look for Celtic crosses or stones that have survived the rebuilding.

Let your feet, not your mind guide you. If you find yourself automatically following an alleyway or passage, continue even if it seems a dead end. You may discover an unexpected way through that you recognized on an instinctive level. You may actually feel a buzzing beneath your feet as you connect with the ley energies.

Using a Pendulum

One of the easiest ways of following leys is to use a pendulum, either the crystal kind or a key on a piece of string. Use anything tied to a cord as long as it does not swing too freely in the breeze. A favourite charm, a plumb bob from the hardware store, even a ball on a string will serve. The length of the string depends on what feels right. You need to be able to feel that your unconscious arm movements are controlling the string, but the cord should not be so short that it cannot move freely. Experiment with different lengths. Think of your pendulum as a dog on a lead; all dogs require different lengths of leash and varying pressure.

Ask your pendulum to demonstrate a positive and negative response. You do not need to set tests to discover these as you can talk to your pendulum as the outward expression of your psyche. Each person and pendulum have a unique way of interacting. Your positive response could be a gentle clockwise circling, a forward and back motion or an ellipse. I know one woman whose pendulum circles anti-clockwise for 'yes' and clockwise for 'no'. Your pendulum may stop when you go off course and start once you are back on the right track.

Stand at a rocky outcrop or a church. Your pendulum will start to move. Begin to walk in the direction the pendulum swings. Let it move naturally and lead you. Note any landmarks you pass. You may feel the emotions of those who have walked the leys in past times, see shadows or even presences. These are quite natural and cannot harm or even touch you. They are imprints of the past. As you walk the leys, you will leave your own mark, so try to walk them with positive thoughts and leave your anxieties at home.

Ley Ghosts

A great number of ghosts appear in natural sites, near woods, on roads and close to water, places where ley energies are particularly strong. It may be easier for ghosts to manifest themselves along the ley lines. Unlike family ghosts, who will cross the world to visit a relative and are seen only by the loved one, ley ghosts are seen by different people but always at the same place, usually close to where they died or experienced some great tragedy.

For example, at Salmesbury Hall in Lancashire, close to one of England's major motorways and also the site of ancient ley energies, the ghost of the medieval Lady Dorothy is seen wandering along the roads near her former home. Lady Dorothy wanted to elope with her lover. He was murdered by her family and Lady Dorothy was sent to a convent where she died insane with grief. She and her lover were buried close to the Hall and their bodies were discovered when a road was built in the nineteenth century.

Since then, the Lady in White has been seen frequently and has nearly caused several accidents on the A677 road that passes Salmesbury Hall. Her most recent sighting was in 1981 when a greengrocer almost crashed as she appeared suddenly in the middle of the road in the early morning and as rapidly disappeared. On another occasion, a driver, thinking she was a hitchhiker, stopped and opened the door to offer a lift. Again she disappeared instantly.

In Norfolk in East Anglia, England, where ley energies are particularly strong, ley ghosts abound. One example is Wayland Wood in Norwich which is said to be the scene of the original Babes in the Woods. The children were supposedly abandoned by a wicked uncle's servants and their misty forms may be seen wandering hand in hand and crying. Are they ghosts or will o' the wisp manifestations that have been woven into a story which we find makes sense in human terms? In Chinese terms, there is said to be bad ch'i at Wayland. Has this been caused by the murder of two innocent children?

There are also the notorious black streams. Are these a psychic as well as physical phenomenon which attracted dark deeds to the woodland? Norfolk has many 'natural ghosts' especially close to water of which there are vast tracts which form the Norfolk Broads. Horsey Mere is supposedly haunted by ghostly children who are said to have been drowned in Roman times. They appear for an hour every year on 13 June.

Ghost dogs also appear in great numbers in Norfolk. For example, Peddar's Way at Great Massingham is haunted by a phantom black dog who attacks hitchhikers and a white ghostly hound has been seen at the village of Great Snoring.

EARTH AND SAND DIVINATION

Geomancy, interpreting pictures or patterns in earth or sand, is practised in many cultures and can involve complex rules and rituals. However the simplest kind of earth divination has always taken place on the banks of a river, some deserted shore or in crumbly soil in a quiet garden. The Ancient Egyptians were devotees of sand divination, while the psychiatrist and psychologist Carl Jung believed that sand therapy, using small figures, could unlock the secrets of a mind's conflicts.

The best way to try basic geomancy is to visit a river bank or sandy beach. If this is not possible, borrow some sand from a child's sandpit and place it in a tray or go to the park in the early morning and use the sandpit in the children's playground. Take a pile of sand, close your eyes and swirl it with a stick or run it through your fingers. When you open your eyes, you will see a shape or even a picture. Let the first image or words that come into your head provide the answer. You may find familiar images or a whole scene. Let your intuition guide you as to the meaning.

ANNA'S SAND DIVINATION

Anna had been asked by her brother Harry if she would take care of his children while he and his wife went abroad for a week's holiday. Anna was not married and had stayed at home with their disabled mother until her sudden death. Now she was expected to act as unpaid childminder for her nieces and nephew whenever Harry and his wife wanted to go away. Anna loved the children but had made plans to attend a theatre workshop. Could she let her family down?

Anna used the children's sandpit and swirled the sand with her fingers. When she opened her eyes, she saw a bird in a cage with an open door, a window and beyond that a wide empty expanse. She realized that she was keeping herself prisoner by being at the constant beck and call of her family. Anna had always offered her help, often without being asked, because there had been a tremendous gap in her life after her mother had died. She realized that she was almost looking for an excuse to cancel the theatre workshop, her first major solo venture.

However, unless Anna flew through that window, she would forever live through Harry's family, a situation that would be restrictive to both sides. When Anna told her brother she was going away and could not help, Harry said that they had friends with whom they could leave the children. He and his wife had been afraid Anna would feel left out if she was not asked. Anna went to her workshop and, after initial nervousness, enjoyed it so much she has booked herself in for another.

EARTH MAGIC IN THE EAST

The ancient Chinese art of Feng Shui, wind and water, looks at the flow of ch'i, the life force through the earth. It dates back at least 3,000 years. Good ch'i depends on the balance between the Yang and Yin, positive and negative energies and Feng Shui experts are used with surveyors to recommend whether a house has good vibes and if not, how it can be altered, perhaps by adding a tree, knocking down a porch or adding water in the form of a fish tank or fountain (see *Domestic Magic*, page 127). Mountains, steep slopes and craggy outcrops are Yang, while gently undulating plains, dips and lakes are Yin. So the perfect location for a building is seen to be at the foot of a slope with a sheltering hill behind.

14

EGYPTIAN MAGIC

THE NILE AND THE SUN

Egyptian Mythology and magic was rooted in the complete reliance of the Egyptians on the waters of the River Nile and on the sun. Because of the scarcity of rainfall, life depended on the annual flooding of the Nile which covered the land on either side with fertile silt so that a green belt of crops could be grown.

The proximity of fertile land to the vast desert wastes imprinted on the Egyptian psyche the closeness of life and death, a closeness echoed in the yearly death and rebirth of the land with the flood. This shaped the magic and beliefs of the Ancient Egyptians who enjoyed an unbroken period of more than 3,000 years of isolation and freedom from invasion from about 3100–30 BC. During this period, the civilization of the Egyptians was virtually unchanged, apart from the gradual evolution of ideas during the three greatest periods in Egypt's history: the Old Kingdom (2686–2181 BC), the Middle Kingdom (1991–1786 BC) and the New Kingdom (1552–1069 BC).

CREATION MYTHS

By the time of the establishment of the Old Kingdom (the first major unification of the different tribes), three important religious centres existed at Heliopolis, Memphis and Hermopolis. Each was devoted to the cult of a different god. The myths of each centre suggested that creation was a gradual process: at the First Time, a major landmark in the evolutionary process, the named God had brought forth life. Then followed the Golden Age when laws, morals and institutions were given to mankind. There are various accounts of how man was created, the most picturesque being that from the New Kingdom whereby Khumn the potter and ram-headed God, associated with the chief God Amun, fashioned men from clay.

The Heliopolis creation myths were perhaps the most widely accepted and inclusive of the most popular deities. Atum, the original godhead, came forth from the waters on to the Island of Creation, where he produced Shu, God of the Air and Tefnut,

Goddess of Moisture. Together they created the Earth-God Geb and the Sky Goddess Nut. From the union of Geb and Nut were born Osiris, Isis, Seth and Nephthys.

The Cult of the Sun

An official sun cult was developed during the Old Kingdom. Under the royal patronage Ra, the Sun God, became identified with the Atum and was depicted as a young man in the morning, an adult at noon and an old man in the evening (see also *Sun Magic*, page 410).

Each morning Ra began his journey across the heavens in his solar boat. At night, in the form of a ram-headed man-god, he passed through the underworld to emerge again in the east in the morning. The cult of Ra increased and Kings began to include the title 'son of Ra' in their lineage. In some myths, Ra is seen as father of Osiris.

As royal power declined by the end of the Old Kingdom, the popularity of the sun cult, which was associated with the King rather than the people, was replaced over succeeding dynasties by the god of the populace, Osiris. There was a revival of solar power in the New Kingdom when the Kings of the eighteenth dynasty elevated Amun to the Creator God and linked him with the older cult of Re to become the supreme state deity, Amun-Re.

THE DEITIES

Osiris

Osiris became one of the most important and popular gods in Ancient Egypt, mainly because he promised non-royal believers that resurrection and salvation from death was for everyone, poor as well as rich. Originally he was identified with each dead Pharaoh and his son Horus was identified with the reigning successor.

Osiris married his sister Isis and his brother Seth married their other sister Nephthys. According to legend, Osiris was at first made an earthly king by his father Geb, the Earth God. Osiris ruled wisely, teaching his people about agriculture and the arts. But his brother Seth was jealous and vowed to kill him. He invited Osiris to a feast and showed the guests a fine chest, promising that whoever fitted inside would be the owner. Osiris stepped inside the chest and it fitted perfectly. Seth slammed the lid tight and he and his followers threw the chest into the Nile.

Isis searched for her husband and at last discovered the chest at Byblos on the Phoenician coast. She brought Osiris's body back to

Egypt and conceived a son by her dead husband, hiding herself in the rushes of the Delta marshes while awaiting the birth. Seth discovered the body of Osiris, hacked it into pieces and scattered them throughout Egypt so that he could never be restored to life. But Isis searched once more and, assisted by Nephthys, remodelled the bones into Osiris's form. By magic, she restored her husband to life.

When their son Horus, the Sky God, had grown up, he fought against Seth to avenge his father. The divine judges, including Thoth, God of Wisdom, met in the great Hall of Judgement and decided that Osiris should become not a living king once more, but eternal King and Judge of the Underworld. Osiris was also god of vegetation, the fertilizing, flooding Nile and the corn and so represented the annual dying of the land and rebirth with the flood. He is normally pictured as a man, bound in mummy wrappings.

Isis

Isis represents the ideal wife and mother. As mother of Horus, who was embodied in the Pharaoh, Isis became associated with the Queen Mother. Isis was a great enchantress, taught her powers by Thoth. She is usually depicted as a woman with a throne as a headdress. The tears of Isis at the death of Osiris were said to cause the rising of the Nile.

Horus

Horus was the Ancient Egyptian Sky God, represented as a falcon or a falcon-headed man. His eyes were the sun and moon and his wings could extend across the entire heavens. He was frequently associated with the morning aspect of Ra the Sun God and worshipped as Re-Harakhte.

Thoth

Thoth was the Ancient Egyptian God of the Moon, Wisdom and Learning. He was also god of reckoning, responsible for the calculation of time. He invented writing and the calendar and was patron of scribes and magicians. He was master of the magical hieroglyphs. He is often pictured as an ibis-headed man or as a baboon. The ibis and baboon are Thoth's sacred animals.

Seth

Seth (also known as Set) was the god of evil, darkness and the desert and so was the other side of Osiris who represented the fertility of the flooding Nile and the corn. He often assumed the form of a serpent or was pictured with the head of his cult animal, a creature with square-topped pricked ears and an arrow tail.

Ma'at

Ma'at, Goddess of Truth and Justice, was responsible for maintaining the correct balance and order in the universe. She was daughter of Re who created her to establish unity and order in the world. Ma'at was pictured as a woman wearing a single ostrich feather as a headdress. She was all powerful, even over the King who had to rule with truth and justice to attain eternal life.

THE AFTERLIFE

Death was regarded as a stage of life through which man had to pass to become immortal. At death the immortal soul left the body, but still kept links with this world through the body in the tomb. It depended on the food and offerings left at the tomb for continued sustenance in the next world.

Over the three millennia of Ancient Egypt's flowering, the concept of the afterlife changed. The earliest idea involved a continued form of existence in the tomb, or Mansion of the Spirit as the last resting place of the body was called. Later, it was believed that it was necessary to preserve the body of an individual after his death so that he could return to earth if he wished. Elaborate rituals were carried out to embalm and mummify the body.

Two distinct concepts of the world beyond developed. During the Old Kingdom immortality was assured for the king through his link with the sun cult. After his death the king was reunited with his father Re in heaven. Such eternal bliss might be shared by the royal family and courtiers and so their remains would buried close to the Royal Pyramid. By the Middle Kingdom, the cult of Osiris promised eternal life to all who worshipped him and were deemed worthy on the Day of Judgement before a tribunal of 42 assessors, gods and Osiris. The deceased would then pass into the underworld to spend his days farming a small piece of land. For those who did not relish such physical toil, statues of agricultural workers, called ushabti were included in the tomb so that they might carry out the menial tasks.

After the funeral rites were completed, the deceased affirmed the purity of his soul by reciting the 'negative confession' in which he declared himself free from sin. His heart was then weighed on scales. Thoth, God of Wisdom and Learning, presided over the weights and recorded the results. The heart of the deceased, regarded as the seat of his intellect as well as his emotions, was preserved separately in a jar. This was placed in one of the pans of the scales by the jackal-headed Anubis, God of Embalming and protector of tombs. Ma'at, Goddess of Justice, placed the single feather from her headdress on the other side of the scales. If the two balanced, the man was declared free from sin and allowed to pass for eternity into the Osirian underworld. The hearts of the guilty were thrown to a creature that was part-lion, part crocodile and part hippopotamus.

Sometimes particularly worthy or noble dead souls entered heaven as one of the stars or as one of the crew of Ra's solar boat. Alternatively, they might live on in the tomb where regular offerings were brought for their sustenance.

EGYPTIAN MAGIC

The Egyptians were the master magicians of the Ancient World. Their magical beliefs were deeply entwined with their religion and politics and no other culture has had such a profound effect on the magical theory and practices of both East and West. Egyptian master magicians were said to have divided the waters of lakes, turned sticks into snakes, foretold the future with great accuracy and claimed to command the gods themselves to obey their will.

Magicians, like the scribes, were highly valued and were under the protection of Thoth himself. Many of the early magicians practised alchemy and were versed in the healing and magical powers of gems and crystals.

The Power of Words

The Ancient Egyptians believed that words themselves contained great magical power. For example, it was thought that preserving a name ensured immortality and so the names of the noble dead were frequently spoken and engraved on magnificent tombs. Magical amulets of precious stones, inscribed with various words of power were placed on various parts of the body of the deceased. Conversely, erasing someone's name destroyed their soul.

To preserve their words, the Ancient Egyptians created one of the most beautiful forms of script, hieroglyphics or 'holy writing' as the

Greeks named it. The Egyptians called these script 'words of the gods' for they considered that Thoth, God of Learning, had imparted the secret of writing to man.

Hieroglyphics were also used to ensure a more pleasurable afterlife. On the walls of tombs were inscribed the goods and servants that the deceased wanted to carry into the next world and perhaps a description of the activities that he or she hoped to continue. The names of foods which could sustain the spirit if relatives neglected to bring ritual food to the tomb might also be written.

HIEROGLYPHIC MAGIC

The Egyptian Oracle

Hieroglyphs possessed a magical and spiritual meaning and as the blessings of the afterlife were conferred upon rich and poor, so the ideas of magic filtered downwards. The Egyptians believed that the energies contained within the symbols were released when they were written or spoken aloud. Hieroglyphic cards are one way of harnessing this ancient form of magic to assist with modern life and dilemmas by triggering an inner power, focused on the meaning of the sacred symbols.

Either draw or photocopy the hieroglyphics shown below on stiff white or yellow card. Make them about twice the size used here. Cut them out to form 15 cards slightly bigger than playing cards. You can leave the one side blank.

While making your reading you may wish to surround yourself with some of the crystals associated with the hieroglyphs and amulets: deep blue lapis lazuli flecked with gold for the heart symbol, fossilized wood for the ladder, glowing orange cornelian for the sun, silvery grey haematite for the pillow, a clear quartz for the white eye of Horus, yellow or red jasper for the ankh or key, any gold jewellery you may have for Isis, the Mother and Ra the Sun-God and silver for Osiris, Father of the Moon. These are all rich gleaming stones for life and warmth and you can add a golden brown or red tiger's eye for the fertilizing silt of the Nile. If you wish, light a golden candle for the sun and a brown one for the life-giving Nile mud so that your inspiration may grow like the golden corn.

Consulting the Egyptian Oracle

Place the cards face down and shuffle or mix them. Arrange them in a circle and select the third, seventh and ninth cards, the most magical positions, to give you the three steps you must take to succeed or the three best guiding principles for your present situation or decision. Each symbol listed below was worn as an amulet for protection or power, set in different precious jewels or metals. As well as offering strength and growth to the living, the hieroglyphics on tomb walls or on amulets promised resurrection to those who had died.

The Oracle Cards

Ankh

The key is the symbol of eternal life. Pictures on tomb walls show the ankh being held to the nose of a pharaoh (the nose was thought by the Egyptians to be the source of life), thus ensuring his continuing life after death. The Ankh in a reading represents what is enduring and of great worth. Any relationship or situation in which you are currently involved is one that is worth fighting for or persisting through immediate difficulties or doubts. Persevere and seek what is of lasting worth is the message of the Ankh.

Wedja

Fire was used by the Ancient Egyptians to forge metal, smelt gold and create the beautiful pieces of jewellery for which they are famed. The heiroglyph was based on a bow drill which turned in a shaped piece of wood (the lower part of the hieroglyph) to produce fire by friction. Therefore Wedja came to represent prosperity and any means of money-making or creating material security. Wedja in a reading talks of material concerns and says that it is important to consider the financial implications of any actions and not to take risks. If there are money worries, it may be necessary to try to resolve them rather than just hope they will disappear. Be prudent and try to consolidate money matters is the message of Wedja.

Seneb

This symbol was the first letter in the word *seneb*, meaning health. It has come to represent the whole concept of health and well-being. In the tombs of a pharaoh the three signs, Ankh, Wedja and Seneb were written after his name, endowing eternal life, prosperity and health in the next world. If Seneb turns up in your reading, health matters may be to the fore. Perhaps you are feeling anxious or under a lot of stress that is affecting your physical or mental well-being. Care for yourself and avoid any unnecessary conflict or people who make you feel inadequate. Look after your own health needs and well-being is the message of Seneb.

Boat

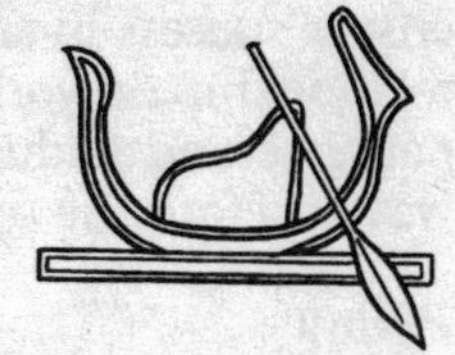

As the Nile was central to the life of the Ancient Egyptians, the boat was the main means of transport and not just for mortals; the sun god Re crossed the sky each day in his solar boat. The Boat hieroglyph represents the means of attaining a goal and overcoming obstacles. When the Boat appears in a reading, it may be necessary to be resourceful and adaptable and use whatever means, even if less than ideal, to attain a goal. The Boat promises that if you are prepared to look beyond the immediate for a solution, a way to succeed will be found. Be adaptable and expand the possibilities is the message of the Boat.

Scarab

This was a profound symbol of rebirth to the Egyptians. It was a beetle who laid its eggs in a small ball of dung to provide nourishment for the young. The Egyptians saw the beetle offspring emerging from the balls as a symbol of rebirth and transformation. In a reading, the Scarab represents a fresh start or transformation, perhaps after difficulty or a particular door has closed. It promises that tomorrow really is another day and that you carry the seeds of happiness and success within you. Look to a new beginning, however dark today, is the message of the Scarab.

Nefer

This means happiness, good fortune and beauty and is based on a musical instrument that resembled a primitive guitar. The perfect form and harmony of the instrument represented fulfilment and pleasure. When Nefer appears in a reading, what matters is your happiness, even if this is not counted as success in the world's terms. Concentrate on your own harmony and let your inner joy shine through. Enjoy each day and find something positive to rejoice in, however difficult the circumstances, is the message of Nefer.

Tet

This represented the tree trunk in which Isis hid the dead body of Osiris. This became symbolic of the backbone of Osiris which was essential for the reforming of his body. The Tet was raised ceremonially at the festivals of Osiris into an upright position and was regarded as a source of strength and stability. Stability was greatly prized by the Egyptians. In a reading, Tet represents the stability and firm foundations that ensure success in any venture. It says that any plans, whether for a relationship or work venture, are, like the tree, well-rooted and with patience and endurance come to fruition. Stand firm and do not waver before the opposition of others is the message of Tet.

Pillow

This symbol represents the pillow which was put under the head of a mummy in the coffin to protect and uplift it. In a spiritual sense, the pillow uplifted the soul of the deceased and ensured triumph of the immortal soul over bodily death. The Pillow is therefore a symbol of seeking support in overcoming difficulties. In a reading, the Pillow says that you should seek help and encouragement from others in achieving your chosen path rather than trying to succeed alone. If you are experiencing difficulties, sympathetic support can give you the impetus to succeed. Do not stand alone but seek the help of others to achieve your aims is the message of the Pillow.

Heart

This was the source of good and evil thoughts. As the seat of life, it required special protection after death and its sign is the urn in which the heart was preserved separately from the body. In the afterlife the heart was weighed in the balance against the symbolic feather representing right and truth and so it represents ideals and principles. In a reading, the Heart may appear if your principles and essential beliefs are under threat or you are wondering whether to compromise over what is important for the sake of peace or even out of love. In your heart you know what is the right path and you should be guided by these principles. Be true to yourself and do not compromise your core beliefs is the message of the Heart.

The Eye of Horus

This is a powerful symbol and represented the white or Sun (Ra) eye, especially at the summer solstice or longest day when the sun is at its height. Although the Egyptian festivals did not mark the solstices, nevertheless the sun was vital to life and growth of the crops and so in magic had a special power. The Eye of Horus marks the full power of the sun, the left-brain assertive energy that casts away inertia and doubts and illuminates every corner of the being with light and power. If you get the Eye of Horus in the reading, you have the strength and desire to succeed in whatever you choose and should be confident in your own abilities and power. Be confident and make a supreme effort to succeed in your chosen path is the message of the Eye of Horus.

Menat

This is the symbol of nourishment, reproduction and fertility, the coming together of male and female. This fertility is both human and of the land, represented by the annual flooding of the Nile. Menat talks, therefore, of abundance, giving and increase. If you get Menat in a reading, you should give freely whether of your time, your self or your love to those close to you. The more generous and open you are in your approach to life, the more you will receive in return. Be generous in spirit and action is the message of Menat.

Vulture

This represents the protection and power of the Divine Mother Isis and was used as a protection for the deceased with the ankh for life engraved on each talon. Isis demonstrated the power of maternal protection when she cared for Horus in the marshes against his evil uncle who would have destroyed him. When the Vulture appears in a reading, it tells of the need to nurture and care for others when they may be vulnerable. The power of the Vulture is a creative one and says that in caring for others lies personal growth and satisfaction. Protect and nurture those close to you who may be in need is the message of the Vulture.

Collar of Gold

This was placed around a dead person's neck on the day of the funeral to allow the soul to escape from the earthly bindings in which the body had been wrapped. The symbol is one that has come to represent independence from the need for material security or from those who would stifle identity.

When the Collar of Gold appears in a reading, it may be a sign that you need to assert your separate identity or that you have become too involved in the problems of others at the cost of your own needs. It may represent a step towards independence at work or in your personal life. Be aware of your own needs and identity is the message of the Collar of Gold.

Ladder

This represented the means by which the dead could gain access to the heavens. The floor of the heavens was seen by early Egyptians as a rectangular iron plate with four iron pillars at the cardinal points. The gods and fortunate dead lived on the iron platform. Osiris used a ladder created by his father Ra to ascend into heaven. The Ladder represents the transition from the material world to a higher level of awareness or to our unconscious spiritual wisdom. In a reading, the Ladder says that you should trust your intuition and inspirations rather than listening to logic or to the advice of others. You should follow your dreams, even in a small way, and listen to the voice of wisdom that comes from deep within your spirit. Listen to your dreams and visions and follow your inner voice is the message of the Ladder.

Shen

This represents the orbit of the sun around the Earth and so was a symbol of time. As an amulet placed upon the dead, it promised eternal life so long as the sun endured. In the mortal sphere it says that it is important to move forward and not look back to past failures or even forward to imagined better times. It talks of acting now and not waiting for ideal perfect future time. Time does not wait, so seize the moment is the message of Shen.

A SAMPLE READING

Adam was hoping to sell his apartment in the city and buy a small house in the country to begin a freelance computer agency. However, he was unable to obtain the necessary price for his home to fund the initial expenses of his venture. To continue with his plan would involve borrowing a great deal of money that would prevent him from equipping the business to a sufficiently high standard to succeed in his chosen field. Should he give up or begin with inadequate equipment? Adam shuffled the cards and picked in the third, seventh and ninth positions Wedja, symbol of prosperity, the Pillow, symbol of seeking help from others and the Boat, symbol of resourcefulness and adaptability.

Wedja, not surprisingly, suggests that it is important for Adam not to take financial risks either to overreach his borrowing capacity or to compromise the standard of equipment. But lack of immediate finance may not be a reason to give up the idea as the next symbol confirms.

The Pillow suggests seeking help from others, whether a grant-aiding body or by considering going into a partnership. Adam had not wanted to be restricted or accountable by accepting grants and interest-free loans from enterprise organizations, but now he decided to investigate this area with a more open mind. As for a partner, Adam could find no one who worked in the same area who wanted to move out of town. The third symbol, however, shed light on the nature of the help.

The Boat talked about the need for adaptability and resourcefulness and using any suitable means, even if less than ideal. Adam's sister had a large farm with a stable block that housed the farm offices. She had offered Adam a room at the top of the house and temporary office space for a reasonable rent until he could sell his apartment for the right price. Originally Adam had decided against this because he wanted to start in the ideal situation and resented his sister helping him as she had so many times in the past.

Adam had already considered these options but had dismissed them out of hand. Often a reading will encourage the questioner to reassess the situation and explore avenues which have not been fully explored before. Adam decided to take up his sister's option and accept a grant for equipment. The conditions proved less restrictive than he had feared. He is now running his new business in less than ideal premises but with first-rate equipment while waiting for his apartment to yield the capital necessary for his own premises.

Conflicting Readings

It may be that two symbols seem to contradict each other. For example the Collar of Gold for independence and the Pillow for seeking help may appear in the same reading. Usually the third symbol provides a bridge and it may be that accepting help in the short term is necessary to attain independence later. However, if a questioner is very confused about an issue, the symbols may reflect conflict in the problem that, like Adam, the questioner may be desperate for help but equally anxious to be fully independent.

15

ESKIMO (INUIT) MAGIC

THE PEOPLE

The Eskimos live in small areas along the coasts of Greenland, Canada, Alaska and north-eastern Siberia. The name Eskimo comes from an Algonquin Indian term for 'raw meat eaters' which has been inaccurately applied to them. They prefer the name Inuit (Yuit in Siberian and some Alaskan speech) which means 'the people'. Inuit myths mirror the experiences of those whose horizons are bounded by frozen oceans and the snowy wastes of the long winter. The Eskimo world is controlled by the innua or spirit powers. Every natural form, including animals and the sea itself, has an innua. Such forces sometimes assume the role of Torngak, becoming guardians of individual Eskimos. Bears possess especially strong innua and if the spirit of a bear becomes an Eskimo's Torngak or guardian spirit, the Eskimo may be eaten by a bear to be reincarnated as a shaman.

THE SHAMAN

The shaman or Angakok is the magical man and to some extent law-interpreter of the community. Eskimo shamanism bears strong similarities to that of Central Asia and Siberia. Angakoks have many powerful torngaks as their familiar spirits. For example, it is believed that in a previous life a shaman might have been swallowed by a whale. The processes of being dismembered by a bear, a whale or other fierce creature and then being reassembled are relived psychically and ritually during a shaman's initiation. The name Torngak comes from Torngasak, the spirit who is called the Good Being by Eskimos. Torngasak himself is often seen as a bear. Unlike other cultures, the Inuit mythology has no single creator being nor a pantheon of deities.

THE WORLD OF THE SEA

Because of the importance of the sea as the source of most food, the most powerful spirit in the Inuit cosmology was a very ancient fertility mother, the Old Woman who lived under the Sea. She is given different names throughout the Arctic: Nerivik in Alaska and Arnarquagssag in Greenland. The most common name is Sedna, Sea-Mother, divinity of the sea and all sea animals.

There are different versions of her origin but all regard her as the source of the creation of marine life. In the most common myth, Sedna was a beautiful Inuit girl who turned away all suitors but was captivated by a handsome hunter who let his kayak sway on the waves while he sang to her in her hut. He offered her necklaces of ivory in the land of birds and a tent covered with the finest furs.

Sedna was lured into the canoe but her suitor was not mortal, rather a bird spirit with the power to assume human form. She was heartbroken when she discovered the truth. Her father, Angusta, who was searching the oceans for her, heard Sedna weeping and rescued her in his canoe. But Kokksaut, the bird phantom, pursued them and when Angusta refused to hand back his daughter, changed once more into a bird and created a terrible storm. The waves demanded the sacrifice of Sedna. Angusta become afraid that he had so offended the sea and spirits of the air that he would be killed and he cast Sedna into the waves.

When Sedna tried to cling to the boat, her father seized an ivory axe and cut off her fingers. The girl sank into the water and her fingers became seals. Three times she tried to reach the kayak but her father hacked at her wounded hands until she was lost beneath the waters. Her knuckles became walruses and whales.

Sedna's father returned to his tupik (tent) and fell asleep. Sedna's dog was tied to the ridge pole. During a high tide, the sea swallowed the tupik and both man and dog were drowned. They have since reigned over a subterranean realm called Adliden where the souls of the dead are imprisoned to atone for sins committed during their lifetime, a punishment that may be temporary or last forever.

The Inuit believe that Sedna controls storms at seas and can either provide or withhold sea creatures for the hunt. When the Eskimos do not catch seals or other sea creatures, the shaman dives in astral or soul form to the bottom of the sea to entreat Sedna to set the sea animals loose. He passes first through the kingdom of the dead, then through an abyss with a wheel of ice and a boiling cauldron of seals. The shaman finally enters a tent under the sea, furnished with the skins of the finest sea animals. There the dark, gigantic Sedna listens to magical chants of the shaman and tells him either that the tribe must move to another place to seek the sea creatures or that she will send shoals to the current hunting grounds.

THE WORLD OF THE SKY

The Eskimo cosmology includes a celestial world above and an underworld below. When a shaman travels to the sky realm, the joyous abode of the good dead, he asks for assistance from the ancestors in removing sickness from an individual or sorrow from the community.

Although the Inuit did not believe in a single supreme spirit, some tribes believed there was one ancestral spirit who was especially responsible for each family. In the Sky World, the seasons were reversed so that winter on Earth was summer in the Sky. The sun and moon were sister and brother, Seqinek and Aningan or Akycha and Igaluk. Their path around the heavens was seen as a perpetual race in which the moon, at first close to his sister the sun, lost ground until she finally overtook him at the end of his cycle, which explains why the moon can be seen during the day.

The sun is pictured as a beautiful girl who carries her torch through the sky. The moon man is a great hunter who can be seen standing in front of his igloo. He has a sledge loaded with seal skins and his team of spotted dogs occasionally chases their prey down to Earth where they are seen as shooting stars. The moon man lives with his demon cousin Irdlirvirisissong, a female trickster figure who tries to bring laughter to travellers on the road to the heavens or those who see her on Earth. If anyone does laugh, however, the clown woman will dry them up and devour their intestines.

The Inuit in north-west Greenland say that the constellation called the Great Bear, or Nanook once lived on Earth but was chased into the sky by a fine pack of dogs. The dogs ran so fast that they flew up to the sky and became the Pleiades. Across the sky, almost directly opposite the Great Bear, is Casseiopia which the Eskimo see as stones supporting a giant oil lamp. Orion is seen as three huge snow steps, leading from Earth to Heaven. The Aurorea Borealis or Northern Lights dancing in the sky are seen as deceased family members as they dance round their fires at celestial festivals.

The movement of the stars provided information essential for a life centred on hunting and fishing. The position of the stars indicated the time of the annual migration of the caribous, the first appearance of the fish shoals, the coming of the big freeze, the thaw of spring, the summer hunting of walrus and whale in the inlets of the open sea.

ESKIMO RITUALS OF THE HUNT

The sea is of greater importance as a source of food to the Eskimo than the land and winter is the longest season. These physical factors influence the nature and timing of the rituals. Caribou or reindeer hunting, for example, takes place chiefly in the autumn. Tekkeitserktok, God of the Earth, is offered sacrifices at this time since he owns all caribou.

Each form of hunting had different gods to be propitiated. For example, Nootaikok, the spirit of icebergs, will send seals if he is called. The spirit within a living bear could be charmed so that he might be caught and killed, but such killing must be only for need.

Eskimos must appease the spirits of the animal they kill for food or there will be a bad hunting period. When the tribes of Hudson Bay slay a bear, they paint the head with bright colours and sing sacred songs around it. Usually the hunter's wife would perform the rituals to avoid bringing down the anger of the spirit of the dead creature. No work could be followed for three days after bearded seals were hunted down and any discarded parts were taken back to the place where the creature was caught so that it might be reborn.

There are taboos against hunting land and sea animals at the same time. For example, fish and meat may not be eaten on the same day. Before seal hunting, weapons are cleansed by holding them in the smoke of burning seaweed to remove the taint of the land.

Amulet belts of bird skulls, teeth and talons were often worn to invoke the protection of Koodjanuk, an important spirit who was seen as a very large bird with a black head, hooked beak and white body. He could offer protection and healing, especially in connection with the hunting of birds whom he created. Similar amulet belts could be created for different creatures and their guiding spirits, such as Aumanil who guides whales to the hunting grounds. The shaman acts as intermediary of the unseen and because he understands the secret language of animals, can travel either to the depths of the sea or to the sky realms when a hunting taboo has been violated.

ESKIMO FESTIVALS

Because the intense cold and darkness makes hunting almost impossible during the harshest winter, December and January are especially favoured for festivals. On the longest night of the year a ceremony is carried out by two shaman who go from hut to hut, extinguishing all the lights and rekindling them from a new flame, chanting: 'From the new sun comes light.' The festival symbolizes the return of the sun and the promise of good hunting weather in the spring.

The Eskimo year is divided into 13 months, beginning with the winter solstice. From this date the moons are counted until the moon can no longer be seen in the bright summer nights. The Central Eskimos have a sunless month that every few years is lost so that the solar and lunar years coincide.

Whaling festivals are important: some are elaborate, but others, like the Hudson Bay festival, are quite simple. After the first kill of the season, the hunters and old women representing Sedna, the Old Woman of the Sea, sit within a circle of stones to eat the first whale meat and make offerings to Sedna from whom the bounty of the seas comes.

Other ceremonies mark the return of other animals. As the ice melts to allow the hunting of sea animals once more, the tribal shaman will enter a trance and travel psychically to the bottom of the sea to harpoon the Old Woman of the Sea to persuade her to release the animals of the sea once more. This journey forms the focus of a major festival.

In Alaska, masks play an important role in such festivals. By wearing masks of creatures in tribal dance, representing, for example, the soul of the salmon, hunters believed they would attract the souls of the salmon and thereby their physical forms into the waiting nets.

Many magical gatherings among the Inuit were inspired by the ecstatic trances of the shaman as he was suddenly possessed by the spirits of nature or the souls of the dead. At such times, he would utter prophecies in the magical languages understood by the older members of the tribe, foretelling the coming of whales, seal or caribou to a certain area.

Although the shaman played a central role in tribal divination, other members of the tribe also followed their own personal premonitions and divinatory practices. Information was given in the dreams of non-shamans. Experienced hunters could also, they believed, understand the language of the animals and birds and so know where the best hunting was to be found.

Drum festivals are considered an especially powerful form of magic and often take place in the home village and around the hunting localities where special festival houses of snow are built. Eskimo shamanism is a drum religion, where a shaman drums until the spirits come in and speak through him, the drum calling the spirits to the earth. The tribe's dancing echoes the drum beat, usually a tambour with a handle beaten with a drumstick and sometimes rattles made of puffin beaks.

DRUM DIVINATION

This method was also popular in Eurasia, especially in parts of Lapland. A shaman's drum would be illustrated with symbols of the sun, moon, stars, animals, fish, seals, whales, canoes, hunters, fishers and the tent made of skins, whose axis is seen to symbolize the axis of the three worlds of Sky, Sea and Land. A ring was placed on the horizontal surface of the drum. Often a whalebone ring was used, but the Siberian Arctic dwellers used a copper one. The drum was beaten or shaken until the ring settled on an image and remained there, even when the drum continued to move. The image was seen as the significant one for the individual or tribe and would offer guidance on the hunt.

Although primarily a shamanistic art, drum divination is one that transfers easily into the realms of modern personal divination and can offer a guiding image to journeying through life. If you have an old drum, a large tambourine or a large, round plain-lidded container made of plastic, you can easily recreate the method of banging or shaking the drum. Alternatively, you can make a mock drum top from a piece of stiff white card about 30 cm (12 inches) square, cut into a circle which you can shake from side to side.

Decorate the surface with the 16 suggested images or others from the Inuit world that seem more relevant to your world. The images should cover the surface and be arranged in three bands with the sky images at the top, the animals and fish below and the sea creatures underneath.

The suggested images are:

The moon man, Aningan, represents the winter and darkness and so suggests that a period of rest and reflection, however short, may be helpful in your life.

The sun woman, Seqinek, the light principle and the coming of summer, says that now is the time for positive action and seizing happiness while the opportunity presents itself.

The clown woman, Irdlirvirisissong, represents illusion and deceit and warns that to resort to trickery or seek an easy answer will not bring positive results.

Nanook the bear represents primal strength and noble purpose and says that any enterprise should be undertaken in the spirit of altruism and idealism and not for self-gain.

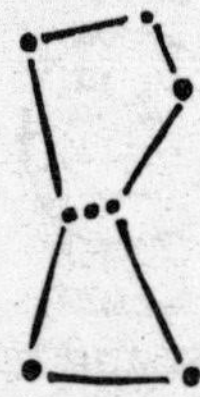

The Aurora Borealis, the Northern Lights, are the fires of the beloved ancestors and represent happiness through a long-term view or commitment that involves close friends or family. It is especially linked with parents and grandparents and the family group.

The Snow Steps or Orion which link the Earth and the Heavens, represent the need to shed practical considerations and concern about details and aim high.

The harpoon is the symbol of defining an aim or target, not being diverted by fear of failure and concentrating on it for now to the exclusion of everything else.

The drum is the power of inspiration and full potential. It is vital to be creative and find an innovative solution to an old problem and to keep the momentum going.

The canoe represents the means of achieving a goal and says that resourcefulness and a refusal to be deterred ensure success.

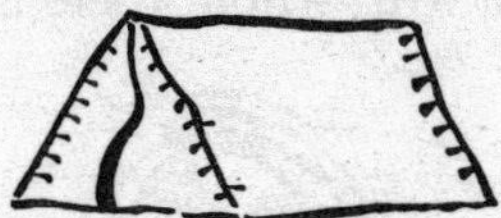

The tipuk, or tent, whose ridge pole represents the axis of the three worlds, is the symbol of unity of mind, body and spirit and the need to seek personal harmony.

The igloo offers shelter against the icy blasts and says that help should be sought and accepted from the existing circumstances if times are hard.

The caribou or reindeer represents movement and sudden action after a period of waiting. He speaks of the need to be ready to seize the right moment.

The whale, one of the symbols of death and rebirth as a shaman, promises new more fulfilling beginnings after an ending which may be painful.

Koodjaanuk, the creator bird and spirit of healing, represents the need for and possibility of healing and reconciliation whether inwardly or with those with whom there is conflict.

Sedna, the Old Woman of the Sea, is the source of nourishment and also potential destruction. Sedna warns that power and love can be used creatively or destructively so it is important to make any choices wisely.

The amulet offers protection, often at a time of fear and uncertainty. Look to a wiser source for advice and help.

The Method

If you live in a cold climate, you may wish to wait until dusk and light a fire in your garden or open space. Even in warmer climes, you can wait till the cooler time of evening and carry out your divination as the sun sets. If you have a drum or tambourine, you may wish to tap it rhythmically to create the mounting tension and as you do so echo as a chant any current concerns or desires.

Use any large plastic or copper ring, perhaps a napkin or serviette ring, large enough to encircle a single image. Place it on the cardboard circle or the tambourine. Then shake it until the ring settles over an image. Place the 'drum' carefully on the ground and read the image which will give you not a direct answer to any questions you may have, but a source of power and direction. You may dream of the image or may wish to use it in daytime visualization as the beginning of a journey through lands of ice and snow.

RING DIVINATION

Another Eurasian and Inuit form of divination involves a ring made from an antler that was covered with skin. Skin, representing an animal's fat or life source, was traditionally considered a very potent source of magical energy. The skin is smeared with fat on one side and held close to a fire. As the fat melts, the spirit of the hunt is invoked. Walrus, whale or seal bone rings and fat are also used according to the kind of animals being hunted. The glowing ring was thrown into the air and if it landed upwards, the hunt or fishing expedition would be successful. If not, the enterprise was abandoned until later.

SCAPULIMANCY

The shoulder bone of a reindeer was also used for a form of divination known as scapulimancy. The bone was smeared with fat and heated until it cracked. The shaman would then interpret the cracks, much as the ancient Chinese used to interpret the cracks on heated tortoise shells, the earliest form of the I Ching.

DRUMSTICK DIVINATION

This was practised by the Eurasian people of the frozen North as well as the Eskimos. A single drumstick would be tossed three times to discover whether the outcome of a hunt or some other venture would be favourable. This was done by ordinary people as well as the shaman, using pieces of bone marked on one side to indicate the positive face. Landing face upwards was considered a good omen and the more positive throws, the better the omens for success.

The method works just as well using chopsticks. Three sticks can be marked on one side with a small coloured spot (I use red) to indicate the 'yes' side. Concentrate on the choice you have to make, then throw the chopsticks and see whether the 'yes' sides are revealed.

Three 'yeses' or three 'noes' are strong indications for action/inaction and no further questions may be needed. Two 'yeses' represents a positive decision but not so strongly, so this is a 'yes, but'. A second question or a rephrasing of the first will often resolve the matter. In a case where there are many hidden doubts or unspoken reservations, several questions may be needed to overcome the doubts. Two noes is a 'no, but' and sometimes the matter will be resolved by waiting. On the other hand, more questions may unearth reasons why caution is necessary.

The first question is often influenced by conscious expectations but if subsequent questions are asked quickly, the unconscious and sometimes real issue may find expression.

EXAMPLE OF DRUMSTICK DIVINATION

Tom had just retired and wanted to open a furniture-restoring business at home. However, his wife Marion, who was taking early retirement, felt that she and Tom have worked all their lives and that this was a time to develop interests together and spend some time travelling while they are young and sufficiently healthy. Tom simultaneously threw three chopsticks marked with a red spot on the yes side.

Question one was should I start the business? The answer was yes (2). Question two was should I travel as my wife wants? The answer was yes (2). How could both be right? This led Tom to ask the last question. Could I combine the two? The answer was yes (3).

Tom decided to buy a large motor home and use it as a basis for restoring small pieces of furniture, making his speciality an 'on the spot' service around Europe. The business might not be wildly successful in financial terms but would pay the travelling expenses for trips around the area in which he was working.

Although pleased with the outcome, Tom was suspicious that the chopsticks he used were weighted in some way. However, with other questions he found both sides appeared equally and that he could not unconsciously influence the fall of the sticks.

FAIRY MAGIC

WHO ARE FAIRIES?

Fairies are small magical creatures, endowed with the powers of shape-changing and invisibility, who are found in one form or another in almost every culture. 'Fairy' comes from the Latin *fata* or fate. The Fates were three women who spun and controlled the webs of life. Fairies are especially associated with the Celtic tradition of Wales, Ireland, Brittany and Cornwall, Northern Europe, Scandinavia and in Iceland.

There are several explanations for fairies. They are variously believed to be nature spirits, Lucifer's fallen angels or guardians of the souls of the dead. They are invisible except to those who have second sight or when they choose to reveal themselves. They live either in plants or under the earth in a land where there is no time. They pester human beings who have messy houses or do not leave food or drink for them.

However, they can reward mortals with gifts and wishes for kindness offered to a fairy in disguise for they are masters of shape-shifting. Many fairy stories centre around the theme of a poor boy who helped a poor old woman who was really a fairy in disguise and was rewarded with magical gifts that enabled him to make a fortune and marry a princess. Fairies also assume the form of crows, usually if they are up to mischief.

A HISTORICAL EXPLANATION

In Northern European tradition, they are believed to descend from the small, dark, Neolithic people who retreated to remote areas, especially islands, to escape from Iron Age invaders. Here they could carry on their agriculture and the hunter/gatherer way of life from their round earth homes, using their flint-tipped arrows and flint knives and spears, sometimes known as elven or fairy shafts.

They carried with them the tradition of worshipping the Goddess and, because they became so elusive, tales grew up of their fairy kingdom and powers of invisibility. These peoples become known as 'the little people', the fairies, and their reaction to the metal sword-wielding invaders is reflected in their legendary fear of metal, especially iron.

The deities of the Old Religion were also either demonized or translated into fairies. The Goddess survived in myth and secret worship as the Good Fairy, the Fairy Godmother or Queen of the Fairies. The Celtic Maeve, Queen of Connaught and warrior Queen, became Mab, Queen of the Fairies or Titania, described in Shakespeare's *A Midsummer Night's Dream*. The Horned God became the Fairy King Oberon, while the trickster-god role, for example Loki in the Norse tradition, became the mischievous Puck of Shakespeare's play. A Fairy tells Puck:

Over hill, over dale,
Thorough bush, thorough briar.
Over park, over pale,
Thorough flood, through fire,
And I serve the Fairy Queen,
To dew her orbs upon the green,
The cowslips tall her pensioners be,
In their gold coats, spots you see,
Those be rubies, fairy favours,
. . .
I must go seek some dewdrops here,
And hang a pearl in every cowslip's ear.

She talks of Puck's mischief:

Are not you he
That frights the maidens of the villagery,
Skim milk,
. . .
Mislead night-wanderers, laughing at their harm?

The quarrel between the King and Queen of the fairies is seen as wreaking havoc on the land:

. . . and
the green corn
Hath rotted ere his youth attained a beard;
The fold stands empty in the drowned field
. . .
The spring, the summer,
The chiding autumn, angry winter, change
Their wonted liveries; and the mazed world
By their increase, now knows not which is which.
(*A Midsummer Night's Dream*, Act II, Scene 1)

ARE FAIRIES REAL?

J.M. Barrie wrote in *Peter Pan* that when the first baby laughed for the first time, the laugh broke into a thousand pieces and that was the beginning of fairies. Tinkerbell, the fairy who first found Peter and took care of him in Never Never Land, also warned that every time someone says he or she does not believe in fairies, a fairy dies.

The Neolithic theory is just one explanation of fairies and the tales that grew up about them. In that case, they would have died out or merged with other peoples and lived on only in myth. But there are many people in the modern world who claim to have seen fairies. Julie, who is now a medium, told me that as a child she had a big garden and in part of it where she played were little spirit friends who were like fairies. To Julie, they were not just pretend friends. In fact, she says that she has seen them in adult life, especially in a particular place in Devon. 'My own children have seen them too. Once when we were together we all saw them, when my son was nine and the youngest only about four.' She described them as 'very fleeting, like butterflies, but not as small, about the size of squirrels'.

Felicity, a psychology student, remembers a field near her house in the country where 'as a child I used to see fairies in the long grass. They were typical fairies, a sort of greeny blue, the kind you see in Flower Fairy Books. They used to talk to me. At the time I never told anyone. I was convinced they were real at the time. When we moved after my parents divorced, there wasn't a field so I did not see them any more.'

Pat, who is now 50 years old, also saw fairies when she was about four at the bottom of the garden belonging to the old lady who helped to bring her up: 'It was a big garden with a stream running at the bottom. They were very tiny, dressed in pink gossamer and used to play around by the stream. I told them my wildest dreams. They used to fly and hover with their tiny wings. I did not tell anyone as I knew they would have laughed.'

THE TOOTH FAIRY

Even modern children subscribe to a belief in the Tooth Fairy who exchanges teeth that have fallen out for money. One of my children was given a replica of a Victorian tooth pillow, embroidered and edged with lace. It had pillow with a pocket for keeping teeth safe. The Tooth Fairy is a character who stems back into antiquity, for it was feared that witches would wreak magic against children by using hair clippings or teeth that had fallen out. Such fears were natural in days of high infant mortality. It was also thought important to keep a child's first tooth and lock of hair throughout life so that when he or she died, the spirit had a complete body. The teeth and hair were placed in the coffin.

I talked to some children in a playgroup in Berkshire, England, about the Tooth Fairy. Five-year-old James assured me of their existence: 'There's tooth fairies. I have seen them, I think. My big brother is seven. He had three teeth come out when he was six. They came out on different days, so the tooth fairy took them away on different nights.'

Three-year-old Nadia explained: 'If your teeth are wobbly, the Tooth Fairy comes to take them and she makes another grow and she gives you money, but it hasn't happened to me yet.'

Tamesin, aged seven, nearly missed the Tooth Fairy: 'Once I swallowed one of my teeth when I fell over. Damien my brother said, "Oh yeah", but I did. So I wrote a letter to the Tooth Fairy telling her what had happened and put it under my pillow and I still got my money.'

THE COTTINGLEY FAIRIES

The most famous case of 'fairies at the bottom of the garden' is probably the Cottingley affair over which there is still controversy some 80 years later. In 1917, cousins Frances Griffiths, aged 11, and Elsie Wright, aged 16, claimed to have played with fairies in a glen at Cottingley, in the Yorkshire dales in North England. They produced photographs which baffled the experts, including Kodak and Sir Arthur Conan Doyle, the creator of Sherlock Holmes and an ardent spiritualist. One photograph showed a group of fairy-like figures dancing in front of a girl, the other a winged, gnome-like creature near a girl's beckoning hand. Some 60 years later, the cousins admitted that four of the photographs had been faked. They had made cut-outs of fairies and placed them in the glen.

This is not the end of the story because Frances said that they did take one genuine photograph. She told Joe Cooper, a psychic researcher and author of many psychic books: 'It was a wet Saturday afternoon and we were just mooching about with our cameras and Elsie had nothing prepared. I saw these fairies building up in the grasses and just aimed the camera and took a photograph.'

Elsie insisted all the photographs were fakes. But along with Frances, she claimed that there actually were fairies in the glen.

The reason the children had faked the pictures was to prove to jeering adults that the fairy folk did exist.

CHANGELINGS

Legends describe the changeling as a wizened, misshapen baby, hairy and with a monstrous head, which is left in the cradle as a substitute for a human child snatched by the fairies or underground elves. It is said to eat ravenously but never grow (or if it grows, to be horribly deformed) and to cry continually. The fairies or sprites carry human babies to fairyland where they are highly prized.

In *A Midsummer Night's Dream*, Puck says:

The King doth keep his revels here tonight;
Take heed the Queen come not within his sight;
For Oberon is passing fell and wrath,
Because that she as her attendant hath
A lovely boy, stolen from an Indian King.
She never had so sweet a changeling;
And jealous Oberon would have the child
Knight of his train, to trace the forests wild;
But she perforce withholds the loved boy,
Crowns him with flowers, and makes him all her joy.

Folklore offers various remedies to make the ever-crying changeling laugh or to trick it into revealing its true age and identity. The story of the soldier and the egg exists in various versions in many parts of Europe. A soldier returns home from the wars to find his younger brother still in the cradle after some 20 years. The soldier empties an eggshell, fills it with water and begins heating it over a fire. The changeling asks what is happening and the soldier replies that he is brewing beer. This amuses the changeling enough for it to laugh out loud and say: 'Old, old I am but in all my years I have never seen a soldier brewing beer in an eggshell.'

The deception now revealed, the soldier attacks the changeling with a whip and it vanishes. The long-lost brother, now a grown man, is restored to the family. According to some versions of the tale, the young man is not at all happy at the reunion because in fairyland where he had been imprisoned for all those years, he lived in flowery bowers and feasted on nectar, a far cry from the rigours of life on a farm.

Other versions of the tale neglect the egg brewing and go straight into the whipping option at which point the fairy or elf who carried out the substitution appears, crying: 'Do not attack my child for I never did yours any harm.' She then returns the missing baby.

As the changeling is so widespread in folklore, it is interesting to speculate what basis there could be for it in reality. Was it the way for parents in less enlightened times than ours to come to terms with disabled children? I asked a doctor with an interest in paranormal experiences about the medical aspects.

'The description of a changeling is not identifiable as a particular syndrome,' he said, 'rather a series of disabilities that separately or together would mark a child as different. When parents have a child that looked unusual, one acceptable hypothesis in times past was that the devil had got into the child somehow.

'Dietary shortages in times past could explain much of the lack of growth and normal development, especially in poor families. In earlier days, a high proportion of children failed to thrive and infant mortality was as high as 50 to 60 per cent. The changeling theory was a convenient explanation for unfortunate parents who produced a socially unacceptable child.'

For the child taken to be a changeling, life could be hard, especially if the parents decided to use the whipping method of unmasking him. In 1843 the *West Briton* newspaper reported the case of a J. Trevelyan of Penzance, Cornwall, England who was charged with ill-treating one of his children. The child was said to have been regularly beaten by the parents and the servants and from 15 months old had been left to live outside. The parents' defence was that he was not their child but a changeling and the case against them was dismissed.

'A century and a half ago,' the doctor told me, 'the railway had only just broken through to Cornwall and until then it had been virtually cut off. When Wesley [founder of methodism] went there in the 1780s he found a land rife with paganism and folklore. Cornwall at that time was appallingly backward with gross poverty, great ignorance and conditions that horrified Wesley.'

AN ESCAPE FROM THE FAIRIES

Fairies also captured wanderers at night, especially on the nights of the magical festivals. The Fairy Queen, according to legend, would spirit away handsome young men to serve her. One of the most famous tales, made into a song as well as a story, is that of Tam Lin, a knight who slipped from his horse and was captured by the Queen of the Fairies. She bound him round with magic and posted him to guard one of the entrances to the world of humans at the well of

Carteraugh close to the Borders of Scotland. Young women were warned not to drink at the well, for every time they did and picked one of the roses that overhung it, Tam Lin would appear and demand that the girl either gave him a green mantle or offered up her virginity.

One bold young woman, Janet, decided to see whether the myth was true and plucked a rose from the well. She and Tam Lin fell in love and he longed to escape from the Fairy Kingdom to marry her. The next night was Hallowe'en and Tam Lin explained that there was an opportunity that only occurred every seven years for him to escape. The Fairy Ride to Hell would take place and the Fairy Band had to ride on horseback along the road. Tam Lin told Janet to wait for him at the crossroads at midnight on Hallowe'en. As Tam Lin rode by in the Fairy Procession, Janet pulled him from his horse and held tight. Just as he had warned Janet, the Fairy Queen turned Tam Lin first into a newt, then a snake, a tiger, a bear and finally red hot metal. But Janet held fast and as he became molten metal, she plunged him into the magical well. The spell was broken. Tam Lin emerged from the water in human form and the two were soon married.

DIFFERENT KINDS OF FAIRY FOLK

There are two main types of fairies. One belongs to a nation of fairies who live in Fairyland with a king and queen. There is no concept of time in Fairyland. No one grows old or dies. The second sort of fairies often attach themselves to a household and are very independent. They choose a family they like and move in.

Brownies

From Scotland, brownies are a friendly species of fairy folk. They live with families and work around the house when the family is asleep.

Elves

They are said to have no souls. They originated in Germany and can be mischievous, although they can prove helpful to those they see as deserving or in need.

Land Wights or Landvaetir

These are guardians of the earth. They are recognized especially in Northern Europe and Iceland where certain fields and hills were sacred to them. No living creature or plant could be destroyed within the hallowed ground. Equally, no one could look upon the sacred land with an unwashed face. Other wights also acted as guardians of settlement and villages, travelling along the fairy paths at dusk to their watch posts at crossroads, sacred trees and standing stones and preventing any harm entering the settlement until morning.

Goblins and Gnomes

Both are bad-tempered creatures who were originally French household spirits. They like to live in dark places, but can be helpful around houses, especially those attached to a work place. Gnomes are very fond of mines and like working underground, digging for treasure.

Leprechauns

They come from Ireland, are 60 cm (2 feet) high, work as shoemakers and are very wealthy. They can be mean with their money and have crocks of gold that they will not give up. They often bury their pots of gold at the end of the rainbow so that no one can find them. They disappear at the slightest disturbance.

Dwarfs

They are good blacksmiths and skilled at baking, tailoring and making prophecies. They can appear and disappear at will and love parties. They do give good advice but are light-fingered, especially where gems are concerned. If a dwarf likes you, he may give you a present which will turn into gold. They usually dwell in caves and are guardians of precious minerals and metals. The Roman author Pliny writes of dwarfs in Africa, perhaps referring to reports of pygmies and they feature in many Teutonic and Scandinavian legends, especially as metal smiths.

The Will o' the Wisp or Friar's Lanthorn

This is not a fairy at all – at least according to scientists. This flame-like phosphorescence floating over marshy ground is due to the spontaneous combustion of decaying vegetable matter. But folklore experts say that Will o' the Wisps guard lost treasures. They elude all who attempt to follow them and lure many lost travellers to their end on marshes and bogs.

Trolls

They can be either dwarfs or giants and live in caves by the sea or in mountains. Fishermen are terrified of them. The Norwegian composer Grieg immortalized them with the *Hall of the Mountain King* in his Peer Gynt Suite.

BELIEFS ABOUT FAIRIES

If food is left on the table all night, the little people will take it and bring good fortune to the house. To ensure a prosperous year, food should be left on the table at New Year when everyone has gone to bed (see also *New Year Magic*, page 362).

Fairy Paths

In Ireland, sacred leys (see also *Earth Magic*, page 153) are known as fairy paths. They link ancient earthworks with other sites of power. At times of the year such as May Eve and Hallowe'en, people are advised not to walk along them because fairies and other non-worldly creatures use them to reach their celebrations. Houses are not erected on these traditional pathways, which are often straight and marked with hawthorns (the fairy tree) at regular intervals.

PROTECTIVE FAIRY MAGIC

Although some people believe that the secret guardians of settlements and households have been driven away by indiscriminate urbanization and pollution, nevertheless, it is possible to use the benign powers of the Earth to protect your home and to help you in material matters.

John, who lives in a new town in Berkshire, England, had to work during the nights and his wife was terrified because every night someone tapped at the window. The police were unable to do anything. He asked for the protection of the guardians of the land on his home. That night John's wife heard the tapping and saw a huge shadow outside. Then she heard a shriek and was never troubled again.

Positioning your Sentinels

If you feel nervous at night or are troubled by hostile neighbours, you need to establish a 'fairy path' and sentinel points for your guardians to stand after dark and at times when you need protection. Trees are good places for guardians, especially oak, ash or hawthorn, as are any intersections, such as a place where two paths cross or the garden path forms a right angle with your front door or patio. You need six or eight significant markers to form a protective ring around your home.

You can also use stones, two either side of the front and back entrances and one at each of the four corners of your plot. If you live in an apartment, place stones in pots either side of your entrance door and at the four outermost corners of your home. The stones need not be large but should be tall and rounded on top, like miniature standing stones. If you can take them from a hilltop or an old site, they will be especially magical. Obviously you would not take stones from an old monument, but those on the ground at the edges of the site or in the next field will share the same ancient energies.

At dusk, whenever you leave home or feel vulnerable, see the calm, wise brown faces of the earth sprites turning away all who would harm you or invade your psychic space. Each morning, offer a small flower, preferably a brown or golden bloom, to your fairy guardians and ensure that they always have fresh flowers and a tiny dish of water. If the markers are in soil, plant a tiny clear quartz crystal or pure white stones to give energy to your guardian.

Garden Gnomes and Money Rituals

Garden gnomes are elemental spirits. They are not like the Disney characters in *Snow White* but older. If you are lucky enough to see one in your garden, he is more likely to offer you advice rather than treasures. Your garden gnome can, however, help out with problems with money or practical matters.

If you do not have a garden gnome, buy one from a garden centre (he can be as gaudy or unadorned as you like) or make your own from an old tree stump. You do not need great wood-carving skills. Often you can find pieces of wood that already possess features and just need a little smoothing down. If you enjoy pottery, you can make and fire a brown or red clay gnome and draw in his features.

Write what it is you need on a piece of square orange paper, wrap it around a coin that is gold or silver coloured – the value does not matter – and bury it at his feet just as the sun is setting. Remember to leave a dish of water and some seeds for him to share with the birds. On the fifth day you will be given the answer to your problem from an unexpected source.

FAIRY RINGS

Fairy rings are circles of inedible fungi, often red with white spots, that feature in all the best fairy stories. They grow naturally in grassy places in Europe, Britain and North America and often spring up after rain. According to magical lore, they provide convenient magical circles where fairies and witches meet, dance and sing at night. In Britain, fairy rings are also called hag rings because, according to lore, they are created by the dancing feet of witches.

Legend says that if someone stands in a fairy ring under a full moon and makes a wish, it will come true. Another belief is that to see fairies, who are usually invisible except for those with second sight, one must run around a fairy ring nine times under a full moon. But do not attempt this on May Eve or All Hallow's Eve, the two major fairy festivals, because the fairies will be offended and carry you off to Elfland.

A Fairy Ring Empowering Ritual

You may be lucky and find a real fairy ring or ring of mushrooms in the woods. If not, take into a clearing in the woods or a secluded corner of a park, nine red and nine white crystals or stones. Put them on the ground, starting at the twelve o'clock position and forming a circle going round clockwise. If you are in a safe place, you can carry out this ritual after dark with the full moon casting light into your circle.

Begin in a position outside the crystal circle where you are facing the moon. Walk nine times clockwise around the circle, saying in your mind or out loud if you are alone, your desire or the particular strength you need to succeed or find happiness. Leave the circle for a while and sit quietly in the moonlight. Then walk round the circle anti-clockwise to pick up first your red crystals and then a second time to pick up your white stones, burying one of each colour in the centre of the original circle to renew the energies of the earth you have used in your ritual. Before you go to sleep, write a step-by-step plan of how you will attain your goal. Leave blanks if there are any difficulties and you will find when you wake that you can fill in the gaps, as if by magic.

A FAIRY WISH RITUAL

Fairies are said to fly as butterflies, dandelion seeds or thistledown. Although gardeners and farmers do not welcome the practice, from time immemorial children and young lovers have blown dandelion clocks and sent fairies on their way, at the same time seeking the answers to questions about love and good fortune.

You can use soap bubbles, either the ordinary children's kind or by making them from liquid detergent and water. Use a big bubble blower. Find a symbol of whatever it is you want: a key for a new house, a toy car for a new vehicle, a coin for money, a flower for love, a toy plane for travel, for example. Place the symbol on a tree stump, preferably a hawthorn (the fairy tree) or between two oaks, which are said to be a gateway to fairy worlds. Blow your bubbles in a circle round your symbol, higher and higher, all the time seeing your ambitions coming true. In each bubble you may see a fairy carrying your wishes.

On the way home, if you see thistledown or a dandelion clock, blow it and help the fairies on their way. Take your symbol home and place it on your window ledge. At night, leave a little gift, a flower or a ribbon for the fairies next to your symbol. Each morning, hold it before you begin the day, then go out and make your dream come true.

17

FERTILITY MAGIC

THE ORIGINS

In ancient times, the fertility of the people and the fertility of the soil were inextricably linked. Couples made love in the woods or fields at times of sowing or peak growth times, symbolically fertilizing the crops as well as ensuring their own fecundity. In the mid-West of the United States, a token plant set by a pregnant woman was believed to ensure the success of the whole crop, while in Indonesia rice crops are traditionally encouraged to produce the maximum amount of seed by a couple making love in the fields at the time the rice is blooming.

Scientific research gives this process some support. Pierre Savon, who comes from New Jersey, investigated ESP in plants. He discovered an electronic reaction with high peaks on a tone oscillator attached to his plants at the time he was making love with his girlfriend 130 km (80 miles) away. He found that the moment of orgasm provoked the strongest reaction.

Fertility Festivals

The sacred marriage between earth and sky was practised in many cultures at the time of spring. In Ancient Babylon, the sacred marriage took place each year between the god Tammuz and the goddess Ishtar. The festival of Akitu or Zag-Mug celebrated the rising of the waters of the Tigris, followed by the Euphrates and the coming of the spring rains to bring fertility at the spring equinox. Like many of the harvest gods, he died every year and was fetched from the underworld by his consort who restored him to life.

Among the Aborigines in Northern Australia, the monsoon season was heralded by sacred sex rites to celebrate the union of the Rainbow Snake and the Earth Mother. The Rainbow Snake is represented in the ritual as the Aboriginal male and Kunapipi, the Earth Mother, by the female Aborigine, symbol of the reproductive qualities of the earth (see also *Aboriginal Magic*, page 1).

May Eve was a special time in Europe for young couples to spend the night together in the woods, having leapt hand in hand between the Beltane (Celtic summer) fires to ensure fertility (see also *Fire Magic*, page 211). The Maypole, around which young girls danced on May morning after bathing their faces in the dawn dew, was a symbol of ancient tree worship and represented one of the old world trees, such as the Norse Yggdrassil. It represented the supreme male power of the corn god and dated back into the mists of time. Maypole dances involved winding red, blue, green, yellow and white ribbons, representing the union of earth and sky, winter and summer, water and fire in spiralling shapes to represent the spiralling earth energies. The May Queen was the final appearance of the maiden aspect of the Goddess before she became the Mother Goddess and so the Maytime is one associated with fertility.

The old saying 'Cast not a clout till May is out' refers to the may blossom of the hawthorn whose appearance marks the beginning of summer in the Celtic year. This is the one time of the year the bough may be brought into the house. Rudyard Kipling wrote of the ancient fertility ritual of 'a-maying' in his poem, *Oak and Ash and Thorn*:

Oh do not tell the priest our plight,
For he would call it sin,
For we have been in the woods all night,
A conjuring summer in,
I bring good news by word of mouth,
Good news for cattle and corn,
For now the sun is come out of the south,
With oak and ash and thorn.

OVERCOMING INFERTILITY

In times of high mortality rates and before welfare systems, it was vital to produce many children if someone was to survive to provide care for parents in old age and to carry on the family trade. Where there was wealth and property, the desire for a male heir was paramount.

Henry VIII estranged England from the Catholic Church, divorced Catherine of Aragon and beheaded Anne Boleyn in his quest for a male to carry on the dynasty. For although his daughter Good Queen Bess 'had the stomach and the heart of a man', there was no tradition, except for the ill-fated Queen Mathilda, for a woman holding the throne. Women under pressure would resort to fertility potions and spells to produce an heir, for the females were always held responsible for the lack of a child.

MIDSUMMER FERTILITY MAGIC

At Midsummer when nature was at its height, flowers were blooming, the trees were in full leaf and the crops turning golden, natural fertility energies were at their height. According to tradition, the yellow herb St John's Wort, which first blooms at Midsummer, should be picked at midnight on Midsummer eve (23 June), by a woman wishing to become pregnant. She should walk naked alone in a garden and not speak a word. She must then sleep with the plant under her pillow and within nine months would, according to popular tradition, have a child (see also *Sun Magic*, page 410).

The natural energies of the golden flower may have increased a woman's fertility by lowering her anxieties. Or it may be that a naked woman wandering the fields or garden alone at night had more earthly aid in becoming pregnant; in either case, the result was the same. Many a farmer's only son or the heir to a stately home and fine lands owed his origin to one of these ancient rituals.

MAGICAL STANDING STONES

Another traditional belief was that an infertile woman could become pregnant if she visited ancient standing stones at midnight. One of the most famous fertility rings were the Rollright stones in Oxfordshire, England. These stones were supposedly the remains of an invading king and his knights who were turned to stone in Celtic times by the legendary hag of Rollright.

At midnight, a woman who wanted to become pregnant would go to the stones alone, remove all her clothes and press herself against the Kingstone so closely that her breasts and thighs were chilled. Within nine months she would bear a strong son.

FERTILITY AND NATURE

Because of the connection between the fertility of the soil and human fertility, fruits, flowers and herbs were regarded as symbols of fertility. Among the Kara-Kirgiz people of Turkmenistan, barren women would roll themselves on the ground under a solitary apple tree in order to become pregnant.

In Northern India, coconuts are considered fertility symbols and are sacred to Sri, Goddess of Prosperity. Coconuts are kept in shrines, blessed and given by priests to women who wish to conceive.

Among the Maoris, certain trees and their resident tree spirits were credited with holding the key to fertility for women. A barren woman would embrace a tree on which the navel strings of babies were traditionally hung. Such a tree was also one where the cords of sacred ancestors once hung. If the woman hugged the east of the tree, she would have a boy. The west side produced a girl.

In the European tradition, a green bush was placed outside the house of a girl whom a young man wished to marry, a symbol of the ancient fertility powers of tree spirits. In Bavaria, 'may bushes' were planted outside the home of newly-married couples, while among women in parts of Eastern Europe remains the belief that if you want a child, you should climb a fruit-bearing tree and hang out one of your undergarments. If the next morning an insect or caterpillar has crawled into the garment, it will transfer the fruitfulness of the tree to the woman if she wears the garment the next day.

The Guarani Indians in South America believed that if a woman ate a double grain of millet she would become a mother of twins.

An old English custom from Yorkshire says that if you want to have children, go to a hayrick on a Friday and pick a wheat straw for every boy you want and an oat straw for every girl and bind them into a straw garter. Wear the garter over the weekend and if it is still in place on Monday, your wish will be granted. But you must not tell your husband or partner. The magic worked both ways. In Austria, pregnant women would be given the first fruit of a tree so that the tree would be fruitful the next year.

SYMPATHETIC FERTILITY MAGIC

Sympathetic magic, where you imitate the desired event to stimulate its occurrence in your own life, has always been an important means of encouraging fertility.

In Sumatra, a woman who wanted to conceive a child would make a wooden image of an infant and nurse it in her lap. In Medieval Europe, a cradle belonging to a woman who had many children was similarly used.

Some older fertility methods were rather violent. One Oceanic ritual involved a man who has fathered many children dangling a fowl over the head of an infertile wife and husband. The unfortunate fowl was sacrificed as the woman simulated giving birth and suckling a doll made of red cotton. The villagers came to congratulate the woman on the birth of her 'child' and nine months later, it was believed, the birth of her own child would occur. In Hungary, a barren woman was struck with a stick that had been used to separate coupling dogs.

OVERCOMING ANXIETIES

Modern fertility magic is much gentler but follows the same principles. Because many women do have babies later in life, anxiety about fertility can be especially acute. In up to a third of cases no medical cause can be found for infertility in couples. Because science and technology are so instant and we no longer celebrate the passing seasons and the fertility of animals and plants, the idea of letting nature take its course has become alien. So anxiety can set in early.

Even for women using artificial insemination or IVF, relaxation, positivity and a receptiveness can help to make conditions more favourable for conception. In 1989 a London hospital began research into folk remedies and introduced sessions of African dancing, mask making and drumming to overcome anxieties that prevented conception. Earlier, Morris Dancing, May Revels and a jug of mead served the same purpose.

THE BEST TIME

May to mid-June is an especially powerful time for fertility rituals, but you can harness the energies on any new to full moon period.

Modern Rituals

Modern fertility rituals usually involve using crystals or eggs (which both have the shape of the cosmic egg, symbol of new life). Herbs and oils of passion and fertility include carnation, ginseng, geranium, grains of paradise, jasmine, hibiscus, olive, orange, patchouli, parsley, rose, rosemary, saffron and lemongrass. You can make a love pouch of some of the herbs and petals, scented with an oil such as patchouli. Use a tiny drawstring purse or sew them into a small piece of fabric. You may wish to add a tiny moonstone for the fertile powers of the moon. Keep this under your pillow when you make love.

The following ritual has been used successfully by women who were having problems conceiving. It is based on a traditional fertility ritual used in medieval times and is not magic or occult, but relies on overcoming all the conscious blocks that can get in the way of fertility. However, it offers no promises. It is important to have medical checks but if everything is fine, then if the ritual does not work, it may just not be the right time to have a baby. In this case, hard though it is, it is important to start something new and really concentrate on it. This is why sometimes a childless couple who foster or adopt find themselves expecting a baby precisely because they had dismissed the idea from their minds and relaxed.

The ritual begins on the new moon and continues until the full moon is in the sky. Menstrual cycles average 28 to 29 days, roughly the same length as the lunar cycle. It is said that ovulation occurs most frequently at or near the full moon and this is why lovers find the full moon so romantic.

A Lunar Ritual

Use either a crystalline egg, such as a dragon's egg, or two matching agate geodes that can be bought inexpensively from a good New Age shop or mineral centre. Make sure that the top and bottom fit together and leave a hollow inside. An ordinary empty egg shell dyed in a gentle colour, such as pink or green, the colours of Venus, is just as effective.

The egg represents the cosmic egg from which all life came. Easter Eggs are a powerful fertility symbol (good news for chocaholics). Place a tiny moonstone or a tiny doll inside the shell and place the egg on the window ledge at the beginning of the moon cycle. Open the egg and let any moonlight shine on the moonstone, but close it during the day.

On the first day of the full moon, insert a sharp needle or tiny jewelled paper knife into the eggshell or within the crystal egg and leave them in the moonlight. This is a symbol of the male and female coming together in love. It is simply a symbol and not witchcraft or magic. Next morning wrap the needle and moonstone in a special shawl or scarf and keep them in a drawer until the next new moon.

Alternatively, if a woman has a very regular menstrual cycle, she can begin the ritual on the first day and insert the needle in the egg around the time of ovulation. She can tell the day either by using a thermometer to calculate it or by the mid-cycle pain and a restlessness. As before, leave the egg on the window ledge but calculate the first day of the menstrual bleeding as the first day of the new moon and leave the egg on the ledge till the fourteenth or whichever day ovulation occurs. Insert the needle or tiny knife in the egg as before. Wrap the egg and needle and place them in a drawer until the next menstrual bleeding occurs. The ritual can be repeated over several months until the bleeding stops with pregnancy.

Make love not by the thermometer, but whenever you and your partner wish during the moon cycle. Light a pink or green candle if it is after dark and place moonstones round it.

A NORSE FERTILITY BIND RUNE

Bind runes, the combination of two or more runic shapes, were used as symbols of power in the Viking world (see *Norse Magic*, page 375).

A fertility bind rune drawn on paper and placed beneath the pillow can be a focus for ancient earth fertility energies not only for anyone who wishes to conceive a child, but also to give life to any venture or relationship that needs to bear fruit.

X Gyfu, the Viking rune of creative giving and loving relationships, takes on the meaning of fertility when combined with

Ing, rune of the Ancient Corn Hero God who brought fertility to the land each year.

Beorc, the rune of the Earth Mother Goddess of the same name, completes the ancient fertility trinity: Ing the father, Beorc, the Mother and Gyfu the union and ultimately its product. One example of how they might be combined is shown here.

You can join the three individual runic forms in different ways, upside down or horizontally, to create your own unique focus of energy. Everyone's fertility bind rune should be different. You can even make a repetitive pattern design of the three main fertility runes or combine the Mother and Father Runes with Gyfu.

A Wooden Bind Rune

For a more permanent bind rune, mark your joined runic shapes on wood, perhaps birch, tree of the Earth Mother Goddess Beorc. Carve the mark with a chisel, burn it into the wood with a red hot screwdriver or wood-burning tool or paint it with a fine brush or permanent pen in red, the colour of fertility. If you wish, gouge a hole in the bind rune so that you can hang it round your neck from a ribbon or silver chain.

A Stone Bind Rune

Go to a beach or river bed and find a small stone with a natural hole in it so that you can hang it from a cord either above your bed or round your neck. Scratch your fertility bind rune with a screwdriver or paint the symbol. Alternatively, you can use an ordinary stone and carry it in your pocket or place it under your pillow at night, again following the new full moon cycle.

MAKING A FERTILITY DOLL

In parts of Mexico, a tiny woven doll, like those used as worry dolls, is enclosed in a tiny brightly woven basket with a lid and carried by women who wish to become pregnant.

A natural alternative is to make a grass baby three months before you wish to conceive. On the new moon take a thin cotton sock, stocking or small porous fabric bag. Fill it seven-eights full with sawdust and shake well to remove all the loose pieces. Add fast-growing grass seed to the top and tie firmly so that you have a ball. If you wish, draw on the eyes, nose and mouth or glue on buttons or sequins for features.

Place your grass baby on a saucer and add water to the saucer each morning. Before the full moon your baby will be sprouting grass hair. When it is long, cut and continue the cutting/watering ritual until the new moon appears again in the sky. Make a new grass baby for three months to open your eagerness to have a child to the cosmos.

CHOOSING THE SEX OF A BABY

Every baby, boy or girl, brings unique gifts and to concentrate on one sex may lead to unnecessary disappointment and pressures on a precious infant. However, if you want to try a bit of moon magic to tip the scales in favour of a boy, you can place a pale blue crystal, such as a blue moonstone or blue lace agate, in an egg shell dyed pale blue on your window ledge on the night of the new moon and leave it until the full moon rides the sky. For a girl, use a pale pink crystal, such as a rose quartz in an egg shell dyed pink, again for the same moon period.

A more traditional method involves placing a tiny silver knife under your pillow if you want a boy and a silver thimble for a girl.

DISCOVERING THE SEX OF AN UNBORN BABY

Most women instinctively know the sex of their unborn child but often we do not trust our instincts. When I was working as a teacher and expecting my first baby, Alice, the school cleaner, told me unhesitatingly I would have a boy, which I did. She based her knowledge on the fact that my bulge was high in front rather than spread more evenly, but I suspect that her knowledge was based on her own deep instinctive wisdom. I have also heard the reverse said, that a baby carried high is a girl and one carried low is a boy, so the real key appears to be intuition rather than reliance on rigid rules.

Pendulums

Suspending a needle or pendulum over the womb is one of the most popular methods of determining the sex of an unborn baby. It is best done by the pregnant woman, since like all methods, it relies on her own intuition and psychic link with the unborn baby. Traditionally a clockwise swing indicates a boy and an anti-clockwise swing a girl, corresponding with the positive (yang) response for a boy and negative (yin) response for a girl. These do not mean positive and negative in the sense of good or bad, but are like a battery where positive and negative are both necessary. If the needle or pendulum swings to and fro, twins may be a possibility.

You can just as easily establish your own personal response whether with a needle on a thread, a crystal pendulum or a key on a cord by asking the pendulum to demonstrate its yes/no/boy/girl response in advance. Pendulums are remarkably obliging (see *Earth Magic*, page 153).

Numerology

Another popular method of determining the sex of an unborn baby is by using the Pythagorean system of Numerology (see also *Time Magic*, page 439). Use the grid shown here to determine the value of a letter that is, C, L and U = 3 and H, Q and Z = 8. Write the full name as on the birth certificate of the mother (her maiden name) and father and the month in which the unborn infant was conceived. Add together the numbers for all the letters. Divide the total by seven. If the whole number obtained (ignoring any remainder), is even, the child will be a girl, if uneven a boy. This method works only for singletons or single sex twins.

1	2	3	4	5	6	7	8	9
A	B	C	D	E	F	G	H	I
J	K	L	M	N	O	P	Q	R
S	T	U	V	W	X	Y	Z	

So if Anna Jane Jones and Alan Paul Wood conceive a child in May, the calculation is as follows.

A	N	N	A	J	A	N	E	J	O	N	E	S
1	5	5	1	1	1	5	5	1	6	5	5	1
A	L	A	N	P	A	U	L	W	O	O	D	
1	3	1	5	7	1	3	3	5	6	6	4	

1+5+5+1+1+1+5+5+1+6+5+5+1 = 42

1+3+1+5+7+1+3+3+5+6+6+4 = 45

and M A Y is

4 + 1 + 7 = 12

42 + 45 + 12 = 99 divided by 7 = 14 ignoring the remainder. Therefore Anna and Alan should have a girl.

BIRTH AND CHRISTENING CUSTOMS

When you bring a new baby home for the first time, you must carry it upstairs and then downstairs or in a one-storey home, stand on a high step or chair with the infant. This is said to ensure that a child will rise to greater things.

A baby born at midnight on New Year's eve, New Year's day or Hallowe'en will have great psychic powers.

A child was blessed in pre-Christian times shortly after birth by his or her father who would take the infant to the sea or use a bowl of salted water and make the sign of the cross upon the left shoulder to prevent the influence of malevolent spirits who were believed to inhabit the left side.

It was believed that only a mother should cut her baby's hair and, until the age of one, she would be expected to bite the fingernails short, not cut them, to avoid anything sharp cutting the magical protection around the child.

A first tooth lost was purchased by the Tooth Fairy for a silver coin and placed in a birth book along with the first lock of hair cut (see also *Fairy Magic*, page 187). There were two reasons for this custom. The first was to protect the child from witchcraft, since it was believed that witches used hair and nail clippings to gain power over their owner. The second stems from an even earlier belief that when a person died he or she should be intact so that the spirit would survive; so hair and teeth from the beginning of life were preserved and placed in the coffin.

The practice of hanging toys on cradles, prams, pushchairs and strokers comes from an early custom of hanging bells directly above a sleeping infant's head so that the sounds and shiny surfaces kept away mischievous spirits who might harm the child.

FERTILITY FOR PROJECTS AND JOINT VENTURES

Fertility magic can be used not only for conceiving a child, but also for helping any new project to take root or a new relationship to bear fruit. If any idea is slow to come to fruition or a relationship is becoming stagnant, fertility magic can bring back life and enthusiasm.

You can adapt any of the rituals described above. If you carry out the new moon egg ritual, instead of a moonstone, use a tiny symbol of whatever it is you want to bring into fruition, such as a tiny silver heart for love or a small silver coin for a money-making venture. Where possible use silver symbols and place them inside the egg. Pierce the egg with the knife as before.

SEX MAGIC

Sex magic practised in a loving stable relationship can provide a powerful release of energies for any venture. However, used for unfair gain, power or casually without love, it is less than useless. Research into plants has discovered that when treated with love, they respond by growing and flourishing. Love is the strongest mover of magical energies. Eastern tantric processes involve diverting sexual energy at the point of climax, but the Western forms of sex magic encourage a natural climax of energies that carry desires and needs with them into the cosmos.

The best time for sex magic is one of the old festivals, such as dawn on the Longest Day, at midnight on May eve (30 April), the beginning of the Celtic Summer, or Candlemas, the evening of 31 January which was the ancient first day of spring or one of the intersections of the year such as New Year's eve or Hallowe'en

(31 October), the beginning of the Celtic New Year at midnight. The first night of the full moon is also a good time.

If possible, make love in the open air if you can be private, perhaps in a secluded garden or with the windows open. If you can find a deserted beach, tide turn is most powerful of all, either at the sea or a tidal river. However far you live from the sea, you can use the nearest sea or tidal river as a marker.

Try to spend the evening together alone, perhaps walking on darkened hills or through a fragrant garden and talk of your dreams and joint plans. Be especially gentle and loving. It is important that only positive energies are created, so do not discuss differences or doubts. Have a bath in fragrant herbs and oils and perhaps use a massage oil, such as lavender, to soothe away the world. Before you make love, sit quietly in the star or candlelight, not touching but breathing as one and let your bodies join harmoniously with no thought other than love and commitment to each other and to your joint plans.

Use the moment of climax to concentrate on a joint venture that you wish to be fruitful and see your energies cascading like stars into the night sky. Spend time afterwards talking quietly about your future hopes and dreams and do not hurry back to the real world too soon.

Should your venture be to create a child, you may see gentle lights hovering. Some parents are convinced that babies are old wise souls who choose their parents, so open your hearts in love and you may be blessed.

18

FIRE MAGIC

DEITIES AND MYTHS

In every culture, the discovery of fire transformed life; men and women could cook their food, fire kept them warm and protected them from fierce beasts and let them shape metals. It was hard to believe that such a precious gift would be given willingly by the gods and many myths tell how heroes stole the fire.

In Greek myth Prometheus, a Titan, stole the fire from Hephaestus, God of Fire and Metals because Zeus, King of the Gods, had denied its use for mortals. Zeus punished Prometheus by chaining him to Mount Caucasus where an eagle ate his liver by day. The liver was renewed each night so that his torment could begin afresh next day. Eventually Hercules rescued Prometheus by killing the eagle. In Maori legend, the inventor hero Maui stole fire for the people.

Fire gods began as sun gods, but gradually the role of fire was assigned to a specific fire god, sometimes linked with the smelting of metals, as with the Greek Hephaestus. In India, the great Fire God was Agni, sometimes regarded as an aspect of the Sun God. He ruled not only over the fires of lightning and heaven, but the sacred fires on Earth as well. Agni carried sacrifices from man to the gods on the dark canopy of smoke from the sacrificial fires on Earth. In Ancient Mexico, Xiuhtecutli, the Fire God, was also the god of the domestic hearth. Every morning and evening Mexican families offered him food and drink. His body was flame coloured and a yellow serpent rested over his back to represent the flickering flames.

FIRE FESTIVALS

Fire has been central to festivals throughout the world, especially on the major solar festivals such as the summer and mid-winter solstices. It represents the power of the sun and life and was used to persuade the sun to continue to shine at times when it was feared its power was declining. Yule logs were burned on the mid-winter solstice and fields circled with blazing torches at the summer solstices when the oak, king of the waxing year, was burned.

At other festivals, such as those of the Celtic and Northern European tradition, fires are linked with the fertility of the land.

By transforming a sacrifice, whether symbolic or in ancient times animal or even human, through fire into ashes and then returning the ashes to the soil, people were symbolically endowing the soil with life. The fires also had a purification element, driving away both disease and malevolent influences that were believed to fear fire. For example, on Beltane, an ancient Celtic and Northern lunar festival for fertility that marked the coming of summer, cattle were let out of the barns and driven between twin fires to purify them. The festival's name comes from Bel or Belenos who was the old Sun God.

Human fertility, like that of the cattle and corn, was linked with the fertilizing fire. Young men would leap over the Beltane fires with the girls with whom they had spent the night looking for the first may (hawthorn) blossoms to decorate the houses. Women who wished to become pregnant would also jump over or run between the fires and, it was said, would have a babe by the next Beltane fires. A Beltane cake was baked, divided into portions and placed in a bag. The person who picked out the piece marked with a charred cross was the *carline*, the mock sacrifice – and in ancient times, the real fire sacrifice.

The Germans call the festival *Walpurgisnacht*, the night of the witches. Hilltop fires were built to drive off the witches and stop them gaining new powers to ruin the coming harvest. The direction in which the smoke blew, the intensity of heat and even how far the fires could be seen would indicate the extent to which their magical powers might extend. Similar festivals were held in other parts of the world. For example, in South Africa about April, the Matabeles would light huge fires to the windward of their gardens so that the smoke would ripen them.

NYD FIRES

Nyd or need fires, the central holy fires of the Teutonic and Celtic peoples, were kindled at the spring equinox (Easter) or Beltane (May eve). The fire was kindled with nine different kinds of wood at midsummer and other times of new life. Sticks were rubbed together or a more elaborate oaken spindle was turned in an oaken log-socket, from which all other fires were lit. Sometimes a sacred fire was kept burning from which all other fires were lit at ceremonial times (as with the Olympic Flame and those burning on the graves of unknown warriors who have fallen in battle). The vestal virgins kept burning a sacred flame dedicated to Vesta, Goddess of the Hearth, at her shrine at Nemi and in Rome itself in her shrine in the forum, where sacred oak was burned on the fire.

The need fire ceremony can still be seen in the Easter Fires and Midsummer Fires in parts of Europe and the extinguishing of candles on Good Friday (a relic of the spring equinox ceremonies) and the lighting of the Paschal Candle from the new fire which must be kindled naturally.

Bonfires were lit outside the churches and sometimes a Judas Man burned (the Judas Man was a scapegoat, a Christianized form of the older pagan wicker or straw effigy which represented a community's collective evil). Charred sticks were taken from the fire and placed on newly kindled home fires or kept through the year as protection against thunderstorms. Need fires were also lit when animals were sick. The beasts would be then driven through twin purifying fires. There is a rune called nyd that talks of this inner 'self-kindling flame and represents the inner spark we all have' (see *Norse Magic*, page 375).

PYROMANCY

Pyromancy is the art of divination by fire. Because of its changeable and unpredictable nature, fire was seen as a perfect medium for interpreting omens. In earlier times, sacrificial fires were considered the most potent to study. The future would be promising if a fire burned vigorously and the fuel was quickly consumed. It was also considered a good omen if a sacrificial fire was clear, the flames transparent rather than dark red or yellow and the fire crackled. A fire that burned silently, was difficult to light, blown about by the wind or slow to consume the sacrifice indicated that the coming days and events were not so propitious.

Ordinary people as well as seers divined the success or otherwise of future plans by observing the flames of torches or by throwing powdered pitch on to fires. If the pitch caught and flamed quickly, the outcome of any action would be favourable. The flame of a torch augured well if it formed a point but was less promising of success if it was divided. However, if it did divide, three points were considered best of all. Sickness, financial difficulties or sudden misfortune were foretold by the bending of a flame.

Pyromancy at Home

In the modern world, few believe that portents of great fortune or disaster can be foretold from fire or any other medium. However, fire scrying, both by studying the flames and by reading pictures from the sparks or embers, is a visually evocative way to awaken our inner knowledge and wisdom. As children, many people watched fire fairies in the flames and saw magical kingdoms in the embers. This ability to scry (see pictures) naturally does not disappear but often lies dormant in adult life, blocking a valuable source of intuition and wisdom.

Light a bonfire in the garden or a small open fire in a grate. Sit quietly and watch the flames and let your natural intuitions guide you to the answer to a specific question or in the general direction of your life. You may find the answers come as words, pictures or general impressions. Do not doubt your fire wisdom for it comes from one of the oldest magical traditions.

MODERN PORTENTS

The Flames

If the fire catches immediately and flares upwards, any venture you are planning will take effect swiftly. A fire that is slower to burn may indicate that you need to persevere to get a venture off the ground. If a fire refuses to light, you may need to seek another approach.

If the flames are clear, red and crackle, success and happiness should follow; remain confident and let your inner voice guide you. If the flames are dull, yellowy and silent, you may need to overcome obstacles and opposition. If a fire spits a lot, you may be facing unexpected envy.

If the fuel is quickly consumed, results will not be long in coming. If the fire is slow-burning, there may be delays.

If the flames seem to bend in one direction or are blown by the wind, there may be a lot of pressure on you to conform or confusion created by others. Keep steady and ignore interference or doubts.

If the fire is suddenly extinguished, you may find you have to go it alone, but this should not deter you if an issue is important.

Smoke

Smoke rising directly upwards says that you should aim high. Smoke blowing in one direction suggests that you may have to choose between two courses or people and that one is specially favoured. You can use this as a form of divination in itself, designating different directions for alternative options and being guided by the first direction the smoke takes. Thick, choking smoke means that you must avoid getting diverted from the main issue or avoid making a decision when facts are uncertain or perhaps opinions unreliable. Evenly spread smoke says that you need to balance any conflicting demands rather than choose between them.

Fire Pictures

You may see moving pictures in the constantly flickering flames, maybe houses, boats or people, perhaps one image rapidly succeeding another. See what each image suggests and if they are forming a coherent picture or message. If the picture is incoherent, try to sketch or write down a note of the images very quickly. Look at them just before you go to bed and again as you wake. However unlikely the pictures or story they create, they hold an answer for you.

The glowing embers may offer a more static but just as vivid an image. Let the coals or wood connect to form bridges, islands, perhaps whole towns as they did when you were a child. Use them, but not to tell stories of fairy kingdoms, but a story of the real world that is your own and how it might be enriched.

Ashes

Even the ashes can offer images if you take a scoop full and shake them on black or white paper. The first image you see is the one that is coming from deep within. Do not worry about conventional meanings, although you may wish to look at suggested symbols in *Tea Leaf Reading* (page 425) and *Herb Magic* (page 268). If you see a butterfly, a bird or boat, ask what each means to you, a meaning perhaps that formed in early childhood.

Finally, look at the shape of the fire. Is it a circle of harmony or a square saying that dreams must fit into the here and now and not some remote tomorrow? Is it an irregular shape that may look like an animal or bird, a triangle of new possibilities or a heap, saying that you must build the mountain you wish to climb step by step? Let the shape offer its own message.

If you have any regrets or sorrows that are holding you back, collect your ashes and bury them. Plant an acorn or other seed from a tree in the ground so that new wood will grow.

CANDLE MAGIC

From early times candle magic has formed a powerful focus for fire rituals of all kinds. Undyed yellow beeswax candles were used in pre-Christian and Christian times, for bees were regarded as messengers of the god and were sacred to the Earth Mother and later the Virgin Mary.

Whether you use a virgin beeswax candle or a white kitchen candle, it will carry your wishes and desires to the cosmos where they will rebound, giving you confidence and the determination to succeed. We almost all lit birthday candles as children and, as we blew out the flames, we knew that our wishes would come true. It is no different for adults, just that the certainty has been dimmed a little.

First decide upon your need. Although some people practise candle magic without a specific focus, it works better if it has a purpose.

The Candle of You

You may use any candles you wish but your astrological colour can personalize a candle ritual. As always, there is disagreement as to the correct astrological colours. Even in this book there are variations according to the culture or tradition from which the magic came. The differences are not inconsistencies, for there are no magical certainties or rules set for all times and all places. If a candle colour feels wrong, substitute one that feels right for you. Kate, who attended one of my Inner Magic classes, was a Capricorn, but hated the idea of a black or brown candle. She worked in forestry and green was a natural choice, so she used that quite successfully.

Aries (21 March–20 April): red
Taurus (21 April–21 May): pink
Gemini (22 May–21 June): pale grey
Cancer (22 June–22 July): silver
Leo (23 July–23 August): gold
Virgo (24 August–22 September): green
Libra (23 September–23 October): blue
Scorpio (24 October–22 November): burgundy or indigo
Sagittarius (23 November–21 December): yellow or orange
Capricorn (22 December–20 January): brown or black
Aquarius (21 January–20 February): violet or dark blue
Pisces (21 February–20 March): white

A Birthday Candle Ritual

On your birthday, light your birthday candle when you have a quiet time, either in the morning or before you go to bed. As you light the candle, see your essential self or those qualities you desire expanding and illuminating your being, giving you confidence, empathy and purpose. Circle the candle with small gifts you have bought for yourself, such as tiny crystals, flowers, bath oils and any other gifts or cards you have received. Finally, add photographs of yourself when you were young and as you are now.

Although you are older, see how your beauty has increased with the wisdom and experience of the years and do not look back with regrets, but forward to all those things you still can do.

Write the most important of these unfulfilled desires on a piece of paper the colour of your candle and let the flame burn it slowly, seeing your wish rise upwards and return in a shower of golden sparks or sunbeams to fill you with joy or hope. This will be your year. Let the candle burn down naturally, knowing that the light is now within you.

Zodiacal Candles throughout the Year

You can light a zodiacal candle at any time you need to strengthen your identity or you feel threatened or anxious. Sit in its light for a few minutes, letting pictures come and go as they will. When you are ready, blow out the candle and send that power emanating throughout your being. Often in candle magic we send love and light to others who need it. Today it is for ourselves, for unless we are strong and happy within ourselves, we cannot give to others.

Candle Magic for Love, Success and Happiness

This is most potent on the first day of the new moon, when the crescent is first visible in the sky. You can use a diary or daily newspaper to tell you which is the first day of the new moon (see also *Moon Magic*, page 336).

You may wish to invite a few friends to bring their zodiacal candles and a candle for their wishes (listed below), but candle magic is just as potent alone. You and your friends can sit in a circle on the floor with your zodiacal candles and candles of what you need most. Use any crystals of the same colour you may have to circle the candles. Some people surround the candles with their jewellery and coins as symbols of wealth, with fruit and vegetables as symbols of plenty, tiny dolls if love or fertility is involved, flowers for health and even books if learning is to be done.

Candle Dressing

Dress each candle with an appropriate oil, working in the oil from the bottom to the centre in spiralling anti-clockwise movements and then from the top to the bottom in spiralling clockwise movements.

Begin with your zodiacal candle. As you light each candle, see yourself in the desired situation, the person you are now, with all your strengths and failings, happy and complete. Turn out the light. Visualize golden showers of coins, stars of health, silver hearts of love or a pink shower of sparkling harmony falling upon you and enveloping you in light and happiness. Look long and deep into the candle flames and let images, words, colours or impressions form.

When you are ready, write your wish on a piece of paper of the appropriate colour of your need. Light the paper in the flame of the candle of your need and put it on a saucer. If the paper burns entirely, it is said you will fulfil your wish very soon. If it goes out partially burned, your desire will take longer to come to fruition.

If you are with friends, blow out your candles at a pre-arranged signal, letting their light go to whoever needs it most. You might like to think of absent friends and family who are ill and sad and perhaps softly say their names. If you are with friends, enjoy a simple supper of fruit, vegetables, bread, honey and fruit juice, fruit wine or tea. Use soft lighting and talk of your dreams and plans and do not let any harsh words, however witty, spoil the magic and optimism of the evening. If you are alone, eat a light meal and instead of extinguishing your candle, let it burn quietly away as you dream by it, allowing its visions to flow within you.

Candle Colours for Wishes and Needs

White for any new venture or relationship
Red for fertility, sexual matters and survival issues
Orange for independence, health and confidence
Yellow for career, any creative adventure and for money
Green for love, friendship, family and children
Blue for travel, success in exams and study
Violet or indigo for inner happiness and psychic awareness
Pink for reconciliation, peaceful sleep and inner peace
Brown for home and home moves and any practical matter
Silver for secret dreams and inner wisdom
Gold for ambitious plans, long-term goals and altruism
Black for moving on and accepting others as they are

Zodiacal Oils for Candle Dressing

Most of these oils can be bought easily from a large supermarket, a herbal or New Age shop. They add a new dimension to your natural zodiacal qualities.

Aries: cedarwood and pine. Cedarwood is useful for all matters of the spirit and pine for protection.
Taurus: rose and geranium. Rose is for love and geranium (also known as rose geranium) for fidelity.
Gemini: lavender and lemongrass. Lavender is for harmony and lemongrass for magic.
Cancer: jasmine and sandalwood. Jasmine is for good dreams and sandalwood for sexuality.
Leo: orange flower (neroli) and juniper. Orange flower represents happiness, especially in marriage, and juniper is a protective oil.
Virgo: patchouli and lily. Patcholi is for material success and lily for self-reliance.
Libra: marjoram and magnolia. Marjoram represents insight and magnolia intuitive awareness.
Scorpio: lemon balm and myrrh. Lemon balm is for healing and myrrh for self-exploration.
Sagittarius: rosemary and frankincense. Rosemary enhances memory and frankincense spirituality. Be careful using frankincense unless it is diluted, as it can be a skin irritant.
Capricorn: cypress and vetivert. Cypress represents letting go of the past and vertivert money.
Aquarius: lemon verbena and coriander. Lemon verbena is for romance and coriander for reconciliation.
Pisces: camomile and ylang-ylang. Camomile represents your inner world and ylang-ylang sensuality.

General Oils for Candle Dressing

As well as using the above oils on your zodiacal candle, you can choose one of the oils listed above to complement the purpose of your candle wishes. You can try combining oils for joint properties; for example, orange flower (neroli) mixed with and lemon verbena combines happiness in an established love relationship with a touch of romance.

Moon and Sun Oils for Dressing Your Candle of Need

Moon and sun oils can add either the gentle wisdom of the moon or the power of the sun to your candle wishes.

Any of the moon oils are perfect for candle magic involving love, reconciliation or inner happiness. They include jasmine, lemon balm, myrrh and sandalwood and offer the unconscious wisdom and intuitive awareness of the moon.

Sun oils, such as frankincense, rosemary, orange and cedarwood, offer power and confidence where success or action is needed in the outer world,

Alternatively, explore your local New Age shop or large supermarket and see which oils match your favourite fragrance or personal associations.

Candle Options

If you have two choices, light two candles on a metal tray, using perhaps blue for logic and green for following your heart, red for acting, pink for waiting, white for go and a dark colour for stay. You can choose your colours according to what feels right or use a golden candle for the Yang (action) option and silver for the Yin (wait) option. You can even make it a choice between two people or jobs. Decide whether for you the first candle to go out represents the yes or the no option. It would seem to me that the longer-burning flame stands for the enduring or best choice, but there are no hard-and-fast rules in magic.

As you light each candle, endow the flame with all your hopes and fears about each option. Leave them to burn in your quiet candle place and occupy yourself with pleasant tasks or simply let your mind roam free in the candlelight until the first candle goes out or burns down. Sometimes one may go out very quickly, giving you an almost instant answer. But in more complex issues, the choice may not be so clear.

Wax Divination

Wait until the second candle burns down. Look at the shapes formed by the wax on the tray and let the first image, picture or even words that come into your mind act as a guide. You may find that the wax images give you an entirely different perspective on your choice. You can also use this method with a single coloured candle or a series of them.

19

FLOWER MAGIC

FLOWER FESTIVALS

Flower festivals occur in many countries, especially those of warmer climates where flowers grow abundantly. The festival of Flora, Roman Goddess of Flowers, lasted from 26 April to 3 May. Japan celebrates its main flower festival on 8 April, the birthday of Buddha. Children carry flowers in procession, offering them at tiny temples. Hydrangea and other floral teas are consumed and homes are decked with flowers. This festival is rooted in traditional ancestor worship. In earlier times, family members would go to the hills in spring to bring back the first wild flowers for the family shrine as a sign of regeneration. Flowers are part of major Buddhist, Hindu, Chinese and Japanese celebrations and the dates of the festivals coincide with the time of blossoming of flowers and trees, especially the cherry blossom in Japan.

In Ancient Greece, the Sacred Marriage of Zeus to Hera was celebrated in January, as new life began to bud. Hera, as well as being the chief Mother and Fertility Goddess, guardian of marriage and childbirth, was also Goddess of Flowers. Her statues were decked with lilies, which became part of the bridal bouquet or headdress throughout Western Europe and the Mediterranean.

FLOWER LEGENDS

In classical myth, many flowers were said to have divine origins, emanating either from the blood of the slain or from the tears of spurned lovers. Other flowers have associations with the fairy folk.

Carnation

The carnation is called the flower of rejoicing because it was first seen, according to legend, in Bethlehem at the birth of Christ. Because it was believed that carnations grew spontaneously on the graves of lovers, the flowers became associated with funerals.

The carnation is used for divination in parts of the Far East. A cluster of three carnations on a single stem is placed in the hair of a young person and left there until the flowers begin to wilt. If the top flower dies first, it is said the later years of the wearer's life will be hardest. If the middle flower dies first, the middle years will be more difficult. If the bottom flower dies first, the earlier years will be more problematic. If the flowers remain fresh for a long time, life will be happy throughout.

Carnations are also associated with Mother's Day, especially in the United States. In 1908 Anna Jarvis, who lived in West Virginia, instigated the first Mother's Day service on the second Sunday in May. She took carnations to the service as they had been her mother's favourite flowers.

Daisy/Marguerite

The daisy was said to spring from the tears of Mary Magdalene at the crucifixion and was traditionally known as 'the day's eye' or 'God's smile'. This was because the flower opened with the sun in the morning and closed at night.

Medieval knights wore daisies when they went into battle as a sign that they rode in the name of a lady whom they loved. A knight wearing a double-headed daisy affirmed that the love was reciprocated. The daisy, a flower of Venus, is the most commonly used for love divination, as lovers pluck the petals chanting, 'He/she loves me, he/she loves me not'. It is said to be a talisman for all who are pure of heart and loyal in love. A daisy root can bring back an absent lover if placed under a pillow at night.

Forget-me-not

This is a symbol of undying love as well as lasting friendship. In Austrian legend, a man and his betrothed were walking hand in hand beside the Danube River on the night before their wedding. A small blue flower was being carried away by the current and the woman began to weep that so lovely a flower should be lost forever. Unable to bear her sorrow, he leaped into the water to save the flower, but was swept away. In a last heroic gesture, he cast the flower on to the bank with the words: 'Forget me not, my love.'

Foxglove

This is a flower of the fairy folk and when a foxglove bows its head, it is a sign that a fairy is passing by. It is very lucky if grown in a garden from seed. It must never be transplanted since it may be home for a fairy and for this reason should only be picked after asking permission from the 'little people'.

Heather

White rather than purple heather is considered the luckiest, perhaps because it is quite rare in the wild. It is said that if a person comes upon white heather growing naturally, he or she can pick it and any wish that is made will come true.

Heather was associated with Celtic magic and divination. In Celtic legend, when Oscar, son of Ossian the renowned Irish Bard and warrior hero of the third century, lay dying on the battlefield at Ulster, he sent his true love Malvina a sprig of purple heather. As she heard the message of love carried by a faithful messenger, her tears fell on the flower, which turned pure white. Since that time white heather has represented eternal love.

Hyacinth

This blue, pink or purple spring flower bears the name of Hyacinthus, son of Amyclas, King of Sparta. Hyacinthus was loved by Apollo. However, Zephyr, the West Wind, became jealous of their happiness and as they were playing quoits, Zephyr blew Apollo's quoit off course. The quoit struck Hyacinthus and he died. His blood fell as a lovely pink hyacinth, which thereafter represented sorrow and love lost.

Lotus

The lotus has been a sacred plant in many cultures, including Ancient Egypt and the Orient. In Hindu tradition, a golden lotus brought forth the God Brahma. It also symbolizes the Buddha in both India and China. In Japan it is the motif of Paradise.

Many water lilies are called lotus, but the true lotus is the *Nelumbium lutem*. The lotus was also regarded as a symbol of fertility in Ancient Egypt and used for wreaths which decorated the brow of Isis. Used on wallcoverings in homes, the lotus is said to bring health and domestic happiness to all who live in the house.

Lily

Lilies were dedicated to all maiden goddesses, especially Diana. It is a symbol of purity and in the classical world was said to spring from the milk of Hera herself.

In Catholic countries, the lily is associated with the Virgin Mary and was the flower of St Catherine who converted her father Emperor Costis by means of the Madonna lily. It was said that the lily had no perfume until, at Catherine's prayers, it gave forth a wondrous scent as proof that Christ was Lord.

Lily of the Valley

The lily of the valley was created by Eve's tears as she was expelled from the garden of Eden. According to Irish tradition, lilies of the valley form ladders that fairies can climb to reach the reeds from which they plait their cradles.

According to early legend, St Leonard was wounded while fighting a dragon and tiny lilies grew on the spot where his blood fell. Another legend says that the first lily of the valley loved the nightingale, but because she was so shy, she hid in the long grass to listen to his song. The nightingale became lonely and at last said he would no longer sing, unless the lily of the valley bloomed every May for all to see. Now when the moonlight shines upon the delicate white bells, the nightingale sings his sweetest and the returning song of her tiny bells can be heard in the stillness.

The flowers are still called 'Our Lady's tears' in Britain and parts of Europe, for they are reputed to be Mary's tears for the sorrows of the world.

Marigold

These are said to be flowers of the sun and bloom all year, like the sun opening their petals at dawn and closing them only when dusk falls. Marigolds are named after the Virgin Mary who wore them as her special flower. More generally the marigold is not a happy flower in the language of flowers and is often mixed with other flowers to mean sunshine as well as showers.

Narcissus

In Ancient Greece, the youth Narcissus, son of Cephisus, so admired his own beauty that he gazed constantly at his own image in a pool and ignored those who sought to win his affection, not least the young nymph Echo who called him in vain. One day, reaching out to embrace his reflection, he slipped into the deep still waters and drowned. A single Narcissus, the white daffodil-like flower, tinged red in the centre for the nymph's pierced heart, was found floating on the surface of the water by Echo. To this day her voice calls her lost love in rocks and hollow places, especially near water. An alternative legend tells that Narcissus was gazing into a fountain and thought the image he saw in the water was the nymph of the fountain. As he reached to embrace the lovely youth, he was drowned.

Rose

The rose is the most magical flower of all. It is said in Christian tradition to have first appeared in Bethlehem near the site of the stable. During the early centuries of the first millennium, a young Christian was sentenced to be burned at the stake. She prayed to God for help and golden, glowing angels turned the fire into yellow and red roses. She was freed and many pagans were converted to Christianity.

Sunflower
The water nymph Clytie was so sad that her love for Helios, the Greek Sun God, was not returned that she sat on the ground day and night, watching his fiery chariot pass across the sky as the sun rose, reached its height and descended into the ocean. She watched for so long that her limbs became rooted in the earth and she was transformed into a sunflower, symbol of constancy. Her gaze is forever fixed sunwards as she climbs towards her love, but she must die each year and let new seeds fall.

Violet
The Thracian poet and musician Orpheus had charmed Pluto, God of the Underworld, with his music, into returning his dead wife Euridyce to life. But Orpheus was told that he must not turn round to see whether she was following when they left Hades together. As he was about to put his feet on the earth, Orpheus turned momentarily and Euridyce vanished forever. The second loss was more than Orpheus could bear.

Eventually he was torn to pieces by Thracian women who were angry at his continuing grief and indifference to their beauty. Where his lyre lay, the first violet bloomed, embodiment of pure love. The lyre was taken by Zeus and placed among the stars and the violet has been dedicated to Orpheus ever since.

Another myth tells how Jupiter fell in love with Io, the priestess of Juno, and turned her into a white heifer, to escape the anger of Juno. He created fields of white violets for her to eat as she wandered the Earth.

THE LANGUAGE OF FLOWERS

The language of flowers was popularized in the nineteenth century, but was formalized as a system of communication, especially between lovers, in the early eighteenth century. The English author Lady Mary Wortley Montagu was living with her ambassador husband in Turkey at this time and discovered the hidden meanings that could be concealed in a bouquet of flowers.

However, the language of flowers was used by the Ancient Egyptians, the Chinese, Indians and Ancient Greeks. During the time of Elizabeth I in England, flower meanings appeared in verse and Shakespearean plays: gilliflowers as symbols of gentleness, cowslips of wise counsel, pansies for thoughts, the flowering rosemary for remembrance and marigolds for married love.

Bouquets containing floral messages were a safe and secret way of sending loving thoughts, a promise or offer, warning or instruction even across language barriers. Many of the flowers can be found around the world, but you can easily adapt the flora of your environment. White flowers often indicated innocence or secrecy, red love or passion and yellow warnings or jealousy. Delicate colours indicate gentler emotions or wishes than brilliant hues. Spring flowers can talk of new hopes, summer blooms of high passion or fulfilled love, while autumn blooms speak of waning or gentler affections. A full-petalled flower represents an intense emotion while a small flower can indicate uncertainty. A tall flower talks of lofty ambitions or spiritual desires, while a flower that grows close to the ground or folded can show affection, friendship or uncertainty.

There are many variations in flower meanings and sometimes the reasons for the associations have been lost. Those listed below combine several systems where meanings are fairly consistent. If flowers have special meanings for you or someone close, use your own personal interpretation. It is quite possible to send floral messages using wild flowers, garden flowers or blossom or even silk flowers.

Flower Meanings

The first meaning is the general sentiment behind the flower and the second longer phrase is the actual message contained by each flower. Many of the meanings centre around love and friendship, but can be adapted to other fields.

Acacia: friendship. 'I value our friendship very much.'

Almond blossom: unwelcome advances. 'Your attentions are displeasing to me.'

Anemones: anticipation. 'I hope to see you very soon.'

Apple blossom: admiration. 'You are both beautiful and worthy of respect.'

Azalea: caution. 'Be careful we are not seen together.'

Bee-orchid: misunderstanding. 'Forgive me. You misunderstood my words.'

Begonia: warning. 'We must hide our love. We are being watched.'

Bluebell: constancy. 'I will be faithful to you.'

Broom/gorse: devotion. 'My only aim is to make you happy.'

Bulrush: discretion. 'Be more subtle in your approach.'

Buttercup: riches. 'All I own I will share with you.'

Camellia: courage. 'Be brave in adversity.'
Campion: love after dark. 'Meet me at dusk.'
Carnation (pink): encouragement. 'Thank you for your token/ message. It was welcome.'
Carnation (red): intense love. 'I must see you very soon. Your absence is too painful to bear.'
Carnation (striped): refusal. 'I cannot see you again.'
Carnation (white): affection. I have fond feelings for you.'
Carnation (yellow): disdain. 'You have proved unworthy of my affection.'
Cherry blossom: growth. 'May our love grow a little each day.'
Chrysanthemum (brown): friendship. 'Let us still be friends, even if love has faded.'
Chrysanthemum (red): passion. 'I love and desire you.'
Chrysanthemum (yellow): discouragement. 'My heart belongs to another.'
Chrysanthemum (white): truth. 'I will never lie to you.'
Clover: fortune. 'May luck and health shine on you.'
Cornflower: delicacy. 'I am vulnerable, so be gentle with my feelings.'
Crocus: youthful gladness. 'You make me feel young again.'
Cyclamen: protection. 'I will keep you from all harm.'
Daffodil: regrets. 'I am sorry. Can we try again?'
Dahlia: instability. 'Your changing moods make me uncertain how to approach you.'
Daisy (field): innocence. 'You are my first real love.'
Daisy (double): mutual love. 'Your love is reciprocated.'
Daisy (Michelmas): parting. 'It is better we do not meet again.'
Dandelion: the oracle. 'The future is ours.'
Evening primrose: inconstancy. 'Your love is not for me alone.'
Ferns: meetings. 'Meet me.'
Flax: appreciation. 'Thank you for your kindness.'
Forget-me-not: remembrance. 'Do not forget our love.'
Geranium (dark): melancholy. 'I am sad.'
Geranium (pink): uncertainty. 'Please explain your intentions.'
Geranium (red): choice. 'I choose you rather than any other.'
Grasses: submission. 'I accept the way things must be.'
Harebell: hope. 'I hope you may change your mind.'
Hibiscus: gentle beauty. 'Your gentle nature is matched only by your beauty.'
Hollyhock: fertility. 'May our love bear fruit.'
Hollyhock (white): ambition. 'I want to succeed.'
Honeysuckle: commitment. 'Accept this token of my love.'
Hyacinth: lost love. 'I regret our separation.'

Hydrangea: inconstancy. 'Why have you changed your mind?'
Iris: communication. 'I need to see you soon. I have a message I must give you.'
Jasmine (Africa): dreams of love. 'I see you in my dreams.'
Jasmine (US): reunion in dreams. 'We may be separated but we are together in my dreams.'
Jasmine (Europe): dreams of desire. 'I desire you night and day.'
Jasmine (India and Asia): reunion. 'Our dreams of being together will come true.'
Jonquil: appeal. 'Please answer my question.'
Lavender: love returned. 'I love you too.'
Lilac: the first stirrings of love. 'You have awakened new emotions in me.'
Lily: purity. 'My love for you is spiritual.'
Lily of the valley: return of happiness. 'I had to go away, but I will come back soon.'
Marigold: unhappiness. 'Your jealousy is destroying our relationship.'
Mimosa: sensitivity. 'I understand your feelings.'
Orange blossom: chastity. 'I seek a permanent commitment.'
Orchid: abundance. 'You will want for nothing with me.'
Pansies: fond memories. 'Remember the happy times we spent together.'
Passion flower: spiritual love. 'We are twin souls.'
Peony: forgiveness. 'Please forgive me for my insensitivity.'
Poppy: sleep. 'Life will seem better tomorrow.'
Roses (as part of a bridal bouquet): lasting happiness. 'Our love will last forever.'
Rose (Carolina): love with danger. 'Our liaison will arouse anger in others.'
Rose (pink): shyness. 'I am afraid to show my feelings.'
Rose (red): love. 'I love you with all my heart.'
Rose (white): silence. 'Our love must remain a secret.'
Rose (wild): distant admiration. 'I love you from afar.'
Rose (yellow): envy. 'I am jealous.'
Snapdragon: rejection. 'You mean nothing to me now.'
Snowdrop: consolation. 'At least we have each other.'
Star of Bethlehem: mending quarrels. 'Can we forget the harsh words we spoke?'
Sunflower: obsession with money. 'You cannot buy my love.'
Tulip (mixed colours): beauty. 'Your eyes hold my soul.'
Tulip (red): declaration of love. 'I want to tell the world how much I love you.'
Tulip (yellow): unrequited love. 'Do you not care for me at all?'

Verbena: enchantment. 'You have cast a spell over me.'
Violet: trust. 'I will not betray your trust.'
Wallflower: faithfulness in misfortune. 'I will love you in sad times as well as happy ones.'
Ylang-ylang: euphoria. 'I am intoxicated with joy.'

Using the Language of Flowers

You may wish to begin by sending a bunch of a single kind of flower or even a single flower, for example daffodils (regrets) after a disagreement or lily of the valley if you have to go away from a loved one.

Bluebells can promise faithfulness. A single cyclamen bloom would promise 'I will keep you from all harm', while an iris would convey, 'I need to see you soon'. At first you may wish to enclose a small note reaffirming the sentiments of the particular flower or telephone shortly after the flowers are received. After a while you can share the language with close friends and loved ones and even create a floral system of agreed meanings to fit with the local flora (useful if a relationship is secret).

Seasonal Variations

The modern world has helped the language of flowers. With the improvements in communication and hot-house cultivation, many flowers have long seasons so it is possible to combine what are traditionally spring and summer or even autumn flowers and to obtain tropical flowers all the year round, even in cooler climates. Lavender once grew mainly in mountainous regions around the Mediterranean but now appears naturally in almost all parts of the world.

You do not need to send complicated messages; two or three different kinds of flowers can express a wealth of sentiment. It is better to buy the individual flowers yourself and make up your own bouquet, as florists may substitute different species or colours. For example lilies and orchids can offer the double reassurance: 'My love is spiritual but with me you will want for nothing in worldly terms.' Even the most impoverished lovers can send messages. Daisies, dandelions and buttercups tied with twine can promise: 'You are my first love and your love is reciprocated, the future is ours and what I have is yours.'

Giving Flowers in Person

The way a flower is given can also convey a wealth of meaning. Roses are most commonly used in this way, but any flower with a thorn or leaves attached can be used. A single rose on a plain stem offered flower uppermost shows positive hopes and intentions. A rosebud surrounded by thorns and leaves offered upright conveys uncertainty that love is returned.

If the recipient inverts the rosebud and hands it back, he or she is equally uncertain but not entirely rejecting the overture. If, however, the recipient removes the thorns and returns the rosebud upright, he or she is saying that there is true feeling. However, if the leaves are removed, there is no hope of the love progressing.

Secret Trysts

Even if there is no need for secrecy, it can be fun to pass messages of which no one else is aware, using prearranged floral symbols. The white rose is the sign of secrecy and confidentiality so if you include a white rose, the recipient knows that you want to keep the meeting quiet.

There are various ways of conveying time, but simplicity avoids possible mistakes. 'Meet me' or 'do not meet me' can be conveyed by an iris (inverted for do not meet me) or by a green fern (meeting) or other long grass or rush on a separate stem for counting. The first fern given is either upright or inverted according to whether the meeting will or will not take place. The rest of the ferns are upright and the total (including the first) should be counted to give the day. One fern means today, two means tomorrow and so on through the days of the week.

You can even be specific about time by adding small many-headed flowers for the hours (using the 24-hour clock). You can adapt any of these methods to fit with the flora in your area or create your own meanings according to your personal choice. In the language of flowers there are few rigid definitions and it has always been a system used in a very personal way.

FLOWER DIVINATION

This was one of the earliest forms of divination. Young lovers would go out into the meadows or hills and pluck petals. The last petal answers the question, 'She loves me/not, he will/will not be true'.

The method could also be used for any option such as go or stay or act or wait.

The Dandelion Seed Clock Oracle

This can be used to calculate time. Use dandelions that are long-stemmed and full of seed-clocks (some say these are full of fairies but gardeners think them the very devil). Ask your time question, 'When will I be married/have a new job/improve my financial situation?' Decide in advance the time scale, whether weeks are more realistic than days. Blow gently and repeat the question between each blow. Watch your oracle fairies carrying your wishes for happiness, love or success to the skies and feel your own mounting optimism. When your seed clock is empty and you have released all the wish fairies, mark in your diary, the week indicated by the oracle clock and begin to work towards achieving your goal. Magic always benefits from earthly effort.

Choices with Roses

If you have to choose between two people or two options, buy two identical rosebuds that are entirely closed. Place them side by side in two narrow glasses or vases, add the same amount of water and leave them in the light but not direct sunlight. Under each vase place the name of a person or option, written on green or pink paper for love, blue for career or travel, or yellow for communication and learning. The first rosebud to reach full bloom gives you the correct choice.

However, if the roses bloom at identical times, watch the way that they fade. It may be that one sheds its petals almost instantly, while the other lasts a long time. It may be that one option would bring instant happiness or success while the second option, although slower to come to fruition or involving a less exciting person, may offer long-term security.

He/She Loves Me/Loves Me Not

Rather than using daisies, choose a larger flower with many petals, such as a chrysanthemum. Ask a question involving two options or people and as you say out loud 'yes' then 'no' for each petal plucked, visualize yourself happy, complete and strong, regardless of the choice you make. That way your conscious mind will not intervene. If you pick two petals at once, count that as one 'yes' or 'no'.

MAGICAL FLOWER RITUALS

In Eastern Europe, it was believed that if you took the soil from beneath a lover or potential lover's shoe print and put it in a pot with marigold seeds, the love would bloom with the flowers and last like the flower winter and summer.

You can also plant a rose on a special love anniversary or the birth of a child, red for a boy and white for a girl, and as it blooms each year be reminded of the feelings of that first moment.

20

FOOD MAGIC

THE ORIGINS OF FOOD MAGIC

Food as a sustainer of life became an early symbol of magic. Writing wishes on food was believed to endow the eater with the power of the wish. Writing 'Happy Birthday' on a cake in edible paste dates back to Ancient Greece and the worship of Artemis, Goddess of the Moon. Her birth date was celebrated with moon-shaped honey cakes with candles on top. Because tradition said that bad spirits were attracted to celebrations, it was important to wish the person a happy birthday, blow out the candles and then eat the wishes inscribed on the cake.

Hot cross buns predate Christianity by many centuries. The buns marked with the old astrological cross, symbol of the earth, were eaten at the spring equinox (see *Seasonal Magic*, page 398), so offering the protection of the Earth Mother and promising a summer of plenty. In Christian tradition, hot cross buns made on Good Friday were said to keep fresh all year and were hung in sailors' homes and churches near the sea to keep sailors from drowning.

The Christmas pudding, originally a semi-liquid concoction, was eaten at the mid-winter solstice (see *Christmas Magic*, page 75) in Western Europe as it contained all the fruits and grains of the Earth and, because of the coins and charms placed in it, the metals of the Earth. Stirring the pudding on Stir Pudding Day, the last Sunday before Advent in the Christian tradition, ensured that the family would have enough money during the winter. The stirring was carried out by all the family, starting with the youngest, each stirring the mixture nine times clockwise.

MAGICAL FEASTS

Feasts were an integral part of both public and private celebrations, whether for birth, initiation, marriage or death. At festivals of the dead, such as Hallowe'en, held on 31 October in Europe and North America and the Festival of Bon, celebrated in August in Japan (see *Hallowe'en Magic*, page 260), favourite foods of deceased family members would be provided should their ghosts return.

Wedding Cakes

In many cultures, the centrepiece of the wedding feast or breakfast is the cake. Such cakes date back to Roman times when the couple would eat a cake made of flour, water and salt to ensure that they should never suffer poverty.

Gradually the cakes became richer, although it was not until the seventeenth century that ornamentation was added. The rich contents indicate the good things of life. The bride cuts the cake to ensure her fertility. Everyone must eat a piece to strengthen the fertility magic and pieces are sent to absent friends. An unmarried girl would pass a crumb of her piece of cake through a wedding ring three times before putting it under her pillow. She would then dream of her own husband. A bride would keep a piece to ensure her husband remained faithful and a tier is often kept for the christening of her first child.

In earlier times, the cake plate was broken over the bride's head at the wedding as a symbol of her husband's authority and the number of large fragments were said to indicate the number of children she would bear.

MOTHERING SUNDAY CAKE

Simnel cakes were baked for Mothering Sunday. Simnel is the finest part of the flour. The traditional simnel cake, called Marchpane in medieval times, with its balls of golden marzipan, was a reminder that the golden sun was increasing in power. It is said that the first simnel cake was created and named after its creators, Simon and Nell who could not agree whether the cake should be baked or boiled and so did both. The English poet Robert Herrick, who lived at the beginning of the seventeenth century, wrote:

I'll to thee a Simnell bring
Gainst thou go'st a mothering,
So that when she blesseth thee,
Half that blessing thou'lt give me

The simnel cake is also associated with Easter and especially with Easter Sunday. The yellow marzipan cake circle represents the Risen Christ (Sun or Light of the World) and the eleven silver balls represent the Apostles who were faithful.

PANCAKE DAY

Celebrated in Catholic Europe and the United States, Shrove Tuesday, or *Mardi Gras* as it is called in France, began as the day on which good Christians would go to confess their sins and be forgiven or shriven before the 40 days of Lent. The pancakes were intended to stave the hunger of the faithful while they waited for the shriving bell to call them to church.

In Britain, the day before Shrove Tuesday was called Collop Monday. Then the meat which was forbidden over Lent was used up in collops or patties made with eggs and bread. Tuesday's pancakes, much richer and tastier than those of today, used up the rest of the honey, fat and other little luxuries not allowed during Lent.

In 1620, the English poet Taylor wrote in his *Jacke-a-Lente* a fierce criticism of the carnival, which he notes began with the ringing of a bell called the pancake-bell whose sound 'makes thousands of people distracted and forgetful of either manners or humanitie'.

> 'Then there is a thing called wheaten flour which the cooks do mingle with water, eggs, spice and other tragical, magical enchantments and then they put it by little and little into a frying pan of boiling suet where it makes a confused dismal hissing . . . until at last by the skill of the cook it is transformed into the form of a Flip-jack, called a pancake, which ominous incantation the people do devour very greedily.'

The pancake eating was followed by a festival described by Bishop Hall in his *Triumphs of Rome*: 'Every man cries *Sciolta*, letting himself loose to the maddest of merriments, marching wildly up and down in all forms of disguises; each man striving to outdo each other in strange pranks of humorous debauchedness, in which even those of the holy order are wont to be allowed their share. For howsoever it was forbidden by some sullen authority to clerks and votaries of any kind to go masked and disguised in those seeming abusive festivities, yet more favourable construction hath offered to make them believe that it was chiefly for their sakes, for the refreshment of their sadder and more restrained spirits that this free and lawless festivity was taken up.'

In the evening children would go from door to door begging and singing verses such as:

Beef and bacon's
Out of season

I want a pan to
Parch my peas on.

Then they would hurl sticks and stones at the doors which were shut against them. The worst offenders were the apprentices in London.

Tradition says that if you eat pancakes on Shrove Tuesday and grey peas on Ash Wednesday, you will have money in your purse all the year.

HARVEST FESTIVALS

The gathering of the harvest tended to be more restrained in its merrymaking. The deities to whom the feast was dedicated would eat the essence of the feast and look kindly on the needs of the people through the winter. This harvest could be grain crops, yams, fruit or the first catch of hunting or fishing.

Harvest festivals developed from the ancient and universal festivals of the first fruits, offerings that were dedicated or sacrificed to the deities or spirits of the harvest. This was called 'offering the soul of the crop' and was especially important in societies that revered the Corn Spirit who was cut down as the last sheaf of corn. This practice goes back to Ancient Egypt and beyond. Even today at Lammas (or Loaf-masse) in the Christian church, the first loaf, baked from the last corn to be cut, is offered on the altar at the end of July (see *Seasonal Magic*, page 398).

MAGICAL COOKERY

Astrological Associations

Food magic can be linked to the astrological signs. You can eat the foods and spices of your birth sun sign to strengthen your resolve and confidence. You could also choose to eat the food associated with a sign whose qualities you need at a particular time, perhaps adding a food of Leo for courage or a Libran food for even-handedness.

If you are planning a romantic meal, you can combine the foods of your own star sign with that of your loved one. You could perhaps set the table with your appropriate zodiac candle (see *Fire Magic*, page 211) and have napkins and place settings using your sun sign colours (see *Colour Magic*, page 87).

How to Use Astrological Foods

For the strengths of your own sign, try to include at least three foods or spices from your zodiacal foods in a meal with several different items. If you are having a snack, eat one of your zodiacal foods and add nothing else to strengthen your identity and unique qualities. You can use the sun sign foods as ingredients in recipes or separately and so long as your zodiacal ingredients predominate, either by weight or kind, the effect is there. For example a slice of bread would be made from mainly wheat and so is a Taurean food, although there are other ingredients.

To borrow the strength of another sign, use two or three of these foods or spices and again make sure the chosen food/foods predominate by weight or number.

With ingenuity, you can create meals almost entirely of the appropriate foods. However, the easiest way is to use a single herb in your cooking for your astrological strength or combine two for love. For example, a pudding combining the spices ginger and cinnamon would bring a Cancerian and Leo into close harmony.

Aries (21 March–20 April)
For determination. Red meat, especially lamb and mutton. Strong-tasting food, such as goat's milk and cheese, onions, leeks, hops and capers. Hot spices such as cayenne pepper and mustard, also tarragon and horseradish.

Taurus (21 April–21 May)
For patience. Wheat and its products, lentils and chick peas (also called garbanzo beans), fruits such as apples, pears, plums, grapes, figs, mushrooms, artichokes and asparagus. Herbs such as lovage, marsh mallow, mint and thyme.

Gemini (22 May–21 June)
For adaptability. Hazel nuts, soya products, buckwheat, carrots, vegetables which grow above the ground except for cabbages, cream and butter. Herbs and spices include caraway, black and white pepper and sweet marjoram.

Cancer (22 June–22 July)
For hidden talents. Milk, white fish, fruits and vegetables with a high water content, white and red cabbage, pineapples and kiwi fruits. Herbs and spices include ginger, rosehips, lemon verbena, sea salt, and nettles.

Leo (23 July–23 August)

For courage. Honey, salmon, mullet, sweet corn, olives, and green vegetables with a high iron content, such as spinach, kale and watercress. Oranges and bananas. Herbs and spices include angelica, coriander, chamomile, cinnamon, saffron and rosemary.

Virgo (24 August–22 September)

For attention to detail. Almonds and nuts of all varieties, except hazel. Potatoes, rye, corn, oats, turnips, rice, swedes (also called rutabaga) and all vegetables grown under the earth. Herbs include fennel, parsley, savory and dill.

Libra (23 September–23 October)

For even-handedness. White meat, tomatoes, beans, yams, marrows, sweet potatoes and all autumn fruits and berries. Mangoes, pumpkins and squash. Herbs include sorrel, mint, thyme and vanilla.

Scorpio (24 October–22 November)

For penetrating vision. Sharp pungent food, curries, red, green and yellow peppers, rhubarb, anchovies, hops, bass, mackerel and lobster. Herbs and spices include garlic, basil and vinegar and soy sauce.

Sagittarius (23 November–21 December)

For focused action. Game, bulb vegetables, aubergines (eggplants), celery, figs, sultanas, raisins and other dried fruits, mulberries, blueberries, cranberries, and grapefruit. Herbs include arrowroot, basil, chervil, chicory and parsley.

Capricorn (22 December–20 January)

For perseverance. Beets, barley, sloes (for gin), starchy foods, such as pasta, and flat unleavened breads, such as pitta and naan, quinces. Herbs and spices include oregano, paprika, celery salt, and bouquet garni.

Aquarius (21 January–18 February)

For independence. Lemons and limes, cheese, airy foods, such as mousse, ice cream and meringues, seeds such as pumpkin, sesame and sunflower, seed cakes and breads. Herbs and spices include allspice, aniseed, chives and sweet cicely.

Pisces (19 February–20 March)
For hidden awareness. Eggs, waffles, prawns, shrimps, mussels, rainbow trout, squid, lettuce, sugary foods, watercress, melons. Spices and herbs include nutmeg, sage, all chutneys and cloves.

MAGICAL FOODS

Certain foods have had magical associations throughout the ages and have rituals attached to them. You may like to try some of these old rituals or use the food or fruit as a symbol of a particular energy or area of focus.

Apples: Love and Good Health

Apples are quite unfairly regarded as the fruit of the temptress, the fruit that Eve took from the Tree of Knowledge, although the apple is not named specifically in the Bible. Legend has it that all the apples of paradise grew a bite on one side to commemorate the bite taken by Eve.

An apple led to the Trojan War, according to Greek myth. Eris, Goddess of Discord, angry because she had not been invited to the wedding of sea goddess Thetis and the human Peleus, crept in and threw a golden apple between the goddesses Hera, Athene and Aphrodite. She said the most beautiful of them should have it. The divine beauty contest was judged by Paris, son of the King of Troy. Aphrodite, goddess of love, promised him the most beautiful woman in the world if he chose her as the most beautiful goddess.

Paris could not resist such a bribe and Aphrodite helped him to abduct Helen, wife of the Greek King Menelaeus. Hera and Athene were so angry that they helped the Greeks in the Trojan War and brought about the downfall of Paris and the destruction of Troy. From this connection came the use of apples (see also *Love Magic*, page 289) to divine one's future love.

To Find Your True Love's Name
Peel an apple and twist the peel for each letter of the alphabet. The letter of the alphabet you have got to when the peel breaks is the initial of the first name of your future love.

It is said that lovers can also discover whom they will marry by twisting the stalk of an apple and going through the alphabet, a letter for each twist. The letter reached when the stalk comes off is the initial of the first name of the future spouse.

To find the initial of the second name, tap the apple with the stalk, going through the alphabet once more, until the stalk pierces the skin of the apple.

To Find if a Lover is True

A traditional method involves throwing apple pips or pits on to a fire while chanting:

If you love me, pop and fly
If you hate me, lay and die.

A loved one is named. If the pip bursts open with a crack, it is proof of love. If it burns quietly, then there is no real affection on the part of the named person. If there is more than one suitor, you can throw several apples pips on the fire at once, naming each one and the first to crack gives the name of your true love.

Finding a New Love

A traditional method involves flicking an apple pip or pit with thumb and forefinger while chanting:

Kernel come,
Kernel hop over my thumb
And tell me which way
My true love will come.
East West North or South
Kernel jump into my true love's mouth.

Where the pip lands shows the direction from which your future love will come.

Some people flick the pips on to a map and then visit the town or even country on which the pip landed in the hope of finding true love.

American Apples

The profusion of apple trees in the United States is credited to Johnny Appleseed, an American religious eccentric born in 1774, who for 48 years roamed the frontiers of North America with a sack of apple seeds, planting apple trees and creating orchards.

Apples and Health

Iduna, Norse Goddess of Youth, kept the Viking gods and goddesses young with her magical golden apples. For this reason, apples are often associated with health and long life.

One of the most potent and simple symbols for family health is a bowl of apples on the table. Apples are also a token of fertility not only in producing children, but also bringing plans to fruition.

Beans

Beans, hung on a necklace are believed in many cultures to protect children from all harm. Romans threw beans on to the fire to keep away ghosts. In Ancient Egypt, beans were placed in tombs as a symbol of immortality. Beans recently discovered in tombs more than 3,000 years old have produced shoots once they are restored to the light.

When you have suffered a reversal or lost confidence in yourself, plant a bean in a pot, using soil on which you have made an imprint with your shoe. This imprint technique is also used with marigolds, grown in the footprint of a lover. As you plant the bean, bury all your sorrows and fears. Each day, water your bean and see new life being poured into it. Place your pot in the sunlight and feel your own optimism stirring. Transfer your bean to the garden when it is strong and watch it grow and eventually flower. By this time you, too, will be strong and confident.

Bread

Bread was regarded in all societies as a gift from the gods and so should never be cut, only broken. Grace before meals was traditionally said over bread.

If you eat the last piece of bread or cake uninvited, it is said that you will die unwed. However, it is considered lucky to toss the last piece of bread and reach for it. Two people reaching for the same piece of bread means company is coming. If you are offered the last piece at a stranger's table, you will marry a fine-looking spouse with an income equal in thousands to the number of people at the table. On the other hand, if you toast bread on a knife, you'll be poor all your life.

Bread Wishes

Bake a loaf or some bread rolls. You can use bread mixture if you are in a hurry or do not enjoy cooking. Use the time your bread is rising to rest in the sunshine or sit quietly by a fire. Many of the old bread and cake making rituals, such as the Christmas Eve dumb-cakes (see *Christmas Magic*, page 75), are carried out in silence to allow visions to form. Let pictures of your real needs come and make your wishes.

When your bread is ready to cook, place a dough image of what you most desire on top or write the initial of your wish or even the person you desire. When the bread is cooked, eat it while warm and as you consume the image of your wishes, remember the magical belief that eating your wishes endows you with the power to make them come true.

Corn

Corn is symbolic of the Corn God of the ancient fertility religions and is also associated with the Great Mother in the Native American Indian tradition. It is said that a golden-haired squaw, one of the guises of the Mother, came to a warrior in a dream and ordered him to burn a grass-covered prairie. He was then to drag her by the hair across the burning fields and pause at regular intervals. Each time he stopped, ears of corn grew and on each one tufts of the squaw's hair sprouted. The golden tufts of corn are said to remind the people not only in America, but all over the world that Mother Earth will nourish them.

A Corn Ritual for Plenty

Corn dollies or Corn knots, tied with red ribbon, are believed to bring fortune to a house. If you cannot buy one, make a simple shape from the corn cut at Lammas (the end of July) or the first corn harvest in your part of the world. Hang your corn knot over the fireplace and on the first day of spring, scatter the seeds on to the fields or open land and bury the doll or knot.

Eggs

Eggs were the symbol of the cosmic egg and so were regarded as fertility tokens. They have been connected with life, birth and hope from early times. At Easter time, in the Northern magical tradition, the first eggs of spring were painted and placed on the altar of Ostara, Goddess of Spring.

This was the origin of the Easter Egg as a symbol of new life (see also *Seasonal Magic*, page 398, and *Fertility Magic*, page 199) for egg rituals to conceive a child. In earlier days, the egg yolk was believed to represent the solar deity and the white of the egg the White Goddess who carried within her the embryo of new life.

The gift of eggs to the mother and child brought health and good fortune to a new infant.

It was considered a good omen if an egg broke when dropped and also lucky to crush the shell of a boiled egg after it was eaten. Eggs should, however, never be taken out of a house after dark or the fertility and fortune would leave with them.

Blue-tinged eggs are lucky for lovers and brown eggs mean happiness. Pure white eggs symbolized money, speckled eggs travel and green- or yellow-tinged eggs quarrels and jealousy.

An Egg Ritual for Prosperity

Place a coin of the highest denomination inside half a pure white eggshell that has been carefully divided when the new moon is first visible in the sky. Leave it open on the window ledge day and night until you can see the full moon. Then place the top half of your eggshell on top of the coin, wrap the eggshell and money in a dark scarf and leave it in a drawer until the moon has disappeared from the sky.

On the first crescent, take out the coin, bow three times to the moon and begin any money-making schemes with confidence. You may find money comes unexpectedly, but it is always as well to assist magic with earthly endeavour, so that your wishes are fulfilled in the real world.

Nuts

Nuts of all kinds, especially hazel nuts, are common fertility symbols. In Ancient Greece and Rome, stewed walnuts were eaten by brides to ensure their fertility. At weddings in the South-west of England, the oldest woman in the wedding party or congregation would give the bride a bag of hazel nuts to ensure her fertility (see also *Fertility Magic*, page 199). In parts of France, even today, a bride and groom are showered with nuts instead of rice or confetti at the altar and the floor of the venue for the wedding breakfast is covered with nuts.

In Eastern Europe, the nut is used to prevent conception. A bride places one walnut in the bodice of her dress for each year she wishes to remain childless. After the ceremony, she buries the nuts.

The almond represents young love. In Greek legend, the Athenian prince Demophon was shipwrecked while returning victorious from the Trojan Wars and met Phyllis, a Thracian princess. Demophon asked Phyllis to be his bride, but before the wedding ceremony could take place, news of his father's death arrived and he had to return at once to Athens for the burial. He promised to return and named the day. Months passed and he did not come back. Overcome with grief, Phyllis killed herself on the very day he returned, delayed through no fault of his own. The gods changed her into an almond tree. The grieving Demophon declared undying love and so the tree blossomed. But because it has early flowers and can be damaged by late winter frosts,

Victorians regarded almonds as a symbol of the imprudence of youth.

A Nut Ritual for Fertility

Like many fertility rituals, this is best carried out on the first day of the new moon. You may wish to count this literally from the day the crescent is visible in the sky or you can link it to the first day of a new menstrual cycle if you want a baby. Because this is a psychic incentive and not a physical method of conception, lovemaking should take place spontaneously whenever you and your partner feel the time is right during the first 14 days.

On the first day, lay a perfectly peeled hazel nut or other smooth nut on a silver cloth or on silver paper near the window in your bedroom. Each day, add a new, perfectly rounded nut and let it lie by day and night, through sun and moon, until the fourteenth night or when you see the full moon in the sky. Wrap your nuts in the silver and leave them covered until the moon disappears from the sky or the end of your menstrual cycle, if it appears. Plant the nuts in a sheltered position and water them regularly. Repeat the cycle, if necessary, until you relax into its rhythm.

If you are seeking fertility in a project or relationship, take a positive step each day during the first 14 days of the moon and use the remainder of the month for planning and letting the ideas grow.

Salt

Salt was called the emblem of immortality, since it was used as a preserver of food through the long winter months. Its name comes from Salus, Roman Goddess of Health whom the Greeks called Hygeia. Because salt was so highly prized in Rome, soldiers of the Emperor were sometimes paid in salt, hence the expression 'worth his salt'.

Salt was also used as an early antiseptic. In honour of Salus, nursemaids would put a pinch of salt into the mouth of new-born infants and salt was put into the first pail of milk from a cow who had just calved.

In magic, salt was scattered around thresholds and in protective circles against all malign influences. Spilled salt would be cast over the left shoulder into the 'eye of the devil' who was believed to lurk on the left side.

A Salt Ritual for Protection

If you feel a room in your house is especially dark or gloomy or you have been waking with inexplicable night terrors, place a small quantity of sea or a coarse-grained salt in a small dish on a small table in the centre of the room. Salt represents the Earth element and grounds your room in the calm, benign influences of the Earth. Pass a lighted incense stick over the dish or use a protective fragrance, such as lemon or peppermint, to blow away negativity. Next pass a lighted candle of protective pink or purple over the salt to bring light. Then blow out the candle, sending the light to every corner of the room. Finally sprinkle a few drops of rose water or any floral oil made from pink flowers and let the healing waters restore love to the room. Leave dishes of salt in each corner for a few days and you will feel the atmosphere lighten.

Tomatoes

Tomatoes were once called *pommes d'amour*, love apples. In Germany, they are still called *liebesapfel*. The love connotation probably came from the well-rounded shape and the brilliant scarlet hue. Like many aphrodisiacs, the tomato is the fruit of Venus or Aphrodite. The love connection remained in Europe until the beginning of the twentieth century to be replaced by a more general meaning of health and money.

A Tomato Ritual for Health and Prosperity

Follow the Italian custom and place a large, fresh tomato on the window ledge of the main room to encourage good health. Place a second over the fireplace or on a shelf near a source of heat for prosperity. Replace your tomatoes when they begin to become soft or lose their colour and use them in cooking, making a wish for the health and prosperity of someone close as you stir the dish.

APHRODISIAC FOODS

Like the tomato, certain foods have acquired the reputation for being aphrodisiacs. The term aphrodisiac comes from the name of the Goddess Aphrodite, the Greek Venus, who was the mother of Eros. She was so called because she came from a wave (*aphros*) and any foods, traditionally under her auspices, gained the reputation of love foods.

Aphrodisiacs have varied throughout the ages. For example, the Ancient Egyptians considered lettuce an erotic food, while Nicholas Culpepper, a botanist, doctor, astrologer and herbalist who first published his *Complete Herbal* in 1649, declared artichokes as 'provokers of lust'. Oysters are said to be one of nature's true

21

THE GYPSY

WHO ARE THE GYPSIES?

Gypsy is a corruption of the word Egyptian, as these wandering folk were once believed to come from that country. They accepted this version of their origins as they kept no record of their history and only in the last century were their origins traced to India through the many words with Sankskrit roots in their language. They were also called *Gitanos* in Spain, and Bohemians in France, but they call themselves Romanies, the Lords of the Earth.

It is uncertain when they began to leave India. Some authorities say their migration began as early as the fifth century, others say the ninth. Certainly a major migration took place in the eleventh century and they travelled across Iran into Asia Minor and the Byzantine Empire, moving into Europe by way of Greece during the early fourteenth century.

By the sixteenth century they had spread across Europe, often earning a living by fortune-telling using astrology and palmistry. They avoided intermarriage with outsiders, whom they called Gajos or Gorgios, and lived and worked in extended family groups called cumpanias. But what really separates them from other people is their determination to live and die under the stars.

Because of their refusal to fit in, they were often targets for persecution. The first Gypsies arrived in North America when they were deported from England (the first official mention of their residence is in 1695 in Virginia) and hundreds more were deported to Louisiana by Napoleon. This may have been meant as a punishment but as the author Martin Cruz Smith put it in *A Gypsy in Amber*, sending Gypsies to such a wide-open continent was like sentencing birds to the sky.

LEGENDS OF THE GYPSIES

Many legends centre around the Gypsy wandering life, mingling pagan and Christian traditions (some writers have noted how the Gypsies would adopt the religion of whatever country they were in). One legend says that Gypsies were doomed to roam the earth without shelter because they had turned away Joseph, Mary and

Jesus when the Holy Family was fleeing to Egypt. Another legend says they are doomed to wander because a Gypsy smith (the old Romany name Petulengro means blacksmith) forged the nails for Christ's cross. As a result the entire race was doomed to wander the earth forever.

However, a Romany counter-legend relates that a young Gypsy boy saw the nails beneath the cross and was so moved by the agony of Jesus that he stole one and would have taken them all had he not been seen by a centurion and had to flee for his life. Because of his kindness, Gypsies were granted the right to steal small items without blame.

One legend tells of the Romany Saint Sara. Queen of a French Gypsy tribe on the banks of the Rhone, she had a vision that the three Marys, Mary Jacobe, the mother of the disciple James, Mary Salome, her daughter, and Mary Magdalene, the patron saint of repentant sinners, were in a ship off the French coast. Sara ran to the shore where she found the boat in danger of sinking in the stormy sea. She cast her robe upon the sea and it became a bridge across which Sara brought the three Marys safely to the shore. In gratitude they baptized her and afterwards she lived in Provence helping all who were in need. In another form of the legend, Sara was an Egyptian servant girl of the three Marys.

Her resting place is in the Church of Les Saintes Maries in Provence where every year on 24 and 25 May Gypsies come from all over Europe on pilgrimage. Sara is not recognized as a saint by the Catholic Church but she is buried in the crypt where Romanies keep watch on the two special nights in May and dress her statue with flowers. Afterwards the statue is touched with garments and artefacts of sick family members in the belief that this will heal them. Decorated effigies of Sara are carried through the streets on raised carts to the sea where they are immersed in the water to bring fertility to the people.

GYPSY RITES AND FESTIVALS

The Festival of Snakes

Among Eastern European Gypsies, 15 March is the Feast of the Snake, a half-pagan, half-Christian ritual which regards snakes as symbol of the Devil and of treachery. Therefore, killing a snake on this festival (also on the Ides of March when Brutus killed Julius Caesar) ensures good fortune for the rest of the year.

During Easter a snake or lizard carcass is bound with red and white wool to represent blood and death and taken around the encampment, defiled, abused and finally cast into running water. Running water was the lifeblood of the Romanies and while fire could easily be kindled, finding an available source of clean water was the first consideration at any stopping place.

According to Romany legend, after the Crucifixion, Mary, Mother of Christ, was comforted by a mother frog. Mary blessed the frog for her compassion and said that wherever a frog was found, the water would always be pure enough for humans. For this reason the frog, although not the toad, is considered lucky by Gypsies, especially if it hops on to the steps of a caravan as this indicates that fresh water is easily accessible.

Green Man Rituals

Both in Southern and Eastern Europe, the spring festival centred around the Green Man or Green George. He was the spirit of plants, trees, vegetables, fruit and vegetation, the male spring deity, consort of the Earth Mother and an early forerunner of both Robin Hood and St George. A Gypsy clad in greenery would play Green George and represent the rebirth of spring after the death of winter.

In some Gypsy communities on St George's Day, 23 April, or sometimes Easter Monday, a young willow or birch tree was cut down and dressed with flowers and ribbons. Accompanied by Green George, it was taken to a river and cast in as a substitute for Green George to appease the water spirits.

The legend of the stolen nails from Christ's cross is recalled in the Easter Green Man ceremonies, where a boy dressed as the Green Man takes three nails that have been immersed in water for three days and knocks them into a willow tree, pulls them out and throws them into running water.

DEATH CUSTOMS

When a Romany dies, a family vigil is kept over the body to keep away ghosts until the funeral. Romanies used to believe that until a body had been cremated, the soul was bound to the Earth. Even today, all the belongings of the deceased, such as bedlinen, tools, china, pots and pans, are burned. In earlier times, the deceased was cremated in his or her wagon so that the spirit might fly free of all earthly constraints.

Today, a Romany might be buried with his or her valuables, jewellery and even a china cup and plate for use in the next world, but this is a fairly recent innovation. Red, rather than black, is the Romany colour of grief.

ROMANY SUPERSTITIONS

Many superstitions were grounded in the Romanies' complicated attitude towards women. For example, on marriage a man would join his wife's clan, or cumpania, and a great deal of power resided in the woman. It was she who would be punished in cases of adultery as she was regarded as the temptress. But women's and men's clothes were never washed together and a woman could not pass in front of a man if he was sitting down. A woman could not step over anything a man had to eat and could not cross a stream which was used for drinking water.

A man would drink from water after his horse, but not after his dog because dogs cleaned themselves and were therefore unclean.

Pregnant Romany women would discover the sex of the unborn child by going to a glade at full moon where wild red and white roses were growing together, spinning round 11 times moonwise (anti-clockwise) with their eyes closed and then picking a flower. If it was red, the child would be a boy, if white a girl. A double-headed flower was especially fortunate and indicated an easy birth and possibly twins.

A Gypsy woman gave birth in a specially constructed tent which was destroyed when the child was a month old. During this time a woman was not allowed to cook or wash for a man. It was said to be unlucky for a woman to give birth without having had her ears pierced.

Omens

Falling stars were believed to herald a birth or the coming of money. Some animals and birds were also heralds of good fortune. A wagtail seen near the end of a journey would indicate a fortunate place to camp. White horses, especially seen looking over a gate, were also omens of good luck. A ring from plaited horse hair pulled from the tail of a wild stallion was considered especially fortunate (obviously anyone who managed to pluck the hairs without being kicked to death had a charmed life anyway).

Bees were messengers of the gods. If they flew into a caravan or tent, they were said to bring good news and were always told family news in return. A robin tapping on the wagon roof or window indicated protection.

The weasel represented bad fortune. If a betrothed girl met a weasel, she would hurry to running water to wash away the taint so that her future marriage would be happy. A *vardo* (caravan) would change direction if a weasel crossed its path. However, weasels could not be killed or misfortune would befall the entire cumpania. The weasel's cry when angry and afraid was called the Devil's sneeze.

It was believed that when a tree, or *rook* as it was called in Romany, was felled, woodsmen Gypsies must cover their ears so the cries of the tree could not be heard. *Rookomengro* or squirrel trees should not be felled as the squirrel was a lucky animal.

GYPSY WISE WOMEN

Much Gypsy magic was rooted in the rich knowledge of herbalism passed down from mother to daughter. Gypsy cures were often very effective. In Romany *drab* means grass or herb so the *drabarni* were the herb or wise women of the clan.

The elder tree was one of the most valuable sources of medicine, and so its wood was never burned by Romanies. Elder blossom ointment healed bruises and skin disorders, elder flower oil soothed burns and elder syrup from the elderberry relieved coughs, colds and chest complaints. Other medicines plucked from hedgerows or taken from fields and orchards included honeysuckle for sore throats, lime against sickness and flax to ease childbirth.

Herbs were also used as charms against illness and again proved powerful, perhaps because the Gypsies' belief in these cures bolstered their natural immune system. For example, burdock seed would be worn in a tiny muslin bag around the neck to prevent rheumatism. Gorse was carried in the pocket to keep away fever.

FORTUNE-TELLING

Fortune-telling is known as *dukkerin* or *dukkering* by the Romanies. Palmistry is a very common form of divination, although Gypsies who developed strong intuitive powers would often study a person's face rather than the hands.

Fortune-telling with a crystal ball was popular at fairs or race meetings where an elaborate booth could be set up. The family crystal was kept carefully in a dark cloth except when in use and was handed down from generation to generation. It was believed to tell the future only when used by members of the blood line.

Tea-leaf reading, which may also have come via the Gypsies from the East, is dealt with in a separate section (see page 425) since it is an art that has spread far beyond the Romany and even the psychic community.

THE GYPSY LOVE CARDS

Tarot packs are often associated with Gypsies, but mostly they used ordinary playing cards. Although playing cards are often associated with gambling, the chief questions asked by women when Gypsy fortune-tellers called at their doors were about love. Men who met a Gypsy woman at the side of the road would seek advice not about money or business, but about a lover or wife or, if single, whether love would come. But Gypsies hardly ever give a real reading to an outsider.

All you need to use the Gypsy love cards is a pack of cards. You need not seek advice only about romantic issues. Any question about a family matter of the heart or close friendship will be answered by turning the cards. You may wish to read for yourself, which in spite of superstition is not at all unlucky, or for a friend or family member. You are not attempting to tell the future. The true purpose of any reading, practised by Gypsy or Gorgio, is to use your natural intuitive powers to bring all the hidden factors to the surface and discover the best way forward along a rarely smooth path.

The Method

Shuffle the cards and lay out three face down. Turn the cards over from left to right. Then lay out a second and a third row, each of three cards.

Row 1: The Cards of your Relationships

These three cards concern your current or projected relationship as it is now and any questions or doubts you may have. Now lay three cards immediately below this row.

Row 2: The Cards of Outside Influences

These three cards talk about the influences of others on a relationship or potential relationship, such as opposition or pressures to marry or have children. Turn over these three cards and read them one at a time, then see how they fit together. Now choose three more cards and place them face down below Row 2.

Row 3: The Cards of Suggested Action

These three cards offer the way forward. Turn them over and read them one at a time and finally see your whole reading as a picture that has built up.

The Love Card Meanings

These have been modified to reflect the original meanings and to take away the purely fortune-telling aspect that can deny personal choice.

The Suits

Once you know the suit meanings, you can obtain an overall impression from the number of each suit. A mixture suggests that your approach to the love matter is balanced. If one suit predominates, that suit may represent the key issue in your life at this moment. If, for example, there is a predominance of Hearts or Diamonds, you may find that emotion in the first case, or practicality in the second, is swamping the relationship. Look especially at the row where they predominate. If there is a preponderance of Clubs in the row of outside influences, it may be that you are being pressurized by other people's dreams. If Spades dominate, you may be being forced by others to consider major issues before you are ready.

Diamonds talk about the practical issues in a relationship that, if unresolved, can lead to conflict. These include questions of money, security and domestic arrangements, all of which can chip away at romance and passion. For example, if a woman feels resentful about doing most of the housework, then her partner may resent spending every Sunday with her mother.

Hearts deal with the emotions, with passion, loyalty, jealousy, resentments, trust and emotional blackmail. Often this is an area where outside influences can cause the most problems since parents, children and friends can all have emotional stakes that may conflict with the needs of a couple.

Clubs talk about communication in love; all those ideas and dreams a couple may have that are just as important as sex and sentiment. Communication can so easily get lost amid the practicalities of life or, worse still, become muddied by past failures and fears of rejection that can make lovers see criticism and unfair comparison where none is intended.

Spades are not about bad luck but represent the challenges and changes imposed by fate and fortune. Some of these challenges involve decisions arising from the natural development in a relationship: when to live together, whether to have a family, whether to work or stay at home with young children, move house, care for elderly relations or when to plan retirement. Or they can involve an unexpected pregnancy, promotion or illness that can seem to herald an ending but, in fact, can offer new opportunities and a new path.

The Card Number Meanings

Look at the numbers and, as with the suits, see if any numbers predominate overall or in any particular row. If there is a majority of high numbers, a matter is nearing fruition or needs powerful action. I have given detailed examples of the Aces to show how you could combine suit and number meanings.

The Joker

Use your own instincts rather than listening other people's advice or the old solutions. You may have to take a step into the unknown, which can be exciting in love.

Aces

These talk of new beginnings or a new approach to an old problem. Sometimes it is worth adopting a new perspective or starting in a fresh environment in a relationship rather than abandoning a love match in difficulties.

Ace of Diamonds: Try new practical arrangements or a change of location. If you are single, you may find a new relationship begins in shared activity, whether work or social.

Ace of Hearts: If you are beginning a new relationship, you may need to learn to trust someone again in spite of previous heartache. Or it may be time to begin a new stage in your relationship, perhaps a deeper commitment.

Ace of Clubs: You may be uncertain about how to communicate with a new partner and need to trust your instincts. It may be that if you are going round and round a problem, you need a new perspective, free from the old resentments.

Ace of Spades: You may find yourself facing a major change if fate has imposed an opportunity or reversal of fortune. Be confident and see the positive advantages.

The Numbers

The Twos are to do with balancing things within a relationship, whether the demands of work and home or two people who may both be demanding your attention. Or you may find that you and your partner are talking at cross purposes. Sort out your priorities, make any choices necessary and accept that you cannot keep everyone happy all the time.

The Threes talk of expansion, whether taking on additional responsibilities, such as a mortgage, a child or an elderly relative, or simply moving on to a more permanent level of commitment. Whether in practical or emotional spheres, the issues concern extra input and perhaps a new extra opportunity that may bring responsibility but promises a deeper happiness.

The Fours are the cards of taking a chance and not letting the desire for security prevent us from trusting and sometimes taking a risk. We may be risking the loss of material benefits or rejection, but if we limit ourselves to what is certain, we may never know true happiness.

The Fives speak of accepting that life and people are rarely perfect and not letting temporary disillusion or boredom destroy the benefits or potential positive qualities of a relationship. Taking a long-term view may overcome doubts.

The Sixes are the cards of harmony and idealism and reflect not only outer calm but an inner peace or need for it. So it is not a time for action but for enjoying today for itself and resolving any differences so that you can present a strong united front in any relationship.

The Sevens are to do with our dreams and searching for something more than life in material terms. This can be a time for discovering what you really want in a relationship and beginning to make some of your dreams come true, however the outside world may mock or try to cast doubts.

The Eights are the cards of responding to setbacks or limitations in plans. They are full of movement and change, whether in abandoning what is no longer fulfilling, in changing location or an aspect of life, so that a relationship can escape from negative factors or people that may be bringing undue pressure.

The Nines talk of the place of one's own identity and separate needs in a relationship and suggest that only if you are strong and happy in your own life can you fulfil the needs of others. It can also indicate that one partner or both partners may be pressurized by demands, whether inside or outside, and needs a little space.

The Tens are the cards of completion and so are the cards of total commitment and fulfilment. Whether the card reflects a period of material security or contentment in the home and family, emotional joy, communication on a deep level or making a major decision, when it appears in a reading, you can be sure that you are doing the right thing and your relationship is on track.

The Court Cards

A predominance of court cards in a reading, especially in the row of outside influences, show that it is the personalities that are the real issue and stumbling block in family or love relationships or that you are seeking someone special.

The Jacks represent a child or teenager in a family situation or the other member in a partnership who is either young or is acting in an immature fashion. It is important to welcome the enthusiasm and fresh ideas of a Jack, especially if life has become restrictive. However, if the Jack in your life is being inconsiderate, you should insist that he or she takes share of the responsibility.

The Queens can refer to any wife, mother or older female relation who occupies a caring position or a personal nurturing role in a family or love relationship. The love and counsel of the Queen may be important right now, but it is important for the Queen to avoid unnecessary interference or becoming worn out by acting as Mother Earth.

The Kings represent a husband, father or any older male relation and offer strength and protection. It may be that the wisdom and authority of the King is necessary when a family member or partner is feeling troubled or vulnerable, but it is important for the King to recognize that vulnerability is not the same as weakness or to become remote from the emotional life of the family or his partner.

If the Queen and King persona refer to the card reader or questioner rather than someone in his or her life, they can be applied to either sex to refer to the need of the questioner to nurture or be strong. This more flexible interpretation is also true of many modern families where traditional roles have been replaced by a more flexible partnership that represents a woman's strength and a man's nurturing qualities.

A SAMPLE READING

Alison met Chris, a much younger man, after several years of living alone after her divorce and gradually he began staying the night at her home. Now Chris has suggested that he moves in while he finishes his first degree as a mature student, with a view to marriage once he graduates.

Alison's older sister Abigail has warned her that Chris is only after a comfortable home and settled love life while he is studying and will leave her as soon as he has a job. She shuffles the cards and picks the following cards.

J
J
J
J

Q
Q
Q
Q

4
4
4
4

Q
Q
Q
Q

2
2
2
2

9
9
9
9

6
6
6
6

4
4
4
4

7
7
7
7

Row 1: the Cards of the Relationship – the Jack of Hearts, the Queen of Diamonds and the Four of Diamonds. The Jack of Hearts is perhaps how Alison sees Chris: her young lover who holds her heart but who brings joy rather than security. The Queen of Diamonds reflects her own practical caring role towards Chris and perhaps an unexpressed worry that she is also providing all the material and financial side of the relationship. Chris, although young, is very definitely not a 'New Man' and Alison does most of the chores. The Four of Diamonds suggests that Alison fears losing her own material security. It also indicates an unexpressed fear that she is being used for the practical benefits she offers and that Chris will leave her once he no longer needs her.

Row 2: the Cards of Outside Influences – the Queen of Spades, the Two of Clubs and the Nine of Hearts. The Queen of Spades probably stands for Abigail who has a strong influence on Alison and who feels that she has always been too soft for her own good. Abigail has made many major decisions for Alison (hence the Spades) and is now trying to force Alison to accept that Chris is not a viable long-term prospect. Even if Abigail is right, Alison must make her own decision. The Two of Clubs suggests that Alison is perhaps confused in what she feels and so is transmitting a mixed message both to Chris and to Abigail. The important thing is to be sure what she wants and to talk to Chris, especially about her own emotional insecurity. The Nine of Hearts seems to throw Chris's long-term commitment into question.

Row 3: the Cards of Suggested Action – the Six of Hearts, the Four of Hearts and the Seven of Clubs. The Six of Hearts advises Alison to enjoy her love for now as it obviously gives her great happiness and satisfaction, even if she cannot rely on it forever. The Four of Hearts says that Alison should take a chance if that is what her heart dictates, rather than demanding guarantees, especially those imposed by her interfering sister. The Seven of Clubs offers Alison hope for the future and says that if she and Chris begin to communicate about the things that matter to them and make plans for their future together, then she may find that the doubts created by Abigail lose their power.

PUTTING THE READING TOGETHER

Row 1: the Jack of Hearts, Queen of Diamonds, Four of Diamonds.
Row 2: the Queen of Spades, Two of Clubs, Nine of Hearts.
Row 3: the Six of Hearts, Four of Hearts and Seven of Clubs.

Hearts predominated and appeared in every row, suggesting that Alison did have strong emotions for Chris and that she was basically very happy and in love. Spades appeared only in the outside influences, implying that Alison did not want to force the issues of marriage now, but rather was responding to her sister's pressure.

There were three court cards, quite a high proportion considering that there are only 12 in the pack. Therefore the personalities, rather than circumstances, were the real issue: her love and trust for Chris who had given her no reason to doubt his commitment and her obligation and love for her sister. The relationship between the practical caring Queen of Diamonds and Chris's romantic Jack of Hearts seemed to work for now and could change once Chris was settled in his new career.

No single number predominated, although two fours implied that Alison was aware that she was risking at least her self-esteem if the relationship should founder. But love is not without risk and the Nine and Six supported the idea that she should enjoy happiness for now. The Two and Seven, both of Clubs, emphasized the importance of clear communication between Alison and her lover that might help her to feel secure in her love.

Alison stayed with Chris and he did not leave her as soon as he graduated. Chris proposed marriage but it was Alison who was hesitant as their relationship was working so well. So they are living happily ever after – for now. And even for an extra piece of silver, a Romany could not guarantee more.

HALLOWE'EN MAGIC

THE ORIGINS OF HALLOWE'EN MAGIC

Hallowe'en or All Hallows Eve, on 31 October, is a major magical and, more recently, commercial festival throughout Europe, America and many other parts of the world. But there are other and earlier festivals that mark the time when the worlds of the dead and the living move closer.

Samhain

One such festival was Samhain, which means summer's end. This was the Celtic New Year, the second major fire festival of the Celtic Year, and ran from sunset on 31 October to sunset on 2 November. It is primarily a festival of cattle and may go back to pre-agrarian times.

It originally marked the onset of winter, when the cattle were brought from the hills for the winter and either put in byres or slaughtered for meat. Sometimes a sheaf of corn would be carried as a reminder of the dying vegetation and an evergreen bough as a promise of the return of life. The Celts believed that with the onset of winter the ghosts of the departed would come shivering from the woodlands and bare fields for the shelter of their former cottages. Food would be left in the kitchens or parlours for them. Hearths were cleaned and a fire was kept burning continuously until the first day of the true spring, marked by the spring equinox around 21 March. Hunting was frowned on during this day or the next for fear that a stray arrow might accidentally wound a wandering soul.

A Time of Misrule

All Hallows Eve or Hallowe'en preceded All Hallows (meaning saint), which is now called All Saints Day in the Christian calendar. It was a time when witches, fairies and goblins were said to wreak mischief. Masks and disguises were worn, especially by those returning from huts in the hills to the family home for the winter, so that evil spirits would not recognize them and spirit them away. Faces were blackened with soot and clothes worn inside out or back to front as a disguise. Disorder ruled. People played tricks and children were allowed to go from house to house begging food, trick or treating. Turnip heads holding a lighted candle were placed in windows to frighten off evil spirits (in America the pumpkin took over this role).

Hallowe'en Fires

The lighted candle inside the turnip or pumpkin is a reminder of the Hallowe'en fires. In Britain, Bonfire Night on 5 November has replaced the Hallowe'en fires that still burn brightly on this night in Ireland and parts of Northern Europe. Formerly in Ireland, all fires were extinguished on All Hallows Eve and could be rekindled only from a ceremonial fire lit by the Druids on Tlachtga (now the Hill of Ward).

The bonfires were originally lit to guide the wandering ghosts of the good dead home. They also prevented witches and malevolent fairies stealing away any souls before their winter departure to fairyland. The bonfires of Hallowe'en were also used to purify the cattle who were driven between the twin fires. Above all, the fires gave power to the sun, as it moved towards its lowest point at the mid-winter solstice six weeks later.

HALLOWE'EN LEGENDS

In Irish mythology, Hallowe'en was the time when the Otherworld became visible to mankind and when spiritual forces were let loose on the human world. There are many Irish Hallowe'en tales of fairy enchantment and battles between good and evil on Hallowe'en night when the misshapen violent Fomorii, the evil gods of Irish myth, came forth to wreak harm, enslave whole tribes and take their riches for themselves. They sometimes appeared with only a single hand, foot or eye. However, the Tuatha De Danaan, the tribe of the Goddess Dana, using the magic of Hallowe'en, defeated the Formorii at the second Battle of Magh Tuireadh and became the leaders of Ireland.

On Hallowe'en in Ireland watch out for the Fairy Rade (Ride), led by Finvara, the King of the Dead, and his Queen Oonagh. Mortals who cross their course on Hallowe'en night are in danger of being captured by them. Often Finvara's hosts of fairy folk attend a fair with revelry and dancing and all kinds of wonderful goods displayed. However, should a mortal sample any of the fare or attempt to buy any of the magical items with fairy gold found scattered in a fairy ring on Hallowe'en, he or she will be enchanted forever. It is supposed to be dangerous to be out at night from Hallowe'en until the end of November as Finvara is out dancing every night. If he sees you, you must join in the revels and dance until you drop.

In Britain, especially in the North, Hallowe'en is a night of enchantment. Within the gorge of Cliviger is the highway from Todmorden to Burnley, a Yorkshire–Lancashire route. This was an area particularly bothered by witches and candles were lit in every window an hour before midnight on Hallowe'en. Folks watched the flames with great care, for if they went out, evil would follow. If they burned steadily, witches would have no power over the dwelling.

Legend says that William Towneley of Hapton loved Lady Sybil who had sold her soul to the Devil but she spurned him. He was advised by the witch Mother Helston to go hunting on All Hallows Eve all around Eagle's Crag. His hounds chased a white doe cornering her on the crag foot so that William was able to throw a silken leash around her neck and lead her to Hapton. In the morning there stood Lady Sybil ready to marry him. It is said that the spectral white doe is often seen around the Crag at Hallowe'en being chased by phantom horsemen.

When she stayed at Balmoral Castle in Scotland, Queen Victoria became very fond of the Shandy Dan Hallowe'en bonfire rites, in which a huge straw effigy was burned to the accompaniment of bagpipes.

On this night on the Isle of Lewis in the Outer Hebrides, tributes of ale were offered to the sea god Shony and a fisherman would wade out into the waves to pour the ale on the water and ask for a fine catch.

HALLOWE'EN DIVINATION

Although Hallowe'en no longer marks the transition between one year and the next, the barriers between past, present and future are still regarded as especially close on this night and so it is still an auspicious time for divination, especially concerning love.

If you go at midnight on Hallowe'en to a crossroads, a place of great magical power (see also *Earth Magic*, page 153), and listen to the wind, you will hear all you need to know for the coming 12 months. Children born on Hallowe'en will be protected throughout life and enjoy second sight.

There are many love rituals associated with Hallowe'en. Some of these were recorded in the poem *Hallowe'en* written by Scotland's great poet Robert Burns. The modern woman has many options apart from finding a husband, but both men and women can still try out the rituals on Hallowe'en night to divine the identity of a future love or see if a present love will endure.

Many of the rituals involve food. For example, if a young person eats a raw or roasted salted herring before bedtime, in his or her dreams, the future husband or wife will bring a drink to quench the thirst of the dreamer.

A blindfolded young girl is led out to the cabbage patch to pull one up. The amount of dirt clinging to the roots indicates the size of the dowry; the shape and size of the cabbage foretell the appearance and height of her intended. She must then nibble the raw heart and its flavour and sweetness will reveal her future husband's disposition. She then takes the stalk home and puts it behind the outer door. The first person to call in the morning will be her future husband.

If a man places a piece of wood in a glass of water or small bowl before going to bed, he will dream of falling off a bridge into a river. Whoever rescues him will be his love.

Two unmarried maidens should hold the end of a string with a raisin threaded in the middle. They chew on the string and the first to eat the raisin will be first married.

Apple Divination

The Roman festival of Pomona on 1 November was a celebration of the ripening of fruits. Apples were also associated with the Celtic Otherworld, with love and fertility and divination. It was believed in Medieval Europe that a single woman could see her future husband's image if she peeled an apple before a lit candle in front of a mirror on Hallowe'en night.

Ducking for apples or apple bobbing is still a popular Hallowe'en game and was a form of Druidic marriage divination. The idea is to use the mouth only to pick an apple from a bowl of water or hanging from a string. Whoever picks the first apple can place it under his or her pillow. He or she will then dream of a future or present love if the relationship is to be permanent.

If a young girl ate an apple while combing her hair before a mirror at midnight on Hallowe'en, she would see her future husband in the glass looking over her right shoulder.

Nut-Crack Eve

Another name for Hallowe'en is Nut-Crack Night. Nuts were also a sacred Druidic food because the hazel was one of the magical trees.

For this reason hazel nuts in the shell are considered the best kind to use for divination.

To discover whom you will marry, name each nut you put in the fire after one of your suitors or potential partners. The nut that cracks first will be your true love. Place five nuts on the fire, one for each of five people who must play the game. The first nut to crack will be that of the first person to marry, the second nut to crack foretells a long journey for its owner, the third will come into money, the fourth will find love over the sea and the fifth will have many secrets. A third version of this ritual involves a man and woman. They both place a nut side by side in the fire. If the nuts glow and burn steadily, their relationship will be a calm, harmonious one. If the nuts fly apart or crack suddenly, the relationship will be a tempestuous one.

Other Forms

A young woman should go to a kiln and throw a bobbin of blue yarn in the pot, all the time winding it on to a new bobbin. Suddenly she will feel someone hold the thread and if she calls, 'Who holds my yarn?', her future love will answer his name.

Place three plates in a row, one empty, one filled with clean water and one with dirty water. A blindfolded young woman reaches out with her left hand and if she touches the clean water, her future spouse will be young, attractive and unmarried. If she touches the plate of dirty water, then she will marry a much older man, perhaps a widower. If she reaches for empty plate, she will remain unmarried.

Place four cups on a table, each the same size. Place a silver coin in the first, a ring in the second, heather in the third and leave the fourth empty. Put a blindfold on each young unmarried person in turn. Twirl him or her around three times clockwise and anticlockwise and let him or her reach for the cups. If he or she picks the ring, that foretells marriage within the year. The heather foretells good luck. If the blindfolded person picks the coin, money is coming, but the empty cup means he or she will need to make a way in the world by hard work.

Take a dish of mashed potato, a traditional food of Hallowe'en, and hide a ring, a silver coin, a sea-shell, a button, a heart-shaped charm and a key in it. Turn off the lights, give each member of the party a spoon and fork to take a scoop of mash. The one who finds the ring will be happily married, the coin promises great wealth, the button a family, the heart charm a passionate love affair, the shell travel to far off places and the key a new home.

OTHER FESTIVALS OF THE DEAD

Souling

All Saints and All Souls Days were celebrated from about the third century on 1 and 2 November and officially introduced in the seventh century by Pope Boniface IV. In the early Christian tradition, on All Hallows Eve, souls were released from purgatory for 48 hours and soul cakes and wine were left out for them. All Souls Day on 2 November is a holy day in the later Christian tradition for prayer for souls in purgatory.

On All Souls Night, 'soulers', children and young adults, went from door to door singing special Soul songs. One that has survived into the modern folk tradition is:

A Soul, a Soul, a Soul Cake,
Pray good mistress a Soul Cake,
An apple, a pear, a plum or a cherry,
Any good thing to make us merry,
One for Peter one for Paul,
One for Him who made us all,
The roads are very dirty,
Our shoes are very thin,
We haven't got a pocket to put the soul penny in,
If you haven't got a penny, a halfpenny will do,
If you haven't got a halfpenny, God bless you.

In return for the song, the young people would be given hot soul cakes and money to pay for masses for the souls of the departed. It was believed that the more soul cakes you ate, the more you would be blessed by the spirits of the dead, since each cake represented a soul.

The Mexican Day of the Dead

The Mexican festival of *El Dia del Muerte* (the Day of the Dead) is known as All Souls Day in the Catholic calendar. People in towns, cities and villages make a path with bright yellow flowers from the cemetery to their house to guide their deceased loved ones back to their homes. The houses are filled with ornaments, pictures of the dead, the things they personally used, the foods they liked, flowers and incense.

After the celebration, the relatives eat the food prepared for the dead remembering how much they enjoyed the dishes in life. *El Dia del Muerte* is celebrated on 2 November for adults and 1 November for children.

The Bon Festival in Japan

The Japanese remember their dead in August with the Bon Festival, the Festival of Lanterns. At twilight on 13 August they make fires and burn incense in front of their houses to welcome departed souls back home. They lay flowers, fruits, other food and drinks in front of the small altar specially prepared in the house and chant prayers or have them said by a Buddhist priest.

On the evening of 16 August they make another fire and burn incense at the gate to send off the souls for another year.

A NEW APPROACH TO HALLOWE'EN

Hallowe'en has become merely a commercial festival with plastic masks and black hats. Even trick or treating has become a hazard for children, given the dangers of going from door to door, perhaps after dark. Yet it is a magical festival and, above all, a family occasion, a time for baking the favourite recipes of a much loved dead grandmother, for settling down with the old family photograph albums and retelling all those old family legends, the funny stories, the moments of courage or endurance and rejoicing in the security of the family or close friends.

One should relate all those ghostly tales: how grandma saw her soldier brother appear at the window the night he was killed in a distant war, an aged relative who came back seemingly across the dimensions to peep into the cradle of a new arrival or whose favourite scent or tobacco was suddenly detected at the wedding of a favourite great-grand child. Such stories are common but we rarely talk about them for fear of disbelief and ridicule.

Yet, as the Celts believed, ghosts are usually family members returning in love, in much the way as they did when we lived. If on Hallowe'en, one of the festivals of the Dead or a family anniversary you are lucky to sense or see a loved one, you should not be afraid but be glad of such tangible proof that love survives the grave.

Candles of Hallowe'en

In the old magic, a huge orange candle would be lit at dusk on Hallowe'en to burn until dawn. This was believed to ensure luck would remain in the household all year.

On the night before Hallowe'en, choose a big golden pumpkin and if you have children, make a festive occasion of hollowing out the pumpkin. Even the youngest child can scoop out loosened flesh with a spoon. Save the flesh to make a pumpkin pie for the next evening. If you have no children, invite friends to join you in the pumpkin-making. Cut out teeth and eyes and place a wide-based golden or orange candle on a flat dish inside the pumpkin.

As dusk falls on Hallowe'en, light your pumpkin candle and place him in the window at the front of your house or apartment. At midnight, blow out your candle and let its golden light give you both protection and enthusiasm in the dark winter days ahead. You can, if you wish, follow the even older custom and use a large turnip.

Herbs, Oils and Incense of Hallowe'en

Myrrh, sage, nutmeg, cypress and pine are all substances connected with this time. Burn pine oil and myrrh incense and decorate the house with pine cones and greenery. Flavour a Hallowe'en casserole with sage and a pudding with nutmeg.

Foods of Hallowe'en

These include apples, sweet corn, cranberry and other berry muffins and pies, hazel nuts, mashed and baked potatoes, turnips and swedes (rutabaga). But it is an occasion for cooking foods loved by departed family members and leaving a little in a dark brown pottery covered dish by the fireside, along with their favourite flowers, berries or leaves as a symbol that their memory remains at the family hearth or its equivalent. Place a photograph or memento of the loved one close to the food and share happy memories of time you spent with them.

Crystals of Hallowe'en

Circle your pumpkin with dark crystals of deep blue, purple, brown and black: sodalite, dark amethysts, golden tiger's eye, smoky quartz, deep brown jasper and jet and obsidian (apache tear). Hold your apache tear up to the light of the candle and see the light shine through promising that winter will not last forever.

23

HERB MAGIC

THE ORIGINS

Herbalism is not a New Age concept. Herbs have been used medicinally and magically in many different cultures and ages. Indeed the two functions ran parallel until the seventeenth century and increasingly they are moving closer once more. For the mind can heal the body and the psyche can influence the conscious mind.

What is more, according to old magical beliefs, eating a food endowed a person with its qualities, so herbal cooking and herbal magic are also linked. Often the easiest way to use a protective or energizing herb is to add it to a meal (see also *Food Magic*, page 233). You can experiment with the herbs listed in this book or branch out on your own (checking any unfamiliar herbs in recipe books) now that most supermarkets usually sell fresh as well as dried culinary herbs.

The first evidence of herbs used for magical healing was discovered by an American anthropologist at a 60,000-year-old Neanderthal burial site in a cave in the Zagros mountains of Iraq. Among the human remains was a wreath of seven herbs, including yarrow and groundsel, all of which are endowed with healing properties according to modern herbalism.

The first herbal healing book is attributed to the Chinese Emperor Shen Nung, about 3000 BC. Its title translates as *The Great Herbal* and it forms a basis for Chinese medicine today. In Ancient Egypt the *Ebers Papyrus*, which dates from about 1500 BC, lists herbs and their uses. The Mother Goddess Isis was believed to endow all medicinal knowledge, based on herb lore.

The Greek healer deity Aesculapius, son of Apollo, was the father of Western medicine and used herbs to found his craft. Magical beliefs became attached to herbs and many of them continue, such as the Ancient Greek fondness for mugwort for protection. The yellow-brown button flowers of mugwort bloom in June or July in northern latitudes and the herb becomes medicinally potent at that point. The flowering herb was tied to a traveller's clothes to prevent fatigue, protect against poisons and to ward off wild beasts. Mugwort, a herb of Venus, is in modern herbal medicine a tonic for anyone under stress and an anti-inflammatory substance.

Nor is the concept of 'green magic' new. The Medieval herbalist Hildegard Von Bingen talked of *viriditas*, the greening power that gives new life to mankind. Herbalism was originally part of everyday life, with natural remedies handed down from generation to generation. The village wise woman of Medieval times was especially skilled in herbal lore, but every older woman would have knowledge of herbs and remedies to heal mind and body that she would pass down to her own daughter.

Such knowledge became a threat to the Church and to established male physicians, for it was based on ways that had existed for thousands of years and recognized the importance of treating the whole person and his or her life and not just the illness. Up to a quarter of a million people were executed for witchcraft in Europe alone from the fourteenth to the seventeenth centuries, many of them village wise-women. This wave of executions spread to New England in the seventeenth century, culminating in the Salem Witch Trials of 1692. Twenty people were executed on the gallows, 150 were imprisoned and countless more fled the colonies.

With the killing of herbalism's practitioners, the natural wisdom that had always been passed on orally was lost in many places. However, in remote areas of Wales, Ireland, and Brittany, secret remedies are still handed down through the generations (some suggest they go back as far as ancient Druidic magical lore).

Native North American Indians, the Aborigines and Maoris kept their natural traditions, which were adopted by the white settlers. For example, tea tree oil and eucalyptus are both Aboriginal healing remedies. Captain Cook named tea tree oil, used medically as a germicide and antiseptic, because he and his men brewed the leaves as a substitute for tea. The Aborigines used the crushed leaves of the blue gum tree to produce eucalyptus to heal wounds. As with most herbal remedies, the native natural lore of the Native North American Indians and the Aborigine and Maori people is scientifically valid.

The most famous herbal book is *Culpeper's Complete Herbal* written by Nicholas Culpeper, the seventeenth-century astrologer, physician and ardent Parliamentarian. It contains herbal remedies that are effective today and gives planetary associations for most herbs.

HERBAL REMEDIES AND SCIENCE

The Gaia Hypothesis, named after the Greek Goddess of the Earth, was first proposed by James Lovelock, a British biologist, in the early 1970s. While working for the Jet Propulsion Laboratory of the

National Aeronautics and Space Administration in Pasadena, California, Lovelock began to see the Earth as a biological self-regulating mechanism, a living entity that adapted to its needs and maintained such factors as constant surface temperature, the same percentage of salt in the seas and a constant amount of methane and oxygen in the atmosphere over millennia. This homostasis (maintenance of 'sameness'), he stated, continues in spite of natural variations, such as the sun radiating 25 per cent more heat than it did when life on the planet first appeared about 3.5 billion years ago.

Evolutionary biology suggests that all the needs of a species are met by its environment, including healing of body, mind and the psyche. Herbal healing long predates the vast modern pharmaceutical industry and if the Gaia Hypothesis is correct, it follows that herbs would have evolved to cope with emerging diseases. The humble foxglove (*Digitalis purpurea*), for example, has been known for centuries for its efficacy in treating heart conditions.

During 1995, British scientists found that the compound galanthamine, which comes from daffodil bulbs, increases production of a brain chemical that is depleted in Alzheimer's sufferers. One of the chief researchers involved in the daffodil project, Professor Gareth Roberts, believes that clinical trials will help to reveal the effectiveness of the compound and enable a suitable dosage for Alzheimer's sufferers to be calculated. Although the compound would slow down rather than prevent or cure the disease and the costs of production would be high, there was hope that real help could be offered to sufferers of a disease that destroys memory and causes unpredictable, confused behaviour in elderly people.

This discovery would not have surprised our ancestors. Increasingly, plants that have been used in healing for thousands of years are now being rediscovered as valuable modern cures. According to Culpeper, garlic was used to cure blood diseases because of its ruddy hue and was believed to be good for what modern medicine calls cardiovascular troubles. Scientific research in India in 1973 and 1975, where garlic is still held in high regard as a folk remedy, found that garlic helps to reduce the body's level of cholesterol. Researchers at the Tagore Medical College in Udaipur fed male subjects a diet that included 100 g (3½ oz) butter a day. Subjects who ate the butter had an average 16-point rise in serum cholesterol, whereas subjects who were given either garlic oil or garlic with the butter had an average drop of 15 to 16 points in their cholesterol levels. Similar research in California during 1987 reported that cholesterol levels in subjects who added 1,000 mg a day of garlic for six months to their normal diet experienced drops of up to 78 points, whereas control subjects lost only three points at most from their cholesterol levels.

Since the late 1950s the US National Cancer Institute has tested more than 30,000 plants and found that nearly 10 per cent had positive results in anti-tumour tests.

LUNAR HERB GARDENING

Whether for medicinal, culinary or magical use, herbs have always been considered best when grown by the user, whether in a specially arranged herb garden or in pots on a kitchen window ledge.

Because of their magical associations, the planting, care and cutting of herbs, even more than other plants, have been governed by the phases of the moon. Again research on both sides of the Atlantic and in the Antipodes has suggested that the old beliefs are supported by botanical studies (see also *Moon Magic*, page 336). In lunar gardening, the lunar month of 28 days tends to be divided into two, the waxing phase, lasting 14 days from the new to full moon, and the waning phase from the full moon to the end of the lunar month (use a newspaper or diary to tell you which phase the moon is in).

Planting on the Waxing Moon

The majority of herbs should be planted during the waxing phase of the moon. Herbs planted during this period prosper more than those grown during the waning half of the lunar month. The days closest to the appearance of the full moon are best of all.

Herb Planting Months

Although herbs can be planted at any time of the year, except for the very cold times, the best periods are said to be during the sway of the Water signs – Cancer, Pisces or Scorpio – again in the waxing period of the Moon. There are exceptions. Garlic, one of the protective herbs, should be planted during the waxing period of either Scorpio or Sagittarius to ensure its pungency. Parsley, one of the traditional divinatory herbs, is said to grow best when planted on Good Friday, the only day the Devil has no sway and an auspicious day for gardeners. Parsley must otherwise 'go to the devil' nine times before it grows. Parsley planted during the new moon phase in the Water signs of Cancer, Pisces and Scorpio and also in the Sign of Libra, is said to thrive well. Sage, another divinatory herb, should be planted during the week of the full moon in the sign of Pisces, Scorpio or Cancer. Valerian, the soothing herb of body and mind, should be planted during the waxing half of the month in either Gemini or Virgo.

Cutting Herbs

Cutting herbs for use or to trim them back is best done during the waning half of the lunar month. The best periods are said to be during Aquarius, Aries, Gemini, Leo or Virgo. The moment the moon turns full is sometimes favoured as the plant retains its full vitality. Essential oils are said to be richest in those herbs cut at the full moon.

Friday, because of associations with the Crucifixion, is considered a bad day for planting or cutting herbs and Sunday retains the religious taboos of not working on the Sabbath. In Ireland there is a belief that herbs pulled on a Sunday lack flavour if eaten and their medicinal value is poor.

MAGICAL HERB GROWING

If you have a herb plot, bury a small clear quartz crystal, green jasper or moss agate in each corner of the plot. If any herb looks as if it is going to wilt, place a piece of jade in water for 24 hours and use the water for the plant. If you have individual pots of herbs, plant a tiny quartz crystal in each (you can buy boxes of mixed tiny crystals at most mineral shops). This will energize the soil and protect your plants from predatory insects. Basil is a natural insect repellent so include this in any plot.

HERB DIVINATION

Because of their healing and magical properties, herbs are excellent for home divination. This is very different from scrying with liquids (see *Water Magic*, page 472) since it offers a three-dimensional image. Parsley, sage, rosemary and thyme are, as the old folk song *Scarborough Fair* tells, traditional divinatory herbs, used by people in their kitchens or in a cottage garden (see also *Domestic Magic*, page 127).

Parsley, ruled by Mercury, has dual associations with fertility, birth and death. Sage is symbolic of wisdom, like its ruler Jupiter. Both sage and thyme were frequently put under a student's pillow or rubbed on the brow to aid memory and learning. Rosemary, herb of the sun, is associated with remembrance, especially of past loves and happiness. Thyme, the herb of Venus, represents the happy home and domestic bliss.

You can mix the divinatory herbs or use any that you have around the kitchen as long as the individual leaves are solid and separate rather than powdery. Use chopped dried herbs, gathered freshly and dried at home if you have the time and inclination, or buy them from a supermarket. Sit at a table with your herbs. Think of a question or a person who is occupying your thoughts. Shake a handful of herbs on a piece of white kitchen paper with a rough surface until an image is formed. If an interpretation does not spring to mind, gather the herbs together in the paper and toss the paper or swirl the herbs around to see what new patterns emerge.

Herb pictures are often whole scenes, viewed from a distance, like coloured sand pictures that you can buy in glass. You may identify figures or buildings or the picture may be a symbol for some event in your life. If your herb picture does not make sense immediately, go and sit at the other side of the table and change your perspective. Once you have identified one element the rest follows.

DON'S HERB DIVINATION

Don wanted a child but his wife Gill did not, as her career involved a great deal of travel which she loved. The only way she would agree to have one was if Don worked from home and cared for the baby. Don believed that mothers should bring up children, although he was prepared to do his share of the chores at evenings and weekends.

To put his question to the herbs, he used bright green chives and shook them on to textured white paper. He saw a house surrounded by a hedge on top of a hill. A woman holding a baby was inside the hedge. Don understood his real problem immediately: he wanted to stop Gill from travelling away from him. He realized how much he hated Gill's going away and that deep down he was worried that she might meet someone else. The baby was not the real issue, but his own insecurities. He decided to shelve the issue of a baby and talk to Gill about his fears.

MAGICAL HERBS

There are many ways you can use herbs as a focus for your own energies to attract money, love, happiness or to keep away negative influences.

You can use a particular herb in cooking. For example, vanilla, a herb linked with romance, is particularly suitable in a dessert when you are having a cosy supper for two by the fireside. You can keep a pot of herbs, such as sage for money, surrounded by a circle of coins. You could sew a herb, such as dried lavender, into a tiny pillow for quiet sleep or burn a protective herb, such as myrrh, as an incense in the corners of a dark room to feel safe.

Alternatively you can make a herb garden with your herbs labelled until you recognize them so that you can pick a sprig of fresh herb to carry with you in a tiny bag for whatever strength or focus you need on a particular day. You can sit near the appropriate herb patch on a warm evening and let healing coriander fill you with a sense of well-being and vigour.

There are no limits to the ways you can use herbs to enrich your life if you trust the wisdom that runs in your blood from your distant ancestors who treated the hedgerows and fields as their garden. Do not be tempted, however, to create your own remedies from herbs growing wild. Some can be poisonous if the wrong dosage or combination is used. Moreover, many wild herbs suffer from the indiscriminate spraying of fields with pesticides. Buy carefully labelled herbs for cooking or medicine and if in doubt, go to a shop which stocks a wide range of herbal products as well as leaflets on their use and the correct dosage.

Herbs for Communication and Travel
Caraway, dill, fennel, lavender, lemon verbena, sweet marjoram, black, hedge and white mustard, parsley, savory.

Herbs for Courage
Basil, chives, honeysuckle, horseradish, rose geranium, nettle, pepper, tarragon, yarrow.

Herbs for Happy Dreams and Peaceful Sleep
Clary sage, clove, pink or carnation, jasmine, lemon balm, meadowsweet, myrrh, sweet cicely and wisteria.

Herbs for Personal Joy and Family Happiness
Apple blossom, citron, feverfew, frankincense, garden mint, hyacinth and sesame.

Herbs for Good Health
Angelica, salad burnet, coriander (or cilantro), eucalyptus, hyssop, juniper, mugwort, pine and poppy seed.

Herbs for Love and Romance
Gardenia, marsh mallow, mimosa, rose, sorrel, tansy, vanilla and vetivert.

Herbs for Money
Basil, dill, cinnamon, ginger, honeysuckle and spearmint.

Herbs for Good Luck and Overcoming Obstacles
Clover, comfrey, fern, heather, horsetail, nutmeg, shamrock and vetivert.

Herbs for Psychic Awareness and Inspiration
Cypress, dittany of Crete, orange or tangerine, hibiscus, lemongrass, lily and poplar.

Herbs for Protection
Cedarwood, cinquefoil, frankincense, garlic, heliotrope, lilac and peppermint.

Herbs for Success
Bay, bergamot, chamomile, lovage, marigold, rosemary, rue, saffron and sweet pea.

Herbs for Wisdom and Learning
Agrimony, borage, chervil, cumin, endive, hyssop, sage, thyme and violet.

(See also the astrological associations of spices and herbs in *Food Magic*, page 233, and for oils and incense see *Air Magic*, page 14.)

Magical Herb Sachets

Often when you visit a psychic fair or New Age shop, you see highly priced sachets of mixed herbs for use as charms for love, success, travel or money. In former times, people would make their own love or happiness charms, gathering wild herbs and petals and wearing them in tiny bags around their necks or pinned out of sight.

You can make herbal charms easily at home, using tiny linen or muslin bags, leather purses or any thin fabric tied with ribbon. Because you make the charms yourself, you can endow them with all your dreams and desires. You do not need to follow any complex recipes since each person has his or her own idea of the right mixture. Use any of the herbs above to help achieve your current need or aim. Experiment by mixing two or three herbs and try to include one fragrant ingredient. Most department stores have tubs of pot-pourri petals and where there is a floral herb, you can use some dried petals or essential oil; for example of rose for love, heather for good luck or lavender for tranquillity. Or sprinkle a few drops of an oil such as lavender or rose on the herbs.

Your bag or herb purse need only be small, but as you add your chopped or dried herbs, see yourself in the desired situation or with the person you love and endow the herbs with confidence and positive thoughts. If you wish, add a tiny rose quartz for harmony and protection. Carry your herb bag with you or, if it is very small, pin it to an undergarment. Sleep with your herbs under your pillow.

Every week at the same time, open your bag and replace any herbs that have lost their smell or add a few drops of oil. Bury any you remove in the earth or scatter them to the winds. Once your charm has worked, bury the remaining herbs and keep the bag for another time.

INDIAN MAGIC

HINDU MYTHOLOGY

'There are more gods than men,' it is said of the mythology of India. For this reason I have concentrated only on the principal Hindu deities and their functions. One of the main features of Hindu mythology is the constant struggle between the gods and the demons for supremacy. Like the gods, the demons were created by Brahma or Prajapati, Lord of All Creatures, and are said in some accounts to be dispossessed older brothers fighting for their rightful inheritance. Often in early myth demons are confused with the human enemies of the invading Indo-Aryans. The constant battle between deities and demons continues throughout Hindu myth with no certain outcome and the gulf between good and evil is not as clear-cut as in Western mythology. In one conflict, Shiva, one of the three Supreme Beings, was compelled by the demons to give them greater power and strength than the gods. But Shiva tricked them and his wife, in her dark, destroyer aspect of Kali, went in to battle and defeated them.

THE VEDAS

The Rig-Veda, the earliest sacred literature, is made up of more than 1,000 hymns, describing creation and extolling the achievements of the early deities, especially Indra, King of the Gods, and his twin brother Agni, God of Fire. These hymns date from about 1700–800 BC, a period that is often called the Vedic Age. They are written in an ancient form of Sanskrit, the language said to have been bestowed upon mankind by Sarasvati, Mother of the Vedas, wife of Brahma and Goddess of Music, Wisdom and Learning.

THE DEITIES

Brahma

Brahma was the first Supreme Being, incarnation of the soul of the universe and grandfather of the celestial beings. In earlier times, he was known as Lord of the Golden Seed. In the Brahamanas, sacred writings produced about 500 BC in Sanskrit, Brahma was identified as Prajapati. It is said that Prajapati pursued his daughter, the Dawn. She fled from him as a doe and he turned himself into a stag. She turned herself into a cow and he into a bull, so one by one all the creatures of the Earth were created. His golden seed fell into the cosmic waters and developed into the universe, a golden egg which split in two. The upper shell was Heaven and the lower shell the Earth, while the yolk became the sun. In later Hindu mythology Brahma was regarded as one of the three forms of the Supreme Deity.

The Early Deities and Creation Myths

Indra

Indra was the first King of the Gods, the Thunder God who brought rain to the land and fertility to the soil in his battle against the Drought Demons at the end of the annual dry Indian summer.

He was the son of Prajapati or, in other accounts, of the Earth Mother and Sky Father. His first great victory came soon after his birth when he defeated Vritra, the serpent who lay coiled around the world mountain. As Dragon of Drought, Vritra was keeping the cloud-cattle captive and so depriving the people of rain and fertility. This battle is said to be re-enacted every year by the deities before the beginning of the rainy season.

Indra then fashioned the Earth. After measuring space with the sun, he set up four corner posts and erected the walls of the world. He made the wide doors of the world facing the East. Each morning they were opened to admit the sun and every evening Indra cast the sun back into the darkness, where it travelled beneath the world to a mirror world of brightness. A Vedic hymn celebrates this creation: 'Indra measured six broad spaces from which no living thing is excluded; he it is who made the wide expanse of the earth and the lofty dome of the sky.'

Indra is no longer of great importance in the Hindu pantheon, unlike his brother Agni.

Agni

Agni, the God of Fire, is sometimes regarded as Indra's twin brother and featured prominently in Vedic hymns. Agni is the vital spark in mankind, birds, animals, plants and life itself. He was manifest in lighting, in celestial sun flames, in the sacred blaze rising from the altar and in household fires (see also *Domestic Magic*, page 127).

Agni was the divine priest and acted as messenger to the gods, interceding with them on behalf of mankind. He conducted the gods to receive the sacrifices of mankind. The priest would chant: 'Agni, the divine ministrant of the sacrifice, the great bestower of treasure. May one obtain through Agni, wealth and welfare.' He is still important as the god of domestic and ritual fire.

Varuna and Mitra

Varuna and Mitra represented universal order or *rita* in the early hierarchy of the gods. Mitra presided over friendship and ratified contracts and Varuna oversaw oaths. Mitra shone as the sun and presided over day, while Varuna was the moon and presided over the night and the waters. Their universal law governed men and deities alike. Mitra became the Mithras of the Persians and his worship later spread throughout the Roman Empire.

Later Deities and Creation Myths

The deities Brahma the Creator, Vishnu the Preserver, and Shiva the Destroyer, form the *trimurti* of gods behind modern Hinduism. The Sanskrit *trimurti* means 'having three forms'. Vishnu and Shiva are opposing forces and Brahma the balance between them. In modern times, many Hindus worship either Shiva or Vishnu as Supreme God.

Vishnu

Vishnu is second in the *trimurti* of supreme gods. He is preserver of the universe and the embodiment of goodness and mercy. He is believed to have assumed earthly form in nine incarnations. Five were in human form of which the most important were Rama (the ideal man) who married Sita, the ideal woman, and Krishna, the cowherd and prince who came to Earth in human form to slay the demons masquerading as wicked earthly kings.

Followers repeat Vishnu's thousand names as an act of devotion. He is pictured as either standing and holding weapons or reclining on a serpent.

Vishnu and the Ocean of Milk

Milk is sacred to Hindus in the same way holy water is in other faiths. The cow is a sacred animal and milk is offered to statues in temples. In September 1995 statues of Ganesh (or Ganesha), Shiva and other deities were reported to be drinking the milk that was offered to them, drawing millions of Hindus throughout the world to their temples to offer milk. India came almost to a standstill.

In one of the most famous myths told about Vishnu, who was a relatively minor god in the Rig-Veda, the gods decided to churn the ocean of milk so that they could obtain *soma*, the elixir of immortality. In these earlier times immortality was by no means guaranteed, even for a deity who might expect a span of a thousand years. The gods asked the demons to assist and in return promised them a share of soma.

The churning pole was the world mountain that rested on the bottom of the ocean. Vasuki, the great serpent, was used as a rope to turn the churning pole. So great was the motion that the whole Earth was in danger of disintegrating. Vishnu therefore transformed himself into a giant tortoise and took the pole on his back to steady it. Wonderful treasures came from the ocean, including Lakshmi who became Vishnu's wife.

The soma was trawled from the ocean like a huge cheese, but instead of sharing it as agreed, the gods and demons fought over it. The demons seized it and Vishnu transformed himself into Mohini, a lovely enchantress who tricked the demons into handing it over.

Shiva

Although he is regarded as the destructive aspect of the *trimurti*, Shiva is the god of both creation and destruction, good and evil, fertility and abstinence. He is the Lord of the Dance which will one day bring about the destruction of the world. His symbol is phallic, representing creative power.

Shiva has three eyes: the sun, the moon and fire. The third eye allows him to see inwards and also to destroy whatever it looks on. He was not one of the original Vedic deities but became one of the supreme gods, according to legend, at the time when the universe consisted only of water, before the cosmic seed was scattered.

Vishnu and Brahma were arguing about who was the greatest god when a great pillar of flame appeared between them. Brahma assumed the form of a goose so that he could fly upwards and see how high it was. Vishnu took the form of a boar and dived into the water to see how low the pillar of fire extended. However, neither god could discover its end. Shiva appeared from within the flaming pillar that was symbol of his masculine power and the other gods bowed before him.

Shakti

Shakti is the female energy or power of Shiva. Her name is also used for the wife of any god. She is the Mother Goddess and, like Shiva, creator and destroyer in her different aspects.

Shakti provides the energy that activates Shiva who represents male divine power. Her life-giving force also animates other gods in difficult tasks. This combination of male and female energies is seen in *chakra* magic. Although there are several female goddesses, they form aspects of Shakti and often their identities merge. One of Shakti's forms is as Parvati.

Parvati

Parvati is the benign and gentle Mother Goddess, consort of the god Shiva and the goddess daughter of the Himalayas. Her name means 'mountain' and she is associated with all mountains. She and Shiva are often pictured as a family in the Himalayas with their sons Ganesha, God of Wisdom and Learning, and the six-headed Skanda, the Warrior God.

Durga, the Warrior Goddess

Durga is the slayer of demons and dragons, although she is gentle and loving to all who worship her. She came into being when the Buffalo Demon could not be killed by any god. The gods were so angry that their energies merged to form the goddess; her head came from the energy of Shiva, her arms from Vishnu, her waist from Indra and her fiery eyes from Agni. She killed the Buffalo Demon, first enticing him to fall in love with her and then beheading him. Hers is the protective aspect of the Goddess. Durga is usually mounted on a lion.

Kali, the Dark Mother

Kali, the Dark Side of the Mother Goddess, came into being when Shiva, whose body was covered by white ashes, taunted Shakti for her dark skin. In fury she carried out rituals until her skin became golden inside.

Shakti shed her black outer skin like a snake and it formed the avenging destroying persona of Kali, her four arms holding weapons and the heads of her victims, and her tongue lolling out, covered in blood. Kali is often pictured dancing on Shiva whose body she trampled on, destroyed and then danced on once more to restore him to life, transforming Shava (Sanskrit for corpse) to Shiva (the living one).

Ganesha

Ganesha is the elephant-headed God of Wisdom and Learning, remover of obstacles and deity of new beginnings. He was born fully grown. When his father, Shiva, returned home he did not recognize his son and, thinking him an intruder, decapitated him. When his mother Parvati grieved for her child, Shiva replaced his missing head with that of the first creature he met, an elephant. Ganesha featured prominently in the world milk miracle in 1995.

CHAKRA MAGIC

Chakra is Sanskrit for wheel and its form of magic belongs to the Hindu and Buddhist yogic tradition. Yoga comes from the Sanskrit word *yui*, 'to harness horses to a chariot' and is a search for the mystery of the universe through finding one's own self. Although yogic practice varies in intensity from exercises taught in a village hall to a profound spiritual and physical doctrine, its origins were not intellectual and *chakra* magic relies entirely on personal experience. Therefore *chakra* magic provides a simple but powerful personal approach for anyone who wants to utilize and focus the body's inner energies.

The seven *chakras*, which vary in name and function according to different systems, were pictured as whirling lotus petals of various colours. They form symbolic energy centres based at the cardinal points of the body, which will be explained below. You cannot see *chakras* physically. However, Japanese experiments have demonstrated that energy levels in the hypothesized locations of *chakras* of people who had worked in this field of spiritual development for years were measurably stronger than those of a control group. The universal life force is said to enter the aura (see also *Colour Magic*, page 87) through the Crown *chakra* at the top of the head and is filtered down through the other *chakras*, each of which transforms the energy into a usable form for the function it governs. Energy also passes in the opposite direction from the Root *chakra* situated at the base of the spine.

Kundalini

Kundalini means snake or serpent power in Sanskrit. It is the basic energy that drives the *chakras*, and is pictured as a coiled snake sleeping at the base of the spine. It travels up the body on a spiralling psychic pathway, activating the various energy centres. Kundalini is often identified with the female energy of Shakti, consort of Shiva. When the female energy of Kundalini reaches the Crown *chakra*, it is said to join with the male force, identified with Shiva. This male life force is said to enter the Crown from the cosmos and when it joins with Kundalini, together they can offer enlightenment.

CHAKRA CARDS

An easy, yet very effective, way to explore *chakra* magic is to make a set of seven *chakra* cards to represent the seven main energy centres. *Chakra* cards work in two ways. They may identify any blockages. When a *chakra* energy becomes blocked at a certain point, it can be expressed as physical 'dis-ease' in the particular area of the body where the blockage occurs or as a more general irritability or lethargy. They may also identify the specific *chakra* that can be helpful at particular time. Each *chakra* is traditionally represented by one of the colours of the rainbow. For example, the *chakra* at the base of the spine is red. It can offer primal power, if there is a basic survival issue at stake, while the green heart *chakra* helps with a decision that requires sensitivity and intuition.

Blockages and energy sources are interrelated because the strength you need may not be flowing naturally if energy is blocked at a certain point.

Making the Cards

Make seven cards out of stiff white cardboard, either as circles or rectangular about the size of a large Tarot card. On each one draw either the appropriate symbol or a circle in each *chakra* colour.

Chakra Meanings

The Root Chakra or Maladhara

This is the Earth *chakra* and its colour is red. It is rooted at the base of the spine. Its symbol is the bull. Draw a red bull or a red circle on your Root *chakra* card. This is the energy centre of the physical level of existence, survival and animal strength. It uses red, raw energy to overcome fearsome odds. Blockages can be reflected in problems with legs, feet, bones and bowel discomfort. On a psychological level, unreasonable anger at trivial causes can be a symptom.

The Desire Chakra or Svadisthana

This is the moon *Chakra* and its colour is orange. Although seated in the reproductive system, it focuses on different aspects of physical comfort or satisfaction, such as eating, and drinking. Its creature is the fish. Draw an orange fish or an orange circle on your Desire *chakra* card. This is the energy centre of wanting, the *chakra* of physical pleasure and happiness and is the home of the five senses. The Desire *chakra* will put you in touch with your all-reliable 'gut feelings' and help in matters of fertility in the wider as well as physical sense. Blockages can be reflected in problems with the reproductive system, bladder and circulation system. On a psychological level, irritability and disorders involving physical indulgence can result.

The Power Chakra or Manipura

This is the sun *chakra* and its colour is yellow. It is seated just below the navel. Its creature is the ram. Draw a yellow ram or a yellow circle on your Power *chakra* card. This is the energy centre of digesting experiences, taking what is of use from life and casting aside what is redundant. This *chakra* comes into its own when you desire power in a situation, want to achieve an ambition or are planning a career move. Blockages can be reflected in digestive, liver, spleen and stomach problems. On a psychological level, obsessions and over-concern for trivial detail can result.

The Heart Chakra or Anahata

This is the *chakra* of the Winds. Its colour is green and it is situated centrally or slightly to the left of the chest, close to the heart. Its creature is the dove. Draw a green dove or a green circle on your Heart *chakra* card. Here the spiritual nature of the *chakras* emerges. This *chakra* controls love, emotions and altruism towards those close to you and to the world generally. The Heart *chakra* can be used for relationship issues and when sympathy and sensitivity are needed. Blockages can be reflected in heart palpitations, coughs and colds, lung problems and in ailments in the hands and arms. On a psychological level, free-floating anxiety or depression can follow.

The Throat Chakra or Vishuddha

This is the *chakra* of time and space and its colour is blue. It is situated close to the Adam's apple in the centre of the neck. Its creature is the elephant. Draw a blue elephant or a blue circle on your Throat *chakra* card. This *chakra* represents an important transition point from the personal to a wider view of the world. It controls ideas, ideals and clear communication. The Throat *chakra* is at its most useful when truth and principles are an issue or you are surrounded by double-dealing for it is the *chakra* of speaking truly. Blockages can be reflected in problems with the neck, shoulders, glands, teeth and throat.

The Third Eye, Brow Chakra or Savikalpa Samadhi

This is the *chakra* of freedom and its colour is purple. It is situated in the centre of the brow, just above the eyes. Its creature is the cobra.

Draw a purple cobra or purple circle on your Brow *chakra* card. This is the centre of inspiration and an awareness of a world beyond the material and immediate. The Brow *chakra* controls psychic awareness, prophetic dreams and harmony. Blockages can be reflected in problems with eyes and ears and in headaches. On a psychological level, insomnia or nightmares can result.

The Crown Chakra or Nirvakelpa Samadhi

This is the *chakra* of eternity and its colour is white. White, the source of pure light (all the other colours combined), pours upwards and outwards into the cosmos and downwards and inwards from the cosmos back into the Crown. The Crown *chakra* is situated at the top of the head in the centre. This is the centre of creative and spiritual energy and represents either pure spiritual awareness or complete happiness in earthly terms. Its uses are for making dreams into reality and for finding true personal happiness rather than success on other people's terms. Blockages can be reflected in problems with sinuses, the skin, scalp and whole body. On a psychological level an inability to rise above everyday and material concerns and a rigid attitude can result.

Using the Cards

Shuffle the cards and lay them face down at random. Choose one and turn it over. This is your current key *chakra*. You may be surprised at the choice of card which may offer an unexpected solution or locate a physical problem away from the area you expected. On a purely physical level, a headache may be rooted in a stomach problem and a neck tension from holding yourself in check emotionally, so do not try to rationalize too much. In the same way, you may need to summon reserves of strength from an unexpected quarter. For example, sometimes an emotional issue needs a blast of root survival energy if you are to avoid being so swamped by sentiment that you sacrifice a vital part of your being.

The Meaning of the Key Chakra Card in your Life

Read the key factors of your chosen *chakra*. If you have any of the listed symptoms, physical or psychological, then the *chakra* may need clearing.

If you have no symptoms, this is the *chakra* that holds particular strengths for you right now and you should concentrate on amplifying its energies. This will give you the surge of power or confidence you need. You should use your *chakra* cards only once a week at the most to get a clear reading. Using the *chakras* is not an instant method for changing your life.

How to Clear a Chakra

Many people find it helpful to link particular crystals or colours with each *chakra* centre and I have suggested a suitable crystal for each at the end of this section. However, you can just as easily use the same clear crystal quartz or pure white stone both to unblock and strengthen all seven *chakras*.

Find a stone or crystal that is pointed at one end and rounded at the other. Hold the crystal about 5 cm (2 inches) over the *chakra* you are attempting to influence and move it in a circular motion using the hand that feels most natural. If you feel that you need to clear a *chakra* indicated by your *chakra* card, use the rounded end, directed towards the appropriate area of your body to draw out any negativity or pain, whether emotional or physical. Circle the *chakra* with an anti-clockwise movement to clear any inertia or pain and see it unravelling as a long dark cord. When the thread is unravelled, cast it in your mind's eye into the sky and see it taken up as a star or sunbeam. Now use the pointed end to provide a blast of physical and psychic power.

How to Activate a Chakra

If there is no blockage in your *chakras*, begin with this stage. Move your stone or crystal clockwise 5 cm (2 inches) over the desired *chakra*, seeing it filled with brilliant light passed down via the Crown *chakra*, mingling with a clear transparent flame that has travelled upwards from the Root. Let your hand automatically trace the route through which the energy will flow. Because we are dealing with psychic rather than physical connections, we all have unique *chakra* pathways, so trust your own wisdom, rather than trying to follow diagrams. Finally rest your crystal on the place where you feel the *chakra* to be and sense the regular, firm vibration like a well-tuned engine.

AN ALTERNATIVE FORM OF CHAKRA MAGIC

It is believed by many people that whatever kind of cards we use in magic, we instinctively choose those that suggests ways forward in our lives by identifying either underlying strengths or potential stumbling blocks. No one fully understands how we are unconsciously guided to the right card.

However, if the card method seems too random, you may prefer to trace your own energy lines and centres with a pendulum or a simple clear quartz, an amethyst, rose quartz, blue lace agate or any other stone that for you symbolizes personal healing powers and natural energies. Use the crystal exactly as you would a pendulum, except that you are cradling it in your palm. Hold it about 5 cm (2 inches) above your body and let it trace a route. As you move the crystal, you will feel it drawing a warm line just below your skin, telling you where your psychic pathways are.

In spite of the vast literature on the subject, there are no definitive links that are true for everyone. Trust yourself, it is the key to all magic. Your pendulum will hover or pull towards one particular *chakra*. If it moves anti-clockwise, you may feel that the *chakra* is static or perhaps whirling too fast. However, if your crystal or pendulum has a steady clockwise pull over the chosen *chakra*, there is tremendous power surging here that you can use to your advantage in a current situation. Once you have identified the *chakra*, use one of the following stones to unblock the energies.

The Root Chakra

Use earthy-red opaque stones, such as red jasper or red tiger's eye, one of the banded red/brown agates or any pebble you have that is dark reddish brown to black.

The Desire Chakra

Use rich orange crystals, cornelians, amber, orange jasper, banded orange agate, gentle orange calcite or orange sandstone pebbles.

The Power Chakra

Use yellow and golden crystals, such as citrine, golden amber, yellow jasper, rutilated quartz, soft yellow moonstone or yellow calcite.

The Heart Chakra

Use pink and green crystals or stones of all kinds, from brilliant green malachite or deep green aventurine to softer jade, amazonite and moss agate. Pink stones of this *chakra* include bright rhodonite or rhosochrite, the healing rose quartz and pink kunzite.

The Throat Chakra

Use lapis lazuli, blue howzite, turquoise, aquamarine or blue lace agate.

The Brow Chakra
Use sodalite that varies from a true navy blue to soft purple, amethyst, sugilite and peacock's eye (bornite).

The Crown Chakra
Use clear crystal quartz or a bright white stone from a shore or hillside for this *chakra*.

Your Chakra Crystals

Have a special box with a lid in which to keep your *chakra* crystals or stones. Wash them after use under running water and keep flowers or greenery next to your box if possible.

Once a week, at the same time, you can light a white candle and place your crystals by your bedside so that the light of the candle shines upon them. Visualize the different lights pouring into you, removing pain and doubt and restoring the balance of harmony into your life. Blow out your candle but keep the crystals by your bed all night.

A Simple Chakra Ceremony

If you face a major challenge or if you feel suddenly unwell in a particular part of your body, light a candle in the colour of the associated *chakra* and pass the appropriate crystal (see the list above) through the flame. Light an incense, such as pine or rosemary, and pass the crystal through it to symbolize the Air element. Sprinkle water and salt on your crystal for the Water and Fire elements and place it beneath your pillow while you sleep.

In the morning as early as possible, carry out the same ceremony outdoors, then pass the crystal over the appropriate *chakra* and feel the blockage clearing and the energy pouring in. Take the crystal with you during the day and try to hold it over the appropriate *chakra* at noon and again at dusk.

25

LOVE MAGIC

ST VALENTINE'S DAY

The fourteenth of February, St Valentine's Day, is perhaps the best known festival of lovers. It is an occasion for great bards and schoolboys alike to express their love in verse:

Tomorrow is Saint Valentine,
All in the morning betime,
And I a maid at your window,
To be your Valentine.

William Shakespeare.

I love you, I love you, I love you almighty,
I wish your pyjamas were next to my nighty.
Don't be mistaken, don't be misled,
I mean on the wash line and not on the bed.

Discovered by Bob Pegg in an old school desk in West Yorkshire.

The Origins of Valentine's Day

St Valentine was a young priest who defied an edict of the Emperor Claudius II that soldiers should not be allowed to marry as it made them poor fighters. St Valentine conducted the weddings of a number of young soldiers and was executed on 14 February 269, thereafter becoming the Patron Saint of Lovers. It is said that while Valentine was in prison, he restored the sight of the jailer's blind daughter and that she fell in love with him. Legend adds that as he was taken to be executed, he wrote on the wall a message for his love: 'Always, your Valentine.'

But in pre-Christian tradition 14 February was the time of lovers at the ancient Roman festival, Lupercalia, which was held where Romulus and Remus, legendary founders of Rome, were said to have been suckled by the she-wolf. The Horned Fertility God, in the form of the Lycean Pan or Lupercus as he was called in Rome, was central to the festival as he offered protection to the flocks from wolves. Partners were found by drawing lots among the young men and women who kept that partnership throughout the festival.

Because goats were sacred to Pan, the young men dressed up in goat skins and ran round the town, beating young women with goat thongs.

With the advent of Christianity, Christian festivals were grafted on to the old pagan rituals and gradually the celebrations on 14 February became dedicated solely to St Valentine and not his pagan forebear. There was a medieval custom on Valentine's eve of casting lots to choose a Valentine. Young men or women would put an equal number of names of the opposite sex into a container and the chosen name picked out by a young man would determine his partner for the Valentine celebrations and maybe even eternal bliss. Young men would wear the slip of paper with the girl's name on their sleeves (one explanation for the old saying 'wearing your heart on your sleeve').

14 February has yet another love connection. It is the day on which birds are said to choose their mates, according to Chaucer's *The Parliament of Fowls*.

For this was on St Valentine's Day
When every Fowl cometh to choose her mate.

If an unmarried girl saw a bird during the morning of 14 February, it was believed that she would divine her future love. Most Valentine rituals were devised in less liberated days when the ambition of every young woman was to find a husband. Nowadays, many a young man is seen with his packet of bird seed on Valentine's morning.

If you see a hen and cockerel together early on St Valentine's Day, it is a sign you will be married. The number of animals you see as you leave home will tell you how many months will elapse before the nuptials take place. The old myths promise that if a girl sees a crow, she will marry a clergyman, a robin a sailor, a goldfinch, a millionaire, any yellow bird, someone who is well off, a sparrow means love in a cottage, a bluebird poverty and a crossbill quarrels. A wryneck portends the lass will remain an old maid and a flock of doves promises happiness in every way.

One custom that has died out is that no lass or lad should step over the threshold on Valentine's morning without sporting a yellow crocus, the flower of St Valentine, that is said to bring luck in love.

It is said that the first man a young woman sees on Valentine's morning will be her true love. However, any girl who wanted a glimpse of her future husband would have already visited the local churchyard on Valentine's eve and as the clock struck 12 run around the church calling:

I sow hemp seed,
Hemp seed I sow,
He that loves me,
Come after me and mow.

Her future husband then appeared in a vision.

Valentine cards have flourished on both sides of the Atlantic as well as in many other parts of the world, although in the United States the scope of Valentine cards has been widened to include family members and good friends as well as lovers. Love notes, often illustrated, began early in the Middle Ages and hand-cut illustrated Valentine messages have been found from as early as the 1500s. The first Valentine card was printed in 1761. The beginning of the penny postal service in Britain in 1840 caused the real expansion of the Valentine card industry.

Printed cards of the Victorian era were assembled by hand and very delicately created from lace, woven silk panels, feathers, pearls and multi-layers, often delicately cut and woven like cobwebs. You opened them out by lifting a central thread. They tended to be very sentimental. For example, a John Windsor card in the possession of the British auctioneers Phillip's bears the hand-written message:

If while my passions I impart
You deem my words untrue,
O place your hand upon my heart,
Feel How it beats for you.

After about 1900, postcard Valentines, as opposed to the frothier confections, came into vogue. These were slightly more jovial although by no means risqué. One with a picture of Cupid declared:

Alas my Cupid looks so shy,
He is not really, nor am I.

Another depicting a telegram said simply:

Wise date,
Can't wait,
Be quick,
Love sick,
No joke,
Heart broke.

However, it has always been considered very unlucky to write your name on a Valentine card. If you do, tradition warns that you will never marry your beloved. On the other hand, if you have received an anonymous card and want to know the identity of an admirer, the nineteenth-century astrologer Zadkiel advised obtaining a crow quill and pricking the fourth finger of your left hand. With the quill write in blood (this spell is obviously not for the squeamish) on the back of the card the day, hour and year of your birth, the current year, the moon's age, the name of the present morning star, and the star sign into which the sun has entered. (He helpfully adds that you can find all the relevant astronomical information in the latest copy of Zadkiel's almanac available at all good booksellers.)

If you have not fainted from lack of blood by this time, go to bed at midnight on the first Friday after you receive the Valentine, with the card in your left shoe under your pillow. Then lie on your left side and repeat three times:

St Valentine pray condescend
To be this night a maiden's friend;
Let me now my lover see
Be he of high or low degree.
By a sign his station show;
Be it weal or be it woe,
Let him come to my bedside,
And my fortunes thus decide.

It is promised that you will dream of your secret Valentine sender and whether you will end up marrying him or not.

LOVE DIVINATION AND RITUALS

Although St Valentine's day was the zenith of love divination and rituals, love magic continued throughout the year, especially on the major agricultural festivals, such as May Day and New Year celebrations, such as Hallowe'en, the beginning of the Celtic New Year.

Midsummer Love Divination

There are several version of this Midsummer eve ritual, on 23 June or the eve of the Longest Day, 20 June in an earlier tradition. In the most popular, three, five or seven young women of good reputation should go to a garden in which there is no other person and each gather a sprig of red sage. Then they should go into a room, set a stool in the middle and on it place a basin of rose petal water and put the sprigs of sage in it.

They should tie a washing line across the room on one side of the stool and hang on it petticoats (or the modern equivalent) turned inside out. The young women should sit in a row opposite the stool, not speaking, and a few minutes after midnight, each one's future husband will take a sprig out of the rose water and sprinkle her petticoat with it.

A man or woman may try to make someone love them or to bring back a straying lover, using a doll or a pair of dolls as symbols. We should not try to influence the mind of another person. An unwilling lover is a hollow victory. However, we can make ourselves more open to a new relationship or enhance our own relationships by magnifying the positive vibes.

Equally, if you have quarrelled with a lover, a ritual may banish negative feelings on your side and so open the way for reconciliation. You may like to try some of the old rituals that adapt easily to the modern world.

TRADITIONAL LOVE RITUALS

Dreaming of Love

This ritual is best practised, according to custom, on a Wednesday or Friday. Open a prayer book bound with the scarlet and white ribbon at the marriage service and put a sprig of myrtle on the page that says 'With this ring I thee wed'. Place it under your pillow and you are promised a dream of your own wedding and will see the identity of the groom.

Love Divination in Water

This ritual aims to see how an existing relationship will progress. Put two corks or acorns in a large bowl of water. If they float instantly close together, the relationship will develop rapidly. If your partnership is long-standing, you are close on a very deep level. If the corks or acorns float completely separately or in opposite directions, perhaps you have an unresolved worry you need to share or are not ready for a deep commitment in your present relationship. Go slowly. If your corks or acorns float close and then away and back again, your relationship is full of the normal ups and downs but perhaps needs more romantic input to rekindle the flames of passion.

Seed and Plant Divination

Because of the associations of the fertility of humans with that of the land (see also *Fertility Magic*, page 199), much love divination is centred around the growth or use of plants and seeds.

Onions

The most common method was for a young girl to scratch the name of several suitors on separate onions and put the onions in a warm place. The first to sprout would be her true love.

Another love ritual on Midsummer eve (the evening of 23 June in more modern tradition) requires peeling an onion, laying it in a clean handkerchief under your pillow and repeating:

Good St John, please do me right,
And let my true love come tonight,
That I may see him in the face,
And in my fond arms him embrace.

Your love will appear in a dream.

Carrots

This less pungent vegetable works equally well. Cut the end of two or more carrots to choose between potential suitors or to make love decisions. You might choose one carrot top for yes and the other for no, one for go and the other for stay, one for declaring love and the other for holding back. You may wish to write the names or the decisions to be made and leave them under each choice.

Place your carrot tops on saucers and add just a little water when the carrots become dry (too much will cause the carrot to become mouldy). Leave them in a warm place. See which carrot sprouts first and that will give you the answer. You should have to wait only a few days. Use this time not to think about the love decision or the people, but to make your present world more fulfilling.

Mustard and Cress

Mustard and cress seeds planted on two or more saucers on either cotton wool or damp tissue are an even faster method of divination. Scatter your seeds generously on the saucers representing the alternative people or love choices. As you do this, visualize the person or decision involved in each and endow it with positive feelings. If the seeds become dry, water them gently, seeing the water giving life to your future possibilities and happiness.

Pea Divination

This method was traditionally used by unmarried people seeking to be wed, but can be used to divine any future permanent relationships. Take a pea pod in which there are nine peas and suspend it over the doorway by a white thread. If the next person who enters the door is not a member of the family and is unmarried or unattached, your own wedding or a new permanent relationship will take place within the year.

Beans

According to old custom, if a woman or man wishes to attract a lover who seems indifferent or to bring about a reconciliation, the seeker should place seven beans in a circle on the road along which the loved one will walk and keep watch unseen.

If the lover strides over the beans or treads on one, he or she will come and declare undying devotion. However, if the loved one makes a detour, the charm has not succeeded. The love match is not intended and the seeker should turn his or her attention to someone more responsive.

Lucky Clover Divination

A two-leaf, as opposed to the elusive four-leaf clover, is used in divination for the name of a future lover or spouse. Go to a field full of clover or shamrocks. Search for one with two leaves. A three-leaf clover from which a leaflet has been removed will not work. Place the two-leaf clover in your right shoe and as you walk along chant or repeat silently in your head:

A clover of two,
Put it in your right shoe,
The first man (girl) you meet in field, street or lane,
You'll have him (her) or one of that name.

Snail Divination

If you put two snails in a dish of flour and leave them overnight, by morning they will have left the initials of your true love in their trail.

Mirror Divination

Mirrors have always retained magical significance. It was believed that you could see the soul reflected in a mirror, hence breaking a mirror was in Roman times considered to mean bad luck for seven years, the time it took for the soul to regrow. As with a crystal ball or the smooth surface of water (see *Water Magic*, page 472), the shiny surface of a mirror was believed to act as a focus for magical visions, especially in matters of love.

Traditional Mirror Marriage Divination

A girl stood in front of a mirror lit by a candle flame just before midnight and spoke the following words:

Mirror, mirror tell me,
Am I pretty or plain,
Or am I downright ugly
And ugly to remain?
Shall I marry a gentleman,
Shall I marry a clown,
Or shall I marry old pots and pans
Shouting through the town?

As the clock chimed midnight, a vision of the true love would appear in the mirror over the girl's right shoulder.

MODERN CANDLE LOVE DIVINATION

The old rituals are still widely practised. Tony, who lives in the United States, wrote to me about his experience of love divination, not for himself, but for a friend.

'I don't use mirrors for scrying, I use a candle flame. A few weeks ago, a friend of mine asked me if I could see if there was any chance of him finding the "right" girl. I gazed long and hard into the flame and received a vision of him walking hand-in-hand with a short, dark-haired, green-eyed young woman.

'I told him about the vision the next day and he laughed, until last week, when he met a girl who fitted the description I gave him. In another vision, I saw her again, but this time, there was a halo of light around her, in which was a silver letter "A". I was talking to him the next day, the day he met the young lady, and I told him about my second vision. Oddly enough, the young lady's name is Ashley.'

A Love Ritual using Candles and a Mirror

Like Tony's friend, many people believe that somewhere out there the right person is waiting and it is just a question of tuning into the same wavelength so that you will meet and recognize the other. Whether or not a love link works so directly, you can use candle and mirror rituals to open yourself to the possibility of love or to send loving messages telepathically to someone with whom you have started a relationship that you would like to become more permanent.

In a darkened room, use a large oval shape-mirror of the kind owned by all the best princesses in fairy stories. Light a pink and green candle, the colour of Venus and of love. Surround them with tiny green and pink soft candy sweets. Take two pink roses for new love and place one in front of each candle so that the candlelight reflects on it. In turn eat each sweet and as you do so see yourself in the mirror being surrounded by a soft pink and green aura that increases until the whole mirror and the candle flames are suffused with pink and green.

Now blow out the candles: first the pink to overcome any barriers, then the green for letting the love in your heart find another who will respond. See the light in long thin rays bound off the mirror and go off into the darkness. In the after-image you may see a figure, perhaps of the person with whom you have started a relationship or someone you do not yet know. Do not be disappointed if he or she is quite ordinary (marriages with handsome princes and willowy princesses have a very high failure rate).

Do not seek your new partner or put pressure on an existing relationship. Let nature take its course. Your loving rays have opened you to all kinds of happy possibilities, but like any flower, the seeds of love must grow in their own time. Concentrate on making other aspects of your life happy and love will come, when the time is right.

LOVE AND MARRIAGE CUSTOMS

Many modern love and marriage customs have their roots in old rituals and superstitions. In seventeenth-century New England, Americans followed the practice of bundling. A betrothed couple was encouraged to spend the night together in the weeks before the wedding, but they had to be fully clothed and a bundle of clothing was put between them.

In Holland, a would-be bride would leave a ladder at her window so her intended might climb up to her room. Her parents, however, provided her with a gong and tongs to raise the alarm should her intended attempt to cross the barrier of clothes in the middle of her bed. Such visits by a serious suitor were considered an honour, but if the young lady became pregnant, she would have to conceal the baby under her cloak at the wedding.

SUPERSTITIONS

A girl who sits on a table while she is talking will never be married. When a girl leaves home, she should always look north as she leaves the door or she will never marry. Love letters should be written on Friday, the day of Venus or Frigg, the Norse Goddess of Love and Marriage. If a couple first see each other in a mirror, they will always be happy. To preserve love, break a laurel twig in half and each lover keep half.

Weddings should take place in June as this is the month of Juno, Roman Goddess of Marriage. Once married, a husband, not a wife, should lock the door to prevent quarrels.

Yellow wedding veils were worn in Roman times and in both East and West the bride was required to keep her face covered until the wedding. The original bridal canopy was used so that malevolent influences could not cast an evil eye upon her before the ceremony.

In Anglo-Saxon times, the bridegroom's men would bring the bride to the church and the bride's woman and bride maidens would accompany the groom. In Roman tradition ten witnesses were required: five bride maidens and five 'best men', dressed identically to the bride and groom so that mischievous spirits, who hovered at a distance at all celebrations, would not know which were the happy pair.

If the bride hears bird song as she wakes, her marriage will be free from quarrels. If a spider walks over the wedding gown the couple will be prosperous.

The bridal bouquet served as a symbol of plenty and the ferns and greenery were originally ears of corn for fertility. Orange blossom is a Saracen custom, representing chastity and purity. The confetti now thrown over a bride was originally wheat or rice, so that when the crop grew tall she would be with child. In some cultures, such as Ancient Rome and present-day France, nuts are thrown for the same reason.

'Something old, something new, something borrowed, something blue' is an old wedding tradition. The 'old' is traditionally a garter or handkerchief from a happily married woman so that her happiness will rub off on the new bride. 'Something new' was the wedding gown itself. The 'borrowed' was a piece of gold to symbolize future prosperity and a symbol of the sun. 'Blue' is often a blue ribbon to represent the power of the moon to make dreams come true.

WEDDING ANNIVERSARIES

At one time, each anniversary represented a different material. These were often things that the bridal couple would need as their wedding gifts wore out or something, such as fruit and flowers, representing the addition of children to the family. Now the custom has been reduced to a few anniversaries, such as Silver and Golden Weddings.

Yet traditional recognition of anniversaries by those who attended the original wedding can provide a focus not only for the couple, but for the loving energies and intent of all present. Anniversary gifts need not be expensive. Even a Golden Wedding can be marked by golden flowers or gifts wrapped in gold paper. Candles can be lit and the couple and those present burn candle wishes or promises for the future. Anniversaries of togetherness can also be celebrated by couples who have lived together for many years.

Key anniversaries include:

First: Cotton
Second: Paper
Third: Leather
Fourth: Fruit and flowers
Fifth: Wood
Sixth: Iron
Seventh: Woollen
Eighth: Bronze
Ninth: Pottery
Tenth: Tin
Eleventh: Steel
Twelfth: Silk
Thirteenth: Lace
Fourteenth: Ivory
Fifteenth: Crystal
Twentieth: China
Twenty-fifth: Silver
Thirtieth: Pearl
Thirty-fifth: Coral
Fortieth: Ruby
Forty-fifth: Sapphire
Fiftieth: Gold
Fifty-fifth: Emerald
Sixtieth: Diamond
Seventy-fifth: Diamond or More Recently Platinum.

MAORI MAGIC

NATURAL GODS

Maori magic is rooted in the nature of island existence, surrounded by mighty oceans, skies with clear stars and beautiful sunsets. The Maoris are a Polynesian people who settled in New Zealand or Aotearoa, the Land of the Long White Cloud, in about 750. Dutch settlers reached New Zealand in 1642, but European colonization did not begin until the early nineteenth century.

Because of their long isolation and rich mythology, Maoris developed a strong artistic, social and economic tradition of their own, while keeping links with the cosmology of the East Polynesian world. Because New Zealand is surrounded by huge tracts of ocean and the Maoris depended so much on its 'fruits' one of the principal deities is Tangaroa the God of the Oceans, fish, sea fairies, mermen and maids. He breathed only twice a day giving rise to the tides and sometimes appears as a huge fish.

New Zealand lies in the South-western Pacific Ocean, 1,600 km (995 miles) South-east of Australia. It is in an unstable zone, marked by earthquakes whose god is Ruau-Moko, who was never born but still stirs inside his mother the Earth. The land has snow-capped mountains, fertile green plains and volcanic regions famous for their bubbling hot springs and explosive geysers. Forests run the length of the country from North-east to South-west. The climate varies from sub-tropical in the North Island to wet temperate on the South Island. Because of the varieties in climate and rich terrain, the Maori gods are those of the natural world.

The first realm was Te Kore, the nothingness, from which came the wai ora, the waters of life. Te Kore was the life force in undeveloped form. In this realm, the primal parents, Rangi the Sky Father and Papa the Earth Mother, were locked in perpetual embrace. With the birth of their first child, Tangaroa, it is said that Papa's body became so filled with the waters of life that they burst forth to make the oceans.

Te Po, the Night, now came into being. However, Rangi and Papa were so close to each other that their six children were unable to move or see the light. Tane-Mahuta, God of the Forests, trees, birds and insects, became a tree and forced the sky upwards. He clothed his father with Kohu the God of Mist, Ika-Roa, the Milky Way and the shining stars. Tane-Mahuta then clad his mother with forests, ferns and plants. The sorrow of the parted Rani and Papa can still be seen in the morning mists ascending from the earth and rain descending from the sky. Tawhiri-matea, God of the Winds and Elements, was so angry at the sorrow of his parents, that the war that still causes storms and tempests broke out among the gods. As a result of the separation, the universe had two spheres: Te Rangi was the sphere of sky, heaven and day, Te Po the sphere of night, dark and the underworld.

The third realm in which humankind lives is Te Ao Marama, the world of Light, which lies between Earth and Sky. The waters of life flow into this world and are part of everything, even the rocks of the Earth, the plants and the insects.

One story of the origins of people and their mortality is that Tane asked his mother Papa to give him a mate. She offered him pine trees, exotic plants, flax and pools of water, but Tane wanted a woman. Papa told him to make a female body from the Earth and to lie on the Earth embracing it. So Tane formed a female being, Hine-ahu-one. Their daughter was given the name Hine-a-taura. Tane took her also as his wife, but when Hine-a-taura discovered her origins, she fled into the darkness below where she became known as Hine-nuite-po, Great Woman of the Night. A dying man was said to creep to sleep in the womb of the Sleeping Mother Death.

When man dies, he can enter the realm of the gods, either by the entrance to Rarohenga, the Underworld, under Cape Reinga in the far north or, if he is a high chief, he is taken by spirit canoe to the heavens where his eyes become stars. When Maui-Tinihanga, Maui of the Many Devices, a demi-god hero, realized his own death was drawing near, he pursued Hine-nui-te-po. He knew if he could crawl through her body and come out the other end without waking her, he could overcome not only his own death but undo the curse of mortality for his descendants. However, just as he was inside, a fantail bird called out and woke the Goddess of Death and Decay. So men must die.

Maui is the hero credited with bringing fire to the Maoris by obtaining it from its guardian Mahuika, the ogress clan mother. He also created the land of the Maoris, fishing up Te Ika a Maui, the fish of Maui, which became the North Island of New Zealand. His canoe remains on a mountain Hikurangi on which the first light fell when sky and earth were separated. The city of Wellington stands on Whanga-Nui-a-Tara, the great Bay of the Sea Goddess Tara that was formed from one of the eyes of the great fish.

Maui's greatest achievement was when he caught the sun. He decided that the days were too short for work and the nights too long. With his brothers he went to catch the sun, Tama Nui-Te-Ra to make it travel more slowly across the sky. Maui used the strong hair of his sister, Hina-Ika, Lady of the Fish, to make a net to pull the sun into the world. Then he released it, letting it fly across the sky. In the West, the land of Avaiki, Maui used the net to lower the sun gently into the seas. This progress can be seen every day.

The Maoris claim their ancestry from Rangi and Papa through the lineage of the deities and hero ancestors. Those who claimed descent in a line of first-born males from an original ancestor were accorded the highest rank in Maori society. For example, a chiefly family in the Cook islands traces 65 generations back to Atea, another name for Rangi and Papa. The high-born Maoris inherited *mana*, power or prestige, from these original god ancestors. Mana links the world of man with the world of spirit and was the gods' favour, a spiritual energy that assured the warrior safety in battle and the farmer rich crops. A woman has mana when she bears a chief many healthy sons to carry on the line and the *tohunga* or priest has mana when his incantations and *karakia*, charms, bring success to the tribe, whether ensuring safety in childbirth, rain or causing the animals and birds to be plentiful for hunting.

Mana was regulated with a system of *tapu* or *taku*. Tapu means sacred and therefore implied separateness from ordinary ways of living; it took the place of law as well as of religion. So seriously was this taken that a tohunga or priest who had carried out a magical ceremony was so tapu he might eat only food served on the end of a stalk to avoid any physical contact with others.

Communication between the ancestors and their descendants was central to Maori existence. The ancestors guarded their descendants by intervening or even appearing personally. When any two groups met, the ancestors of both parties would be present as well as the newly-departed dead and had to be welcomed. Ancestors may offer warnings, often by causing the strange movements of ancestral treasures, such as images of the gods and symbols of the chieftainship that had been handed down through the generations and which contained the mana or power of the ancestors. The eldest born of a tribal chief, as a direct descendant of the gods, was seen as having a special relationship with the ancestors and gods and could interpret such omens and signs.

The Maori year had 13 months, fixed by one or more risings of stars. Hakari or feasts were said to have originated in offerings made to the gods at times of tribal as well as seasonal significance, such as a birth-naming ceremony, a marriage or the ritual interring of bones. They were also often dedicated to the sun, using large poles with pennants representing the rays and a fire at the centre. The New Year Festival in June was held at the rising of the constellation of the Pleiades on the East coast and at the rising of Rigel in the North. The rising and disappearance of the Pleiades marked significant phases of the seasonal cycle. The New Year coming of the Pleiades was celebrated by festivals that marked the time of sowing. Cleaning ceremonies were also carried out, as in many other cultures, at the time of the New Year. The Hahunga or harvest festival, in the tenth month (March), acknowledged the gathering and storing of the crops.

The gods of nature and local deities, whether tribal or family gods, allowed the harvest to ripen and made the land and sea fruitful in return for correct observation of the natural rites of worship and by man's own diligent efforts in bringing the natural processes to fruition. For example Rongo ma-Tane, God of Agriculture, fruits and cultivated plants, is worshipped and his abundance considered sacred, for all foods that are grown are regarded as his children. The *kumara*, sweet potato, a staple Maori food, was considered so magical that if one was buried in the path of an approaching enemy, he would be driven away.

These gods communicated pleasure or displeasure through celestial or natural phenomena. Lightning, thunder, winds and rain are all personified as children of the Sky Father and Earth Mother. Gods could also send their *aria* or semblance as lizards, dogs, birds, insects (particularly the green mantis), trees, rocks, rainbows, comets and stars. For this reason, the natural world formed the basis for divination and the study of omens.

MAORI DIVINATION

Because of the ever-changing natural environment, divination among the Maoris involved interpreting these fluctuations. For example, a leaf might be cast into the wind and the way it flew and fell would be interpreted by the tohunga as a favour or otherwise from the deity invoked. Kites, in the shape of men or animals, were flown and the directions they moved in were used to foretell the likely success of a venture, especially in war.

Interpretation relied on the intuitions and inspirations of the tohunga. Therefore Maori divination is especially suitable as a focus for modern personal decision-making, because there are no fixed meanings but rather triggers for our own inner voices to tell us the best way forward. Rituals were carried out by the tohunga for matters of tribal importance, although ordinary Maoris and even children would use the simpler divinatory rites to discover whether they were favoured by the gods. Although many of the tribal rites involved the success of war parties, they might also divine whether a time was auspicious for fishing or hunting.

There were several variations of the niu ritual. In war divination, the deity Tu-Matauenga would be invoked for his blessing, as well as the appropriate tribal gods and ancestors. War was considered a positive way of expressing loyalty to ancestors and avenging any recent ghosts of those lost in war or killed by the forces of an opposing chief's malevolent magic men (tohunga makatu).

In one version of the ritual, a tohunga placed a mat on the ground and, after fasting and prayer, took fern stalks in his hand, one for each of the chiefs who were going to war. Each 'home tribe' stick was given the name of a particular chief and tied with a piece of flax. The same number of fern stalks without flax ties were chosen to denote chiefs of the opposing tribe. The set of 'enemy warrior' sticks was fastened upright through the mat. The tohunga took up the 'home warrior' sticks and threw each in turn at a stick without a tie. If the named stick dropped to the left of the chosen upright stick, the named chief would fall. If it dropped to the right, the named chief would survive enemy attack. This was done for all the chiefs on the war party, using different 'enemy warrior chiefs'. The results would determine whether the time was auspicious to proceed with the raid.

Casting Stones

Niu Kowhata is a more personal divinatory practice, traditionally performed on the banks of a river, pond or lake. It can be used for determining a future personal course of action. The left side is taken as the female, spiritual, waiting side and the right as the male, active, life force. The place that a stone lands is influenced by our hidden inner wisdom that determines the unconscious thrust of the hand in a particular direction, suggesting a course very different from that consciously considered. A stone thrown straight ahead may veer apparently without reason. But the direction always confirms the 'best' course.

Think of a question about a possible course of action with two options, such as go or stay, declare love or remain uncommitted, change jobs or continue in your present position, explore the world or stay close to home. The change option you could designate Option A. If it is a choice between two people, then designate the more outgoing person, Person A.

Choose three stones of the same size and colour and take them to a lake, pond or river. Throw the first straight ahead into the water with a gentle, upward circular movement. Throw the second behind you over the left or spiritual shoulder, again gently, and the third directly upwards.

Stone One
The stone thrown into the water represents the likely success or rightness of any action or change, that is Option A or the choice of Person A.

If it falls straight into the water without sound or splashing, Option A or Person A will not be fruitful. If it skims the water, there will be partial success if you opt for A. If the stone splashes and makes ripples as it hits the water, the signs are good. The more rings or ripples, the greater the impact of acting on Plan A or choosing Person A. If this is a positive overall picture, you would choose Person or Option A.

Stone Two
The stone thrown backwards offers information as to whether the change or choice of person should be immediate or if it is better to wait for the right moment.

A stone that falls behind you to the right indicates that immediate action should be taken. If it falls behind you to the left, it counsels delay. You can judge how long by how close the stone is to you. If the distance is great the delay should be for weeks or even months. A central position suggests that proceeding cautiously will ensure the greatest success.

Stone Three
This stone, thrown upwards, offers insight as to whether the proposed plan or choice is one where the approval of others is important. For example, if your family members hate your new lover, should you ignore their advice?

If the stone falls in front of you, the auguries are good for ignoring the advice of those close to you if it differs from your own desires. If the stone falls behind, then other people's opinions should be considered, although not followed blindly. If the stone goes to the left, listen to your inner voice. If it goes to the right, seek independent counsel.

Reading Natural Omens

Maoris were also deeply influenced by the omens of the natural world, known as *aitua*. They also relied on dreams and tohunga would appeal to the gods to answer their questions during sleep. Here, too, natural signs were considered highly significant, sometimes those meanings coming directly from myth.

For example, Ngirungiru, the white-breasted blue tit, is the Maori lovebird, symbol of love remembered. According to myth, Ruarangi's wife was stolen by the King of the Fairies but the singing of the lovebird reminded her of her home. Therefore, to see the lovebird was a sign of the importance of home and family, perhaps at a time of domestic strife.

In Maori mythology, the frog was a god of the waters, rains and rivers and it was believed that killing one would cause downpours and floods. A frog in dreams or on one's path was a warning of floods or unduly heavy rain.

A short, sharp shower in an otherwise blue sky was seen as *waewae tapu* (sacred footsteps) and suggested that the ancestors had drawn near and so it was important to listen to the wisdom of the ever-present past.

The Maori God of Rain had many names, Ua-Roa (Long Rain), Uanui (Hail) and Ua Nganga (Rainstorm). His son is Hau Matingi the God of Mists or Fog. So a long rain might suggest long-term favour.

Tipua Kura involves the unusual movement of sacred tribal artefacts and natural objects which behave in ways contrary to natural laws. For example, a log floating upriver might indicate an uphill struggle or unexpected obstacle.

Each tribe had sacred heights, whether the peak of a mountain or a sacred mound, where the movement of storms was interpreted. If lightning flashed vertically towards the home village, this was seen as inauspicious for the home tribe and so ceremonies had to be held to propitiate the gods. Lightning flashing away from the village indicated that the tribe was protected. Sheet lightning indicated war or problems stemming from human rather than divine error, perhaps the breaking of tapu.

Rainbows, which are frequent in New Zealand, were used as a vital source of divine counsel. A low rainbow directly ahead would indicate that a projected journey might be difficult. A high-arched rainbow promised favour on any enterprise and one forming a circle assured total success and happiness.

In modern industrialized societies, we often fail to recognize the power of the elements. Although omens are no longer taken so literally, there is good reason for using the natural world as a focus for our own intuitions. If you want to practise using omens, see what pictures appear in the lightning or what words are suggested by the thunder. They may well cast light on a current question.

You may find that already from your own personal as well as regional mythology and dreams, certain natural symbols have consistent significance. You may like to keep an omen journal listing phenomena, such as rainbows, shooting stars and a ring around the moon, and what they mean to you. Such collections are a wonderful legacy to future generations and one that accords with the sacred inheritance left by the ancestors in Maori tradition.

The Shells of the Gods

The Maori nature gods were intimately connected with every aspect of life and their attributes personified wisdom about the nature of human existence. Their lessons are as relevant in the modern technological world as under those clear skies. Take 12 hollow shell halves, about the size of a large coin, with a clear markable interior. Try to find shells identical on the outer side. You may wish to go to the coast and see the cloak of Rangi, the Sky God, turn red with the dawn and stay until Maui gently lowers the sun in his net below the western horizon. If there has been a shower and the sun is shining or a rainbow forms, your reading will be especially luminous.

If this is not possible buy 12 mother-of-pearl shells in a soft colour or failing that, 12 large, oval pearl buttons will do. Number each shell in black or red permanent paint or with an indelible marker.

Shell 1: Rangi, Sky God
Shell 2: Papa, Earth Mother
Shell 3: Tanc-Mahuta, God of Forests and light, trees, birds and insects
Shell 4: Maui, the inventor
Shell 5: Tawhiri-Matea, God of the Winds and Elements
Shell 6: Tangaroa, God of the Oceans and Fish
Shell 7: Haumia Tiketike, God of Foods Growing Wild
Shell 8: Rongo-ma-Tane, God of Cultivated Foods
Shell 9: Kuku Lau, Goddess of Mirages
Shell 10: Ruau-Moko, God of Earthquakes
Shell 11: Tama Nui-Te-Ra, the Sun God
Shell 12: Hine-Nui-Te-Po, Goddess of the Underworld

Place your stones in a shallow pool dug in the sand and filled with sea water or any deep bowl of water that reflects colours of the ocean. Pick just one shell with your eyes closed and let the deity be your guardian.

Each time you do a reading, which can be every day if you use a bowl at home, see which deity speaks to you and whether one appears regularly as your guardian. If you have a question, it may be answered by your choice.

Rangi
The Sky Father offers creative energy for new ventures. He talks of power and confidence and promises that you can succeed in achieving your worldly goals if your aim is direct and unflinching.

Papa
The Earth Mother is the nurturer, offering love, acceptance and patience. She talks of relationships and love as the key to happiness. Fertility of ideas and giving of one's abundance are the keys to personal fulfilment.

Tane
The God of Forests and light offers gradual growth into the light. He provides the sure foundations of a tree and shows how small enterprises can grow to great heights. He says that it is important not to be shaken by the doubts of others.

Maui
The inventor offers ingenuity, adaptability, a certainty that there is a way round any obstacle, if necessary, by creating a solution. Be resourceful, there is always a way, he insists.

Tawhiri-matea
The God of Winds and the Elements speaks of change and the need to free ourselves from the petty restrictions that stop us expressing our essential nature. Let the winds of change clear the clutter from your life, he advises.

Tangaroa
The God of the Oceans and Fish talks of limitlessness, fluidity, moving with the tides and the moons and not lingering in the shallows, but striking out for the open sea.

Haumia-tiketike
The God of Foods Growing Wild indicates the need for simplicity, going back to the sources and accepting that sometimes we can lose our path by reliance on the material world. He says we should live according to what is available and not wait for harvest time.

Rongo-ma-tane
The God of Cultivated Foods talks of the need to plan for the future and to be aware of the different cycles of our life and their special demands. His maxim that as we sow, so shall we reap offers control over our lives for we can use today to create the fruits of tomorrow.

Kuku-Lau
The Goddess of Mirages warns us to beware of illusions and taking what seems the easiest path. It is important to be sure any plans we make have firm foundations.

Ruau-Moko
The God of Earthquakes points to repressed negative emotions that can become destructive, unless acknowledged and released in a positive way to bring about change and overcome injustice, whether to ourselves or others.

Tama Nui-Te-Ra
The Sun God tells us to enjoy every moment of sunshine in our lives and not demand guarantees or worry about what might happen tomorrow. It is important, too, to spread joy and fulfil our own special dreams.

Hine-Nui-Te-Po
The Goddess of the Underworld reminds us that we sometimes need to close doors on the past and to accept that a relationship or stage in our lives has run its natural course.

These are just suggested meanings. You can visualize the natural deities whenever you are in the open air or in your dreams and if you allow them, they will demonstrate the personal meanings they hold for you in their mythological forms.

MAYAN MAGIC

MATHEMATICAL MYSTERIES

Civilization first appeared in Mexico and Central America in about 800 BC. The Olmec culture left behind ceremonial centres, pyramids, sophisticated sculpture and writing. At about this time the idea of the 260-day ritual calendar arose.

From about AD 200 until 900, the Maya of Southern Guatemala and Mexico's Yucatan peninsula developed what was perhaps the most civilized and spiritual of all Mesoamerican cultures. The Aztecs who came later were warriors concerned with conquest and built on the creative genius of the Maya.

The Maya built huge and beautiful temples at the top of stepped pyramids and developed the 260-day count into a complex astrological and numerological system that attempted to capture the wisdom of the universe. What is especially remarkable is that they created huge urban complexes of great beauty in what was an area of dense rainforest and limestone plateau. Teotihuacan, for example, was a sacred city laid out as a model of the cosmos as a whole, divided into four main divisions centred around the symbolic axis mundi, the centre of the universe. These vast urban complexes grew maize for food and had priest-kings as local, rather than centralized leaders.

Mayan religion and magic were based around the growing of corn and the need for rain and sun and the priest-kings became experts at forecasting weather cycles. Over the centuries they developed remarkable skills in mathematics and astronomy and were able to predict weather, eclipses, transits of Venus and the return of comets. From these signs they made prophecies that have been startling in their accuracy, all the more amazingly because they did not know that the Earth went round the sun.

In spite of the collapse of the Mayan civilization and the book-burning by the Spanish invaders who arrived in the early sixteenth century and found a culture still reflecting the old ideas, the classic 260-day astrological and divinatory Mayan calendar lives on. It can be found in an oral and simplified form in remote and scattered villages of Mexico, Belize, Guatemala and Honduras and is used to regulate and determine many aspects of life.

THE DEITIES

The Maya believed that nature was a living entity that continually renewed itself. The Mayan universe was made up of 13 higher and nine lower levels. There was constant conflict between the upper life-giving powers of life, warmth, light and fertility, and the lower life-taking powers of night, death, drought, war, disease and famine. Mayan mythology is almost entirely based on the conflict between these primal powers of light and darkness.

A ritual ball game reflected this constant struggle of the universe. The Maya believed that each time it was played, the life-giving powers were enhanced and the darker powers temporarily defeated. The game court, erected near a temple, was formed like the imagined shape of the universe with carved goals at each side and raised seats for spectators. The opposing teams, representing light and darkness, used their hips and shoulders to force a way through to score the winning goal and hence gain supremacy. The game is said to be an earthly version of that played by the sacred twins, Hunahpu and Zbalanque, the sun and moon, who, as forces of light and life, play against the powers of the underworld.

The chief deity of the higher realms was Itzamna who was associated with the powers of sky and sun and breathed life and light into people. Among other tribes he was also called Kukulcan, Man of the Sun and was the fore-runner of Quetzalcoatl, plumed serpent God of the Sun. He was also God of Thunder and the ruling God of the West.

In Yucatan, the sun god was known as Kinich-ahau, Lord of the Face of the Sun. He was linked with the Firebird or Arara and was also called Kinich-Kakmo (Sun-Bird). The sun god ruled the North. Myths recount that the Maya came from the sun. Because the sun rose in the East, so the hero gods came from the ascending light, bringing culture, law and art, writing, architecture, mathematics, ceremonies and astronomy.

Next of importance to the sun god for the growth of the maize was Chac, the tapir-nosed rain god whose nose was the spout from which rain fell. He was Lord of the East. Another major god of the growth cycle was Ah-Mun of the Corn or Yum Kaax, Lord of the Harvest Fields, who wore a leaf-ear of maize in his headdress. Like the sun and rain gods, he was offered human sacrifices at the season's end to ensure the next crop,

Ix che'l was the Goddess of Medicine and Healing and in later times she and Ix-chebel yax became one and the same and was identified with the Virgin Mary. She ruled the South.

In the realms of darkness, Cizin, the death-god, was sometimes depicted with exposed vertebrae and a skull face. On his head was the snail symbol, the sign of rebirth. His was the realm of the West, the home of death, departing with the setting sun. The Bat-God also belonged to the regions of darkness. He was called Zotzilaha Chimalman and lived in the cave of bats, which was on the road to the lands of darkness, decay and death.

THE FESTIVALS

The annual Mayan festivals began in January, with the rain gods' festival of Ocna when new images of the gods and ceremonial artefacts were created. The fire festival of March was dedicated to Itzamana, God of Fire and Life. Rain rituals were also performed at this time. The Maya built a terraced pyramid, its higher steps painted blue to represent the rain falling from the sky and the lower ones covered with mud to represent the wet earth.

Next came the festival of Eckhuah, God of Merchants, and Hobnil, God of Beehives, in celebration of the cacao pod. In May came another fire festival, this time of Pacumchac, God of War. New Year was celebrated in July with rituals of cleansing temples, houses and streets. At this time, domestic and craft utensils were replaced. A new fire was kindled in honour of the gods and incense was burned at the feast of Pocam. Every artefact and tool was painted blue in honour of the sky and the rain and rededicated to service.

At their special festival in September beekeepers offered money and incense to Hobnil. The greatest annual ceremony came in October, in honour of the sun god, Kukulcan the Feathered Snake, the counterpart of the Aztec Quetzalcoatl.

THE CALENDAR

Astrology and divination were part of the same concept to the Maya. An unbroken cycle of 20 named days formed the basis of both systems. This cycle began with the Alligator and finished with the Flower. Each day represented different stages and qualities of life.

The sun as it travelled across the sky during the 24-hour period created the day. The day unit was regarded as a basic measure of time itself. The importance of the day to Mayan calculations is shown by the fact that sun, day and time were represented by the same word in Mayan language.

The Mayans used two calendars, one consisting of a 260-day year, called a *tzolkin*, and the second, the *Haab*, comprising 365 days.

The 260-day *tzolkin* apparently goes back to the Olmec. The Mayans used it with 20 named days. Imix, Ik, Akbal, Kan, Chicchan, Cimi, Manik, Lamat, Muluc, Oc, Chuen, Eb, Ben, Ix, Men, Cib, Caban, Eznab, Cauac and Ahau. However, these were counted in cycles of 13 so that the first day of the year would be 1 Imix, followed by 2 Ik, 3 Akbal, etc up to 13 Ben. The next cycle would begin with 1 Ix, 2 Men, etc.

It is as though we had months that were only six days long. So January would begin with Monday 1, Tuesday 2, Wednesday 3, Thursday 4, Friday 5, Saturday 6, then into February which would begin Sunday 1, Monday 2, Tuesday 3, etc.

Because of the way the Mayan cycle ran, 2 Imix was the fortieth day of the cycle, not the second, or twenty-first as you might expect. The cycle finished at 13 Ahau.

The 365-day *Haab* which corresponds to our solar year (the time the earth takes to orbit the sun) comprised 18 months of 20 days and a short month, Uayeb, of five days which were considered particularly unlucky. The names of the Mayan months were Pop, Uo, Zip, Zotz, Tzec, Xul, Yaxkin, Mol, Chen, Yax, Zac, Ceh, Mac, Kankin, Muan, Pax, Kayab, Cumhu and unlucky Uayeb. The first day of the month was known as its 'seating' and so the days were recorded as the seating of Pop, then 1 Pop, 2 Pop, 3 Pop and on to 19 Pop, the seating of Uo.

The two systems ran together so that each day had two names, its *tzolkin* name and its *Haab* name. So the first day of a cycle would be 1 Imix Seating of Pop, followed by 2 Ik 1 Pop. Because the years were different lengths they got out of step after 260 days when the next *tzolkin* would begin on 1 Imix, the seating of Kankin, and continue 1 Ix, Kankin.

The two calendars did not come back into step for 52 *Haabs* when the cycle would start again at 1Imix, seating of Pop. This is sometimes called an Aztec century because the Aztecs, who also used this system, thought the turn of the century vitally important. There is evidence that they feared the world would end at the end of the cycle. When it did not there were great celebrations and they rebuilt their temples and pyramids.

However, the Mayans were more concerned with a larger period of time, the *Long Count*, which stretched over vast periods. We are said to be living in the Fifth Age, which, according to the scholars who have tried to reconcile the Mayan system with ours, began on 13 August 3114 BC and will end on 22 December 2012.

Birth Day Signs

The most significant factor in understanding an individual's fate was the day on which he or she was born. Priests and astrologers consulted the *Book of Fate* to assess the prognosis of a new born infant as well as on political or religious matters. The 'birth day' sign could indicate potential characteristics inherent in the birth symbol.

Unlike Western sun sign astrology, people born at different times of the year would share the same symbol and by implication core characteristics because of the 20 signs constantly rotating in 13 day cycles. The four directions, North, South, East, West, each controlled five symbols. The genii Bacabs guarded the four quarters of the sky: Kan, Muluc, Ix and Cauac, whose symbolic colours were yellow, white, black and red. These stood in the East, North, West and South respectively.

The same 20 symbols were also used for divination. Because there is so much connection between the Middle American systems, the one used here is a representative system that attempts to reconcile some of the discrepancies.

The 20 Day Signs

Each of the day names had a special meaning, for example Imix was the alligator or sea monster sign. Often the signs are seen in two sections. Nine and 19, Water and Rain, are sometimes exchanged according to local variations. The meanings vary according to the region and have been modified slightly to retain their essence but to bridge the vast gulf of ancient usage that has been lost.

The North, South, East and West connotations are not in a block but are more like the Earth, Air, Fire, Water characteristics of western sun sign astrology but need not be considered in the methods used here.

The Meanings

1: IMIX, the Alligator: Nurturing

Area of Heavens: East

The Alligator is a creator of home and family or business. The Alligator's caring, nurturing side means that the interests of those close to you will always be paramount. However, because the Alligator fears rejection, this love can become overwhelming and make others feel constrained.

The divinatory message of the Alligator is be creative and loving but not suffocating

2: IK, the Wind: Versatility

Area of Heavens: North

The Wind is the sign of versatility and adaptability. The Wind has an ability to succeed in many fields and see the points of view of others. The Wind represents responsiveness to the world and human nature especially. However, he or she can give up easily if things get difficult or new ventures beckon.

The divinatory message of the Wind is be adaptable but not fickle. It meets the demands of life with sensitivity and understanding of the real issues. The only danger is that the Wind absorbs so much from others it becomes a mere reflection of the current situation.

3: AKBAL, the House: Security

Area of Heavens: West

The House is the sign of physical and material security. The House represents a steady, practical approach to life that succeeds because any venture has firm foundations. However, the desire for security can mean too rigid an attitude and an unwillingness to accept change.

The message of the House is to move steadily forward but do not exclude new ideas.

4: KAN, the Lizard: Transition

Area of Heavens: South

The Lizard is a symbol of the links between two worlds, whether water and earth, past and future or body and spirit. It represents the integration of opposing factors, talents and the ability to move in different worlds with ease. However, the Lizard can be fickle and indecisive about priorities.

Its message is to integrate different aspects of your life but stick to a course.

5: CHICCHAN, the Snake: Transformation

Area of Heavens: East

The Snake who sheds its skin is a symbol of the power to cast off the redundant or destructive throughout life and start again. It offers the powers of subtlety and the ability to change negative into positive. However, it can be vicious to those who cross it and cast off the good with the bad.

Be free from unnecessary guilt but do not break off what is of value in the past.

6: CIMI, Death: Tradition

Area of Heavens: North

Death is the sign of tradition, loyalty and duties, whether to politics, religion or to maintaining order and stability in daily life. Death therefore represents the conformist but one who is prepared to make personal sacrifices to the common good. However, Death can lead to following others without thinking through the wisdom or justice of the situation personally.

The divinatory message is to uphold what is of value, but do not follow the wisdom of others blindly.

7: MANIK, the Deer: Relationships

Area of Heavens: West

The Deer is the sign of relationships whether friends, family or business and is the connecting force of harmony, using intuition and sensitivity to understand the feelings and hearts of others. The deer is a force for harmony but can be in danger of losing a separate identity.

The divinatory message is create harmony with others, but do not lose sight of your own needs and feelings.

8: LAMAT, the Rabbit: Adventurous

Area of Heavens: South

The Rabbit is eager to roam and explore new territories and has the ability to avoid obstacles and evade danger. It is a symbol of a desire for taking chances in life and not being held back by fear or the need for security. However, the Rabbit can find it hard to make permanent commitments.

The divinatory message is to be bold in seeking new horizons, but pausing long enough to understand.

9: MULUC, Water: Emotions

Area of Heavens: East

Water is the symbol of strong, deep emotions and following intuition rather than logic. Water represents psychic powers and development and an ability to move with the needs of the moment. However, Water falters where practical matters and the need to take responsibility arise.

Follow your intuition but be aware of the need to live in the world is the divinatory message of Water.

10: OC, the Dog: Loyalty
Area of Heavens: North

The Dog is a good friend or family member, although it is happier to follow than lead. It is consistently loyal, no matter what reverses of fortune may occur, and is courageous. However, the Dog can need mature direction and guidance to fulfil its potential.

Remain loyal and courageous even in adversity, but follow the guidance of the wise if in doubt.

11: CHUEN, Monkey: Curiosity
Area of Heavens: West

The Monkey is a symbol of a desire to learn everything about the world and how it works. The Monkey is able to live by wit and intelligence and performs willingly in any social situation. The danger is that values can be as interchangeable as the needs of the moment.

Explore and learn but respect the rights and dignity of others is the divinatory message of the Monkey.

12: EB, Grass: Healing
Area of Heavens: South

Grass is the symbol of peace and healing powers, whether for an individual or the community. It represents reconciliation and compromise. However, because personal negative feelings can be suppressed, Grass can occasionally slip into depression or a flash of inappropriate anger.

Heal any quarrels or discord, but do not suppress your own feelings is the divinatory message of Grass.

13: BEN, Reed: Communication
Area of Heavens: South

The Reed was used for writing and so became associated with both spoken and written communication, especially that of an authoritative source, as it was seen as a regal plant. So the Reed talks of the need to communicate clearly and to listen or read carefully any spoken or written communication for the real meaning.

Be clear and make sure you understand what others are trying to communicate is the message of the Reed.

14: IX, Jaguar: Power
Area of Heavens: North

The Jaguar is symbol of power, moving at great speed through life and yet noble in spirit. The Jaguar will have great impact, whether on life or a specific situation, and inspire lesser creatures with his fire. The danger is that the powerful energies may be dissipated rather than concentrated on vital targets.

Use your power to the utmost but make sure there is a cause.

15: MEN, the Eagle: Vision

Area of Heavens: West

The Eagle is symbol of the visionary, who soars high and so can see the whole picture clearly. The Eagle offers a clear perspective on life or any matter of concern and has startling accuracy of aim for any ambition, whether in personal or work life. However, the eagle can find it hard to settle to mundane daily existence and so can be seen only as a dreamer.

The divinatory message is to be guided by higher motives, but be aware that you need roots in this world too.

16: CIB, the Vulture: The Realist

Area of Heavens: South

The symbol of the Vulture represents an awareness of life with all its darkness as well as light. The Vulture may be critical but is always fair and may find that life's path is not always easy. However, this experience offers a basis for wise counsel to others and an awareness of valued. The Vulture does find it difficult to accept human weakness and so sometimes can seem unsympathetic.

Speak the truth and expose injustice but tempered with compassion is the divinatory message of the Vulture.

17: CABAN, Earthquake: Movement

Area of Heavens: East

The Earthquake is a vital form of restructuring life and so is a vehicle for progress from one stage of life to another. It represents the power to fight injustice, so can be very altruistic, and the power to instigate positive change. However, the Earthquake can also contain suppressed emotion that unless channelled, can become destructive.

Instigate positive change but do not turn any anger inward is the divinatory message of the Earthquake.

18: EZNAB, Flint Knife: Decision

Area of Heavens: North

The Flint Knife represents making a choice and then following that decision through in the real world. The Flint Knife is incisive, cutting through difficulties and doubts. The only danger is in hurting oneself and others by too forceful an approach.

Be clear and put decisions into action, but do so with the minimum of pain is the divinatory message of the Flint Knife.

19: CAUAC, Rain: Renewal

Area of Heavens: West

Rain is the sign of fertility and growth, whether of a new enterprise or personal development. It is the opportunity that may come after a period of waiting and preparation and promises that old problems can be solved through a new perspective or input. The only problem is in being too impatient and giving up when results are not instantaneous.

Choose the right moment for action and then wait for the results is the divinatory message of Rain.

20: AHAU, the Flower: Fulfilment

Area of Heavens: South

The Flower represents perfection, whether in a personal or wordly way. Finding this perfect happiness – the right mate, the ideal career or a lifestyle filled with beauty and joy – is the aim of the Flower and he or she will make every effort to reach this ideal in whatever sphere. The only problem is that real life sometimes does not measure up and the Flower can be disappointed; in refusing to accept second-best, the Flower may end up with nothing.

The divinatory message for the Flower is to aim high but accept that life is rarely perfect in every way.

Mayan Divination Today

Although little is known about divinatory practices at the flowering of Mayan civilization, their descendants, including the Quiche Maya, who live in Guatemala, have magicians or Day Keepers who pass on orally the 260-day count and practise divination on behalf of individual tribal members.

They use crystals or beans in a special ceremonial bag. A seeker asks a question and the Day Keeper draws at random a quantity of crystals or beans from a bag. These are divided into lots of four until all have been used. The final group is the important one, for if only one or three beans or crystals remain, the Day Keeper will proceed no further. Should two or four beans remain, he will continue, counting all the complete piles of four. The number obtained will be added to that of the present-day sign.

For example if the day count had reached 1 – Flower, and there were ten piles of four, he would count on to 11 – Dog and Dog would be the sign that held the answer. The characteristics of the Dog would hold the clue to a course of action, that is to show loyalty to one's friends and seek guidance from someone wiser. The next Day of the Dog would in addition offer especially favourable conditions for resolution of the problems. The divination was, if a matter was difficult, repeated to give another sign and perhaps other auspicious days for action.

Finding a Special Day

There are many complications and little agreement as to definitive correspondences between the ancient ritual calendar and the modern solar one, since so much evidence has been lost. Even in western astrology, the astronomical and astrological years are separated by two whole star signs. Therefore, since divination relies on intuitive links, it is possible to use the old Mayan methods to calculate a symbolic special day, equivalent to a birth day, and then use this for all future divinatory questions.

Buy or make a special bag for your tiny crystals, beads, stones or beans. You may already have a quantity of small quartz crystals or white stones – you will need about 150 in your bag but do not count precisely how many are in there. You can sometimes buy bags of very tiny crystals of all kinds very cheaply, or, like the Maya, you can use dried beans. They do not have to be the same kind and colour so long as the size is similar. You may wish to go somewhere humid to carry out your divination, perhaps the corner of a hothouse if you live in a cool climate. Equally, you may wish to begin a collection of small ferns and palms in a small glassed area as your 'Mayan place'.

Pull out a quantity of beans at random. This may be one or two handfuls according to what feels right at the time. Divide these into piles of four, discarding any incomplete piles. You may, like the Day Keepers, wish to try another day if you end up with one or three in your last pile, but this is entirely a personal choice. Count the complete piles and note the number. Beginning at 1 – Alligator, follow the list in this book and count on the number of piles. You may go through the list two or three times before you reach your day. Do not worry about its number, merely the name for this will be your special day. You may like to find or make a symbol of your special day sign and keep it as a token. This first core sign, picked by divination, is special to you, but if after a few months you feel that you have changed or seek to develop a different side of yourself, you can repeat the process of divination.

Asking Questions

You may have a natural question or simply a desire to find out what characteristics and strengths would help you fulfil your current ambition or need.

Take one or two handfuls of beans or crystals and divide them into piles of four. Again discard any incomplete piles. You may wish to continue another time if you are left with one or three beans in the last pile.

Write down the number and from your list of signs identify your special day. Count on the number of piles until you reach a day sign. If this is your special day sign, you will know the issue is a core one, where your identity is in some way at stake. Look at the strengths of the day sign and see how a person whose special day sign it was would respond in your situation.

Be aware, too, of any weaknesses in that approach. If the day sign does not answer your question, repeat the process with the beans and add the insights of a second day sign to your special one. Remember that the number of days counted ahead will be especially propitious for any action or new endeavours on your part.

AN EXAMPLE OF MAYAN DIVINATION

Doug discovered his special sign was the Snake and he felt that its habit of shedding its skin and moving on expressed his own travelling light lifestyle. He had worked as a freelance television producer, going wherever the work was and keeping a small apartment in the centre of town for his needs. But Jenny, an old girlfriend, had come back into his life and Doug found himself dreaming of a home and children as time was passing. The death of his mother had reminded him of his own mortality.

Doug used a corner of a hot house on location while everyone else was at the bar and picked a handful of pebbles from an old plastic bag (magic can be improvised anywhere). Doug was left with exactly 15 piles and so he counted on from the Snake to the Flower: perfect love. Then he realized that what the day sign was saying was that he was seeking an idealized love, home and family to fulfil his own longing and was not really looking at Jenny as a person.

He also realized that the expectations he was loading on to Jenny were unfair. So Doug decided that he would take time to get to know her again and then see how they both felt about a committed future.

Making your Own Mayan Calendar

Take a wall chart planner or your own diary. Mark your own special sign either on your birthday or on the day you carried out the 'special day' divination. Mark each day going forward with the 20 signs until you have reached the end of the year. This may offer you a guide to significant days, that is, every time your own day sign appears. You may even find that the day signs give you a personal hint as to the day ahead. For example. If it is an Earthquake day, you may wish to make a few changes. You may be surprised as to how accurate this personal day sign scheme is.

METAL MAGIC

MYTHS OF METAL

In the classical world, Vulcan, son of Jupiter and Juno, was God of Fire and Metalworking and protector of all who carried out the craft. In his workshops under Mount Etna, Vulcan, also known as Mulciber the softener, forged thunderbolts for Jove. But because he took his mother's side in a quarrel with Jupiter, his father cast him from the heavens. Vulcan fell for nine days and although the people of Lemnos saved him from destruction, he broke his leg and was lame thereafter.

The classical tradition also gives us the cautionary tale about the obsessive desire for precious metals, especially gold. Midas, the legendary King of Phrygia, begged the gods that everything he touched might be turned into gold. They granted his wish and Midas discovered that although he now had a wondrous throne, artefacts and even golden trees, his hound, his food and finally his daughter turned to lifeless gold at his touch. Midas entreated the gods to take back the gift. The gods sent him to bathe in the River Pactolous and so the river runs over golden sands.

The legendary Wayland Smith, father of British blacksmiths and metalworkers, is an anglicized version of the Norse hero Volund (Wieland in Anglo-Saxon). He was reputed to be a metal smith with supernatural powers who was captured by King Nidhing of Sweden. Nidhing stole Volund's magical sword and cut the sinews of his feet so that he could not run away. Then Volund was set to work creating ornaments, jewellery, armour and weapons for his captors. After regaining his magical sword by creating a substitute for King Nidhing, Volund escaped using swan wings and was reunited with his Valkyr (swan maiden) wife. He settled with her in Alf-heim (Elf land) where he fashioned suits of armour that kept the wearer safe from any weapon. Volund also created magical swords, including that of the Emperor Charlemagne.

Metal and the Christian Tradition

Christianity also had its famous metalworkers. One was St Dunstan who in tenth-century England became Abbot of Glastonbury, then Bishop of Worcester and under King Edgar, Archbishop of Canterbury.

He restored the monastic movement which had nearly been destroyed by Saxon invasions. But it was his other gift as a metal smith that won him a place in the story books. St Dunstan fashioned bells, organs and tools. The Orange and Lemon bells of the old nursery rhyme at his church St Clement Dane in London were named after him. Pictures show him holding the Devil by the nose with a pair of tongs for legend says that St Dunstan was working at his forge when a man with horns, tail and no horse came and asked if he could be shod. Realizing the identity of the stranger, the saint nailed the Devil to the smithy wall and refused to let him free until he promised never to enter house or forge with a horsehoe nailed to the wall.

The Saint is also seen plying his goldsmith's tools, for he is the patron saint of goldsmiths, jewellers and blacksmiths, as well as of the blind and of Trinity House which controls British lighthouses and ships.

METALS AND THE PLANETS

Since Ancient Babylonian times, particular metals have been associated with the planets known to the early astronomers (Uranus was not discovered until 1781, Neptune in 1846 and Pluto in 1930), the sun and the moon and their ruling deities. In Western alchemy it was believed that when the influence of the ruling planet was strong, its metal would grow much faster within the Earth.

The metals, sometimes called by their planetary names, were said to contain an arcanum, a celestial power derived directly from the ruling planet. This arcanum, having been released and perfected through alchemical processes, was said to provide a highly effective medicine.

Planetary Qualities

Gold
The metal of the sun, it contains the pure masculine power and energy for success and achievement.

Silver
The metal of the moon, it contains the pure feminine power of intuition and instinctive wisdom for spiritual and psychic understanding.

Mercury
The metal of the planet with the same name, it contains the power to communicate and learn new things, to interact with others and make a place in the world.

Copper
The metal of Venus, it contains the powers to love and to attract love and to encourage harmonious relationships with family and friends.

Iron
The metal of Mars, it offers the power to stand against injustice and protection against negative influences.

Tin
The metal of Jupiter, it provides wisdom and idealism that make ventures worthwhile.

Lead
The metal of Saturn, it offers mastery over fate through recognizing times of change and finding a way round difficulties.

Modern Substitutes

Magic must move with the times and as some metals have been found to be potentially lethal and new metals have been discovered, substitutions have been made for certain rituals.

Mercury
Mercury is unstable and potentially lethal, unless contained in a thermometer or barometer. Aluminium is used as a modern substitute in magic and is ruled by the planet Mercury.

Gold/Brass
Brass is frequently used as a less expensive substitute for gold, especially in money spells, and is also ruled by the sun.

Iron/Steel
Steel is often used in modern magic as a substitute for iron and its gleaming surface can add a dimension of light to the protective qualities of traditional iron.

Lead/Pewter
Lead is poisonous so for many years pewter has been used as a substitute in magic. Pewter objects can be bought very cheaply from garage sales, antique and second-hand goods shops.

ELEMENTAL METALS

Earth offers a practical approach and firm foundations to any venture. It rules lead and mercury.
Air offers a logical, direct approach when change is needed. It rules aluminium, mercury and tin.
Fire offers a creative, inspirational approach for a new beginning. It rules brass, gold, iron and steel.
Water offers an intuitive response from the heart in sensitive issues. It rules copper, mercury and silver.

Because of its unique nature Mercury is ruled by Earth, Air and Water.

METALS AND THE DAYS OF THE WEEK

According to tradition, each metal is sacred a particular day of the week through its association with the planetary deities. On its 'day' a metal's symbolic powers are especially prevalent, but if you need the qualities of a particular metal to amplify your own, you can use it on any day. These powers echo the planetary strengths.
Sunday: gold or brass for success, power and money
Monday: silver for intuition, psychic dreams and unconscious wisdom
Tuesday: tin for conscious wisdom and transformation
Wednesday: mercury or aluminium for communication, learning and healing
Thursday: iron for strength and protection
Friday: copper for love and friendship
Saturday: lead or pewter for banishing regrets and old sorrows and finding a way round obstacles

You can carry small pieces of the appropriate metal or wear it as jewellery. Alternatively, find household objects made of these metals to focus on the particular strengths you need.

ALCHEMY

The word alchemy comes from *chyma*, Greek for the casting or fusing of metals. The ultimate aim of alchemy in the Western world was to create the Philosopher's Stone that would transform base metal into gold. Gold was believed to grow from base metals within the earth. The gold that would be produced by the alchemists through transmutation would not be ordinary gold, but a perfect form, the gold of the sages.

Work with metals created the foundations of alchemy which was first described around 200 BC. Western and also, perhaps, Eastern Alchemy was influenced by Ancient Egypt which was famed for its skilled metalwork, creation of alloys and metal tinting.

The emphasis of Eastern alchemy was to make a perfect elixir of gold that, when consumed, would give immortality as well as the ability to use celestial knowledge for human benefit.

In both the East and West, gold was from early times associated with royalty, divinity and the sun. Because of this divine link, gold was believed to bestow celestial blessings on mankind and for this reason was the focus for alchemical explorations. Western alchemists described gold and silver as the sun and moon, King Sol and Queen Luna who produced the Divine Hermaphrodite, source of the elusive Philosopher's Stone. An Eastern saying from the seventh century BC proclaimed: 'Gold is indeed fire, light and immortality.'

Alchemy reached its height in the Middle Ages in Western Europe. It remained popular throughout the sixteenth century, being discredited only in the early nineteenth century with the discovery of oxygen and the composition of water. Sadly, much of its wisdom was also lost and the validity of some of this knowledge is only just being rediscovered.

It is said that in the fourteenth century, Nicholas Flamel did transmute mercury into silver or gold three times, whether by magic, science or the mixture of both that made up alchemy.

MAGICAL METALS

Not only the alchemists used metals for magic. From time immemorial, ordinary people have used metals for rituals and many of these old skills survive as customs and superstitions. Metal magic can be adapted to modern needs and act as a powerful focus for intuition.

At the end of the section on the individual methods is a modern ritual or action using the metals or their present-day substitutes. These are only suggestions and often a personal ritual can be most powerful of all in galvanizing the determination to succeed or find happiness and love.

Aluminium

As well as being sacred to Mercury, aluminium is the metal of Odin, the All-Father of the Norse tradition (also Woden), after whom Wednesday is named. Aluminium or aluminium foil can be used for an interactive approach to any problems. Clear communication both with yourself and the outside world is vital.

An aluminium foil ritual

This can be used before an examination presentation or meeting where facts need to be memorized.

Begin in the evening seven days before the crucial day. Place the papers or books you need to master on a square of aluminium foil or an aluminium plate. Light a blue candle for knowledge and a yellow one for communication, as the way you present the facts may be crucial. Let the light from the candles reflect off the foil on to the learning material. See the words endowed with the light and life of mercury and visualize them as a blue ray entering your mind. Study until the candles are burning low and then re-wrap your books and all worries of failure inside the aluminium foil until morning. Blow out the candles and let the light drive away any lingering doubts in your mind.

Brass

Like gold, brass is sacred to all the solar gods, Helios and Apollo in classical tradition and the Norse Sun Goddess Sol and Baldur, God of the Growing Light. Brass can be used for healing, money and protective rituals. A brass ring is said to cure stomach cramps, while traditionally a brass key placed on the back of the neck stops nosebleeds.

In its protective role, brass was used because of its reflective surface to send negative thoughts, conscious or unconscious, back to the sender. Horse brasses were placed on horse's bridles to keep away any harmful spirits. Brass is especially effective in rituals for attracting money.

A Brass Money Ritual

Find a brass plate or dish. A dish of another material covered in yellowy-gold paper with a small brass ornament in the centre will serve as a symbolic substitute. Place a quantity of brass discs from a hardware store or brass coloured coins (of any value) in the dish until it is about half-full. Surround the dish with yellow crystals, such as citrine, golden tiger's eyes, yellow quartz, jasper or calcite, or with yellowy, golden flowers, such as marigolds, chrysanthemums or even buttercups, symbol of modest riches (see also *Flower Magic*, page 22).

Place the dish under a yellow light bulb, if possible in a brass lamp or one with a yellow lamp shade. Imagine the golden rays falling as coins into the dish. Watch them rise until the dish overflows in your mind's eye and cascades like a waterfall. Cover the dish with a yellow or golden cloth or another brass plate or lid if you have one. Switch off the light. Each day, add a coin or brass disc until your bowl really does begin to overflow. As you add each coin, switch on the yellow bulb and recreate the golden waterfall of wealth. You will find that your mind begins to generate money-making schemes. If you begin to doubt, uncover your store of hidden wealth and leave it in the sunlight until your confidence returns.

Copper

This may have been the first metal to be used by early man because it was so malleable. Indeed weapons and utensils made of pure copper have survived. This usage developed and copper was used to make bronze, the first real age of metal.

Because of its softness and rainbow sheen, copper is associated with love goddesses of different cultures: Venus, its ruler, Frigg, the wife of Odin and Mother Goddess of women and fertility, Ishtar, Astarte and Innana. Its powers are for love, friendship, healing and protection.

The healing powers of copper are attributed to its ability to balance the body's polarity. Copper bracelets are still worn to prevent and relieve rheumatism and arthritis, a custom that began in the Middle Ages. In India, Hindus use copper earrings to prevent sciatica and ear infections.

Copper is also worn to attract love. In past times, a copper ring set with emerald or jade was sometimes given by a young man to his beloved as a love token. They were sometimes surrounded by mimosa seeds.

A Copper Love Ritual

Take some copper jewellery, such as a bracelet or ring, and entwine it with roses, Venus's flower, if in season, or with greenery, such as myrtle, tree and flower of love, ivy, apple, avocado or peach boughs. Pass an incense stick or an essential oil (heated in an oil burner or over a radiator) over the ring or bracelet. Use magnolia, ylang-ylang, geranium, rose or thyme, fragrances of Venus. See your loving energies and powers of desirability rising upwards and outwards towards someone with whom you could share love.

Place your copper ring or bracelet and flower on a favourite love poem that you have copied in your own handwriting on to pale green or pink paper, the colours of Venus. Light a green or pink candle and as you read the words to your known or unknown love in the candlelight, see him or her in the flame.

Gold

Gold is sacred to Osiris the Egyptian All-Father and to Re or Ra, Egyptian sun god as well as the classical sun deities. The first examples of gold adornments and utensils have been dated to the Fourth Millennium BC. In Ancient Egypt, gold was also used to adorn royal tombs and in many cultures was regarded as the highest tribute that could be made to the gods. Because of its association with the male solar gods of different cultures, gold has come to represent success, power and male potency.

Druids gathered mistletoe, the all-healer, with sickles of pure gold from the sacred oak trees. Medieval herbalists collected plants with golden implements to strengthen the curative and energizing power of the herbs. Even today, herbs are gathered with non-iron implements to avoid blocking the energies.

Where brass represents money, gold is pure power and for ordinary people throughout the world, as well as the fabulously wealthy, wearing a gold ring or necklace increases courage and confidence. Because of its solar gleam, gold is also regarded as a protective metal. In India, children wear small golden charms to keep them from all harm.

A Gold Ritual for Success

This is a ritual to be performed when the sun is high in the sky on a cloudless day. If possible find a flat plain or sandy place where the sun shimmers on the horizon.

Hold a gold chain with many links up to the sun. Each individual link forms a circle, part of the larger golden circle, an unbroken circuit of energy and potential achievement. Walk directly towards the sun, holding your chain between your two hands, as far apart as it will extend so that the sun's rays shine through the golden circle into each separate golden sun link. As your golden band becomes filled with the energy and positivity of the sun, keep walking towards the ever-expanding horizon of possibility. Let the golden light and power fill every fibre of your being, endowing you with golden light and confidence. Allow the light and sun to expand further and further until the horizon is ablaze. When you are pulsating with power, stop and at the place you stop walking, plant a golden fruit seed or stone in the sunlight as symbol of living gold.

Place the chain around your neck and let the interconnected circles of gold inspire you with confidence in your own abilities to succeed. If, after a day or so, you begin to lose your impetus, repeat the ritual or if the day is dull, place your sun links around a golden candle and allow it to burn until the sun has set.

Iron

Iron is sacred to the Norse Tyr, the defender god with his magical iron sword, as well as Ares, God of War, the classical forerunner of Mars who carried an iron sword. It is used both for endowing physical strength and endurance and for initiating change. Wearing iron or carrying a piece of iron was said to enhance physical strength.

Its other principal power resides in protective magic, whether against illness or malign influence. Iron was reputedly feared by fairies, witches and dragons. In China small chunks of iron were thrown into dragon pools so that they would flee to the sky and produce rain.

Iron first gained its magical reputation when meteorites containing pure iron fell from heaven. This magic metal was used to make simple tools, replacing primitive bone and stone implements. It was seen by early man as a gift from the gods. Iron was manufactured by the Hindus and in the East while European peoples were still using bronze. However, the magical reputation of iron increased everywhere as native peoples found bronze weapons useless against the iron swords of invading tribes.

Because of the legendary fame of the smith gods and heroes, such as Vulcan and Volund, blacksmiths and farriers were regarded as magicians and their forges endowed with magical significance. Horseshoes have been used to bring luck and guard against misfortune since Greek and Roman times. They are still displayed, points upwards so that their luck will not run out. However, those outside forges should point downwards so that the magical power will pour on to the anvil. It is ten times luckier to find a horseshoe than to buy one. Water from the trough in a forge traditionally had healing power.

Iron nails were driven into the beds of women in labour and into infants' cradles as protection against negative influences. A child's bathwater would be poured over him or her, first letting it run over the blade of a scythe to stave off illness.

Placed beneath a pillow at night, iron was said to regenerate the body's ability to reject illness. A piece of iron or an iron or steel object, such as pair of scissors, would be buried under the threshold to prevent negative influences entering (see also *Domestic Magic*, page 127). Alternatively, iron with just the tip showing would be buried near the front door, so that it would attract any unfriendly vibrations. These could pass into the earth and be absorbed to regenerate as positive growth.

An Iron/Steel Ritual

Carry this out if you are facing a difficult situation to which there seems no answer or you need strength to take a decision, initiate change or stand against injustice.

Take seven short, thick shiny nails, the sacred number often used for fixing horseshoes. Place them about 7 cm (3 inches) apart, sharp end uppermost in the shape of a horseshoe with the arms pointing skywards. Within the horseshoe of nails, place a large, wide brilliant red candle (the colour of Mars) on an iron dish or candlestick.

Beginning with the top right nail and proceeding clockwise, warm each nail in the flame of the candle, then push it into the wax. As you do so, endow each nail with strength and determination and let any negative fears or feelings be buried with it in the wax. Then using a stainless steel mirror, disc or lid beam the glow of the candle flame on to a wall so that it moves upwards and catches the gleaming nail heads.

Blow out the candle and take the scarlet energy within yourself. When the candle is cool, take out the nails and place them in a sealed glass jar as a reminder of your own strength and determination. Jars or pockets of nails were seen as protective and a source of enduring power, so keep yours over a fireplace or on a window ledge where they may absorb either the fire of the sun or a domestic heat source.

Lead/Pewter

Lead is sacred both to Saturn and to Saetere or Seater, Anglo Saxon God of Agriculture who carried a wheel (symbol of the cart and also fate) in his left hand and flowers and fruit in the right.

Linked with fate and the limitations of time and space, lead was associated with the dead and with wrappings for the dead. It was traditionally placed above the threshold to prevent harmful influences entering the home and in the modern world it is used as a shield against radiation.

Lead was also the metal of written offerings and charms. Entreaties and prayers for power, fertility of humans and land and less benign wishes were written on tablets of lead in the classical world. The softness and malleability of lead made it easy to record messages that would not decay.

Lead or pewter as the metal of fate is a powerful catalyst for turning limitation into opportunity, for obstacles into a guide to new directions and endings as the doorway to a new beginning.

A Ritual for Letting Go

This ritual is for releasing old sorrows, a bad habit or a destructive relationship. Use an old pewter mug, jug, dish or any made of dull grey metal, the more battered and worn the better. Write what it is you wish to lose in black ink on a dull grey stone. As you hold the stone, let all your sorrow and anger pour into it (the stone may seem to become darker). Do not worry how negative your thoughts are, but do not be tempted to curse or hex a person who has wronged you. To utter a curse is destructive to you psychologically and such magical practices are best left in the Dark Ages.

Place your stone in the pewter container. Wait until the sun is almost set and take your pewter message into the garden or a corner of a park. Dig a hole and bury the message. Plant small white flowers there for a new beginning. Fill your pewter mug, jug or dish with a riot of greenery, bright blossoms, flowers or berries and place it in your bedroom so your new hope is the first thing you see when you wake in the morning (see *Flower Magic*, page 221).

Silver

Silver was especially sacred to the Egyptian Mother and lunar goddess Isis as well as to the moon herself, to Diana and lunar goddesses in many cultures. From time immemorial silver has been used for images of goddesses and silver bells were a special invocation of the power of all mother goddesses. It is a source of psychic and intuitive abilities, especially when its ruling moon is full. A silver ring left in the moonlight and placed beneath a pillow before sleep brings psychic dreams that will give answers to the problems of the day. Keep a silver-coloured pen and pad by the bed and write down any impressions when you wake.

Scrying with Silver

Scrying (seeing psychic pictures or receiving impressions) with silver is especially effective on the first clear night of the week of the full moon (see also *Moon Magic*, page 336). Use a plain silver object with a rounded surface, such as a coffee pot or inverted silver bowl. Alternatively, place circles of thin silver bracelets in a small bowl of clear water and let the moonlight form ripples on the silvery water. Think of a question and half close your eyes. Place the silver near an open window.

You may see images, colours or shadows in the silver or hear half-formed words. If they do not make sense immediately, write them down or draw them on paper with a silver pen and place them under your pillow. The answer will come to you in your dreams.

Silver is a symbol of protection and money. In China, infants are given silver lockets which they wear at all times to provide special protection against bad dreams and night terrors. In many parts of the world, silver is turned over on the new moon so that money will come during the month.

Tin

Tin is sacred to Jupiter, Father of Wisdom and to Thor, the Norse God of Thunder, who was said to have discovered the metal as it ran from stones that had been heated. This legend was attributed to the Christian St Piran of Cornwall, once a great area of tin-mining in Britain. Tin ingots and artefacts have been excavated in lake dwellings thousands of years old.

Magically, tin is the metal of hidden riches and potential as the black, apparently worthless ore reveals its silvery streams. It has been used for divination and in money rituals, for many ancient coins are made of tin. Because it is so malleable, it has been used to make talismans for good fortune.

A New Year's eve divination ritual involved melting a tin ingot in an iron cup over a flame, casting the molten metal into cold water and using the shape it formed as a symbol for the coming year. A heart shape indicated love, a disc indicated money, a boat indicated travel and so on.

Achieving a Seemingly Impossible Dream

Use a row of 'tin' cans with the labels removed as a symbol of tin or obtain a set of tin soldiers from an antique market.

Place them in a straight line and at the top of the row put a symbol of what it is you really want: a toy boat or plane for travel, a model house for a new home, a coin or credit card for money, a heart charm or rose for love. Above the symbol, place a bright blue candle, Jupiter's colour, and as you light it see the fire transforming the dark ore into shining tin.

Hold the first can or soldier and see the silvery stream of your hidden beauty, talent and strength flowing outwards, forming shining steps towards your goal. As the tin takes shape in your mind, you will know the first step. Remove the first tin or soldier and plan to fulfil at least a part of that dream in the real world.

You may wish to carry the first step after extinguishing the candle and sending the light from the candle to illuminate your inner potential (see also *Fire Magic*, page 211). You can then leave the remaining cans or soldiers in place, surrounded by bright blue flowers, until you are ready for the next stage. You may prefer to carry out the whole ritual at once, seeing the shining steps of tin unfolding and repeating any on which you falter.

MOON MAGIC

ORIGINS AND EARLY BELIEFS

A moon goddess first appeared in cave paintings during the Neolithic or New Stone Age which in Europe began about 7000 BC and lasted until about 5500 BC. The moon was seen to have three main phases: waxing, full and waning. These stages echoed human existence, birth, maturity and death.

Women especially identified with the lunar life cycle and the moon goddess came to represent the maiden, mother and crone or wise woman phases of development. Women who wanted to become pregnant would sleep under the rays of the moon from waxing to full to ensure conception.

As the hunter/gatherer way of life gave way to agriculture, the moon goddess's fertility became identified with the fecundity of the earth as well as motherhood. The moon goddess ruled the night, as the sun god did the day, and both were worshipped as the source of all life and goodness. When it was realized that the tides rose and fell with the moon, the concept was applied to bodily fluids and even agriculture. In planting and reaping, the waxing moon was said to increase all growth and ripening while the waning moon decreased the speed of growth and richness of fruit. Gardeners, particularly in country places, abide by these old maxims, which seem to work.

According to legend, every evening the moon gathers unfulfilled wishes, discarded hopes, unwanted memories and disappointments and takes them into herself to be restored as the morning dew.

THE MOON AND REBIRTH

Because the moon disappears from the sky for three days at the end of every cycle and is reborn again as the visible crescent, it became associated with rebirth. In popular myth the moon took dead souls back to her womb whence they came, to await fertilization by the sun and rebirth. Plutarch, the Ancient Greek philosopher, developed a more sophisticated version of this folk magic, describing the moon as a resting place for souls following death. The body was consigned to the earth, domain of the Earth Goddess, Demeter. The soul and psyche then returned to the moon where they were able to retain memories and dreams of former life. The mind progressed further in a second death and splitting of the soul and psyche, travelling from moon to the sun, where it was absorbed and reborn as a new mind. The rebirth process continued as the mind returned to the moon where the waiting soul rejoined the fresh mind and adopted an new earthly body.

The Hindus also believe that unenlightened souls return to the moon to await rebirth, while those who have attained freedom from the wheel of reincarnation take the path to the sun.

MOON CREATION MYTHS

Every culture offers its own account of the creation of the moon and several are contained in different sections of this book. One of the more picturesque myths comes from the Navajo Indians.

First People emerged from the underworld to live on the surface of the Earth. But the Earth was dark and cold and so First Man and First Woman fashioned two disks from glowing crystal quartz to form the sun and moon so that there would be light both by day and night. First the sun disk was adorned with a mask of blue turquoise with red coral around its edge and it offered warmth as well as light. First Man and First Woman next attached eagle and lark feathers to the sun so that its light and heat would be cast to all four corners of the earth. The sun disc was fixed in the eastern sky with lightning darts. First Man and First Woman paused to admire the great beauty they had created for the day and then turned to the night.

The moon disk was decorated with clear shimmering crystals and pearl white shells and, like the sun, fixed high in the sky. But to the sorrow of the First People, their creations were static and lifeless. Two wise old men offered their spirits to the disks that they might live and move forever. First Man and First Woman then marked out the daily path of the sun by fixing 12 eagle feathers at equal points (see *Native North American Magic*, page 348, for the 12 divisions of the Medicine Wheel). At dawn, the sun began to move majestically across the sky, warming and illuminating all in the blackness beneath. At dusk, the sun returned tired from his journey and the moon, also adorned with eagle feathers, began his course.

However, Wind Boy, who thought it unfair the moon should have to travel so far by night alone, blew his strong breezes so that the moon might glide effortlessly across the darkened heavens. However, the moon's eagle feathers blew across his face, temporarily blinding him and so to this day the moon follows an irregular passage across the night sky.

THE MAN OR WOMAN IN THE MOON

Even before the moon deities were given names, legends grew about the man or woman who lived in the moon whose features could be seen at certain times of the month. In Ireland, the man in the moon is said to be a man from Killarney who was cutting hawthorn on the sabbath. For this sin, he was transported to the moon and can be seen sorrowfully gazing down on his native Ireland with his bundle of sticks forever tied to his back.

Another legend makes Judas Iscariot, the disciple who betrayed Jesus, the man in the moon, while a German version has both a man and woman on the moon: the woman is banished to the lunar wilderness for churning butter on the sabbath and the man for casting brambles and thorns across the path of worthy folk walking to church.

In New Guinea, it is believed that the moon was once kept in a jar by an old woman until one day mischievous boys let it out. The lines on the moon are the fingermarks left by the boys who tried to retrieve it and avert the old woman's wrath. But the moon was never caught and so roams free through the skies.

Cambodians say that Pajan Yan, Goddess of Healing, was exiled to the moon by the God of Death because she wished to restore the dead to health and so deprive him of his subjects.

THE HARE IN THE MOON

The hare is sacred to moon goddesses in different cultures. Perhaps the most famous is the hare of Ostara or Eostra, the Anglo Saxon Lunar Goddess and Goddess of the Dawn of the Year. Ostara's hare became the Easter Rabbit who brings chocolate eggs or rabbits for Northern European children. But the Hare in the moon myths probably began in India where the 'man in the moon' is said to be Chandra, Hindu God of the Moon. He is depicted carrying a hare or 'sasa'. In India the moon is called Sasin or Sasanka, which in Sanskrit means 'having the marks of the hare'.

One of several similar Buddhist myths recounts that Buddha became lost in a wood and after several days was weak through lack of food. A hare took pity and offered itself as nourishment to Buddha. It told him to light a fire then hopped in among the flames.

Buddha, overcome by the hare's nobility, revealed his divinity and plucked the hare from the fire unharmed. He then placed the hare in the moon as an eternal symbol of sacrifice, where he remains to this day.

According to Chinese myth, a three-legged toad lives in the moon, its legs representing the three main phases. At lunar eclipses, the toad swallows the moon (see also *Chinese Magic*, page 63).

LUNAR DEITIES

In many cultures the lunar deities tend to be goddesses rather than gods because the moon is naturally seen as feminine, intuitive and the mysterious aspect of nature and because of its associations with the female rhythms and cycles of life. Most famous of all of lunar goddesses and one still central to modern Wicca (witchcraft) is Diana, Roman Goddess of the Moon, the Hunt and Fertility. Lakes are often called Diana's mirror, as she is seen to gaze at her own reflection in them as she rides high in the sky. Although, like her Greek counterpart Artemis, she was worshipped originally as the maiden aspect of the moon, in time she came to represent the full moon also. Sometimes the Triple Lunar Goddess of modern Wicca is represented by the classical deities, Diana (the Greek Artemis), Selene and Hecate.

Isis the Egyptian Goddess was both Moon Goddess and Mother of the Sun. She held a papyrus sceptre and the ankh, symbol of life (see also *Egyptian Magic*, page 164). Caotlicus was the Aztec Moon Goddess and wife of the Sun God. Arianrod was the Celtic Moon Goddess whose home was in the constellation Corona Borealis. Britomartis was originally a Cretan moon goddess, but was adopted by the Greek invaders since she offered protection to all who crossed the seas. Gwatan was the Japanese Buddhist lunar goddess and one of the 12 Buddhists deities, holding the moon disk in her right hand.

Moon Gods

Khonsu was the Egyptian moon deity. His name means 'he who crosses the sky' and he is pictured as a mummified youth holding a crook, flail and sceptre, crowned by both crescent and full moons. He was associated with pregnancy.

Myesyats, the Slavic Moon God, represented the three stages of the life cycle like the lunar goddesses. He was first worshipped as a young man until he reached maturity at the full moon. With the waning phase, Myesyats passed through old age and died with the old moon, being reborn three days later. As he was the restorer of life and health, parents entreated him to take away their children's illnesses and family sorrows.

Alako was worshipped as the Romany Moon God until the nineteenth century and some of the rituals have survived. Tiny stone idols depicted Alako with a quill in his right hand and a sword in his left. Children and marriages were carried out under his auspices, even if more conventional religious ceremonies also took place. When a Romany died, Alako took back his soul to the moon. He was worshipped also at the full moon.

Twin Lunar Deities

Candi was the female counterpart of Chandra, ancient Hindu God of the Moon whose symbol was the hare. Lunar god and goddess presided over the moon on alternate months.

THE LUNAR CALENDAR

The earliest calendars were based on the lunar cycle and moon time is still used in the modern world in both pagan and religious rituals. In the Christian church, Easter is calculated as the first Sunday following the first full moon after the spring equinox (21 March).

The Chinese New Year is also a lunar festival and the Chinese ritual year follows the moons. China did not adapt the Gregorian (official solar calendar) until 1912.

In New Guinea, the natives reckoned months by the moons and they threw sticks, stones and spears at the moon to hasten its progress and so hasten the return of friends and family who were away for a year working on the tobacco plantations.

MOON MAGIC

The full moon became associated with magic in days before artificial lighting and today Wiccans still hold their *esbats* or circles at the full moon when it is believed that magical power is at its greatest. The ancient witches of Thessaly were said to have the power to draw the moon from the sky at their command. The ceremony of drawing down the moon symbolically is still performed by modern Wiccans.

But moon magic is not the province of witches only. It has formed a basis for folk magic, especially among women, from the earliest times. Even today, many people bow before the new moon and turn over the money in their pockets to ensure that they will have enough money for the coming month.

The waxing moon has traditionally been considered the time for growth, increase in money, happiness or new love, as well as healing rituals. The full moon is associated with fertility, success in money and love and an excellent time to get married or begin a new job. The waning moon offers powers to undo unhappiness, illness, bad habits or unwanted ties. The dark of the moon, when the old moon is invisible, is said to be good for rituals of protection and for any undertaking that involves secrecy.

Magical Moon Days and Times

Each heavenly body has its special day of the week and time when its magical influences are said to be especially powerful. Monday is ruled by the moon and during Monday the first and eight hours after sunrise are most magical of all for moon rituals and wishes. After sunset on a Monday, the third and tenth hours are the special lunar ones. Take the hour as beginning from the time of sunrise and sunset which will vary each day and can be found in any newspaper. Traditionally Monday is favoured for rituals and wishes for love, reconciliation, second sight and ventures involving water, travel, the sea, home, family and gardening.

Lunar Associations

Silver is both the metal and colour of the moon. Its element is water and it rules the astrological sign of Cancer the Crab. Therefore those born between 21 June and 20 July are children of the moon and may feel happiest after dark, especially when they can see the moon.

The moonstone, mother-of-pearl, sea-green aquamarine or pale golden beryl are stones of the moon. Moonstones come in different hues – pink, yellow, blue and creamy white – so differently coloured moonstones can represent the different phases. A pink moonstone may stand for the waxing phase, white or yellow for the full moon and blue for the waning moon.

Lunar flowers and herbs include the dog rose, gardenia, jasmine, night stock, lemon, lemon balm, myrrh, poppy seed and wallflower. Lunar animals include the dog, wolf and crab. Its bird is the owl and its special Archangel is Gabriel. Trees of the moon are any growing close to water, but especially the willow, the mountain ash, the mango tree, the rowan, the banana tree and the cactus.

You can use any of these for your own lunar rituals or wishes, for example burning a silver candle or using a silver coin as a focus to visualize money increasing as the moon waxes.

Identifying the Lunar Phases

The most effective way of beginning moon magic is to choose a night when you can see the moon. When it is waxing, the light is on the right and the illuminated moon grows larger night by night from right to left until the disk is fully illuminated. When the moon wanes, following the appearance of a full moon, the darkness increases from the right, covering the light on the left until the moon disappears to return three days later as a crescent.

If you want to study the moon's phases, these are usually to be found in the daily newspaper. Many diaries also include the moon dates. The cycle from new moon to new moon lasts 29.5 days but there is a retardation averaging about 50 minutes a day in the rising and setting of the moon. It takes just over 27 days for the moon to complete its orbit round the Earth.

There are various ways of calculating the phases of the moon. For example, the lunar month is counted as 28 days and on calendars, the lunar phases are divided into four weeks: the week of the new moon, the week of the first quarter, the week of the full moon and the week of the last quarter. These quarter periods will vary between seven and eight days according to the month and this varies each year. There are also eight recognised phases within the lunar cycle.

Magical Reckonings

Since the earliest times, moon magic has operated on the three aspects of waxing, full and waning. The phases are fluid and last for about nine nights each, with the first night being that on which the first crescent appears in the sky. This is the most magical time of all. However, the phases should not be governed by calendars, but by intuition. Because the influences are inner rather than outer, go with your own rhythms and what you feel rather than what the calendar says. If your full moon surge lasts for extra days and nights during one month, go with it and benefit from the extra power to get things done.

After a month or so, you will find your own cycle echoing the ebbing and flowing energies of the moon. You will feel the stirrings of excitement and enthusiasm link in the new moon with a special peak on the crescent. Then as the moon moves towards fullness, you will feel energy and confidence with perhaps the greatest momentum for achievement as the moon reaches its fullness.

Gradually these energies will recede. When you start to feel irritable and easily tired, you will know that the waning period is beginning and you should rest and avoid unnecessary conflict. As the waning moon dies, you will reach the peak of this phase and should withdraw physically and mentally to reflect on the future when the next crescent offers another chance at happiness.

You will find that your own rhythm gradually synchronizes with those of the moon and women in the fertile years may find that their menstrual cycle adapts so that, like the women of old, they bleed on the dark of the moon, the 'wise blood' of the Goddess.

New Moon and Waxing Magic

This is the time to initiate new ventures. Rituals to increase money, especially on the day of the new moon, are perhaps the most common waxing spells. These rituals come from all cultures from when coinage was first used. They were handed down orally and were first recorded about the eleventh century.

A Waxing Moon Money Ritual

If you need money for a good reason, take a silver coin to symbolize the metal and colour of the moon. Stand at an open window facing the crescent moon (old superstitions say that you should not look at the moon through glass). Light a silver candle and hold your silver coin in your right hand for action in the real world (since the left or logical part of the brain is said to control the right hand and vice versa).

Turn over the coin and see silver coins showering down like moonbeams upon you. Say as you place your money on the window ledge:

New moon, true moon,
Silver you grow,
Let now my fortune
Increase show.

Blow out your candle and see the silver light spreading prosperity over every venture you touch. Each day until the moon is full, add to your silver pile and when the moon is full, give the coins to a good cause or buy a small gift for someone you love and you will find your gift comes back many times.

Full Moon Magic

This is especially potent for love magic and matters of the heart (see also *Love Magic*, page 289).

A Full Moon Love Ritual

At the full moon, use a silver-handled knife to cut a small willow bough or any tree growing near water. Take it home and on it hang a silver ring. Light a moon fragrance, such as jasmine or sandalwood, either as an incense cone or burn it as an oil in one of the small burners on sale in many supermarkets. You can place the oil in a saucer and warm it gently over a radiator if you have no burner. Pass the ring endowed with loving feelings through the fragrance and place the ring on your wedding finger, seeing before you your absent lover or the person you would like to meet.

Finally place the ring beneath your pillow, while reciting:

Lady Moon, bring to me,
My lover, whether of high degree,
Low estate or gypsy wild,
Close to home or cross the sea.
Let me dream my lover's face,
My future home, our first born child,
And show me where my love will be.

Sleep with the moonlight shining on your pillow and you will dream of your future love. Plant your tiny bough near water the next day.

Waning Moon Magic

This can be very potent if you have had a period of bad luck or ill health.

A Waning Moon Ritual to Banish Sorrow

On a clear night as the moon begins to decrease in size, go to a lake or pond (Diana's mirror) and take a white stone. Using a sharp black stone or silver-handled knife, scratch on the stone a symbol or word to represent the sorrow, ill-health or negative feelings you want to leave behind.

Cast the stone into the water so that, if possible, it ripples the image of the waning moon. As you throw it say:

Old Moon, Wane Moon,
Moon of Sorrow,
Bring me now
A new tomorrow.

Plant a few seeds by the pool or in your garden to symbolize new beginnings, for in magic you must always replace what you take away.

MOON CRYSTAL DIVINATION

You can use moon crystal divination whenever you want to ask a question or make a decision, but it is especially effective on a Monday during one of the evening moon power hours.

Burn a silver candle if you are working after sunset as this is the colour of the moon. You might like to choose a moon oil for your bath or to burn, such as sandalwood, lemon, lemon balm or jasmine. Choose three different coloured moonstones or moon crystals, mother-of-pearl, beryl or aquamarine, to represent the waxing, full and waning phases.

Make a moon chart or cloth with three circles: the largest outer circle about 25 cm (10 inches) in diameter, a smaller one of about 17 cm (seven inches) in diameter inside the first and a third one of about 10 cm (4 inches) in diameter in the centre of the second. The inner circle represents the waxing moon, the middle one the full moon and the outer the waning moon. You could mark your chart or cloth circles silver on white or black on white. Alternatively, use stitching to make the circles.

Begin with your waxing, full and waning stones in a cloth bag or purse. They must be of similar size and shape and you need three of each colour: perhaps pink moonstones for the waxing phase, white or yellow for the full and blue for the waning.

Ask a question and pick a stone without looking, casting it on to the cloth. The kind of stone and the circle in which it falls will indicate the answer to your question or the best strategy to take in your present dilemma or life plan.

The Meaning of the Cloth and Moonstones

The Inner Circle of the Waxing Moon

Any stone that falls within the inner circle represents a new beginning or venture: friendship, a love affair, a new phase in a relationship or a new idea or work project or opportunity, especially one involving possible advantages in money.

If the waxing moon stone falls into the area of the waxing moon, the idea may be only tentative or the potential relationship still only on the horizon. Take courage and take the first steps.

If a full moon stone falls into the waxing area of new beginnings, the way forward is clear and, given persistence, happiness or a success will be achieved.

If a waning moon stone is in the area of the waxing moon, it is important to clear up old doubts and unfinished business before starting a new venture.

The Centre Circle of the Full Moon

This circle talks of the power and energy to achieve any goal or to experience fulfilment in relationships.

If a waxing moon stone falls into the full moon circle, you may be feeling a new intensity of emotions or be in uncharted waters in an important career, love or life plan. Believe in yourself and you will succeed.

If a full moon stone falls in the area of the full moon, success is assured as long as you are prepared to commit yourself entirely.

If a waning moon stone falls in this area, you may be letting irrelevant issues or the criticism of others distract from the main goal or relationship in your life. Focus your powers.

The Area of the Waning Moon

Here resides all that is redundant, perhaps an aspect of your life that has lost its purpose or pleasure. It is time to move on, whether to a new stage or to initiate a change.

A waxing moon stone in the waning moon circle means that you fear having to start again or stand alone on an issue. Move forward and you will find that there are new opportunities around the corner.

A full moon stone in the waning moon circle suggests that there may be major opposition to any change you are planning, perhaps from those around you who prefer the status quo. Follow your own heart.

A waning moon stone in the waning area of the cloth suggests that change is inevitable, but it is important to explore your fears and discuss your doubts so that the future is how you want it.

A SAMPLE READING

Angela is in her late twenties and divorced. She has returned to the family home but her parents, who disapproved of her husband from the beginning, are now attempting to control every aspect of her life, albeit with great kindness and smothering affection.

She has decided she would like a career change and has been offered training as a nurse at the other end of the country which will involve a considerable drop in salary. Her parents are trying to persuade her to continue her career in banking and have been inviting the unattached son of family friends around at every opportunity.

Angela consults the moon oracle and throws. A full moon stone in the waning moon circle. This suggests that Angela's own impetus for change is being stifled by others, in this case her parents. She should follow her own heart and not theirs. She then casts a waxing moon stone in the waning moon circle. This reflects Angela's own fears about starting again and being alone. But if she does not move forward, she will not be able to discover new opportunities, in this case a career change that may bring her happiness. Finally, she casts a waxing moon stone in the waxing circle. This reflects Angela's own desires for a new beginning and says that she should take the first steps to put her ideas in motion.

Angela did not ignore the warnings and moved to begin her training. Although she is missing her family and material security, she has made friends with another mature student and is finding her new career fulfilling.

30

NATIVE NORTH AMERICAN MAGIC

GREAT SPIRIT

Native North American magic is as varied as the continent it spans, vast distances of high, rocky mountains, dense forests, arid deserts and fertile plains peopled by hunters, farmers and warriors. Central to all forms is the belief that all life stems from a Great Invisible Creator and that this life force is imbued equally in minerals, plants, animals and humankind. The earthly forms of things are said to reflect their perfect form in the spirit world. Black Elk, the Oglala Sioux medicine man, gives the example of the spotted eagle: 'His feathers are the rays of the sun and when the feathers are worn, represents and is the real presence, Wakan-Tanka, the Great Spirit.'

Creation myths vary among the tribes but a representative one is that of the Indians of the Great Plains, an area extending from the frozen wastes of the Mackenzie River in Northern Canada to the North of Mexico and to the West of the Mississippi. They believed the world was ruled by the all-powerful and invisible Great Spirit. Mother Earth was the source of all life. Their ceremonies honoured the marriage between Earth and Sky and the birth of Life. Great gods, such as the Sun, the Moon, Wind and Fire, were intermediaries between the Great Unknowable Spirit and mankind.

RITUALS

The sun was the principal deity for nearly all tribes. The Great Sun Dance on the summer solstice, around a central pole representing the axis of the universe, was based on the idea of sacrifice. Once warriors drove skewers connected to the central pole to their chests to symbolize their connection to all things. Thomas Yellowtail, Sun Dance Chief of the Crow Tribe said: 'As the drum beats, it establishes the heartbeat for the dancers, our tribe and for all mankind.'

To the beat of the drum, braves danced around either a totem pole, representing all the power animals of the tribe, or around a sacred fire, pressing down on the living earth to unite Earth and Sky. These dances marked the great agricultural festivals of the year and also those special to the area. For example, the Buffalo Dance of the Mandans, a Dakota Tribe, marking the annual return of the buffalo herds, was held when the willow was in full leaf.

TRIBAL TOTEMS

A totem represents an essential quality or strength. Animals were often totems because they displayed the skills essential for survival. Many myths tell of braves meeting the chief of an animal clan who would impart his wisdom.

Personal Totems

At 13, boys would go into the forest to fast for several days. The first animal, bird or reptile they met or which acted in a significant or unusual way – perhaps a deer coming very close or an eagle circling above several times – might be taken as a personal totem. Thus such names as Lame Deer or Running Bear would replace a childhood name. Girls, too, would be taken to a safe place where such 'fasting totem visions' might occur.

A Personal Totem in the Modern World

If you live in the countryside, there is no problem seeing wild creatures. If you are a city dweller, visit an animal or bird sanctuary, an aquarium or wildlife park. Make a special journey alone at a time when the place will be quiet and eat only a light meal beforehand. Sit or stand quietly and let the creature make the overtures.

Perhaps, a certain creature has appeared in your dreams or at important times in your life, so you already regard it as 'your animal'. Friends and family may have given you an animal nickname. It was believed that if an Indian woman thought of an animal strongly during pregnancy, her child would resemble that animal. Once you have identified your totem, carry a symbol of it or a small picture to give you strength when you need it.

WHAT IS MEDICINE?

Medicine equals energy, the vital life force in nature, mankind and the Great Spirit. A person's medicine is that power generated by his or her own talents and strengths, used in a positive way to achieve the right path in life.

THE MEDICINE WHEEL

The Medicine Wheel or Circle of Power is central to all Native American magic. Our system draws from several traditions, for there are almost 500 different systems in North America alone. The wheels link the celestial, human and natural cycles. Some were 27 metres (90 feet) in diameter, but research suggests that some were much smaller and placed around ceremonial tepees to be used by both the shaman and anyone seeking a spiritual path. The original Medicine Wheel was made of stones and could be created wherever a tribe camped. Around the wheel are totem animals representing each birth month and season. The totems vary according to each tribe's mythology.

The History of Medicine Wheels

Medicine Wheels may date back 1,500 years. The most famous, the Big Horn Medicine Wheel near Sheridan in Wyoming, dates back perhaps 200 or 300 years. It is about 27 metres (90 feet) in diameter and made of stones. Its primary alignments are to the summer solstice, dawn and sunset points, with secondary ones at the rising of various stars. The Moose Mountain Medicine Wheel in Saskatchewan, Canada, is at least 1,000 years older and also aligned to the solstice. Fifty have been discovered throughout America and Canada, but many have been lost.

Why a Circle?

The circle was central to Native American life as well as magic. Black Elk commented: 'Everything an Indian does is in a circle and that is because the power of the world always works in circles and everything tries to be round. In the old days when we were a strong and happy people, all our power came from the sacred hoop of the nation and so long as the hoop was unbroken, the people flourished. The East gave peace and light, the South gave warmth, the West gave rain and the North with its cold and mighty wind gave strength and endurance.'

Symbolism of the Medicine Wheel

The basic form of the Medicine Wheel was a cross in a circle. The North to South axis represents the connection between Heaven and Earth and the East to West line the path of living within time and history. On our wheel the Four Winds, each representing a season, occupy the Outer Wheel and lie between the four main compass points. Each Wind and season has an animal or bird and relates to our wider life. The 12 animals or birds of the Inner Wheel are personal totems related to the individual's birth or sun months. This is a simplification but is the essence of Medicine Wheel magic and works well in the modern world.

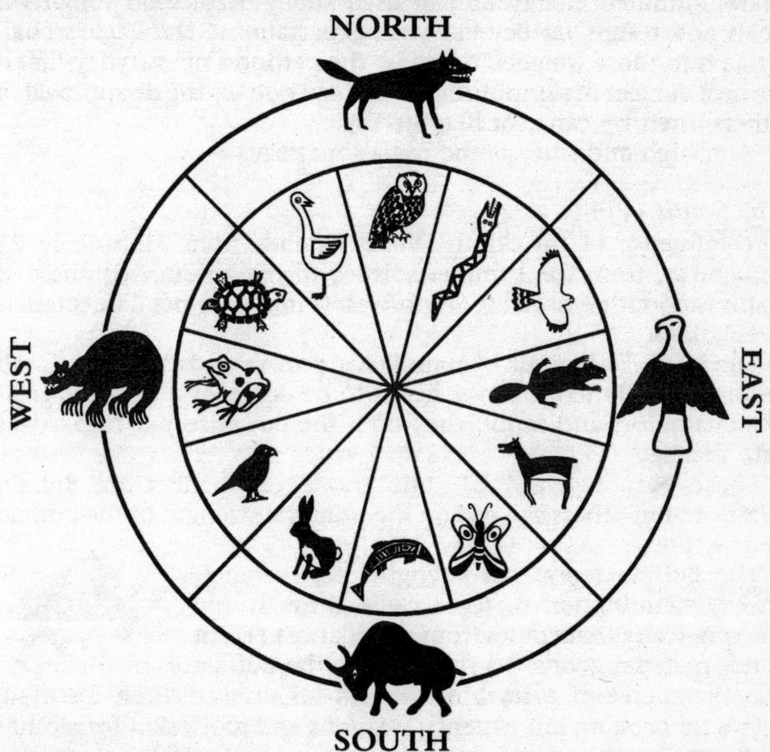

The East Winds

The influence of the East Winds begins at the spring equinox on 21 March, marked on the Outer Wheel in the North-east. Its influence continues until 21 June, the summer solstice, in the South-east. The East Winds' totem is the Eagle. The Winds herald the coming of spring and are associated with new beginnings and a fresh approach to old problems. If you are born during the period of the East Winds, you are an 'Eagle Warrior', but his strength and challenges are available to all who need them.

The Eagle represents the need to stick to principles and a clear vision of possibilities. He is Tribal Chief of all birds and soars high in the sky, yet sees everything below. He is said to carry the prayers of the people to Father Sun. He is associated with the Thunder Bird, the rain-bringer whose flashing eyes are lightning and flapping wings bring thunder.

If you are of the Eagle tribe or seeking 'Eagle' attributes, you can draw unlimited energy and focused strength to reach long-term goals and results far beyond your expectations. The Eagle's challenge is to those weighed down by the pettiness of everyday life. If we heal our fear of standing alone and can outface the disapproval of others, then we can soar like the Eagle.

'Aim high and true,' is the Eagle's message.

The South Winds

The influence of the South Winds extends from 21 June to 21 September, from the summer solstice to the autumn equinox. It spans the South-east to the South-west compass points. The totem is the Buffalo.

The South Winds talk of abundance, growth and giving one's self wholeheartedly to whatever needs to be done. At a time for great personal effort and input, they offer the power to put fresh ideas into practice.

Those born between 21 June and 21 September are Buffalo Warriors, but others can call on the primeval strength of the buffalo at any time

The Buffalo represents strength, perseverance, sheer determination to see a cause through and the generosity that comes from abundance of spirit if not material goods. To the Indians, the Buffalo was the source of everything needed for survival: flesh for food, bones for cooking implements, weapons and tools, skin for clothes and covering the tepees. Even the sinews were used for sewing.

If you are of the Buffalo tribe or seek Buffalo attributes, you can draw the determination and generosity of spirit to give to all in need. The challenge of the Buffalo is to overcome any fear of personal scarcity or loss that can leave us holding on to what we have, risking stagnation and accepting second best.

'Only by giving much can we receive more,' is the message of the Buffalo.

The West Winds

Their influence extends from 22 September to 21 December, from the autumn equinox to the mid-winter solstice. They blow from the South-west to the North-west and the Bear is their totem.

The West Winds herald a time for gathering the fruits of summer's labours and preparing for winter, whether physically or emotionally. It is time for resolving issues and also accepting what cannot be resolved.

Those born between 22 September and 21 December are Bear Warriors, but others can call upon the Bear's self-sufficiency and foresight.

The Bear represents the strengths of independence and planning rather than letting fate take its course. In autumn it builds up its fat for hibernation. It is said a Bear can identify the healing herbs it needs when sick.

The Bear was regarded as an ancestor by some tribes and a bridge between the animal, human and spirit kingdoms. Bears are often seen as guardians of the mineral kingdom because they live in caves. If you are of the Bear tribe or need his attributes, you can take control of your own life through imitating his independence and initiative.

The Bear's challenge is to avoid relying on others and hoping that the answer to problems will turn up 'by magic', which can only lead to living on other people's terms. 'Be self-sufficient, not selfish,' is the message of the Bear.

The North Winds: the Region of Earth

The influence of the North Winds extends from 22 December to 20 March, from the mid-winter solstice to the spring equinox, that completes the cycle of the year. The totem is the Wolf.

The North Winds represent the period of the inner world, resting and growing strong by rest and withdrawal from the colds of winter, whether physical or emotional. This time of withdrawal has become lost in modern life where unremitting action is the root cause of many stress illnesses.

Those born between 22 December and 20 March are Wolf Warriors but others can call on his ability to survive on strategy rather than force.

The Wolf is associated with the dog star Sirius, the home of the gods. An ally of the moon, he can teach us about the Spirit World. It was believed that the souls of especially brave hunters became wolves. The Wolf's power is that of the pack, for there is strength in kinship.

Sometimes we need to withdraw from the world and seek refuge with those we love. We must use our minds rather than threats or violence when faced with oppression or injustice. If you belong to the Wolf tribe or seek his attributes, draw strength through relationships.

The challenge of the Wolf is to avoid undervaluing the familiar and mundane, for if we avoid commitment, we can end up rootless.

'Be loyal and wait for Spring,' is the Wolf's message.

The Creatures of the Inner Wheel

The 12 divisions represent the 12 moons of the year. There are 12 totem creatures, three for each season, approximately matching the dates, but not the meanings, of the sun signs in Western astrology. While your birth totem or chosen totem is always the most powerful personal symbol, you can use the strengths of any totem creature as its month unfolds.

The East

Under the Eagle's sway are the Hawk, the Beaver and the Deer.

The Hawk (21 March–21 April, corresponding to Aries) is a bird of lofty ambitions and plans, hunting fulfilment with voracity. He represents the desire to explore, to search for truth rather than personal gain. Sometimes, like the Eagle, he is associated with the Thunder Bird and the power of the sun.

He was one of the creatures who helped to create the world after the Flood. The Hawk hunts for need and kills for food not pleasure.

If your totem is the Hawk, you may be seeking inspiration for a particular target or dream. You know this goal may not bring you love or gratitude from those less far-sighted but it is still worthwhile. The challenge of the Hawk is to avoid wasting energy in flights that lead to nothing or cruelty for its own sake, often expressed as a sharp wit towards those who cannot not see beyond their noses.

'Be single-minded, but do not hurt others,' is the Hawk's message.

The Beaver (20 April–20 May, corresponding to Taurus) is hard-working, tenacious, comfortable in water or on land and able to adapt to difficulties. He represents the desire to create a secure material environment for himself and loved ones and addresses the practical world rather than that of ideas.

The Beaver emphasizes the importance of achievement in the world of which we are part, not necessarily in material terms but in work finished, problems solved and plans brought to fruition. He offers his perseverance to complete your tasks. The challenge of the Beaver is to avoid seeing material possessions and personal achievements as more important than the people for whom they have been earned.

'Be prepared to work hard for what you want, but do not lose sight of the purpose,' is the Beaver's message.

The Deer (21 May–20 June, corresponding to Gemini) is the creature of gentleness, sensitivity and intuition, easily startled and prone to swift changes of direction or perspective. Her strength is in her responsiveness to others and their environment.

If your totem is the Deer, then you desire harmony with your surroundings and to create peace for yourselves and others. This strength may be quiet but has great effect, for gentle words can deflect anger and avoid potential conflict. The challenge of the Deer is to avoid being over-sensitive to obstacles, difficulties and criticism. Sometimes we need to accept that gentleness can degenerate into weakness and self-pity if we do not stand firm.

'Be gentle, but do hold not back for fear of criticism,' is the Deer's message.

The South Winds

Under the Buffalo's sway are the Butterfly, the Salmon and the Rabbit.

The Butterfly (21 June–21 July, corresponding to Cancer) is a creature of transformation and rebirth. She represents transience, a reminder to enjoy each day for what it is without always worrying about a past that cannot be changed nor a future as yet unmade.

She can give the ability to welcome change and to regard even loss as offering a different path. Through her ethereal beauty you can learn to find something every day in which to rejoice. The challenge of the Butterfly is to avoid superficiality and restlessness that can be as limiting to self-growth as rigidity.

'Value every life experience and do not demand guarantees of permanence,' is the message of the Butterfly.

The Salmon (22 July–20 August, corresponding to Leo) is Tribal Mother of Fish and totem of returning to source. Because the Salmon will swim hundreds of miles to return to her place of birth, leaping high waterfalls to spawn her young, she has come to represent the essential unchanging self in a rapidly moving world.

The Salmon can assure you of who you really are. We all have a core self which, no matter how far we travel or whatever we achieve, will remain permanent despite triumph or misfortune. The Salmon passes through water without disturbing it and follows her life path without hurting or diverting others from their path. The Salmon's challenge is to connect with others so that her core of wisdom is passed on. Only through making contact can the Medicine Wheel operate.

The message of the Salmon is to be true to yourself, whatever the situation, but to let others touch you with their wisdom as you pass.

The Rabbit (21 August–20 September, corresponding to Virgo) is the bringer of fertility and movement to a stage of life that seems without purpose, inspiring action and the growth of inspiration and enthusiasm. Unlike the Salmon, the Rabbit is the connector, making warrens for the safety and shelter of his tribe.

The Rabbit can help you to overcome fear. He faces many predators and lives with danger but knows that you must live in the world as it is, adapting, accepting risks but always multiplying your positive influence. The challenge of the Rabbit is to conserve resources, to be aware that the Earth's riches are not limitless.

'Make the world your home but do not squander its resources,' is the message of the Rabbit.

The West Winds

Within the West Winds' or Bear's sway are the Raven, the Frog and the Turtle.

The Raven (21 September–22 October, corresponding to Libra) is the teacher of magic, seen both as the Great Trickster and Creator. He is sometimes called the Big Grandfather and Raven Man and, like the Hawk, was one of the creatures who recreated the world after the Flood.

It is said he stole the sun, a reference perhaps to the love of ravens for bright things. The Raven is also a messenger of the Great Spirit. He will offer you inspiration and intuition to see beneath and beyond the outer world. His voice is our hidden voice, not of reason or logic but of our inner wisdom that we must learn to follow. The challenge of the Raven is to avoid living entirely by your own rules and believing that any right cause justifies the means.

'Be resourceful without being devious,' is the message of the Raven.

The Frog (23 October–22 November, corresponding to Scorpio) is the rain-bringer, a symbol of the moon and fertility. The Frog represents the power of the waters and especially rain to cleanse, refresh and cause new growth.

The life cycle of the Frog is, like the Butterfly's, one of transformation. The Frog offers emotional strength and fluidity, the power to empathize with others, to soothe those whose feelings are in turmoil and to use your own sensitivity to reach to the heart of any situation. The challenge of the Frog is to avoid becoming over-sentimental or allowing others to emotionally blackmail you. The Frog must also avoid using the same tactic yourself to save a relationship that needs to change or end.

'Follow your heart, not your sentiments,' is the message of the Frog.

The Turtle (23 November–21 December, corresponding to Sagittarius) who, like the Beaver, is at home on land or in water, represents the bridge between the worlds of intuition and practical action. For the Sioux, the world was a huge turtle floating on the waters.

The Turtle offers the slow but certain path to achievement, promising that your dreams have firm foundations but will not be realized overnight. Her strength is the patience to wait for the right moment. The challenge of the Turtle is to avoid retreating into her shell and avoiding the unknown or challenging for set ideas and rigid principles.

'Be patient but do not be inflexible,' is the Turtle's message.

The North Winds

Within the North Winds' or Wolf's sway are the Snow Goose, the Owl and the Snake.

The Snow Goose (22 December – 19 January, corresponding to Capricorn) which migrated from the Arctic during the winter months was known as the creature from 'beyond the North Winds' and heralded the snow. When spring came, the snow goose would depart.

Her visit is a reminder that all things have a time and season and that winter, whether the season or a frozen period in your life, will pass. Because the Snow Goose is associated with dreams, she is also a reminder that it is important to grow strong within, so that when the time is right, the ice will melt and you can move forward. The challenge of the Snow Goose is to remember that we can withdraw from reality only for a short time and that dreams are a rehearsal for action in the real world.

'Wait, but not too long,' is the Snow Goose's message.

The Owl (20 January–18 February, corresponding to Aquarius) is often called the Night Eagle, being the bird of the night and moon as the eagle rules the day and the sun. To the Woodland tribes of South-east America, the Owl is Chief of the Night and a sacred protector of all who must travel or work in darkness.

You can share his ability to see in the dark, to enable you to discover hidden truths, hidden messages behind words, hidden motives. This will offer protection when you are vulnerable to the world's predators. He is the creature of forethought and can prevent you from leaping before you look. The challenge of the Owl is to avoid letting penetrating vision lead to distrust and an over-critical attitude.

'Be aware of the motives of others, but beware of cynicism in yourself,' is the Owl's message.'

The Snake (19 February – 20 March, corresponding to Pisces) is seen as the traditional enemy of the Thunder Bird and is the symbol of the Earth. He can act as messenger between man and his instincts. The symbol of the Snake swallowing its own tail appears in many cultures and represents the circle of existence.

As the Snake sheds its skin, so you can shed what is redundant and move on. This is why the Snake resides at the end of winter so you, too, can cast off your doubts and regrets and begin the year with hope. The challenge of the Snake is not to shed what is good or necessary along with the old. Transformation, using the past as impetus, is very different from the death of the old.

'Move on, using the past as a bridge to the future,' is the message of the Snake.

Using the Medicine Wheel for Divination

The Medicine Wheel can show what strengths and qualities are needed to answer questions or problems. Use the printed Medicine Wheel with six small black and six small white pebbles, crystals or buttons (you may prefer to photocopy the diagram to twice or even three times its original size). Put the 12 stones in a bag, draw three without looking and cast them one after the other on to the Medicine Wheel, while concentrating on your question. If a stone is white, then you need to develop the strength of the animal in whose segment the stone has landed. If black, it is the challenge aspect of the animal that is important. When all three stones picked are white then your progress will be rapid; if all black you should proceed slowly.

Stone One suggests the real issue. The question you have in your heart, not the one asked by your conscious mind. Try to see what the creature is saying about your life. Stone Two suggests a possible course of action. This may be at odds with your conscious intentions but may offer a way forward you had not considered. Stone Three is the likely result of following the suggested action. This may suggest a path different from that of the original question, but which is closer to your real needs.

EXAMPLE

Sue, a journalist, is married with two children. She has been offered a senior position on her newspaper involving worldwide travel and a good salary. Should she take it?

Stone One, a black stone in the wolf segment, suggests that the challenge is to succeed without losing her family life. It suggests that the real question is: 'If I take the job, will I lose close contact with my family?' Sue hardly ever sees the family at the moment which has caused tension at home.

Stone Two also falls on the Wolf, but it is white. The suggested action is to find a career move that will enable her to spend more, not less time with the family. Others might not want this, but the stones reflect our hidden feelings.

Stone Three is a white stone in the Snake. The outcome may be a life change, shedding what is no longer needed. Sue knows she can succeed in the world of the media, but realizes that if she does move off the fast track, it will be a new way of life. Sue has long wanted to run a freelance writing agency and now decides to spend six months working from home, rediscovering the family and then deciding whether to return to the fast track.

A Closer Look at the Stones

A stone in the outer (Four Winds) segments shows that it is a problem that involves the world and that you need to negotiate with the people. If a stone falls in one of the 12 inner segments, the solution to the problem lies with you alone. Stones in both inner and outer ring suggest that you are right on target and that others will see things your way if you persist. Stones outside the Wheel mean that you need to avoid hesitating in your course or listening to those who criticize or doubt the wisdom of your actions. If all fall outside, you need to ask a different question. If a stone lands in your birth month, the issue concerns your identity and is worth fighting for.

Making your Own Medicine Wheel

You can make a simple Medicine Wheel with pebbles in your garden, using personal symbols for the animals and birds. Therefore, if the animals listed here feel wrong, use animals native to your own part of the world. Equally if you live in the Southern hemisphere you will relabel your Wheel to fit with your own seasons; for example, the summer solstice in Australia can be substituted for the mid-winter solstice of the Northern hemisphere and vice versa.

Creating the Wheel

Draw only a single circle for the 12 animals. Put your birth animal segment at the top at 12 o'clock and divide the circle into 12 using the clock numbers. You should make your medicine wheel large enough to step in.

Draw one in chalk if you have a smooth stone yard or mark the circle with a stick in the dirt, drawing sunwise or clockwise. You could follow the old tradition and mark the outline permanently with stones in your garden. For the symbols, write the names of the totems, draw approximations or put symbols, such as a pottery frog and a child's toy bear. You can keep these symbols in a medicine bag, a fabric bag used for your special power symbols.

Choosing Totems

Follow your instincts. We all 'know magic' on the deepest level if we trust ourselves. Use animals and birds that suggest the qualities of each month. If a field or harvest mouse represents the harvest gathering in of September for you, adopt that as your September symbol. We all have our own store of myths about animals derived from childhood.

As you pick an animal, close your eyes and see his or her strengths and also the challenges to weaknesses they suggest. Let the animals speak to your heart and psyche as you arrange the circle. Let your instinct tell you where to put each animal – it is your wheel, the wheel of your life.

Preparing to Use the Wheel

In an ideal world you would withdraw to a high place where the elements combine, by a stream for water, near a rock or ancient tree for the earth, at noon when the sun is shining for the fire. But you can substitute simple earth, air, fire and water symbols: a few flowers for the earth, an incense stick, such as lavender, citron or almond, for air, a golden candle for fire and a dish of pure water (mineral water or water left for 20 hours in the moon and sunlight).

Place these at the four main directions, beginning with fire in the South, water in the West, earth in the North and air in the East. Black Elk explained: 'Is not the South the source of life? And does not man advance from there toward the setting sun of his life [West]? Then does he not approach the colder north where the white hairs are? And does he not then arrive if he lives at the source of light and understanding [the East]?'

Asking a Question

When you have your circle of creatures, stand at the South, facing North, ask a question and throw a large, grey pebble or crystal, this time a grey one, into the circle. Stand or sit in the segment where it lands and let the answers and strengths flow naturally. Now ask the animal what the challenge is, what weakness is hidden that may be holding you back and how you can overcome it. Like the Indians, you must talk to your totems and they will take you to the answers in your dreams or meditation.

Healing Wisdom

Many physical ills are rooted in our own worries that can make our immune system less able to fight off 'dis-ease'. If you have a particular anxiety, identify the animal whose challenge is weighing you down. Follow the Peace Path to the animal diametrically opposite and see how its strength provides an antidote.

For example the Owl's forethought taken to extremes can be constant anxiety far into the night. Stand in the Owl segment and walk towards its alter-ego, the Salmon, who accepts that some things are inevitable and does not waste energy on fighting those things or people who cannot be changed.

Sample Peace Paths

These are based on the illustrated wheel
Owl to Salmon = *forethought – automatic action*
Snake to Rabbit = *casting off – creating*
Hawk to Raven = *external focus – inner vision*
Beaver to Frog = *practical – emotional*
Deer to Turtle = *versatility – steady progress*
Butterfly to Snow Goose = *action – introspection*

NEW YEAR MAGIC

THE ORIGINS OF NEW YEAR MAGIC

New Year marks a time of new beginnings, a time to wipe the slate clean and to make resolutions. Although the year begins at different times in different societies, its significance is the same. From when man first began to measure time, the New Year marked a significant watershed in the wheel of the year and often coincided with the spring or vernal equinox.

In Europe, New Year was marked by the spring equinox and did not move to 1 January until the Gregorian calendar was introduced in 1582. Eleven days vanished from the calendar and Christmas Day changed from 6 January to 25 December. However, the new calendar was not adopted in Protestant England until 1752 and in Scotland the emphasis is still on Hogmanay or New Year rather than Christmas.

Whenever New Year fell, there was a traditional flurry of sweeping and cleaning on New Year's eve, the emptying of rubbish and ashes from the old fire of the year and the settling of accounts.

DIFFERENT DATES

Some primitive tribes have several New Years, depending on the arrival of shoals of fish or animals to be hunted or on the growth of different crops. Often the yearly arrival of certain stars in the sky marked the date. For example, the Egyptians watched for the rising of the Dog Star, Sirius, which presaged the flooding of the Nile when new life was restored to the land.

In Oceania, the New Year is marked by the coming of the constellation of the Pleiades which coincides with the annual time for sowing. In the New Hebrides, turtles' eggs are harvested and among the Dayaks rice is planted when these stars appear.

The Celtic New Year, the modern Hallowe'en, began on 1 November, (see *Hallowe'en Magic*, page 260). In the Isle of Man, just off the coast of England, a Mummers' Hogmanay dance at Hallowe'en recalls this earlier connection.

Among Native American peoples, there were different beginnings to the year according to the location and life of the tribes. For many it began at the spring equinox, for others in autumn, at snow fall, with the rutting season, the migration of animals or the New Fire Festival. However, the celebration was always a renewal not only of the year, but a re-enactment of the birth of the people and the cosmos itself. In the re-enactment of the original creation through ritual, it is believed that its powers are regenerated, bringing down blessings of health, abundant crops and fertility on the tribes.

HOGMANAY

One of the places where the New Year is most enthusiastically celebrated is Scotland. Like much of the Northern Hemisphere, in Scotland New Year's Day occurs on 1 January.

The name Hogmanay comes from the old solar hero giant of the North, Hogmagog. The ancient custom of New Year fires to burn out the Old Year has survived in Scotland and other areas of Celtic, Scandinavian and Teutonic influence. The fires purified the New Year, kindled new energies and burned all the old bad luck. In the older calendar, the New Year Fires were originally lit on what is now the shortest day and so were also a magical device to persuade the sun to shine again (see also *Christmas Magic*, page 75).

Feasts were held because if the year began with a good fire and plenty of food, sympathetic magic (in which you act out what you want to happen) decreed that it would continue to yield prosperity and abundance. Nuts and eggs were often given as symbols of the fertility of the coming year.

NEW YEAR FIRES

In many cultures fires are extinguished and re-lit at midnight at New Year to symbolize new life (see also *Seasonal Magic*, page 398). In the Grampian region of Scotland, fireballs, made of wood and cloth soaked in paraffin and bound in wire mesh, are whirled around heads and limbs in the Hogmanay procession. At midnight the fireballs are hurled into the sea, a survival of an earlier custom of offering alcohol, food and coins to the sea gods.

The Flambeaux festival in Tayside in Scotland involves birch poles, topped with blazing hessian sacking, which are hurled to make a fire at midnight. In an earlier version, participants were dressed as animals as part of the old animal purifying and fertility ceremonies. Dressing up as animals on New Year's eve, especially bulls and goats, has links with the old Horned God fertility worship.

The medieval Christian church so disapproved of these antics that it decreed a three-year fasting penance for those who indulged in them, although in remoter areas until the end of this century, the parson might well have joined in.

Bell ringing, the sounding of hooters, cannon fire, fireworks and, in more recent times, car horns at midnight go back to the primitive belief that malevolent spirits assembled at celebrations, especially at transitions in the year. The noise drove them away.

FIRST FOOTING

In places influenced by Celtic, Scandinavian and Teutonic customs, all the doors of a dwelling are opened just before midnight by the head of the household to let out the bad luck. Then they are closed. A dark-haired man, representing the New Year, knocks at the front door at midnight. When the First Footer is admitted by the head of the house, he offers bread to ensure food for the household all year, a piece of coal for warmth and a coin for prosperity. He then leaves by the back door without speaking and re-enters the front to a chorus of 'Happy New Year'. There are many variations of this ceremony. In Dundee and other fishing communities in Scotland a herring is given to the First Footer.

An older Scottish First Footing also goes back to the Horned God ceremonies. A young man, covered in a cow hide, runs round the outside of the house, while his fellow revellers bang sticks on the walls. On being granted entry to the house, the leader of the bovine revellers chants: 'May Hogmagog bless the house and all that belongs to it cattle, kin and timbers. In meat, clothes and health of all therein, may fortune abound.'

NEW YEAR RITUALS

Cleansing Rituals

All cultures use water and sometimes fire to purify homes for the New Year. In the Highlands of Scotland, it is said that you should drink from a dead and living ford, one over which funeral parties pass, and sprinkle it around your home without dropping the cup.

All exits are sealed and juniper berries are burned till everyone is coughing heartily. The home is thereby purified for the coming year by fire and water. Good fortune will then follow.

Deflowering Wells

The first water drawn from a well on New Year's morning will bring great fortune and happiness. The person who gets the 'cream of the well' sprinkles hay or petals on the surface to let others know the well has been deflowered.

Divine Food

It is believed that it is especially lucky to eat cheese on New Year's eve, particularly the pungent type saved from Christmas. In Scotland it is eaten with gift cakes, a literal translation of Hogmanay from the Norman French for a triangular oat or shortbread biscuit.

Plough Monday

In the Northern magical tradition, Plough Monday was the first Monday after Twelfth Night. It goes back to the Norse and Teutonic traditions and involves a decked and beribboned plough led by an old woman, called Bessie, a form of the Celtic Cailleach Bheur, the old Goddess of Winter. She represents the hag aspect of Mother Earth who in spring will become the Maiden Goddess.

In England, the Morris Men would perform sword dances in the fields to mark the death of the old year and the fertilization of the fields. The day was also called Distaff Day because it marked the occasion when women took up their spinning and weaving once more. Their distaffs were decorated with scarlet ribbons in honour of Frigg, the Norse Mother Goddess who was patroness of housewives.

WALKING STONES AND FAIRIES

Standing stones are believed to have the power to move on New Year's eve and New Year's day. The Rollright Stones in Oxfordshire in England (see also *Fertility Magic*, page 199) are said to drink, move and eat at midnight on New Year, while in Scotland the Stone of Quoyboyne walks to the nearby Loch of Boardhouse. It is said that if mortals watch the moving stones, they will be spirited away forever, for standing stones are doorways to other fairy worlds.

WASSAILING THE APPLES

The wassailing of apples took place on the eve of Twelfth Night and is still practised in different forms all over the world. Cider was poured over the trees in orchards and the trees beaten with sticks to awake the sleeping fertility of the tree. A wassail bowl, made of apple wood, was carried by revellers from door to door to drink the health of the householders and bring luck to their homes. Wass-hail means good health. Beehives and barns were also wassailed and in later times guns were fired at the trees to encourage growth.

NEW YEAR SUPERSTITIONS

If you end the year in poverty, you will continue it in poverty. In Lowland Scotland it is said that unless you finish all your spinning and weaving before the New Year dawns, the Gyre-carlin, a powerful fairy woman, will abscond with all your flax.

You should burn the old calendar at sunrise on New Year's day. Wind it nine times with red wool, throw it into the flames and say: 'Old year burn, old troubles do not return'.

You should not lend anything, especially money, on New Year's day or you will be lending all year. Collect all your debts on New Year's eve to ensure that money comes in and not out during the following 12 months.

If you cry at New Year, you will cry all year. Whatever you are doing when the bells ring out at midnight shows what you will be doing for much of the year. You should not sweep dirt out of the door on New Year's day or let anything be taken out of the house or your luck will leave. Nor should you wash anything in case you wash your good fortune away. Clocks should be wound at midnight on New Year's eve so that there will be good fortune all the year.

Dance around a tree on New Year morning and you will have health, wealth and good luck all year.

NEW YEAR DIVINATION

Whenever New Year is celebrated, it is traditionally powerful for divination, especially at midnight on New Year's eve as the dimensions part (see also *Hallowe'en Magic*, page 260).

Candle Wax or Egg Divination

This can be used for seeing whether New Year resolutions will bear fruit or for predicting whether hopes for the coming year will be realized. Either light a pure white candle at midnight on New Year's eve and let the wax drip into cold water or prick a hole in the first egg laid on New Year's eve and let the egg white trickle into very hot water. Another traditional method is to melt tin over a flame and cast it into a bucket of cold water.

As you let the wax fall, think of any New Year resolution you have made and ask what the New Year will bring. The wax, tin or egg white will form a shape or perhaps two or three and answer your question. For example, a boat or plane might suggest that you would have to travel far to achieve your ambition, a baby that there may be an unexpected arrival in the family that may change your plans. Below are listed 30 shapes that might answer your questions about the next 12 months. If your picture is not listed, trust the first image or words that may come into your mind. The meanings I offer are just one way the images have been interpreted for New Year magic. Follow your own intuitions.

An apple: your venture will bear fruit, especially if connected with love.
An axe: you will need to fight for what you want and clear a lot of dead wood.
A baby: an unexpected new arrival in your immediate circle may change plans.
A bear: someone who will use his or her strength to help you.
A boat: you may find happiness overseas.
A broom: you will be preoccupied with domestic affairs.
A cat: you will find an independent side to your nature.
A coin: new ventures will bring prosperity.
A church: matters of the spirit will be at the fore.
A cloud: any problems will be temporary.
A crown: you will be meeting important people who can further your plans.
A dog: old friends will be loyal to you in any difficulties.
A dome: you may get an opportunity to visit exotic places.
An eagle: you will fulfil your ambitions if you aim high.
A flag: you will have reason to celebrate a victory.
A fox: beware of false friends.
A gate: you can overcome any barriers in your way.
A goose: take notice of any warnings you are given.
A heart: a friendship may develop into love.

A horseshoe: unexpected luck may help you to succeed.
A house: a house move may be imminent.
A kite: you will get the freedom to follow your dreams.
A lion: if you keep your courage, you will succeed beyond your dreams.
A mouse: pay attention to detail and you will win through.
A nest: you will achieve material security.
A nut: a small scheme will grow and flourish, especially concerning money.
A plane: you may travel a long way from home to find happiness.
A rose: new love and perhaps a permanent relationship may follow.
A snail: says that success will come slowly but you will reach your goal if you are patient.

Naming Your True Love

Wait until the turning of the year and use a small Bible and your door key. Find the Songs of Solomon Chapter 8, verses 6 and 7 and recite the words:

Set me as a seal upon thine heart, as a seal upon thine arm, for love is as strong as death.
Many waters cannot quench love, neither can floods drown it. If a man would give all the substance of his house for love, he would be contented.

Place the key at the appropriate section while you write the letters of the alphabet on separate pieces of paper. Shuffle and place them face down in a circle at random. Remove the key, place the open Bible in the centre of the circle and tie the key on to a long red ribbon. Holding the ribbon with your wedding ring finger, walk around the circle clockwise.

The key will swing on the chain. Continue walking round and round until the key remains still over one of the letters. The letter to which the key is pointing is the initial of the first name of your true love.

To find the initial of the surname of your love, collect the letters once more, shuffle them and replace face down in the circle. Recite the verses again, then hold the key over each letter in turn until it stops swinging. You will find that it stops quite definitely over one letter each time.

Replace the key in the Bible, tie it with the ribbon and place it next to your bed. You will dream of your love and he or she will reveal the full name.

THE JAPANESE NEW YEAR

In Japan there is a Greater and a Lesser New Year. The Greater is derived from the ancient Chinese lunar calendar and celebrated on the first day of the first month and the Lesser on the fifteenth of the first month. At the Greater New Year, pine branches are placed in gateways and are ritually burned at the end of the festival. It is a family time with traditional fare, such as soup with rice cakes and sake, served in a family circle.

The Lesser New Year marks the agricultural renewal. Prayers are offered to the gods of agriculture for a fruitful year and straws are used to symbolize the ritual breaking of the ground with rice seedlings.

Such rituals take place even in snowy regions and a shrine, made of a pine branch, is set up for the God of the Rice Paddy. Bird frightening rituals are carried out to stop them eating the new seedlings. In houses, a pine tree is decorated with rice cakes, fashioned to represent silk worm cocoons, tools and fruits, for prosperity in the coming year in all that is produced.

A First Footing ceremony still takes place in some regions where youths, dressed as demons, visit houses and are given food and wine to bring good luck to the house and drive away all that is malevolent.

THE CHINESE NEW YEAR

The Chinese New Year is marked by the first full moon in February. Houses are cleaned, all debts are settled and the paper gods who guard the door are replaced. Chinese characters depicting health, wealth and happiness are written on red paper and used to decorate the entrances to dwellings. Drums, symbols and firecrackers are let off as part of the New Year festival to ward off any malevolent powers.

The God of the Kitchen visits the Jade Emperor in heaven on the eve of the Chinese New Year to report on the household happenings (see also *Domestic Magic*, page 127). The three-day Festival of Lanterns ends the New Year celebrations. Lanterns are placed on public and private buildings and lanterns, huge paper dragons and papier-mâché lions are paraded through the streets (see also *Chinese Magic*, page 63).

The Twelve Chinese Years

On his last New Year on earth, Buddha called all the animals to his side. Only 12 came and as a reward Buddha is said to have given each one a year that would reflect its personality.

Each person is born under the sign of one of the 12 years and the year itself bears the characteristics of the animal. Because the date of the Chinese New Year can vary from late January to mid-February, people born around this period can find that they may belong to the year before the Western calendar date. For example, in 1994, the year of the Dog, the New Year occurred on 10 February, so anyone born on 9 February is a Rooster. In 1995, the Year of the Pig began on 31 January, so anyone born on 30 January is a Dog. To compensate for this difficulty, people born on or around the Chinese New Year are said to be very psychic and open to new ideas.

While Chinese astrology is extremely complex, in folk tradition Chinese people identify themselves with one of the 12 animals, much as in the Western tradition people think of themselves as Librans or Aquarians without worrying too much about ascendants and trines. The Chinese Ten Thousand Year Lunar Calendar, almanacs and computer programmes can calculate the Chinese New Years forwards and backwards if you want to be sure of your exact place.

Birth Years

The years run in 12-year cycles, so if your birth year is not listed below, add 12 or subtract multiples of 12 to bring you to the nearest birth year listed. For example if you were born in 1912, add 12 and that brings you to 1924, the Year of the Rat. So you, too, are a Rat. The order of the animals never varies.

Equally, the years in the list end at 2019, the year of the Pig. If you want to know what will be the dominant features of the year 2031, subtract 12 from that date and you end up with another year of the Pig.

Rat	1924	1936	1948	1960	1972	1984	1996	2008
Ox	1925	1937	1949	1961	1973	1985	1997	2009
Tiger	1926	1938	1950	1962	1974	1986	1998	2010
Rabbit	1927	1939	1951	1963	1975	1987	1999	2011
Dragon	1928	1940	1952	1964	1976	1988	2000	2012
Snake	1929	1941	1953	1965	1977	1989	2001	2013
Horse	1930	1942	1954	1966	1978	1990	2002	2014
Sheep	1931	1943	1955	1967	1979	1991	2003	2015
Monkey	1932	1944	1956	1968	1980	1992	2004	2016
Rooster	1933	1945	1957	1969	1981	1993	2005	2017
Dog	1934	1946	1958	1970	1982	1994	2006	2018
Pig	1935	1947	1959	1971	1983	1995	2007	2019

Secondary Animal Characteristics

We all have another side to our nature. This may be especially strong if you were born close to the Chinese New Year. The secondary animal can explain your conflicting feelings and alert you to hidden strengths. According to the time of the day or night you were born, your secondary animal can be found.

11pm–1am	Rat
1am–3am	Ox
3am–5am	Tiger
5am–7am	Rabbit
7am–9am	Dragon
9am–11am	Snake
11am–1pm	Horse
1pm–3pm	Sheep
3pm–5pm	Monkey
5pm–7pm	Rooster
7pm–9pm	Dog
9pm–11pm	Pig

The animals of the birth times are very stable since they are not affected by the date of the Chinese New Year. However, if you are born at a cusp time, you may find that you share characteristics with the adjoining animal. If your birth year and birth time animals are the same, you may have a very strong personality, but should beware inflexible attitudes.

You will need to take into account your personal birth time, according to the time zone in which you were born. Also, remember to allow for any variations such as summer or double summer time at the place of your birth.

The General Pattern

Each year is ruled by its animal and you may find that all over the world, similar economic and political trends are feeding from the same energies. If the New Year is a year that is the same as your birth animal, it will be a significant year for you. If it is the year of your secondary animal, it may be a time for your hidden strengths to come to the fore.

The Twelve Animals

Rat years
These are good for new schemes, ambitious plans and because they are years of plenty, for money-making, storing money or investments for the future. Beware of taking unnecessary risks or over-extending yourself especially in financial matters.

Rat people
They are hard-working, ambitious, friendly, assertive, devoted to those they love, but can be mean, quick-tempered and less than truthful to further their ambitions. They include William Shakespeare, Leo Tolstoy and Marlon Brando.

Ox Years
These are marked by stability and steady growth, where hard work will be rewarded. They are good years for domestic affairs. Beware of clashing with authority or not keeping your paperwork up to date.

Ox people
They are responsible, stable, hard-working, patient and reliable but they can be unimaginative and materialistic. They include Walt Disney, Vincent Van Gogh and Charlie Chaplin.

Tiger years
These are times of great change and strides forward, especially in fields of exploration. Beware of restlessness, accidents through carelessness and violent outbursts.

Tiger people
They are dynamic, noble in aim, enthusiastic, born leaders and competitive, but can be selfish, domineering and easily angered. They include Ludwig van Beethoven, Dwight D. Eisenhower and Marilyn Monroe.

Rabbit years
These are calm, happy, good for diplomacy, international relations and enjoyment, but beware of over-indulgence and putting off until tomorrow what needs to be done today.

Rabbit people
They are sensitive, well-mannered, joyous and quietly observant, but can be superficial and self-centred. They include Albert Einstein, Queen Victoria and Jomo Kenyatta.

Dragon years
These are good for creative and artistic ventures and matters involving risk. But beware of health hazards and emotional stresses.

Dragon people
They are successful, independent, highly creative and inspire others, but can be arrogant and unable to keep to a routine. They include Joan of Arc, Salvador Dali and Che Guevara.

Snake years
These are good for secret negotiations and undercover investigations, but beware of double-dealing and scandal.

Snake people
They are investigative, persuasive and good at keeping secrets, but can be devious and very jealous. They include Pablo Picasso, Abraham Lincoln and John F. Kennedy.

Horse years
These are marked by positive action, rapid change in both business and the personal worlds and plenty of travel but beware of over-exhaustion and being carried along by change not of your making.

Horse people
They are active, sociable, hard-working and outgoing, but can be unreliable in one-to-one relationships. They include Rembrandt, Theodore Roosevelt and Nikita Krushchev.

Sheep years
These are for humanitarian issues, peace-making, introspection and family matters. But beware of pessimism and over-sensitivity.

Sheep people
They are gentle, peace-loving, kind, tactful and reflective, but can be vulnerable to criticism and easily depressed. They include Michelangelo, Andrew Carnegie and Rudolph Valentino.

Monkey years
These are good for enterprise, speculation, finding ways round obstacles and achieving the impossible. Beware of instability in business and personal matters and the breaking of promises.

Monkey people
They are quick-witted, inventive, versatile, humorous and with an excellent memory, but can be unscrupulous and fickle with friends and colleagues alike. They include: Leonardo da Vinci, Charles Dickens and Nelson Rockefeller.

Rooster years
These are good for politics and money, for overcoming inertia and injustice and for self-sufficiency, especially in smaller money matters. Beware of extremism and perfectionism.

Rooster people
They are honest, efficient, good organizers, especially of money, and high profile, being successful in either the media or the law. They can be abrasive and dogmatic. They include: Prince Philip and Pope Paul VI.

Dog years
These are good for matters of defence, whether at home, work or in international affairs, and for integrity. Beware of rigid attitudes and cynicism towards the intentions of others.

Dog people
They are crusading, protective, loyal and honest, but can be obstinate and suspicious. They include Voltaire, Sir Winston Churchill and Elvis Presley.

Pig years
These are good for bringing long-term projects to a successful conclusion and for the welfare of those less fortunate. Beware of giving more than you can afford and falling prey to cheats, especially in money.

Pig people
They are generous, altruistic, home-loving, diligent and chivalrous, but can be extravagant and over-indulgent. They include: Al Capone, Alfred Hitchcock and Humphrey Bogart.

32

Norse Magic

The Vikings

Norse magic and the gods of the Vikings reflected the hazardous, warrior existence and the harshness of the Northern climes. Their beliefs sustained them on incredible journeys. The early Vikings penetrated many corners of the globe in their oaken longboats. They colonized Iceland in about 815 and journeyed to what is now Turkey, Greece, Russia and even North Africa. The places they visited are marked by stone monuments and artefacts etched with runes, the Norse or Viking magical symbols of power.

In 992, five centuries before Christopher Columbus discovered America, Leif Eriksson, son of Erik the Red who colonized Greenland, sailed west in search of timber and new settlements. He had only 35 men and the seas were tumultuous, but he landed in Labrador which he called Markland, 'the land of great forests' and as he travelled southwards, discovered a green, fertile area where he met early Native American tribes. The explorers wintered there before returning home.

Formal written language did not reach the Nordic world until the eleventh century, along with Christianity. Before then, the early legends of the ancient Northern gods and heroes were transmitted in song and poem through the generations. The Eddas, the sacred prose and poetic sagas, are the earliest written record of these ancient legends. The sacred myths were transcribed by scribes, usually monks, and were often distanced from the original tradition. Many tales were lost or Christianized. What remains gives a rich picture of courage and endurance.

The Creation Myths

Ice from Niflheim in the North and fire from Muspellheim in the South fused together in the vast chasm of Ginnungagap, bringing forth life. The first two beings were Ymir the Frost Giant and Audumla, the primal cow/mother. Audumla licked a pillar of salt ice and brought forth Buri, the first of the gods who married the

Giantess Bestia. She gave birth to three sons, Odin (spirit), Vili (will) and Ve (holiness), or according to some versions Odin, Hoenir (the Shining one) and Loki, the Trickster, God of Fire. The gods fought with the Frost Giants and eventually killed Ymir.

From Ymir's body the gods created the Nine Worlds that were supported by the world tree, Yggdrasil, a gigantic ash. On the top level, the principal realm was Asgard, realm of the Aesir or Warrior Gods. This is where the gods and goddesses had their halls and where Valhalla stood. Here the Einherjar, the slain warriors chosen for their courage in battle by the Valkyries or Battle Maidens, were led over Bifrost, the Rainbow Bridge. In Valhalla the chosen warriors fought by day and feasted each night, waiting for Ragnarok, the final battle between the gods and giants. Also on the upper level was Vanheim, home of the Vanir, or fertility gods, who eventually united with the Aesir.

On the second level, the principal realm was Midgard, the middle world of men, surrounded by a vast ocean and encircled by Jormungand, the world snake. Jotunheim, the realm of the giants, lay in the mountainous eastern region of Midgard along the coast. Asgard and Midgard were connected by the rainbow bridge Bifrost (Trembling Roadway).

On the third level lay Niflheim, nine days' ride northwards and downwards from Midgard. Niflheim, the place of the dead, was relentlessly cold with perpetual darkness. Hel was its gloomy citadel, ruled by the Goddess Hel.

Yggdrasil formed the axis of the Nine Worlds and had three roots, one sunk into Asgard. Under this root was the Well of Urd, guarded by the three Norns, the Goddesses of Destiny. Here the gods held their daily council. The Norns nourished the tree with water from the spring. The first Norn, Urdhr, talked of the past, which in Viking tradition influences not only a person's own present and future but that of his or her descendants. The second Norn, Verdhandi, talked of present deeds and influences, which also influenced the future. Skuld, the third Norn, spoke of what would come to pass, given the intricate web of past and present interaction. This was a forerunner of the modern idea that man influences his destiny by what he is and has been.

The second root of the world tree lay in Jotunheim. Beneath this root was the Well of Mimir and its waters of pure wisdom.

The third root descended into Niflheim, where the dragon Nidhogg and serpents gnawed at the roots. The squirrel Ratatosk ran up and down the branches passing insults between Nidhogg and the all-seeing eagle at the top.

The Creation of Man

Odin and his brothers Vili and Ve were walking along the edge of the land where earth met sea and came upon two uprooted trees, an ash and an elm. These they used to create the first man and woman, Ask and Embla. Odin gave them the breath of life, Vili endowed them with intelligence and a loving heart and Ve gave them their natural senses. Ask and Embla were given Midgard, Mid-Earth, as their home and so began the human race.

At the destruction of the existing order at Ragnarok, the descendants of Ask and Embla, Lif and Lifthrasir, sheltered in Yggdrasil and survived the destruction to repopulate the new world. One of the runes or magical symbols is named Ask or Aesc after the first man and, like the world tree, Yggdrasil, represents endurance and strength in adversity.

THE DEITIES

Odin was the All-Father, God of War, Wisdom and Poetry. However, even he was subject to the power of the Norns. Although he was worshipped principally as the Warrior God, Odin wanted wisdom above all things. Therefore, he went to the spring of Mimir, source of all wisdom and asked to be given knowledge of all things. The Guardian Mimir demanded the payment of one of Odin's eyes for a drink from the waters of everlasting memory. The eye was placed in the fountain and each morning Odin drank of its healing waters.

Odin had his special rune or magical symbol Os, the mouth, symbol of communication. He had a magical spear, Gungnir, that he took from Yggdrasil, the world tree. Odin carved magical runes or signs on this ash spear so that it might always hit its mark and protect him from all harm. So sacred was Gungnir to the Vikings that once an oath had been sworn upon it, the vow could never be broken.

Frigg or Frigga was Odin's principal wife, mother of Baldur, God of Light and Spring, Hermod, Messenger of the Gods, and Tyr, the Spirit Warrior. She was the Goddess of Women, Marriage and Motherhood. Her jewelled spinning wheel formed Orion's Belt for she was goddess of the northern housewife over many centuries. Her only sin was to steal a piece of gold from a statue of Odin to fashion into a necklace. He was so angry that he left Asgard. His brothers disguised themselves as a false Odin, thereby allowing the Frost Giants and Uller the Winter God to invade the earth and bring winter. After seven months Odin returned and May Day celebrations heralded the coming of spring. That is why the Northern winter is so long. Frigga's rune is that of Gyfu, the rune of partnerships and giving to others.

Thor, second among the gods, son of Odin and Jord, the Earth Mother, represented law, order and stability. Thor created thunder and lightning and controlled 'the winds and the showers, the fair weather and fruits of the Earth', according to the old poems. Thor alone was strong enough to wrestle with the serpent Jormungand who was coiled around the world at the bottom of the ocean.

Thor had a magical hammer, Mjollnir, the scourge of the giants, that when thrown at an enemy always found its target and then returned to his hand. Mjollnir acted as a sacred symbol at marriages, births and funerals. In pre-Christian times, the sign of the hammer was made a sacred mark of protection and the thorn (Thor) rune was drawn to call upon the might of Thor against aggressors.

Tyr was the Spirit Warrior, God of Courage and War with Honour. He paid the price of his right hand so that the other gods might bind Fenrir the giant wolf who was threatening the life of Odin. Tyr became a symbol of noble sacrifice with a rune named after him, invoking his nobility.

Freyr or Ing, the God of Plenty, was the most important of the Vanir or Fertility Gods and was associated with agriculture rather than war. He was a relic of the old earth religions where the god of the corn died each year at harvest time and was reborn at the midwinter solstice. Freyr or Ing drove his wagon over the fields after the winter to release the creative potential of the soil. The constellation called the Bear in Western astrology was known in Northern tradition as Freyr's Wagon. The rune of Ing invokes creative withdrawal and fertility. This rune was often carved on walls or over doorways of houses and even churches as a protective device.

Freyr's sister Freyja, Goddess of Love and Beauty, rode in a chariot pulled by two black cats. As Valfreya she frequently led the Valkyries into battle to select half the slain warriors for the glories of Valhalla. She married Odur, the summer sun. When he left her each autumn for southern climes, she would pursue him, her tears falling as gold in the rocks and changing to amber in the sea, until the summer sun returned. The first rune row or aett (set of eight runes) was named after Freyja.

Loki the Trickster God and Shape Changer was either Odin's true brother or foster brother and represented the principle of inevitable change and disruption. His children were Jormungand, the wolf Fenrir and the Goddess of the Underworld Hel. Loki tricked Hodur, the blind son of Odin and God of Darkness, into throwing a dart of mistletoe at his brother, Baldur, solar god of the growing light. Mistletoe was the one plant against which Baldur had no protection and he was slain. Frigg wept on the mistletoe and her tears fell as pearls which became the white berries we have today. According to Norse legend, Baldur could be restored to life only if every living creature wept for him. All did except the evil Loki disguised as an old woman.

In the traditional version of the legend, the young sun god was doomed to remain in the Underworld until Ragnarok. Odin had an infant son Vali, the Avenger, whom on the day of his birth was so strong, he slew blind Hodur with an arrow and restored light to the world. After Ragnarok, Thor's sons, Modi and Magni, together with Odin's youngest son Vali, God of Vegetation, and the resurrected Baldur and Hodur, founded the New Order.

RUNE MAGIC

What are Runes?

From the poetic Eddas, the songs telling the deeds of the Vikings and their gods, come many references to the magic of the runes and their use by deities and heroes alike. Rune means secret or hidden and comes from *ru*, a secret or mystery in the ancient Northern European language. The modern German word *raunen*, to whisper, is also derived from this stem.

Runes were angular markings made by the Germanic peoples, that is, the English, German and Scandinavian races who shared a common heritage and language. These marks, on stone, metal and wood, were used on inscriptions, monuments and for magical divinatory purposes. Stone was one of the main materials of Viking art, which was not a separate craft but used to adorn objects used in everyday life.

Carved runic stones dating from the fifth century found in Gothland portrayed the world of the Viking gods and especially scenes from Valhalla. As well as giving details of Viking ships, homes and weapons, inscribed stones would commemorate great and bloody battles, such as the raid on Lindisfarne, an island off North-east England, in 793. For warriors lost far from home, such stones would commemorate their burial place. Inscriptions would sometimes be made on living rock in natural settings to honour a chieftain or village elder.

As well as having an alphabetical value, each rune symbolized a concept, much like a Tarot card, and was intrinsically magical. To speak the name of a rune or carve it on a sword was believed to call up the power of the deity or nature spirit who commanded the rune. In modern times the power is seen as more personal, that of the intrinsic energies within mankind and the earth.

The first simple pre-runic symbols date from the Bronze Age and early Iron Age where symbols for the sun and the elements were especially prevalent. The runic systems in modern use date from the second or third centuries BC, when the Germanic peoples came into contact with the Mediterranean Etruscan alphabet system through the early trade routes. Although each symbol does represent a letter, the divinatory aspect always predominated.

Casting the Runes

In about AD 98 the Roman author Tacitus described how in Germanic tribes the father of a family or leader of a clan would cast rune staves cut from a nut-bearing tree on to a white cloth. He would pick three at random and use them to interpret the matter in question. There are many forms of runes in use, circular discs and even squares made of wood, silver, pottery or clay, as well as ordinary pebbles or stones.

Odin is credited with the discovery of the runes. Although he had wisdom by giving his eye to Mimir, he still longed for more insight and divinatory powers. So he returned to hang from the World Tree for nine days and nine nights, pierced by his own spear. The old Norse poem *Havamal* (Sayings of the High One) describes Odin's ordeal:

I know that I was hanged
On a windy gallows
Nine full nights,
Wounded with a spear.
Neither with loaf did they succour me
Nor with horn
I peered down;
I took up the runes;
Screaming I took them,
I fell back thence,
Freed.

Modern Rune-casting

The usual method of divination with runes involves casting or throwing the stones of staves. Numbers of runes vary from 24 in the Norse set to 33 in the Northumbrian system, but many people use the 29 Anglo-Saxon runes.

I have used Anglo-Saxon symbols although Runic calendar magic concentrates on 12 key runes rather than the whole set. Runes are traditionally linked with the passing of the year and can be used to harness the energies of a particular month. The earlier system based on the moons has been modified to fit with modern Western calendars. Runes do not predict what will happen in a particular month, rather they indicate the predominant energies that may galvanize personal power.

Using the Calendar Runes

You may like to copy your birth month rune on to a stone or crystal and carry it with you. You could draw all 12 runes on stones chosen from a beach, river side or open space and keep each as a talisman for the appropriate month or when you need a particular quality. Or you can place all 12 of the key runes in a cloth bag and pick one each morning at random to give you the guiding quality of the day.

The Runic Year

ᛁ *January/Snow Moon*

The key rune for January is Is, pronounced eess. This is the rune of Ice and refers to the fifth element in the Norse tradition. The Anglo-Saxon Rune Poem talks of the coldness and beauty of Ice, saying, 'it glistens like glass, is most like a jewel'. The Ancient Norse poem sees ice as a bridge between dimensions that needs to be negotiated with care by those perhaps blinded by fear of going forward.

In the world of the runes, winter was a real force to be reckoned with, bringing mankind face to face with the power of the elements and the limitations of movement and travel. Survival and reflection occupied the long winter months and were a vital time not of progress but regeneration.

During January or at any time that you fear to go forward, your Is rune will help you to prepare wisely for change and to use the waiting time to grow strong. If your birthday falls in January, you have inner resources of patience and wisdom and when the time is right, success and happiness will flow.

ᚢ *February/Horn Moon*

The key rune for February is Ur, pronounced err, the rune of primal instinctual strength. Ur represented the mighty aurochs, huge, wild, horned cattle that roamed the plains of Northern Europe until 1627. Their horns were worn on helmets by Northern warriors, often engraved with the Ur rune, as a symbol of boundless strength.

Ur speaks of the strength and courage to overcome obstacles to achievement. In the Anglo-Saxon Rune Poem, the auroch is 'single-minded, a fierce horn fighter, stamping his moors'. The Norse poem talks of hardship and the obstacles to be overcome. If the month is February or you need sheer might and single-mindedness to overcome seemingly insurmountable objects, Ur will give you courage of heart and mind, as well as physical endurance. If you were born during February, your path may be filled with obstacles but you have the will and power to succeed.

ᛒ *March/Mother Moon*

The key rune is Beorc, pronounced bay-ork. Beorc, the birch tree, is the rune of rebirth and regeneration, associated with the Earth Mother and is an apt rune for the season of spring when new life comes forth. The birch tree, the first tree to recolonize the land after the retreat of the ice-cap at the end of the last Ice Age, 'puts forth shoots without seeding' according to the old Rune verse.

If the month is March or you need a new beginning, especially in family matters or those of love, the power of Beorc promises fertility and new hope for a spontaneous return of enthusiasm and feeling.

Those born in March with Beorc as their rune are naturally creative and loving and will find that even if the present is unhappy, the immediate future promises new hope.

ᚱ *April/Cuckoo Moon*

The key rune of April is Rad, the rune of change, pronounced rard. It involves effort but offers great rewards. Rad is the rune of the wheel, the sunwheel of the turning year and also the wheel on the wagon of Freyr/Ing, the Fertility God, as it passed over the awakening fields. The Anglo-Saxon Rune Poem warns that 'Riding for a hero inside the hall is soft'. It stresses that it is necessary to go out into the world and make life what you want it to be by your own efforts, rather than dreaming or waiting for change to come.

If the month is April or you need to make a change in direction, the rune Rad promises that even though the journey ahead may be hard, it will be exciting.

If you were born in April, you have a natural thirst for exploration and achievement and can, if you are prepared to act, make your dreams come true.

May/Merry Moon

The key rune of May is Peorth, the rune of your unique identity. Peorth, pronounced pay-orth, is the rune of the fortune only you can make, because it is your personal destiny. It is the rune of the Norns, the three Fates. Because of its strong association with fate, Peorth is the rune of the lot of rune cup, in which the ancient warriors tested their luck. The old rune poems talk of 'play and laughter in the beer hall' for gambling and rune casting were seen as one and the same and a joyous process. This lot-casting would determine the virtue of an undertaking and battle itself was seen as an extension of lot-casting in which the gods would grant victory to the most deserving and valiant side.

If the month is May or you feel that your identity or principles are under threat, the rune Peorth can strengthen your resolve and unique abilities.

If you were born in May, you have high principles and a strong identity and should not be afraid to stand out from the crowd.

June/Sun Moon

The key rune for June is Sigil, pronounced see-gul, which is the rune of the sun, moving through the year. The sun reaches its height on the longest day, about 21 June. The sun is seen in the Rune Poems as 'light of the land, hope and guide of seafarers', who, with fine weather, could cross mighty oceans. Because in the Northern hemisphere, the sun reaches its full potential during this month before beginning a slow decline to winter, Sigil represents making the most of the moment without demanding permanence and making a supreme effort to reach any goals, whether personal or success in the world's terms.

If the month is June or you need to make a great leap or effort to succeed, the rune Sigil can give you energy and boundless potential.

If you were born in June, you have boundless creativity and energy and thrive on action. You should not worry about tomorrow, but live each day as it comes.

July/Hay Moon

The key rune for July is Daeg, pronounced darg, the rune of the day or the awakening. Nott, the Goddess of Night, who rode her dark chariot through the sky, was the mother of a radiant son, Daeg, whose name meant Day. As soon as the gods saw the radiance of Daeg, they fashioned him a chariot, drawn by a white steed, Skin-faxi (shining mane). Brilliant beams of light radiated in all directions from its mane. Daeg became a symbol of spiritual as well as physical illumination.

If the month is July or you need some light at the end of a particular tunnel of gloom, Daeg can promise that, given faith and optimism, enlightenment is not far off.

If you were born in July, you are naturally optimistic and a bringer joy. Do not let those who try to cast gloom in your life divert you from your natural belief that life is intrinsically good.

ᛄ *August/Harvest Moon*

The key rune for August is Ger, pronounced gair. This is the rune of the harvest. The Rune poems say that 'heaven's king allows the fields to blossom forth as bright abundance', a reference to Frey, God of the Harvest and a reminder that man is dependent on the benevolence of the earth and seasons to thrive. Also inherent is the idea of 'as you sow, so shall you reap', a reminder that past efforts affect the present and future harvests, a philosophy strongly echoed in the Norse concept of fate as an intricate web of past and present.

If the month is August or you are anxious about the success of long-term projects or relationships, Ger is a reminder that the effort you put in now in will bring rewards in the future.

If you were born in August, you are a natural planner and hard-worker and can be confident your efforts will be rewarded.

ᚠ *September/Woodmoon*

The key rune for September is Feoh, pronounced fay-och. In the Viking tradition, Feoh signified cattle, mobile wealth in the form of roaming herds. While the Anglo-Saxon rune poem talks of the joys of material comforts as long as they are used wisely and given freely to others, the Old Norse and Icelandic poems warn that money can cause strife among those who are kinsmen. Therefore, the meaning of Feoh encompasses the price that has to be paid, whether for success, change or keeping life as it is.

If the month is September or you are considering the cost of making a change or commitment in your life, Feoh can help you to assess the true price, including the hidden costs.

If you were born in September, you are rooted in the real, practical world but use your heart as well as your head, so that any success will enrich you personally as well as materially.

ᛗ

October/Hunting Moon

The key rune for October is Eh, pronounced em. Eh is the rune of the horse, especially the horse that carried its rider into battle. It talks of the harmony between man and rider. Because the horse was so vital to the Viking as he rode into battle or on adventures, perfect harmony was embodied in this relationship between a rider and his horse. If a warrior was killed in battle, his horse would often be buried with him and when a much loved horse died, it would be given an elaborate burial too. Odin had an eight-footed grey steed, Sleipnir, on which he rode into battle. Odin had engraved magical runes on its teeth to make it invulnerable. The rune poems talk of the horse as comfort to 'one who is unquiet or restless'.

In October or when you need harmony and balance in your life, Em can assist in reconciling the demands of different aspects of your life or opposing people who each claim your loyalty.

If you were born in October, you are naturally fair-minded and see both sides of any question. Your own inner harmony will protect you from the conflicts of others.

ᛟ

November/Fogmoon

The key rune for November is Odal, pronounced owed-al. Odal is the homestead, the rune of the practical organization of our lives. Because Odal refers to land passed down through a family over generations rather than leased from an overlord, it represents clan and family values. Although the Norse people were great wanderers, the homestead was still important to them as a symbol of all that was of value in the domestic and social sphere. In the Rune poems, Odal is said to be 'beloved of every human' but this domestic contentment is linked with a good harvest, that is, material comfort. This is also a reminder that the effort on a practical level has to be put in if the fruits of a secure lifestyle are to be enjoyed.

If the month is November or you feel the wintry blasts of life driving you to seek hearth and home, the rune Odal is a reminder of the value of stable relationships and shared experiences, however mundane they may seem.

If you were born in November, you are a home-maker and home-lover in the most creative sense and have the unique gift of putting others at ease wherever you are.

ᚺ

December/Wolfmoon

The key rune for December is Haegl, pronounced hargul. Haegl is the rune of hail and is the cosmic seed or egg. The idea of the cosmic seed is found in the old Icelandic Rune poem which talks of Haegl as a 'cold grain' and the Anglo-Saxon poem adds the concept of Haegl containing frozen life, as it 'whirls for the sky and turns into water'. Haegl carries in it the idea of creative potential waiting to come into fruition, with the rebirth of the sun on the shortest day, about 21 December.

If the month is December or you have temporarily withdrawn from life exhausted or defeated, the rune of Haegl is a reminder that sometimes we can only trust that the dark days will end and our personal sun will shine again. It will not be immediate as there is Is or ice to come in January, but Haegl holds the promise of real happiness after the winter.

If you were born in December, you are a creature of dreams and vision and sometimes the inner world seems richer than the outer. Trust your insights and put them into practice in the outside world when you are ready.

The Runes have moved in a circle. You can, if you wish, draw your runic year as a clock face on a circle of paper and cast a blank stone on it to find the right rune for each day or decision.

SOUTH AFRICAN MAGIC

33

RELIGION AND MYTHOLOGY

In tribal Africa, each person is born into a tribe and remains a member of it, even after death. The ancestors still play an important part in everyday life. Each tribal group has its own religion, although where there are similarities of language, there are great overlaps in myth.

Bantu is the most common linguistic group in Central and Southern Africa with more than 200 forms, including Zulu. Although most modern Africans now embrace either Christianity or Islam, the magical and divinatory practices are still followed in urban centres. It has been estimated that 80 per cent of black patients visit a traditional healer before visiting a medical doctor and that this trend is spreading. Assessments of the number of witch doctors practising in South Africa range from 300,000 to one million. Acting as community doctors, psychologists and spiritual advisers, they are held in high regard. Sections of the white community have started to take these beliefs seriously and at least 20 white people had undertaken the gruelling initiation process to qualify as a genuine *sangoma* or *inyanga*.

Sangomas are said to communicate with the ancestors who, in turn, are said to communicate with god on man's behalf. The belief is that if the ancestors are angry with someone, they can cause illnesses and accidents. The ritual sacrifice of a goat can often re-establish the balance. It is the sangoma's job to tell people what the ancestors are saying and to give them all the necessary steps to take.

The ingyana's role is less spiritual. He is more of a medicine man and uses his expert knowledge of roots, herbs, barks and parts of animals which can be used to cure sickness.

Bantu peoples have the idea of a one god though he is not distinguished from the sun or the sky or even the first ancestor of the tribe.

The High God

The High God lives above the sky which is believed to have a solid roof which meets the Earth at the point at which no one can travel far enough to reach. People have reached this land by climbing up trees or a rope dangling from the sky. The High God who is not a creator god in the accepted sense is sometimes called Mulungu. It is said that in early times Mulungu lived on Earth, which existed before everything, even the High God. But Mulungu went up into the sky because men killed 'his people', as the animals were called, and burned the bushland.

The Ghosts of the Ancestors

Ancestral ghosts, it is believed, go on living only as long as people remember them. Therefore, apart from those of chiefs and heroes, ghosts tend not to go beyond three generations. The dead, according to legend, live beneath the Earth in the same way as they did in life, carrying on their daily tasks and living in huts. Countless myths tell of visits to the underworld, often by following an animal into its hole.

Before a journey or undertaking, a man would seek advice from his father's spirit by consulting a diviner. One method involved taking a handful of flour and dropping it slowly and carefully on the ground. If it formed a cone, the signs were promising. The cone was then covered with a pot and left overnight. If the cone had remained intact by morning, the man would go on his journey full of optimism. However, if the cone had collapsed, a postponement was advised.

Modern Flour Divination

We no longer believe that the spirits are speaking through the flour, warning of danger. However, the method can be effectively used not only for making decisions, but for creating images that can provide further insight.

Use heavy wholemeal or wholewheat flour on dark kitchen paper. Think of a question. Sprinkle flour through your fingers towards the centre of the paper. If it forms a cone, you will know that the answer is yes. If it scatters over the paper, the answer is no.

Whether or not your flour forms a cone, shake the paper and let the flour make images. These may help to explain your answer and suggest pointers towards action.

The Origins of Mankind

Zulus believed that the first man came from a reed. Unkulunkulu, another name for the High God, was said to break off mankind from a reed, which then exploded. Two people, a man and a woman, emerged. It is the custom in some tribes to stick a reed in the ground beside the door of a hut in which a baby is born

The Coming of Death

The Bantu tell how the chameleon brought death into the world. In one version the High God Unkulunkulu sent a chameleon to a village where a man lay dying, with the message: 'Let mankind not die.' The chameleon went slowly and loitered on the way, eating fruit. Meanwhile, the lizard who overheard the message, filled with spite, hastened and delivered the opposite message: 'Let mankind die.' By the time the chameleon arrived, the man was dead and so death came into the world. Both creatures are considered unlucky in Africa and Native Africans will not pick up either.

CASTING THE BONES

The origins of this form of magic are unknown, since it existed before written records. In 1607 the Portuguese missionary Joano dos Santos witnessed the divinatory 'throwing of the bones' in Mozambique.

Even today the bone diviner is consulted on matters, such as the thriving of cattle and crops and the successful outcome of disputes. Originally, the underlying belief was that all misfortune came from the malevolent thoughts of others, specifically witchcraft, and that divination could identify these sources of storm, illness and treachery. Traditionally the bones are said to reveal the will of the gods. Other diviners are convinced that the ancestors speak through them.

It is possible by using an adaptation of bone-throwing to focus on the symbols as a guide to intuition. There is no dark magic in making your bones or drawing your symbols on stones, but a positive harnessing of the awareness that animal and man are interrelated.

It may be that bone divination reached South Africa originally from what is now Zimbabwe or from the early Arab traders. The names of the bones in many areas resemble those of ancestor gods.

Traditional Bone Divination

Bone-casting is traditionally carried out by diviners who interpret the 'fall' of the bone. They are also skilled in medicine and herbalism and use the bones in their diagnosis of illness. Each diviner makes a personal set of divination bones and asks the ancestors to make the bones powerful.

One empowerment ritual involves burying the newly-crafted bones in white ash, white being the colour of the spirits. For the same reason diviners wear white when casting the bones. Untried sets of bones are also placed under white leaves on a growing tree in the moonlight. A more primitive method involves drinking water in which the bones and the flesh of a white goat have been boiled. This is believed to absorb the power and wisdom inherent in the bones. The ancestors are then entreated to strengthen the bones and impart their wisdom in the 'falls'.

There are two different forms of bone divination. One version has four bones to represent the senior male member of a family, a senior female, a junior male and a junior female. These are usually made of ivory, wood, bone or cattle horn. Each bone is decorated on one side to represent the positive aspect and the other is left plain for negative results. The bones are cast on the earth and each 'fall' as it is called, has a specific name and a verse, known as a praise poem, connected with it. Thus there are 16 possible combinations. The diviner considers the problem or question posed and applies the meaning accordingly. Whether a throw is good or bad can depend on the issue to which it refers and the diviner interprets the meaning in relation to the problems at hand.

This divinatory set is based on the oppositions of male and female and senior and junior, as well as negative and positive.

Male/Female

The oppositions and interrelations are reflected in tribal life. When a boy is born, the father will be told by a man hitting him on the shoulders with stick. If the new-born baby is a girl, a woman will pour a jar of water over the new father's head. The male/female divide is also reflected in the natural world. For example, the earth is female and the sky male. The left side is generally associated with women and the right with men, dark is female and light male. These concepts are also seen in other cultures continents away. With many of the divination systems in the book, the similarities are greater than the differences, perhaps because the basic concepts are inherent in human nature and experience.

Male diviners used an external focus for their magic, the bones, whereas females practised clairvoyance.

Senior/Junior

The senior/junior precedence system is at the heart of the family, as well as kinship, villages and totemic groups. The bone pieces are related to family position, at root father, followed by mother, son and daughter. These basic positions can be adapted according to the question asked or the sphere under consideration. The senior father bone can, for example also stand for paternal ancestors, the grandfather, the father's brother, the chief or simply an older man.

Casting the Astragali or Knuckle Bones

This is a more extensive divination system, using anything up to 50 or 60 knuckle bones. These bones come from different animals, with a male and female bone for each creature. The set also includes pieces of tortoiseshell, shells and stones found at sites of religious importance. Again, each bone has a positive and negative side. The Astragali are read both according to the clusters of the bones and which side faces upwards.

The content of the astragalus sets also varies according to the specific totem (power animal and bird groups). These tribal animals are reflected in the sets. A typical South African set would include four flat pieces of ivory, two male and two female. Four other pieces would be taken from the tortoise, each with two distinguishable sides, and four shells, two for the male aspect and two for the female.

The four ivory pieces are studied first. These give insights into the general issue. This, in turn, is related to the position of other key bones, especially the knuckle bone of the steenbuck, which stands for the chief or principal character under question.

Another key bone is that of the antbear, which represents the ancestors and indicates both from its position and its positive or negative aspect whether a venture is likely to succeed. It also indicates the possible well-being and health of the inquirer, which it was believed was controlled by them.

The influence of important or respected people is indicated by sheep bones, while goat bones suggest the doings of ordinary people.

Although each bone has a fixed meaning, the interpretation of the cast or fall varies according to the kind of problem presented. For example, when the four senior male bones fall in a positive position, it can indicate too much activity, but is a good indicator if rain is needed.

A Modern Version of Bone-Casting

Make your bone set on small round bones or if you prefer on white stones, small enough for you to be able to toss four at a time on the back of your hand. There are 14 pieces, eight animal totems or power animals that represent human characteristics and four human bone symbols: senior male, senior female, junior male and junior female. According to whether each symbol presents its positive or negative face and their groupings, you can obtain the answer to any question. Write the names of each totem on one side of the bones, leaving the other side blank. Place them in a bag.

Put a square white cloth or small sheet on the floor. Put your hand in the bag and, without looking, draw four bones out of the full set. Putting them on the back of your hand face upwards, toss the bones or stones and let them fall on the cloth.

The Symbols

The Antbear: the Ancestors

The antbear represents the ancestors because it burrows into the underworld, the realm of the deceased. When the Antbear appears, it says that you should follow tradition and look to the wisdom of the past for the answer to your question.
Positive face: A conventional approach is best.
Negative face: Avoid an over rigid approach.

The Baboon: the Followers

There is an old African legend about the hare who tricked the baboons into chanting that they had eaten the lioness's cubs, although it was the hare who had killed and skinned them. The lioness heard the chant and killed the baboons instead of the true culprit. When the Baboon appears, it says that you should be careful not to follow blindly the advice or opinions of others if you are to make the right decision.
Positive face: Go with the crowd.
Negative face: Think for yourself.

The Bird: the Seeker

As in many other cultures, in Africa the Bird is the messenger of the High God and helper of the other animals. When the Bird appears, it says that you should be prepared to follow your dreams and fly beyond your immediate world in pursuit of what it is you really want more than anything else.
Positive face: Widen your horizons.
Negative face: Do not flit from task to task.

The Chameleon: the Delayer

The Chameleon took so long delivering the message 'Mankind shall not die' that death entered the world. When the Chameleon

appears, it warns that now is the time for action. Tomorrow will be too late.
Positive face: Act now for success.
Negative face: Do not ignore urgent issues.

The Elephant: Brute strength
In one legend a huge elephant was known as the swallowing monster because he swallowed whole forests, villages and cattle. He was eventually killed by a mother and her children who built a fire inside him and cut out his liver to cook. The mother then cut her way out, releasing everyone. When the Elephant appears, you may feel that you are being forced along a path you do not wish to take. Resist, however immense the opposition.
Positive face: Stand up to aggression.
Negative face: Do not ride roughshod over others.

The Hare: the Hero/Trickster
The Hare is the equivalent of Brer Rabbit in West Indian tradition, the trickster who is much admired for his cunning and his ability to escape from any situation. When the trickster Hare appears, you may find yourself on the receiving end of deception and promises that will be broken. Keep quiet about your plans and intentions and avoid being compromised.
Positive face: Use your ingenuity.
Negative face: Beware falsehood.

The Hyena: the Villain/Trickster
The Hyena is also a trickster, but lacks the Hare's charm. When the Hyena appears in a reading, you should beware the temptation to take one short-cut too many or adopt solutions that may hurt or diminish others, however justifiable your actions may seem.
Positive face: Consider an unconventional approach.
Negative face: Look at the effect on others before you act.

The Lizard: Lost opportunities
In some versions of the legend about the Lizard who brought the message of death to mankind, the Lizard was not malevolent. The High God sent him after the Chameleon with the counter message that mankind must die, but because of the Chameleon's delay, the Lizard was too late. Either way, the Lizard's appearance heralds a lost opportunity that must be faced and not stand in the way of the future. By shunning the Lizard, we avoid facing what must be overcome in order to move forward in a positive way.

Positive face: Seize opportunities when you can.
Negative face: Face the future head on.

The Steenbuck: the Leader
The Steenbuck, which traditionally represents the Chief, is a particularly important bone. When it appears, it stands for the most important person in the reading, not in modern terms in rank alone, but the most significant character in your life. The bone warns that you ignore this person at your peril, but that by coming to some agreement with him or her, you may find that great opportunities are offered.
Positive face: Do not be afraid to take the lead.
Negative face: Do not attempt to go against the status quo.

The Tortoise: Perseverance and determination
The Tortoise persists to the end and in all the legends, such as the Hare and the Tortoise, another African legend exported to Greek as one of Aesop's Fables, the Tortoise won the race because of the swifter Hare's over-confidence. The Tortoise inevitably wins the day because he never gives up but moves to success step by step. When the Tortoise appears, you know that if you stick at any situation, you will win through and that to persevere is the answer to any question or dilemma.
Positive face: Keep going in spite of opposition.
Negative face: Do not be stubborn.

The Senior Male: Authority
In African society, the Senior Male represents any authority as well as a father figure. Therefore, it suggests not only that the answer or dilemma is centred around authority, but that controlled strength and assertiveness are needed to move forward.
Positive face: Be confident and direct in your course.
Negative face: Do not be dogmatic.

The Senior Female: Nurturing
The Senior Female stands for the mother, the carer and protector. This bone says that a sensitive approach is needed to any issue or question and that it may be necessary to co-operate with others.
Positive face: You are valued for your caring qualities.
Negative face: Do not become overwhelmed by caring for others.

The Junior Male: Youthful energy
The Junior Male bone, which traditionally represents a mother's brother, her ancestors or any younger or lower ranking male, is a

symbol of youthful enthusiasm, energy and sometimes anger. It talks of impulsive action and idealism.
Positive face: Use your natural enthusiasm for energetic change.
Negative face: Do not be impatient when things move slowly.

The Junior Female: Pliability and compromise
The Junior Female represents complying with the wishes of others and suggests a gentle response and co-operation, rather than confrontation or independence.
Positive face: Look to others for happiness.
Negative face: Do not compromise what matters to please others.

Interpreting the Bones

Once you have cast the bones or stones, examine the clusters. Note how they fall, whether in a group, singly, in pairs or in a cluster of three.

Single Stones suggest that there are separate questions within the issue or you feel fragmented. See how the stones might relate and draw your life together. Pairs of stones represent a conflict, a choice or balance according to whether they are negative or positive and their meanings. Clusters of three suggest that the issue or question involves more than one major factor and so may need compromise.

Count whether you have more positive or negative faces showing. If there are more positive than negative, the answer is affirmative. Two of each says that the answer is not clear-cut. You need to study the symbols carefully and weigh up the options before committing yourself to a cause.

A Negative Reading

African magic is not a gentle magic for its world is harsh and sometimes brutal. It contains more aspects looking at struggle and survival than Westernized systems that concentrate more on love and happiness. But the power animals offer their strength and the bones lay out the continent of the psyche.

Most readings in whatever divinatory system give a positive message and pointers for the future. What if you cast four negative bones? Should you abandon the reading? No, because often by studying the pointers, however negative, you can assess the situation you are in and abandon unrealistic hopes. If you are feeling negative, this will reflect in the reading, but that in itself can be a catalyst for action and actually help you to move forward. As life is made up of day and night, sunshine and shadow, so a 'dark' reading, not in the sense of malevolent but in expressing doubts and fears, can show you the light, albeit weeks away.

Real magic, whether South African, Norse or Chinese, promises no instant solutions, no lovely ladies, handsome princes or pots of money, but it can act as a friend and guide to harness your energies to propel you forward. Like a ball bouncing against a wall, magic can amplify your inner powers and divination focus your determination and direction.

LINDSEY'S BONE-CASTING

Lindsey, a woman in her late forties, had severe financial problems in her small business and had received a letter from the bank, threatening to call in her loans. Would she survive her financial crisis, she asked the bones?

She cast three stones together which fell blank side up and a fourth, also blank side up. The first blank was the Lizard, the second the Chameleon, the third the Senior Female and the fourth the Senior Male.

The Lizard of lost opportunities, in his negative aspect, showed that Lindsey must confront the immediate future head on and face her problem rather than ignoring it. The Chameleon urged the same course, to take urgent action. But their message was not all gloom for it told her to face up to her very real problems rather than hoping for rescue. If the Chameleon could get there first, the legend of doom could be reversed, but that demanded swift action.

The third, the Senior Female bone, expressed the way Lindsey had run her business affairs: helping out employees and waiting for payment from customers with hard luck stories. Now in her difficulties she had found that she had few friends.

The final bone, the Senior Male, was positive, the good fairy of the reading. But it was not telling Lindsey to seek wise advice from a father figure, but to act herself. She tried every port of call and finally found a bank that would take on her loans and offer her a respite from payments for a short time. There was a price (there always is in real life and magic), but it gave Lindsey breathing space to streamline her business and by not replacing a member of staff who retired but taking on the extra work herself, Lindsey is just able to meet her first payment.

Had Lindsey visited a clairvoyant in the Western world, she might have obtained assurances that things would improve and she should take the advice of someone wiser, in this case her bank manager who would have shut down her business. The African bone reading was starker, coming from a land where, even today, life is harsh and survival is hard. Yet because it confronted Lindsey with the painful truth, in a sense it released her and galvanized her to swim for shore.

34

SEASONAL MAGIC

THE POWER OF THE SEASONS

The seasonal agricultural landmarks, even in a largely urban society, symbolize the changing energies of the year. Whether in a tropical zone, a land frozen for many months of the year or more temperate climes, there is a time of new life, the birth of the young animals and birds, the appearance of the first shoots or the return of the herds or shoals of fish, a time of plenty and a time of dearth when the soil rests or is buried beneath the snow.

Once the seasons were particularly marked by the appearance and disappearance of fresh foods. But in an industrialized society, where refrigeration and other methods keep products fresh for months or even years and a plane can transport produce around the globe in not much more than 24 hours, seasonal variations can be blurred. However, the underlying seasonal energies of the land are reflected in the cycles of human life, beginnings, coming to fruition, fading away and regeneration time and time again, as we complete a phase and move on to the next. Each involves a small death and the birth of the next stage. Ignoring the natural cycles of existence and trying to keep up a constant intense pace may account for a sense of alienation, irritability and exhaustion in daily life.

A SCIENTIFIC BASIS FOR SEASONAL ENERGIES

A study in America has discovered that the female biological clock is in tune with nature and responds to the seasons, while men have become biologically deaf to the rhythms. A preliminary survey at the National Institute of Mental Health in Bethesda, Maryland, during 1996 found that an increase in the number of daylight hours causes women, during nocturnal sleep, to secrete lesser amounts of melatonin, the hormone that controls such seasonal urges as migration and breeding in other species. As winter comes and days grow shorter, women's nocturnal secretion of melatonin increases. Most men appear to have lost the ability to react to changing daylight hours and produce the same amount of melatonin regardless of the season. 'Men seem more sensitive to artificial light than women are,' Dr Thomas Wehr, a psychobiologist, told the *New York Times*. 'When it comes to seasonal change, men just don't get it.'

The research scientists found that although men retain the biological machinery to respond to changing day length, they tend not to use it. Some scientists think that the difference may be linked to a vestigial urge towards seasonal breeding among females that harks back to a time when humans also tended to breed at times of peak fertility in the spring and autumn. The findings may also help to explain why women suffer more from Seasonal Affective Disorder (SAD), the winter depression.

It may be that men have simply moved further away from the natural cycles and that if they became more aware of the changing year and patterns of life, stress levels could fall and a more harmonious pattern of activity emerge.

FOUR SEASONS MAGIC

This section uses the four seasons system which accords with the seasonal cycles of most people in the United States, parts of Asia and Europe and can be adapted by those living in the Southern hemisphere.

Internal and External Seasons

As well as responding to the external seasonal clock, almost everyone has an internal seasonal rhythm that reflects ebbs and flows at times of crucial life changes or major decisions. By responding to your own inner seasonal cycles over a period of time you may be aware whether you are feeling the stirrings of spring, the confidence of summer, the determination of autumn or the gentler contemplative energies of your internal winter. Or perhaps it is a time when external pressures and responsibilities are strong and you feel the pull of the Earth to follow the course before you until clearer markers or calmer times are ahead.

If you can ride the crest of the wave or go with the dip, life becomes harmonious and your outer actions mirror your internal needs and energies.

The Chinese Seasons

Western alchemy recognizes four elements (Earth, Air, Fire and Water), but the Chinese system has five interrelated elements that link with the seasons: Earth, Metal, Wood, Fire and Water (see also *Earth Magic*, page 153, and *Chinese Magic*, page 63). Their seasonal associations can offer unusual insights into magical energies.

In the system the seasons are seen to revolve round the fifth element, Earth, which forms the centre. However, it is not a static unchanging core, but like the other Chinese elements, a process rather than an entity that reacts upon and is affected by the other elements, for the cycles are those of constant creation, destruction and recreation.

Each season is controlled by an animal deity: the Green Dragon of spring controls the rain and the White Tiger of the autumn controls the winds.

Spring: the Green Dragon

The Green Dragon represents the East. Its element is Wood (the Chinese word means wide-reaching), which represents spring because that is the time trees begin to grow leaves and spring is the dawn of the New Year. The Chinese New Year falls around the same time as the festival Brigantia or Candlemas in early February, the first spring festival.

In spring, the seeds of new life burst from within the womb of the earth where they have rested in the winter. So the Green Dragon of spring is a symbol of new life and beginnings, like the tree putting forth buds. Because Wood (spring) is rooted in the Earth (the centre) a new spring in our lives arises from using our core strengths to initiate new projects and relationships with sure foundations (Earth). With the first stakes thrust into the sleeping soil, dreams are put into action. Use the courage of the Dragon to tread new pathways and regenerate enthusiasm.

Summer: the Red Bird

The Red Bird represents the South. Its element is Fire because the sun is at the fiercest at midday when it is in the South.

So the Red Bird of summer is a symbol of creative power and clear vision, the height of yang (pure creative energy). Fire (summer) burns or destroys any dead wood in our lives and so removes any obstacles from our path. The warming rays of the sun encourage living wood to grow upwards, creating confidence and optimism in the future. Aim to soar high towards the sun like the Red Bird.

Autumn: the White Tiger

The White Tiger represents the West. Autumn is the time of harvesting and its element is Metal. Traditionally, once the harvest was gathered, territorial disputes would be settled, often by resort to arms. Both scythes and swords were made of metal, the blades of swords being silvery white. It is also associated with death and was the guardian of graves because it was thought that people were born with the rising sun and returned with the setting sun.

So the White Tiger of autumn represents the riches of the earth, financial gain, recognition and realization of earlier efforts. Metal (autumn) is shaped and tempered by fire (summer) into a form that will be useful and powerful and enable us to reap the results of our toil, although perhaps not in a way we expected. When it is melted, it flows like Water and so moves on to the next element, winter. But the metal was taken from the Earth, our core and so is not without sacrifice. In autumn we acknowledge the changes within. Use the fierce, protective energies of the Tiger, Lord of the Land Animals, to fight any opposition and to claim our rightful place in the scheme of things.

Winter: the Black Tortoise

The Black Tortoise represents the winter. Its element is Water because winter is the midnight of the year when the nights are long and the days dark, the height of yin or receptive, waiting energy.

As water is absorbed by the Earth, so this is a time when energies and movement turn inwards and strengthen our Earth core. Water quenches the power of fire, as the colour black absorbs and negates all others. The Black Tortoise represents long life and indestructibility and so winter it is time to wait, withdraw and grow strong. Use the enduring power of the Black Warrior Tortoise to be strong and patient.

Earth

The fifth Chinese element, Earth, is seen as yellow and is located in the centre of the cycle. The effect of the seasons is seen in the Earth and so the Earth represents the outcome of a seasonal change or action upon our world. Inevitably it suggests that life or others are now in control and so you need to be guided by what life offers or accept any limitations.

Chinese Seasonal Divination

This remarkably simple, yet powerful method of divination can be used when you need to plan a course of action or devise a strategy. Use it first thing in the morning before an important day to harness the wisdom that your unconscious mind has been collecting during your time of sleep and dreaming. Your internal seasonal clock, whatever the time of the year, can steer you towards the natural energies that will enable you to reach the right decision.

Making Chinese Season Stones

You can use five different coloured crystals or stones: green for spring and the Dragon, red for summer and the Bird, white for autumn and the Tiger, black for winter and the Tortoise and yellow for the Earth.

Suggested Crystals
Choose crystals of similar shape and size.

Spring: jade, aventurine, chrysoprase or amazonite
Summer: red jasper, garnet, red cornelian, red tiger's eye
Autumn: clear crystal quartz, snow quartz, mother-of-pearl, white moonstone, selenite
Winter: obsidian/apache tear, jet, black onyx, smoky quartz

Alternatively, choose five white stones and draw a green dragon, a red bird, a white tiger and a black tortoise with permanent pen or paint. On the fifth, paint a yellow square, a traditional sign for the Earth.

Reading the Stones

Place your five stones in a bag or purse and concentrate on the predominant issue of the day or decision to be made. Choose one stone without looking and read it. See whether the forthcoming day is one that is ruled by spring, summer, autumn, winter or is a day of fate as ruled by the Earth.

JANICE'S SPRING DAY

It was mid-August when Janice was facing a major decision: whether to accept an offer of promotion at work, continue at her present level or resign and apply to college as a mature student to study the archaeology of Ancient Egypt, her first love. Logic and her colleagues told Janice that she would be mad to turn down a chance to reach the top of her firm. Janice cast the Green Dragon, the spring stone, that confirmed her own desire to recognize the new direction that was beckoning. The Dragon gave her the courage to resist the attractive but ultimately stifling path.

AL'S SUMMER DAY

It was the end of February and Al was planning to travel for three months on the Silk Route to Katmandu from the United States. His travelling companion suddenly changed his mind about going and tried to dissuade Al, pointing out the dangers and lack of comfort he would face.

Al's parents agreed and offered to accompany him on a trip to Europe, which they would pay for. But Al was still tempted by the Silk Route as he had never travelled alone. His summer stone, the Red Bird, was a reminder of the potential that he believed he could fulfil by seeing a new culture and living entirely away from friends and family. He went alone and teamed up with another traveller on the plane. His abiding memory was of the brilliant red birds he saw flying in India.

CONRAD'S AUTUMN DAY

Conrad had worked hard building up his small business and was seeking a loan to expand. However, the bank manager suggested that he was overreaching himself and ought to consider selling to a larger firm that had offered to take his business over.

Conrad had banked with the same company since he was a teenager and was tempted to follow its advice. Although it was March, Conrad drew the stone of the White Tiger, the autumn stone, reminding him of the link between the harvest and fighting for just rewards. He contacted every bank and building society in the area, as well as the local enterprise board, and found offers that would enable him to keep his independence but to expand sufficiently to be a challenge to the firm that wanted to buy him out.

GILLIAN'S WINTER DAY

The sun was shining brilliantly in July, but Gillian was sad as her marriage had recently ended in divorce. Her family were urging her to go out and meet people again and her friends had set up several unattached men to meet her.

On the outside Gillian complied but she felt increasingly isolated. When her mother telephoned to say that she was being included in a family holiday to Spain on which a recently divorced male cousin was also coming, Gillian realized that she was losing control of her life. She chose the winter stone of the Black Tortoise and realized that she needed time alone to grieve and to grow stronger before returning to the social scene. Taking a month of her annual leave, Gillian booked a cottage in a remote country village and refused to give her family the address. When she returned, she moved with her job to another region where she could start again alone.

MIRANDA'S EARTH DAY

Miranda is a single parent of four children whose new partner, John, demanded that she pay more attention to him and not her brood whom he studiously ignored. He wanted her to leave the children with her frail mother and come backpacking with him for the summer. When Miranda expressed doubts, John demanded that she should choose him or the children. Miranda picked the Earth stone which said, do nothing but let life take its course. Miranda refused to choose. Instead she explained that she could not leave young children with a sick grandmother. John stormed off but returned six months later, entirely changed, having missed her desperately. He is starting to get to know the children, but Miranda is still letting the future take its course.

The Western Seasonal Cycle

The Western seasonal cycle is bound up with the elements of Earth, Air, Fire and Water, traditional magical symbols for the forces that make up life (see also *Earth Magic*, page 153, *Fire Magic*, page 211, and *Water Magic*, page 472). Alchemists believed that by combining these elements, a fifth element, ether, could be produced from their essence. This elusive substance would lead the way to the creation of the Philosopher's Stone that could turn base metals into gold and offer the key to immortality. The colours and meanings of Western seasons are slightly different from those in the Chinese system. Use whichever system you prefer at different times. Like all magic, they are alternative ways of approaching the same area of experience.

The Solar Tides and Seasons

The four solar tides and seasons of the year are marked by the equinoxes and solstices. Seasonal influences are especially powerful for major life changes, long-term plans or gains that may take many months to reach fruition. The predominant energies of the seasons also offer a recipe for harmonious living.

Few modern people can actually withdraw physically from life for the winter. But if you do try to slow down and use long winter evenings for quiet contemplation, avoid major change where possible during the winter months and develop the domestic aspects of your world when it is cold and wet outside, you may suffer less from anxiety and constant tiredness than if your pace never varies.

However, if you do need to initiate a new project in the autumn, you can harness internal spring energies by focusing on the symbols of spring. The seasons given below refer to the Northern hemisphere. If you live in the Southern hemisphere, substitute the relevant dates.

Spring

21 March–20 June (for the Northern hemisphere), from the spring equinox to the summer solstice. The time of sowing. Its direction is East and its colour yellow.

The vernal equinox or Ostara Time, 21–23 March (for the Nothern hemisphere), marks the transition point between the dark and light halves of the year. At the spring equinox, the sun rises due East and sets due West, giving exactly 12 hours of daylight. The first eggs of spring were painted and offered on the shrine of the Anglo-Saxon Goddess Eostre or the Norse Ostara to whom the hare was sacred (this is the origin of the Easter bunny). Long before the days of intensive farming methods turned natural cycles on their head, the festival of Eostre was the time when hens began to lay eggs after the winter.

At the spring equinox, bonfires were lit and the corn dolly of the previous harvest (or in Christian times a Judas figure) was burned on the Easter fires. The ashes were scattered on the fields for fertility. It is said that if you wake at dawn on Easter Sunday, you will see the sun dance in the water and the angels playing. Easter is regulated by the paschal moon or first full moon between the vernal equinox and 14 days afterwards.

Spring Rituals

These are rituals for new hopes, new beginnings, new relationships and life changes and anything to do with fertility, children and love.

The Air quadrant promises the impetus for change and growth. For spring energies during this season or at any time of the year when you need a new beginning, use eggs, any flowers or leaves in bud, pottery or china rabbits, birds or feathers as a focus for your own spiralling energies. Carry sparkling yellow crystals, such as citrine, the strengthening stone, yellow beryl, the energizer or a yellow rutilated quartz with streaks of gold, the regenerator, for your spring talisman.

Summer

21 June–20 September (for the Northern hemisphere), from the summer solstice to the autumn equinox. Its direction is South and its colour is red.

The summer solstice or the time of nurturing marks the high point of the year, the longest day (see *Sun Magic*, page 410) and is the zenith of its light and of magic. It is a time for full power and for putting in hard work that will bear fruit in autumn. Modern Druids still celebrate this festival of light with ceremonies at midnight on solstice eve, dawn and noon. Great fire wheels were rolled down the hillsides in honour of the triumph of Baldur the Sun God over death. In medieval times on the day of St John the Baptist, 24 June, bonfires were lit on the highest points to mark the highest position of the sun.

Morris men wear white during the summer months in honour of the Earth or White (Moon) Goddess and practise a form of weather magic. The bells and ribbons were ancient fertility symbols, as were their staffs. The handkerchiefs are waved to drive away the clouds and the six-pointed star, centre of many of the dances and symbol of the English Folk Dance and Song Society, marks the union of the ancient Air triangle fusing with the upwards Earth symbol in the summer.

Summer Rituals

Rituals for success, happiness, strength, identity, wealth, career and travel. The quadrant of Fire promises dynamic results.

For summer energies or when you need confidence and power at any time during the year, use brightly coloured flowers, ribbons, gold-coloured coins, orange or red candles to evoke the power of the sun and your own strength and potential, even in dark times. Carry brilliant red or orange crystals, stones of the sun, such as amber, cornelian or jasper as your summer talisman.

Autumn

21 September–21 December, from the autumn equinox to the mid-winter solstice. Its direction is West and its colour blue.

The autumn equinox or time of gathering was traditionally celebrated as the second 'wild or green harvest', a time of celebration for the fruits and vegetables of the earth and the Earth Mother. It is also a time when the sky and animal god is said to retreat for the long winter. Druids climb to the top of a hill to take leave of the summer sun as the nights will get longer.

Michaelmas, the day of St Michael, the Archangel of the Sun was celebrated on 29 September with a feast centred around a goose. Since St Michael was patron saint of high places and replaced the pagan sun deities, he was an apt symbol for the last days of the summer sun.

Autumn Rituals

These are for harmony and reconciliation in your outer life and relationships, especially those concerning the family, adult children, brothers and sisters and friendships, and for material security for the months ahead. The quadrant of Water promises peace with others, very different from the autumn in the Chinese system where war followed the harvest.

For autumn energies or whenever you need to mend quarrels or seek harmony in your life, choose coppery, yellow or orange leaves, harvest fruits, such as apples, and pottery or china geese. Use also as a focus knots of corn, wheat or barley from the earlier harvest and copper or bronze coins to ensure enough money and happy family relationships. Choose soft blue crystals, such as blue lace agate, blue beryl or azurite, as a talisman of autumn.

Winter

21 December–20 March, from the mid-winter solstice or shortest day to the spring equinox. The direction is North and its colour green.

The mid-winter solstice or the time of waiting pre-dates organized religion. When early man saw the sun at its lowest point and the vegetation dead or dying, he feared that light and life would never return. So he lit great bonfires from yule logs, hung torches from trees and decorated his home with evergreens to persuade the other greenery to grow again. This mid-winter magic forms the origins of Christmas festivals throughout the globe (see also *Christmas Magic*, page 75). The Mithraic birth of the unconquered sun in Persia was just one pre-Christian festival that was celebrated on 25 December.

Winter Rituals

These are for removing unwanted influences and redundant phases, for home and long-term money plans and for older members of the family. The quadrant of Earth promises rest, regeneration and inner awareness.

For winter energies or when you feel pressurized, tired, or face hostility choose evergreen boughs, a circle of red and green candles, small logs of wood, especially oak and ash found naturally, as a focus for faith that tomorrow is another day and for inner vision. Choose deep green stones, such as aventurine, bloodstone, or amazonite, as your winter talisman.

A PSYCHIC CARD GAME

This is aimed at putting you in touch with your inner seasonal needs at times when a situation may not be clear cut, especially if you work under artificial light or at night and travel underground. Then you may lose contact with your internal ebbs and flows. Although you have a thousand and one jobs to complete and you are sleeping only a few hours a night and bringing work home, you may not need the power of the summer which would put you into overload, but some winter inner tranquillity, even for a short time. Or you may be going for broke but have an unresolved matter that is stopping you from succeeding. In this case a touch of autumn magic will restore your inner harmony.

Finding the Right Seasonal Energy

Take an ordinary playing card pack. Remove the joker and shuffle the cards well. You can also use the one to ten cards of a Tarot pack (40 in all), plus the court cards, although there will be 16, not 12 as in playing cards.

Begin dealing them into four piles for the different suits. The aim is to see which suit you complete first. This will give you the predominant seasonal energy you need. The relations of the seasons and cards are as follows.

Diamonds indicate winter and Earth (Pentacles or Disc in a Tarot pack).
Hearts indicate autumn and Water (Cups).
Clubs indicate summer and Fire (Wands).
Spades indicate spring and Air (Swords).

If your life is in flux or you have many important decisions, you can use this method twice a week or even more often. It may be, however, that the same suit turns up for several weeks.

It was winter. Eileen was housebound and becoming more depressed because she had a progressive muscle-wasting disease that confined her to a wheelchair. A local charity had offered her a computer so she could take an Open University course, but Eileen was unwilling to accept that her active days were over. The computer lay idle.

She dealt the cards and first completed spades for spring and a new beginning. She had some imitation Fabergé jewelled eggs she had brought back from Russia in the days when she travelled extensively and placed them on a dish on her window ledge, surrounded by the daffodils her neighbour had brought back from the Channel Islands for her.

One morning the winter sunlight sparkled on the eggs and lit the keys of her computer. Eileen decided that she would not only use her computer but find out the opportunities at the local college for wheelchair users so she could stay in the mainstream of life.

SUN MAGIC

THE ORIGINS OF SUN WORSHIP

The sun is source of light and heat and life to the world and so it was regarded as a deity and worshipped by all early civilizations. At first the sun was worshipped as a living being. Later the sun deities were thought to live in the house of the sun.

Wisdom and the arts of civilization were believed to have been brought from the sun by solar deities or early hero-gods who travelled from the East and returned to the West when their work was done. Quetzalcoatl, the Feathered Serpent and Aztec Sun God, was regarded as Father of the Toltecs and in an earlier time, as the Man of the Sun who left the sun for a season to impart the arts to the people.

THE SOLAR GODS

Solar deities were central to the pantheons of the great civilizations of the past. Shamash was the principal god of the Assyrians and Babylonians and the great judge of the universe because his light penetrated into every corner. According to the Sun-God Tablet in the British Museum, Shamash gave the code of laws to King Hammurabi.

Mithra or Mithras of the Persians, whose religion spread throughout the Roman Empire carried by soldiers who saw him as their personal god, was called the Unconquered Sun. He was born in a cave on 25 December, just after the winter solstice, thus restoring light to the world after the shortest day (see also *Christmas Magic*, page 75). Ra or Re of the Ancient Egyptians (see *Egyptian Magic*, page 164) travelled across the skies daily in his solar boat and through the underworld at night.

Helios of the Greeks, known to the Romans as Sol, was regarded as the sun himself. He ascended the heavens in a chariot drawn by winged snow-white horses to give light and in the evening descended into the ocean. The Greek poet Homer wrote: 'Drawn in his swift chariot, he sheds light on gods and men alike; the formidable flash of his eyes pierces his golden helmet, sparkling rays glint from his breast and his brilliant helmet gives forth a dazzling splendour. His body is draped in shining gauze, whipped by the wind.'

The most famous Greek Sun God was Apollo, son of Zeus and Leto. Apollo and his twin sister Artemis were born on the barren, rocky island of Delos. They were under the protection of the Sea God Poseidon so instantly the island became covered with flowers. Nourished with nectar and sweet ambroisia, Apollo cast off the white mists surrounding him and became a man. He set off with his golden quiver westwards, spreading knowledge and overcoming the forces of darkness. First he slew the evil female dragon/serpent Python, whom Hera, Zeus's wife, had set against her rival Leto just before the birth of the twins. His sister Artemis (Diana) became the Moon Goddess.

As God of the Solar Light, Apollo made the fruits of the earth ripen and at Delos and Delphi where he slew Python, the first crops were dedicated to him. He was also God of Music, Poetry, Archery, Healing and Divination. The last was unusual since prophecy was a function usually reserved for deities of the Underworld.

SOLAR GODDESSES

There were female sun deities, such as Sol (or Sunna) of the Norse tradition who rode her sun chariot drawn by the horses Aarvak (the early waker) and Alavin (the rapid goer), with a golden shield to protect them from the heat of the sun. Sol was the daughter of the giant Mundilfari and her brother was Mani the Moon God.

In Ancient Japan, the chief deity or kami (essence of divinity) was Amaterasu Omigami, the Sun Goddess. All natural phenomena were seen as manifestations of the divine. Amaterasu was one of the children of Izanagi and Izanami, the kami who created Japan as the most beautiful place on earth and sent their offspring to be the kami of nature and the elements: the wind, mountains, waterfalls, trees, ocean, animals and birds. Her name means 'Great August Spirit Shining in Heaven', but she is also called Shinmet, 'Divine Radiance' and O-hiru-me-no-muchi, 'Great Female Possessor of Noon'.

THE SUMMER SOLSTICE

This is the main festival of the sun, held around 21 June on the longest day in the Northern hemisphere when the sun is at its highest point in the sky and sunrise and sunset are at their most northerly points on the horizon.

From Russia, Norway and Sweden in the North to Greece and Rome in the South of Europe, among the Native American tribes in North America and in China, the summer solstice was an important festival from early times as man tried to hold on to the sun's power by sympathetic magic to stop its decline.

In parts of Northern Europe, the sun is believed to bathe in the waters on the solstice eve and so the waters were especially healing the next morning. As with Easter, the sun is said to dance on the morning of the solstice.

Among the Lapps, the main festival of Baiwe, Sun Mother and bringer of fertility to the land and the reindeer, is the summer solstice when sun-rings or grass garlands are woven in her honour and butter is smeared on the doorposts as a sign of her bounty. At the family meal sun porridge that contained rich dairy products was served. The father of the house asked her blessing of warm sunshine over the birch trees and the reindeer and that there might be a rich milking season.

In many parts of Europe the midsummer festival is now celebrated on the day of St John the Baptist, whose festival falls on 24 June.

The midsummer eve fires echo the earlier tradition of lighting solstice fires on beacon hills to celebrate the power of the sun which had reached its height and to try to persuade it to remain high in the sky and not to wane. The effect of so many hilltop bonfires was believed to strengthen the power of the sun. Indeed the Aryans believed they were actually giving fire to the sun.

Fire wheels were rolled down the hillsides, flaming tar barrels swung on chains and blazing torches tossed in the air. Young men would leap over the bonfire, for the higher they jumped, the higher the corn would grow. If they were not singed, they would be married within the year.

Fields were circled sunwise (clockwise) with processions of flaming torches to bless them and a woman chosen as Earth Mother would cast a bouquet of flowers and herbs on to the hilltop fire. The bouquet was tied with red, blue, green, yellow and white ribbons, representing the union of Earth and Sky, winter and summer, water and fire.

For Druids in Western Europe and other parts of the world today, as in Celtic times, the summer solstice (Alban Heruin) is still one of their chief festivals which they try to celebrate in a great stone circle, such as Stonehenge. The Ancient Druid Order (one of several modern-day Druidic groups) met there until an exclusion zone was enforced around the sacred stones to protect them from over-enthusiastic tourists who were not taking care of the ancient monument. The Druidic solstice ceremony starts at midnight on the evening before the longest day and the Druids hold a vigil throughout the night around the solstice fire. As dawn breaks, a second ceremony celebrates the sun rising and a third takes place at noon on the longest day.

Above all midsummer, whether on the original solstice eve (usually 20 June) or the new midsummer eve (23 June), is the time for love rituals and divination.

Midsummer Rituals and Divination

Love Rituals

It was believed that the oak bloomed briefly on midsummer eve but faded before dawn. If a lover could catch a little of the dust from these mythical blooms in a white cloth and put it beneath his or her pillow, he or she would discover the identity of his or her future beloved in a vision.

Any golden or yellow pollen, colour of the sun, gathered at midnight on the magical night of midsummer eve and placed beneath the pillow, is said to be equally effective.

An alternative ritual involves the small yellow flower, St John's Wort (wort is the old word for herb) that traditionally first flowers at midsummer. An unmarried woman should gather St John's Wort on the same eve without having eaten anything all day and she will have a husband before the year is out. If she sleeps with the yellow plant under her pillow, she will dream of her true love.

A Money Ritual

There are also midsummer rituals for good fortune. The fern seed is said to bloom golden on midsummer eve and if the seeds are cast into the air, according to Russian tradition, they will land as a star at the place where treasure is buried. It is said that casting golden fern or other yellow seeds and as they fall, seeing them as golden coins, attracts good fortune.

In the Southern hemisphere, the summer solstice can be celebrated on the eve and day of 21 December, with Christmas following shortly afterwards as the promise of the rebirth of the sun.

Ritual for Protection

St John's Wort or any similar small golden flower or herb can also be used to avert negative influences. Traditionally, this and the other three herbs that bloomed around midsummer were picked at dawn on midsummer morn and hung in a circlet outside the front door of a house, and the words, 'Trefoil, vervain, John's wort, dill, keep out witches at your will', were chanted.

A Modern Ritual for Success

Rise before dawn on the day of the summer solstice and climb to the top of a hill so that you can see the sun rise. As the first rays of light suffuse the sky, run, cycle or roller blade down the hill. As you gather speed, let all the ascending solar energies fill you with purpose, confidence and joy. Spend the day enjoying the open air, even if it is raining or you are in the middle of a town. Make plans for the future and map out the steps you need to take to fulfil a dream or ambition, however modest.

Before dusk, climb the hill once more and as the sun sets in the west, thank it for the gift of life and strength and in a sheltered place light a golden sun candle. As the last light fades, blow out your candle and let the light of your personal sun shine over all who need it. If you are not well, get a friend or family member to drive you to a hill top at dawn and dusk and ask for health and strength or a way to use your inner sun to find happiness.

SOLAR MAGIC THROUGHOUT THE YEAR

The sun, masculine, powerful, courageous and assertive, speaks of our conscious strength to succeed and direct our energies in a linear way. It corresponds to yang, the left-brain, light, convergent thinking and creativity.

The moon, feminine, mysterious, intuitive, nurturing, is the yin power, dark, unconscious, the right side of the brain, divergent thinking, equally powerful but operating in cycles of time. It is wrongly assumed that magic uses only the right side of the brain involving intuition and unconscious powers. That is only half the story and the magic of the Aztecs, Greeks, Egyptian, Chinese, Celts and the alchemists who sought to combine the essence of King Sol with Queen Luna, recognized the need for powerful, direct energy and action as well as intuitive powers (see also *Metal Magic*, page 323).

By harnessing the power of the sun as well as the moon, left-brain, logical magic does not usurp, but supplements the mystique of lunar powers. As well as recognizing the cyclic nature of human lives and lunar magic, solar magic can use the surge of direct energy to propel its energy into real action.

Women and men have within them energies that correspond to both the sun and the moon and the power of the sun can give to woman the focused energy to make dreams into reality, plans into action.

Solar or Lunar Magic?

Solar power is best for matters in the conscious, outer world and material matters, family matters, a better job, money or establishing a strong identity. Things of the spirit, inner issues and emotions, spells for love and kicking deep-seated habits or destructive relationships are better in moonlight where the unconscious powers predominate. You will know instinctively if it is a solar or lunar issue and whether you need a blast of sun power or clarity or more subtle moon bindings or unravellings.

Natural Sources of Sun Energy

You can use any or all of these natural sources of solar power not only at the summer solstice but whenever you need energy, inspiration, self-confidence and joy. You can carry one or more of the crystals of the sun, eat the fruits and foods of the sun, wear gold jewellery and orange or yellow clothes. Place the flowers of the sun in your home or plant any yellow flowers in your garden or on waste ground. Use the sun herbs for tea, cooking, as essential oils to burn or in a bath or begin a sun herb patch or window box.

Find a sun tree and feel its warmth and energy emanating from the trunk. Tie golden ribbons around the branches and leave yellow flowers around the base. Buttercups or dandelions are as powerful as the most expensive yellow blooms.

Gold is the metal of the sun and yellow and red are its colours (see *Colour Magic*, page 87). Orange represents a strong sense of identity and yellow clear communication.

Foods of the sun include all citrus fruits, sweet corn, spicy foods, saffron rice, olives and olive oil. The herbs and incense of the summer solstice include chamomile, cinquefoil, fennel, St John's Wort, pine, saffron, sandalwood, thyme and verbena. Sun trees include almond, ash, laurel, olive, palm and walnut. Flowers of the summer solstice include roses, lavender, marigolds, carnations. Crystals and gems of the sun and summer solstice include clear crystal quartz, diamonds, amber, cornelian and topaz.

Solar Days and Times

The days between the summer solstice and midsummer are powerful solar days so use them for asking for promotion or more money, applying for jobs, making important plans or making a new beginning. Sunday is the day of the sun and especially powerful for solar rituals.

The Timing of Solar Rituals

With solar magic, if you are seeking a new beginning, go for dawn. For full power or realizing your potential carry out your rituals at noon, the height of the sun, and for banishing spells, try sunset.

A Ritual for Sunny Days

At noon, the time symbolic of full solar power, or when the sun is shining especially brilliantly during the afternoon, place a large bowl of water in your garden or yard or use any small expanse of water such as a garden pond. Catch the sunlight in the water so that it turns golden and splash your face with the golden empowering light, feeling yourself filled with energy, enthusiasm and confidence. Now drop in the water a golden or yellow symbol for the area in which you seek success: a coin for money or financial gain, a yellow pencil or pen for examinations or learning and a clear crystal quartz or any yellow crystal or stone for clarity in interviews or communication matters. Float yellow flowers on the surface and see the accumulated gold amplifying your natural abilities.

When the sun has faded and all the golden beams have been absorbed by the symbol, take it carefully from the water, dry it on a yellow cloth and keep it with you during your forthcoming endeavour.

A Sun Power Ritual for a Dull Day

It is more difficult to feel enthusiasm and confidence when it is raining or cloudy. But the sun is there, just waiting to break from behind the clouds, if you are very lucky, casting a rainbow of promise.

Use a pot of marigolds, a sunflower or any other golden flower to attract the sun and its energizing powers. The noon tide will add the full solar potential. Before you begin have an early lunch of golden fruits, vegetables, bread, butter, a globe of golden cheeses or corn-fed chicken and instead of switching on the light if the day is dark, light a golden candle.

Place your flower and any left-over golden fruits or vegetables in the centre of your window ledge or go out into the open air with your flower and use its golden essence to spread sunshine over your garden or work-yard. Concentrate on each petal and see it shedding a golden aura like a sunbeam and the sunbeams together spiralling into a golden ray of sunlight. Let it fill you with joy, optimism and an assurance that you will succeed.

When you no longer need the sunshine, separate it into individual sunbeams to return it to the petals. Thank the flower and give it extra plant food or a warm sheltered corner to grow. If it is raining, put on a bright raincoat or cape and splash through puddles, feeling the innocent joy of childhood returning.

Making a Sun Catcher

In the United States, sun catchers, like dream-catchers, can be brought to hang in windows to catch the sunlight. Hanging clear quartz crystals and amber crystals from threads, using clasps to secure the stones, can catch rainbows and spiralling light, casting energizing light into the darkest corners.

Alternatively, you can sew a web with tiny crystalline beads and rainbow sequins in the centre to hang across a window so that the jewelled sunlight filters through and any dark thoughts, negative feelings from others or sorrows are held in the centre.

SUN DIVINATION

Inner Astrology

There are three key sun stones for you to throw on to your sun chart. You do not ask a specific question, although you may well get answers to key concerns. Rather, the system alerts you in which of the astrological houses your solar energies and strengths lie at a particular time.

The system relies not on charts of formal horoscopes, but on the inner intuitive affinities that we have with the sun. Few can doubt that we are affected psychologically as well as physically by the sun. There are people who become depressed and ill because of lack of sunlight.

But as the moon calls us on an intuitive level, so the sun operates on a psychic level of inner power and focus. It is this psychic force that underlies inner astrology. These solar affinities were first experienced by ordinary men and women millennia ago, as they worshipped the golden orb and regulated their lives by its seasons and rhythms.

The Sun Stones

You will need three yellow or white pebbles, each about the size of a medium coin. You can draw the signs listed below on the stones with a pen or paint. However, you might prefer to buy three round pieces of amber or cornelians, the crystals of the sun, and mark them with permanent pen or paint.

Stone One: your Birth Sign

Your Birth Sun Sign highlights your core characteristics and strengths. When it falls in a particular house, you know that is the area where your personal strengths and qualities should be directed at the time of the reading. When your Sun Sign lands in the House it rules, its influences are especially strong and you will find that you are facing an important issue when you need to stand by your beliefs.

Stone Two: your Polar (Opposite) Sign

This will be the Birth Sign opposite yours on the Sun Wheel. The Polar sign is increasingly regarded as the other self, the shadow side, whose characteristics and strengths can help you to overcome opposition and your own weaknesses. When your Polar stone lands in a House, it indicates the area in which any opposition or difficulties may currently arise. By using the strengths of the Polar sign, you can turn the situation to your advantage. If the Polar stone falls in its own House, the opposition may be fierce but the prize high. However, if it falls in your Birth House, then you may be causing difficulties by an inner uncertainty about the rightness of your actions. It may be deep down you want the opposite of your conscious aims.

Stone Three: the Sun

The symbol is a dot surrounded by a circle and it represents the peak of energy, enthusiasm and potential. When the Sun stone lands in a particular House, it identifies areas in your life that will benefit from a sudden burst of energy or a positive logical approach. If your Sun stone lands in Leo, the astrological birth sign it rules, you will find your creative powers at a height.

Birth Sun Signs

♈ **Aries**, the Ram (21 March–20 April): Polar Sign, Libra. A Cardinal (initiating) Fire sign. Those born under Aries are innovative, assertive, active and with a strong sense of identity, energetic but self-centred.

♉ **Taurus**, the Bull (21 April–21 May): Polar Sign, Scorpio. A Fixed (Stable) Earth sign. Those born under Taurus are patient, practical, cautious, concerned with material comfort and security, but can be possessive.

Gemini, the Heavenly Twins (22 May–21 June): Polar Sign, Sagittarius. A Mutable (adaptable) Air Sign. Those born under Gemini tend to be inquisitive, intelligent, communicative and adaptable, but restless.

Cancer, the Crab (22 June–22 July): Polar Sign, Capricorn. A Cardinal Water Sign. Those born under Cancer tend to be home-loving and nurturing, sensitive, creators of emotional security, but secretive.

Leo, the Lion (23 July–23 August): Polar Sign, Aquarius. A Fixed Fire Sign. Those born under Leo tend to be courageous, proud and loyal, a born leader, but needing the approval of others.

Virgo, the Maiden (24 August–22 September): Polar Sign, Pisces. A Mutable Earth Sign. Those born under Virgo tend to be methodical, skilful, perfectionist and efficient, but critical.

Libra, the Scales (23 September–23 October): Polar Sign, Aries. A Cardinal Air Sign. Those born under Libra tend to be balanced and peace-loving, harmonious and just, but can be unwilling to make a decision.

Scorpio, the Scorpion (24 October–22 November): Polar Sign, Taurus. A Fixed Water Sign. Those born under Scorpio tend to be mysterious, psychic, intense and regenerative, but can be vengeful.

Sagittarius, The Archer (23 November–21 December): Polar Sign, Gemini. A Mutable Fire Sign. Those born under Sagittarius are visionaries, seekers after truth and meaning, optimistic but can be very outspoken.

Capricorn, the Goat (22 December–20 January): Polar Sign, Cancer. A Cardinal Earth Sign. Those born under Capricorn are quietly resolute, prudent, conventional and ambitious, but can be mean.

Aquarius, the Water Carrier (21 January–18 February): Polar Sign, Leo. A Fixed Air Sign. Those born under Aquarius tend to be independent, idealistic, intellectual and humanitarian, but can be emotionally detached.

Pisces, the Fish (19 February–20 March): Polar Sign, Virgo. A Mutable Water Sign, those born under Pisces tend to be sensitive, imaginative, intuitive and spiritual, but can be inconsistent.

The Houses of the Sun

The Houses are drawn according to the Equal House system of 30 degrees each, although individual Sun Signs vary slightly in length.

The First House

Ruled by Aries, 21 March–20 April, the First House concerns the self, identity and core personality. It talks of new beginnings, change, renewal and major decisions.

The Second House

Ruled by Taurus, 21 April–21 May, the Second House concerns possessions and financial matters. It talks of material concerns and security, negotiating pay rises and all financial deals.

The Third House

Ruled by Gemini, 22 May–21 June, the Third House concerns communication, whether by letter, phone or in person, relationships with brothers and sisters, neighbours and younger relatives, transport, especially cars, and short journeys.

The Fourth House

Ruled by Cancer, 22 June–22 July, the Fourth House revolves around the home, family, homemaking and improving and the private world of the individual. It talks especially of older people, especially parents, memories and all the issues involved in ageing.

The Fifth House

Ruled by Leo, July 23–23 August, the Fifth House concerns creativity, love affairs and passions. It talks also of sport, exercise, celebrations, pleasure and risk taking and is the House of children.

The Sixth House

Ruled by Virgo, 24 August–23 September, the Sixth House talks of health and physical matters, especially those caused by stress. It also talks of work relationships, routine matters, especially at work, and of minor rather than major worries that can get out of proportion.

The Seventh House

Ruled by Libra, 24 September–23 October, the Seventh House concerns close relationships and partnerships, whether marriage or business. It deals with relationships and the development and stabilizing of new liaisons. It deals with negative as well as positive aspects and the actions of rivals.

The Eighth House

Ruled by Scorpio, 24 October–22 November, the Eighth House concerns other people's resources, endings that form the seed of new beginnings, changes in existing patterns of life or finance, matters of inheritance, taxes and debts, psychic and mystical matters and secrets.

The Ninth House

Ruled by Sagittarius, 23 November–21 December, the Ninth House influences law, philosophy, religion, publishing, far-reaching ideas and communication (an extension of the Third House), distant travel, new educational fields, intellectual challenges, restlessness and a desire for freedom.

The Tenth House

Ruled by Capricorn, 22 December–20 January, the Tenth House concerns the outward public and social image as opposed to the Fourth House, which deals with the inner private world of home. It talks of professional and career life and 'the good citizen image', vocation and responsibilities.

The Eleventh House

Ruled by Aquarius, 21 January–18 February, the Eleventh House concerns friendships and affiliations, the influence of friends and organizations, social activities. It also deals with hopes, ideas and ideals and emotional detachment.

The Twelfth House

Ruled by Pisces, 19 February–20 March, the Twelfth House concerns limitations, sorrows and difficulties. It talks of self-delusion and escapism, but indicates issues of life which, if faced with courage, will lead to self-revelation and happiness. It also talks of needing wise counsel, rest and avoiding deceit in self and others.

Making the Sun Wheel

Either photocopy the Sun Wheel shown in this section to twice or even three times its size or draw a similarly enlarged Sun Wheel with a pair of compasses and copy the symbols. If you wish to use the Wheel in the book, choose three tiny crystals, one orange for your Birth Sign, one yellow for the Polar Sun Sign and a tiny clear quartz for the Sun. You do not need to draw the signs on them.

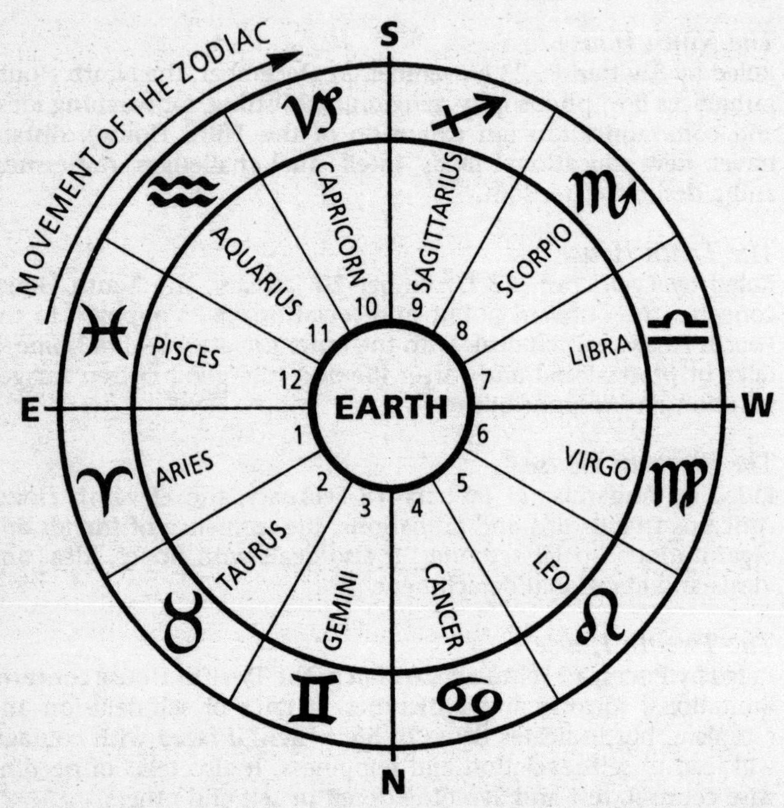
MOVEMENT OF THE ZODIAC
S
E
W
N
EARTH
CAPRICORN
SAGITTARIUS
AQUARIUS
SCORPIO
PISCES
LIBRA
ARIES
VIRGO
TAURUS
LEO
GEMINI
CANCER
1
2
3
4
5
6
7
8
9
10
11
12

Reading the Sun Wheel

Throw your three stones on to the Wheel one at a time, beginning with the Birth Sun Sign and ending with the Sun Stone, and see in which Houses they land. Read your stones in accordance to the House in which they fall. If more than one of the stones lands in the same House, that is a key area in your life that demands attention or resolution immediately to free your energies for other projects. Should a stone fall on the cusp, read as though the stone has fallen on both sides of the division, giving you four instead of three readings.

A SAMPLE READING

Sarah needed energy and confidence to break free from a destructive relationship with Greg, her partner for four years. Her unspoken question was: 'Do I have the strength to make a life alone?'

She threw first her Birth Stone, Libra. Like many Librans, Sarah saw the other person's point of view at the expense of her own and had many times drawn back from leaving her drunken, abusive partner because she felt responsible for him and worried he would not cope alone.

Stone One: the Birth Stone

Sarah's Birth Stone fell into House One, the House ruled by Aries, that reminded Sarah of her own separate identity and strength of character. It is the House of new beginnings and major decisions and so represented a turning point for Sarah, making the scales of Libra come down on the side of her own survival.

Stone Two: the Polar Stone

Sarah's Polar Stone was Aries, the fiery, assertive side of herself that she had buried from childhood, but which now could give her the impetus to move on.

Her Polar Stone fell in the Eighth House, Scorpio, the House of endings and also secrecy. Sarah realized that she needed to break the destructive pattern that was not helping Greg and destroying her own integrity. Previously she had warned Greg that she was going and he had made a supreme effort to stay sober for a week or so, until her resolve had weakened. Now Sarah realized that her Aries shadow side could help her to make a stand, but only if she went secretly and left no address.

Stone Three: the Sun Stone

The final stone, Sarah's Sun Stone, represented all the lovely sun energy and potential she possessed to make a new beginning.

It fell in House Twelve, ruled by Pisces. The Sun was illuminating the House of sorrows, overcoming the limitations and promising Sarah that if she avoided the illusion that her relationship with Greg might magically be reformed (he had refused all help many times), she could move into a new life, wiser and more mature because of her bad experiences.

Sarah did leave and went to stay with a friend a long way away. When she feels stronger, she hopes to help other women who were in her position.

TEA LEAF READING

THE HISTORY

Tea leaf reading is probably the most widely practised intuitive art and is found in the folklore of families around the world. Most people have a grandmother or elderly aunt who reads the leaves and the art is usually passed down through the female line. It is a form of natural folk magic that cuts across cultural and social barriers.

Tea was produced in China as early as 3000 BC for its medicinal properties as well as being a drink. China tea with its firm, large leaves and aromatic fragrance is still considered best of all for divination, whether taken in the traditional style without milk, lemon or sugar or served with all the trimmings of a full English afternoon tea. From China the secrets of its cultivation and divination spread to India and Sri Lanka, the former Ceylon. From India, the Romany gypsies brought the magical art to Europe (see *The Gypsy*, page 247).

Tea did not reach England much before the middle of the seventeenth century and was very expensive, costing £6–£10 per pound. It was not until 1885 that tea from India and Ceylon (now Sri Lanka) reached England in any quantity and so even in Victorian times it was a great luxury, kept in a locked wooden box by the lady of the house.

But the art of divination from the dregs left behind in a cup or glass was practised in Europe much earlier. Wine dregs were consulted, a craft known as olinomancy. From early times, peasant women made herbal brews for minor ailments and to preserve good health and the coarse leaves formed an early source for leaf readings. For example, camomile tea was routinely taken for centuries in rural areas to help insomnia and anxiety as well as minor skin irritations. Afterwards leaves from the brews would be used by the family matriarch to discover the root cause of the distress.

Coffee was introduced into Europe a century before tea and the first London coffee shop was opened to the public in 1652. Because coffee was not so expensive as tea, coffee grounds reading was, for a time, more popular and still forms the chief material for tasseography in countries as wide apart as Turkey, Greece and the United

States. In Merimée's story *Carmen*, the Gypsy tells her lover Don Jose before he kills her: 'I have seen more than once in the coffee grounds that we would meet our deaths together.' (The story was changed for the opera and she foretells their deaths with a deck of cards.)

Traditionally, coffee grounds are considered better for matters of the inner world and dreams, but this is entirely a matter of preference. If coffee is used, it should be the thick Turkish kind or a heavy grain, made by hand, boiled with water and the remaining syrup after drinking drained in the saucer, using the method suggested for tea leaf reading.

PREPARATION FOR TEA LEAF READING

Use firm, separate leave of a traditional brew, such as Earl Grey or Darjeeling. Some people like to keep a special small canister of tea especially for readings. Warm the teapot with water that has not quite boiled and rinse it out. As you do this visualize all the conscious worries and blocks disappearing.

Put a spoonful of tea in the pot for each person plus one for the pot. Let the rest of the water reach boiling point, add it to the pot and leave for three to four minutes, unstirred, longer for a stronger brew. In industrial areas of Britain, the Brown Betty is the traditional teapot used for tea leaf reading, a plain dark brown pot.

Use a large, shallow cup, plain on the inside. A clear glass or heat-resistant cup, a modern alternative, is in practice very effective as you can see your reading from both sides.

READING FROM A FULL CUP

Even with a full cup of tea, traditionalists suggest that indications can be read. For example, a single tea leaf on the surface of cup of tea is said to indicate the possibility of money coming, perhaps an enterprise at which you have worked bearing fruit.

A single leaf on the side of a cup of tea suggests meeting a new friend. If you are unattached, there may be romance. Several leaves floating suggests that you have busy days ahead, while a clear surface promises rest and relaxation, possibly even an unexpected holiday.

A TEA LEAF READING

Leave just sufficient liquid in the bottom of the cup so that leaves are still floating. The traditional method for tea leaf reading is to swirl the remaining tea round in the cup in an anti-clockwise direction three times with the left hand. Place the inverted cup on the saucer to drain the remaining liquid and turn the inverted cup a further three times in an anti-clockwise direction, once again using the left hand (which is controlled by the right side of the brain where creativity and intuitive responses are believed to reside).

Keeping the handle towards you, turn the cup the right way and twist it in all directions until you can see images in the leaves. Read the cup from left to right and if necessary, refloat the leaves in boiling water and drain them again if you can make no sense of the images or want a further reading on the same question. Often tea leaf reading fails because of a conscious block that stops the psyche letting the images take on meaning.

The tea leaves are a focus or trigger for pictures from deep within you and so it may be that a group of leaves suggests an image or even a picture that on closer consideration no longer appears. Go with that first clear picture, dictated by your wise inner voice. In any psychic work, the first spontaneous image, whether the sound of the leaves rustling in the wind or a tea leaf picture, is the truest one. The best tea leaf readers are those who trust intuition and inspiration and see with the mind's eye as well as the physical one.

You may even find that rituals involving using your left hand and turning the cup three times anti-clockwise seem unnatural and actually block your intuitions. The idea behind any repetitive actions in magic is to lull the conscious mind and so allow your subconscious mind an opportunity to take control. The act of drinking tea with friends in itself serves this function. There is no magic in the action itself for the magic is within and if you prefer simply to drain your cup in the saucer, to use a mug or even a paper cup drained on blotting paper in the office or factory, the tea leaf reading will still work.

Reading your own Tea Leaves

It is not unlucky to read your own tea leaves and, indeed, it is a very user-friendly, personal form of divination. However, you may find it easier to read for friends or family. If so, ask them what particular area of concern is uppermost.

Even with strangers, you should not waste time playing psychic guessing games. The tea leaves are there to provides clues to particular questions and if you know the issue from the outset, the reading can be very rich and informative. Ask the person for whom you are reading to pick out any images he or she sees and encourage them to guide the reading.

Can You Tell the Future?

Tea leaf reading is often regarded as a fortune-telling device and occasionally you may find, whether you are reading the leaves for yourself or for friends, that occasionally you get a flash of pure inspiration about the future. This is a bonus. However, the real point of any divination is to uncover your real choices and needs and see where potential paths will lead.

What gets left out by fortune-tellers in the worst sense (and these can include expensive city consultants as much as the lady at the end of the seaside pier) is that element of choice and the fact that what you are seeing are in a sense rehearsals of these choices. So if you see anything that feels bad, it is not a warning of doom or disaster, but a picture of your own or your friend's inner fears of what might happen if a certain course is pursued.

Areas of the Cup

There are agreed traditional meanings according to where tea leaves are sited in the cup. However even here are disagreements and you may prefer to read the cup as a whole picture and then apply the context of locations and situations in the light of this.

The handle of the cup, held towards the reader, is often taken to represent events or people close to home, whether self, family or close friends. The opposite side of the cup from the handle is seen as events or people at work or on holiday or strangers or new places not yet visited.

Past or Future

Traditional interpretations suggest that, with the handle held towards you, any symbols that point towards the handle are events, people or things coming into your life or that of the person for whom you are reading. Conversely, past events and people and those beginning to move out of your life are symbolized by images facing away from the handle.

When Will Events Occur?

Many conventional tea leaf readers interpret leaves at the rim of the cup as occurring in near future, within weeks or even days. Leaves halfway down the cup suggest people or events moving in or out of your life within a few months. The area close to the bottom of the cup is believed to portray the distant future, a year or more. However, you may not find timings particularly helpful.

Joys or Sorrows

The problem with interpreting events as 'good or bad' is that you can actually unconsciously project fears that are then regarded as bad fortune. It may be more useful to regard the areas of the cup as indicating challenges and obstacles to be overcome.

Leaves near the top of the cup may indicate that there are no obstacles to be overcome in a particular issue or that present circumstances promise happiness. Tea leaves from the centre upwards indicate that, apart from a few minor details, any current aims should be attained or generally that life will be peaceful for a while. The lower half of the cup suggests that there may be some challenges and obstacles to overcome to achieve any goal, but that persistence will pay off. The bottom of the cup, traditionally seen as foretelling tears and sorrow, indicates that it may be necessary to compromise to succeed and that setbacks can be turned to advantage with patience.

A pile of leaves at the side of the cup opposite from the handle suggest that overcoming obstacles needs the cooperation of others, while a pile of leaves close to the handle says that the solution lies in your hands. This may be an occasion to refloat the leaves to get a more detailed reading.

The Alphabet

Letters of the alphabet are traditionally seen either as important people in your life or the name of someone new, whether a helpful stranger, a new friend, lover or business acquaintance. The position of the letter is indicative of the relationship: the closer to the handle the closer the relationship either emotionally or in location. If the letter is near the handle, the meeting will occur close to home or involve home events.

Numbers

Numbers traditionally represent the number of months that will elapse before an event occurs. The time scale is usually taken from the area of the cup in which the number occurs. For example, a number eight at the top of the cup would indicate perhaps eight days, above the centre eight weeks, below the centre eight months and at the bottom of the cup eight years.

This time scale is applied to the symbol to which it is closest, for example, a six next to a boat or plane below the centre of the cup might suggest an unexpected journey overseas in about six months. However, some people do not like to try to forecast time so accurately, preferring a general indication of possibilities.

If a number occurs in isolation, it can be interpreted independently. If it is close to a symbol, you may choose to interpret the number meaning rather than using it as an indicator of time.

One indicates a new beginning, energy and decision and says that any action taken, whether in connection with a relationship, work or starting a new venture, promises well.

Two suggests either that relationships are the predominant issue, whether love, family or at work, and that you may need to balance the demands of different people or aspects of your life.

Three is the number of expansion, perhaps an addition to your family or circle of friends. It can as easily be a new step relation rather than a baby. Alternatively, it may represent new responsibility that may not be welcomed but which could lead to future prosperity or satisfaction.

Four is the number of feeling restricted and frustrated but suggests that a slow, methodical path may be the best in the long run and that it is not a time for risks or short-cuts, whether in money or relationships.

Five in tea leaf reading suggests restlessness and a desire for change in a particular aspect of life. It suggests that a change of approach or perspective may be better than giving up.

Six talks of harmony and reconciliation, of recognizing your own worth and achievement and developing links with others, whether socially or in connection with work.

Seven is a very magical number, indicating the unexpected and exciting. Rely on your intuition and take a chance if one is offered.

Eight is the number of widening your horizons, perhaps moving on to another phase and not worrying about past mistakes.

Nine is the number of achievement in a personal way, ambition and independence from the warnings and doubts of other. Believe in yourself for you are on the right track for the unexpected.

Shapes

Circle

Circles or rings are often regarded as the most fortunate of shapes, indicating happiness or success. If the circle is interpreted as a ring, it may suggest a permanent commitment of the heart, perhaps marriage. Although some tea leaf readers say a circle that is thick should be regarded as a ring, it really is an individual interpretation.

If accompanied by a bell, another traditional wedding symbol, the ring would suggest an imminent attachment, especially if near the top of the cup.

A broken circle or ring never foretells the end of a relationship or happiness. Rather it says that the questioner may be worried about a broken relationship or one that seems to be foundering. The surrounding symbols can offer advice as to the problem and most importantly how the reader sees it.

Cross

A cross can indicate burdens, usually imposed by others, or a feeling of being weighed down by the demands of life. Traditional lore gets very gloomy about a cross within a circle, indicating confinement in hospital or even prison. However, the restrictions are usually those of a situation that cannot at present be changed and so needless energy is wasted fretting, instead of planning for when movement is possible or finding something good about each day. A cross inside a square suggests that the questioner is making barriers, perhaps because he or she does not want change.

Square

Squares represent protection rather than restriction. However, if a person is being too protective, the situation may feel stifling and it is time to try to push back the boundaries of personal freedom. Often the square appears close to a symbol of a house, which may suggest that material security, especially concerning the home, is a central issue.

Stalk

Stalks traditionally indicate people and may appear with an initial. Often an accompanying symbol gives a clue to the identity. If not, let your intuition guide you. The stalk will be someone who is featuring in your life at present, either because of a developing relationship or perhaps a problem in dealings with this person.

Two or three stalks together can suggest a family or that there is a choice or conflict of loyalties. Let your intuition guide you. If a stalk is straight, the person is reliable, while if wavy, he or she may waver according to circumstance.

Dots

Dots in groups indicate money, usually money coming in, perhaps from an unexpected source or a project bearing fruit. The number of dots can suggest whether the windfall is likely to be small or larger. Small single dots often refer to correspondence, perhaps a job offer, contract or news that may lead to money-making opportunities. A single large dot may be a gift or payment in kind.

Line

Lines seem to indicate journeys, the length of which can indicate whether the journey is local or far away. Clear straight lines suggest easy journeys, while broken ones indicate that any travel arrangements should be double-checked and if possible, plenty of time allowed and an alternative means of transport or back-up route arranged.

On a less practical level, lines can refer to any kind of venture and if straight, promise a direct route to success or happiness.

Dashes or Broken Lines

Dashes mean either that journey plans may be delayed or interrupted or, more usually, an enterprise that needs ingenuity and perseverance and will not be quickly realized. Some people count small dots as months and long ones as years.

Rectangle

A rectangle can indicate that disagreements or unfair criticism can hinder progress, whether at work or in a relationship. Usually this is due to rigid attitudes on the part of others and so it is important to avoid potential areas of conflict where possible.

Triangle

A triangle is a magical shape and so indicates success and unexpected possibilities. However, if the apex of the triangle is pointing towards the bottom of the cup or away from the handle, opportunities are in danger of being missed unless swift action is taken.

The Size of a Symbol

These may vary considerably. The largest symbol is usually the dominant one. If a symbol is large in relation to the others, it may represent, according to the meaning of the symbol, a large success or sum of money or a major problem.

The Clarity of a Symbol

If a symbol is clear and well-formed, the issue is clear-cut or the offer or relationship is definite. Mistiness and unfinished outlines suggest that all may not be as clear as it seems. It might also indicate that a problem appears larger than it really is because of personal fears.

Asking a Specific Question

Even if there is one definite question in mind, read all the symbols in the cup as the whole picture may indicate that the real question is more complex. The number of good omens and bad omens can be counted to weigh up a decision.

Tea Leaf Pictures

Most images in the tea cup form either images or even a whole picture. Tilt the cup until an image suggests itself. I have deliberately not included any pictures as other people's images, especially two-dimensional ones, can create a rigid stereotype. Let the ideas be dictated by your inner voice.

Psychological experiments have shown that one of the main ways we interpret visual material is not from external cues but according to the images existing in our minds and, most importantly, the context. In any tea leaf reading the context is the question posed by the questioner and the situation in his or her life. For this reason a dialogue is essential if you are reading someone else's tea leaves. How he or she perceives the images is far more important than resorting to set meanings, as they form the focus and key to the whole reading.

TEA LEAF MEANINGS

Personal Symbols

Everyone has a personal symbol system. This started in early childhood in the myths of your culture, the stories you first heard, the animals, birds and trees of your home area and the magical creatures of your dreams. Therefore, any tea leaf reading symbols should be interpreted in the light of your own personal meanings system. If you are uncertain of this, you might like to begin by reading tea leaves without using the suggested meanings given here or in any other book. You will find that perhaps the same 20 or 30 basic symbols occur most frequently and have personal relevance. Write your personal core symbols in a small notebook or journal, along with any others that occur occasionally.

A completely clear cup indicates the complete absence of trouble. You may find that the main symbols appear in dreams of actuality not long after a reading that seemed very significant. The psychologist, Jung, called this phenomenon synchronicity or meaningful coincidence.

Universal Symbols

These are based on what Jung called the archetypes, the idealized forms of the characters that have peopled the world of men and women from the beginning of conscious time: father, mother, fool who may be wise, trickster, angel, demon, loyal dog, noble lion, butterfly of change and rebirth, flower of blossoming love, sword of justice or challenge, priest, soldier, king who symbolizes earthly authority, sun of growth and potential, child as a symbol of innocence. These are but a few and may be images that have already appeared in your personal symbol system.

Traditional meanings given in different books are varied and sometimes conflicting. This is because personal symbols are seen in different ways and different characteristics emphasized even in universal symbols. Sometimes the meanings given may be ones handed down through a family or even from other clairvoyants and so the original reasoning behind the symbols may have become obscured.

I have suggested some core meanings based on what seems general agreement between systems and where there is conflict, I have used a meaning that seems to make sense in terms of symbolic associations in other fields. I have kept the fortune-telling meanings to the minimum so that the tea leaves can be interpreted according to present needs and possible future paths.

You may wish to change or ignore the list and create your own meanings that may alter, even during a reading, in dialogue with friends.

Acorns: small beginnings that promise to bear fruit.
Acrobat: a complete change of opinion or viewpoint is needed.
Anchor: security, often a person, in stormy times.
Ant: hard work, involving co-operation with others.
Aircraft: exciting new prospects through aiming high.
Apple: fertility, whether personal or in a new project.
Arrow: a barbed attack or criticism from an unexpected quarter.
Axe: clearing the way for new beginnings.
Baby: a new beginning or birth.
Basket: abundance that will need to be shared.
Bat: a hidden fear.
Bear: strength to overcome any opposition.
Bees: a need to communicate or important messages on the way.

Bell: a cause to rejoice, also associated with weddings.
Bird: if flying towards the questioner, good news on the way, if away, then the need to try another approach.
Book: check information before acting.
Bone: forgetting old injustices.
Branch: a new friendship, addition to the family or chance of a new direction.
Bridge: mending a quarrel.
Broom: making a fresh start.
Butterfly: enjoying the moment without demanding permanence.
Cage: feeling restricted.
Canoe: being prepared to take responsibility for your actions.
Castle: being in a strong position, so long as you do not let down your defences.
Cat: needing to remain aloof.
Cauldron: inspiration and creative thinking are the key to success.
Chain: joining resources with others.
Cliff: taking a leap into the unknown
Clock: wait for the right moment rather than acting now.
Clouds: confusion over an issue that will clear, given time.
Clover: luck that should be maximized by effort.
Comet: an unexpected bonus or opportunity.
Cow: the need for patience.
Crab: finding the vulnerable side of an unapproachable person.
Cradle: the need to care for anyone younger or vulnerable.
Crocodile: beware of double-dealing in a friendly stranger or new acquaintance.
Crow/Raven: be sure to double check any crucial arrangements.
Crown: potential high achievement.
Dagger/Knife: be aware of a flatterer who criticizes you behind your back
Dancer: harmony is the keynote to success.
Deer: be swift and act without telling others.
Dog: a loyal friend or family member who should be valued.
Door: a chance to move on.
Dove: you may need to act as a peacemaker between family or close friends.
Dragon: a need to confront any opposition head on.
Drum: do not be drawn into the quarrels of others.
Duck: satisfaction at the moment is close to home.
Ear: ignore gossip about those close to you.
Eagle: success in worldly matters and fulfilment of ambitions.
Egg: the fruition of an endeavour or a new birth.
Elephant: happy memories may be rekindled.

Eye: look carefully at any offers and see beyond the surface.
Face: friendship is important, so seek friendly faces.
Fairy/angel: happiness through psychic/spiritual matters.
Fan: flirtations and flattery.
Feather: fair-weather friends.
Fish: using intuition.
Flag: rallying around friends or family who need support.
Flowers: recognition and thanks for what you have done.
Frog: the ability to move in two worlds.
Gate: a barrier to success or happiness easily overcome.
Giant: the need for a huge effort or monumental step.
Glove/gauntlet: a challenge that can be met.
Grapes: your own desires are important now.
Gun: resisting others trying to get their way by force.
Hammer: the need for input and hard work now.
Hand: showing appreciation to those who help.
Hare: a sudden change in direction.
Harp: a harmonious relationship or period in one.
Hat: a welcome visitor, perhaps from the past.
Heart: a new romance or rekindling of a family relationship.
Hen: domestic concerns and taking care of others.
Hourglass: it is important to finish any tasks in hand.
Horn: good news or cause for celebration.
Horse: hard work is necessary to succeed.
Horseshoe: good fortune favours any enterprise undertaken.
House: either moving house or concerns about material security.
Iceberg: hidden factors or feelings.
Island: feeling temporarily isolated.
Jug: a store of energy to help you succeed.
Juggler: balancing different demands on your time.
Key: an opportunity for improvement in your life.
King: a male authority figure.
Kite: new ideas that may not have firm foundation.
Ladder: promotion or career opportunities.
Lamp: light after a period of doubt.
Leaves: a cluster of leaves indicates praise or material rewards.
Lighthouse: help from an unexpected source in time of difficulties.
Lion: courage and high ideals will achieve your dreams.
Mask: hidden malice or anger.
Mermaid: a gentle, dreamy friend may prove a good one.
Monkey: curiosity and new skills to be learned.
Moon: listen to your dreams.
Mountain: an ambition that seems impossible but can be attained.
Mouse: pay attention to small details.

Mouth: be careful what you say or you may be misunderstood.
Nail: direct, forceful action will succeed better than hints or sulks.
Necklace: a bond of friendship or love, if broken needing mending.
Needle: improve your life or relationships by careful effort, rather than move on.
Net: look beyond your immediate environment to find friendship or happiness.
Nun: withdraw from the conflicts and demands of the world for a while.
Octopus: be versatile if a problem seems difficult.
Ostrich: do not avoid tricky issues as they will not go away.
Owl: seek wise counsel from an impartial source.
Padlock: there is a way out of a restricting situation if you are prepared to adapt your ideas.
Palm tree: well-deserved rest and relaxation, perhaps a holiday.
Parcel: an unexpected gift or news.
Parrot: try to be original, however good others' ideas.
Peacock: don't be taken in by appearances.
Pipe: take time to think over a decision.
Purse: you will need to watch financial matters.
Pyramid: seek wisdom from the past.
Question mark: examine any doubts as they may be well founded.
Rainbow: happiness after sorrow.
Rattle: children or someone who acts childishly may demand extra attention.
Ring: a deep emotional commitment, perhaps a marriage.
Rocks: care and tact is needed to avoid upsetting someone.
Roof: you may be worrying about your material future unnecessarily.
Rose: love, friendship and emotional happiness.
Sailor: news or a visitor from afar will bring happiness.
Scales: balance the pros and cons of a situation carefully.
Scissors: cut through any indecision by others that is holding you back.
Ship: travel, especially far away.
Snail: persevere as you will achieve your goal in the end.
Snake: you may be tempted to stray or act in a sly way.
Spade: dig deeper and you will discover the truth.
Spider: a lucky opportunity should not be dismissed because of fear of failure.
Star: try to make your dreams come true if only in a small way.
Sun: enjoy today and do not worry about tomorrow.
Sword: be prepared to fight for what you want.
Table: family togetherness or conferences.

Telescope: look to the long-term advantage.
Tent: break out of a routine that seems stifling.
Tortoise: do not be afraid of stating your needs or opinions.
Tower: being apart from the crowd because of a strong principle or vision others do not share.
Train: exploring new horizons, travel.
Tree: independence.
Tunnel: a temporary depression or sadness that will end.
Umbrella: a person or place that offers temporary refuge.
Violin: avoid being over-sensitive about criticism.
Volcano: sudden, tempestuous change that has been building up for a while.
Wall: obstacles to be overcome.
Waterfall: a sudden and frightening surge forward that offers happiness.
Whale: a huge undertaking or responsibility with great satisfaction at the end.
Wheel: following any changes that life dictates to the best advantage.
Windmill: using any help to move forward.
Window: a sudden insight that offers the answer.
Wings: rising above difficulties.
Wolf/fox: the need to act swiftly but without alerting others.
Yacht: a time to let life take its course.

37

Time Magic

MEASURING TIME

Time has been divided into regular units of measurement from when each moon or sleep was first etched on stone or carved on staves and the lunar phases used to mark out longer divisions. The physical division of time underlies a very powerful form of magic, where ordinary people would recognize certain hours of the day as especially magical and use the energies to strengthen desires and ensure the success of actions.

In Ancient Egypt, the daylight time was measured by a shadow clock, an early form of sundial. Early candle clocks, marked into regular divisions, were used in many societies and served a double purpose in harnessing magical fire energies (see *Fire Magic*, page 211). During the Middle Ages sundials formed the chief measurers of the day and portable sundials were popular from the sixteenth to the eighteenth century.

Until the late sixteenth century, sand clocks were used at sea and also on land, based on the hour glass which works on the same principle as an egg timer.

European clockmakers carried their craft to the United States with the early colonists. Although Switzerland is often regarded as the centre for watch- and clock-making, American craftsmen displayed great mechanical inventiveness and as early as 1650, before even the introduction of the pendulum clock, a clock was erected in a Boston church tower. The first public clock in New York City was built in 1716 for the City Hall at Nassau and Wall Street.

THE SUN AND TIME

The apparent motion of the sun across the sky formed the basis for measuring time from early days and at any locality. When the sun reaches the highest point in the sky during any given day, it is noon. This point is called the meridian. Since the length of the day according to solar time is not the same throughout the year, mean solar time was invented, based on the motion of a hypothetical sun travelling at an even rate throughout the year. The difference in the length of the 24-hour day at different seasons of the year can be as much as 16 minutes.

Standard time, which is based on solar time, was introduced in 1883 by international agreement and the Earth was divided into 24 time zones. The base position is the zero meridian of longitude that passes through the Royal Greenwich Observatory, Greenwich, England, and time zones are described by their distance East or West of Greenwich. Within each time zone, all clocks are set to the same time. In 1966 the United States Congress passed the Uniform Time Act, which established eight standard time zones for the United States and its possessions. In 1983 several time zone boundaries were altered so that Alaska, which had formerly spanned four zones, could be nearly unified under one time zone.

Modern magic recognizes the 24-hour clock and uses the current time in the time zone in which the practitioner is working.

DEITIES OF TIME

Because time was strongly associated with the sun and moon, many of the deities of time were associated with them. For example, Horus, after whom horology, the science of time measurement, is named, was linked with Ra or Re, the Sun God in the Egyptian tradition. Known as the 'face of Heaven by day', Horus represented the passage of the sun through the sky at different times and came to be regarded as God of Time, although it was the lunar Thoth, God of Wisdom who ruled the calendar (see *Egyptian Magic*, page 164).

Old Father Time himself was Kronos or Cronus of the Greeks, who, according to Greek myth, was banished to Rome where he instigated the Golden Age and became associated with Saturn. Time had to move on so that the New Age led by Zeus might begin. Kronos, in an attempt to hold the future back, devoured all his children except for Zeus (Air), Poseidon (Water) and Dis (the Underworld), elements that it is said even Time could not consume.

WHEN DAYS BEGIN

In Ancient Greece, day began at dawn. In the Northern tradition, however, day began at sunset and continued throughout the night and the following daylight until the next sunset. Modern festivals based on more traditional ones are celebrated on what is now the preceding evening, notably Hallowe'en and New Year's eve. Christmas eve, too, is a special occasion.

In the Norse tradition each 24-hour day was divided into eight tides, known as the *aettir*. Each day tide is three hours long, with an *atting*, peak hour, at the middle of each tide.

MAGICAL HOURS

These special hours, 3.00, 6.00, 9.00, 12.00, 15.00, 18.00, 21.00, 24.00, were known as chime hours. It is said that those born on a chime hour are especially intuitive and able to look backwards and forwards into time. Each three-hour period or *aett* has special strengths, qualities and areas of focus. If you need a special energy or are worried about an aspect of your life, you can identify the most appropriate *aett* for your need and spend the hour either looking into a candle flame or into still water in sunlight and letting pictures filter into your mind that will offer wisdom and perhaps an answer. I have used the modern idea of beginning the new day at midnight, but if you wish you can use the traditional sunset to sunset time frame for your magical work.

I have listed the strengths of the time periods and certain issues or problems may fit into one. The times reflect the slower agricultural world where toil began early and any loving and learning were relegated to the evenings when work was done.

0430–0730
Morningtide is the time of awakening, fertility and new beginnings. The chime hour begins at 6 am. Use its energies for new beginnings and on all matters concerning infertility, conception, pregnancy and birth of both babies and projects.

0730–1030
Daytide is the time of work and money-making. The chime hour begins at 9 am. Use its energies for money problems, money-spinning ventures and for success.

1030–1330
Midday is the time of endurance and perseverance. 12 noon is the chime hour. Use its energies for matters that are proving wearisome or long in bearing fruit and for difficult people.

1330–1630
Undorne is the time for change, transformation and illumination. 3 pm is the start of the chime hour. Use its energies for exploring new horizons and travel plans.

1630–1930
Eventide is the time of the family, of home and reconciliation. 6 pm begins the chime hour. Use the energies for questions concerning children of all ages, domestic matters, marriage and partnerships.

1930–2230
Nightide is the time for love, passion and learning. The chime hour begins at 9 pm. Use its energies for love relationships, close friendships and acquiring formal knowledge.

2230–0130
Midnight is for healing and restoration of mind, body and spirit. The chime hour is midnight. For insight into illness, especially of the chronic kind, for the mending of quarrels and the world of the spirit.

0130–0430
Uht is the time of sleep and old age. The chime hour begins at 3 am. Use its energies for concerns over elderly relatives and ageing and for calm sleep.

TIME (ASTRAL) TRAVEL

Because the chime hours are especially magical, you can use them for travelling forward in your psyche in a process known as progression. This is similar to regression except that you look not into the past, but into the future. Rather than seeing a specific future, you may gain impressions of a time yet to unfold, its colours, sounds, scents, even tastes. These images of the future often shed light on your present. Therefore you may wish to begin with a question in mind or if you prefer, let the experience dictate the direction of the wisdom.

Progression

The idea of time travel into the future is not new. Leonardo da Vinci, who drew planes, helicopters, parachutes and snorkels centuries before their existence, and writers, such as the Victorian Jules Verne who predicted journeys to the moon and super submarines capable of travelling round the Earth, were using channels of the psyche that enabled them to touch on the future with accuracy.

The methods suggested for forward travel in this section involve no trance states nor the services of a hypnotist. You are always in control, awake and aware and any visions come from within you or from the deep well of unconscious wisdom and knowledge that can be accessed through your deep subconscious. You will not witness your own death, an Armageddon or a world void of life. Whether a few months or hundreds of years ahead, the experience centres on sensations not specific events and, unlike spontaneous premonitions, link only with positive future scenes. The future you see may look remarkably like the present. You may be only five, ten or 20 years ahead. Consider that if a time traveller were to arrive at standing stones after the tourists and vehicles had gone away, it would be easy for him or her to mistake the date by a century or even a thousand years.

Suggested Techniques

Go on a real journey, for example on an uncrowded train, a long coach or interstate bus journey and let the rhythm of the wheels and the flashing countryside soften the conscious world before your eyes. Choose a seat that faces forward. Take a ferry on a calm sea so that you can sit on deck in a quiet sheltered place, the endless waves and empty horizon lulling you beyond the conscious world. A long night flight on a plane allows you to mingle with the clouds as you cross from light into darkness and back into light.

Nearer to home, walk across a long flat unbroken grassed or sandy area where you do not have to worry about traffic. If you are indoors, move slowly on a walking machine, so that you do not become fatigued but your physical and conscious mind are occupied.

As you are carried or walk along, visualize yourself crossing the horizon at your point of focus over a bridge of sea spray, flowers made from a blur of colours, a white open door in the clouds or a starry entrance. Keep moving. Travel forward on a silk-lined boat on a gentle stream, walk along a road of pure white stone or sand towards a point on the next horizon, the sun or a star. Note the scenes on either side: buildings, trees, birds, animals, flowers, homes or town centres. If you pass travellers or other boats, smile but do not try to communicate, for you exist in their imagination only.

Accept whatever impressions you are offered, rather than going on an information-gathering mission. You may hear snatches of conversation, scent fragrances, smell cooking, taste spices or salt on the wind, touch overhanging boughs, peep through windows or gaps in the houses as you pass. If you see anything unusual, note how it is being used or how the clothes or houses differ from your present world. Keep travelling forward.

Do not waste your journey trying to find evidence of newly-invented technology or pinpointing locations. You can explore the future many times and what you need to learn will unfold over your visits quite spontaneously. Look in the sky. Even if you do not see a state of the art space station, there may be different stars or planets. Perhaps you can see the blue of the Earth above you. Who knows where or how we will travel? Use your mind's eye to look downwards too. Already vast shopping malls exist beneath Toronto streets, to name but one city that has gone subterranean.

When you feel tired, the road peters out, your boat stops, you come to an impenetrable mist or the water course you are using narrows into a trickle and disappears into the rock, you know that it is time to return. Going on would be counter-productive. There will be different sights and sounds while returning.

As you reach your doorway, point of light or your entry point, relax and merge with the crossover. Touch your seat in the plane, bus, train or ferry, sit down if you have been walking or switch off your walking machine and rest in a comfortable place.

If you have not reached the end of your present journey, close your eyes and let the kaleidoscope of impressions form a coherent whole. You might want to write a few lines or sketch a brief outline. You may find that a question that was half-formed has been spontaneously answered or that a new confidence in the future has replaced your doubts.

THE RIGHT TIME (A NUMEROLOGICAL APPROACH)

All of us have special times of day when we feel powerful and responsive to a particular situation, whether an important meeting, presentation, test or romantic encounter. These times are dictated not only by our body clocks, but by natural energies that, whether or not chime hours, harmonize with our unique vibrations.

One of the simplest ways of discovering potentially positive times throughout the day and night is by using numerology. If you begin an encounter on a harmonious frequency, it bodes well for the whole encounter. You can use the 24-hour clock wherever you are. You can also calculate a good day, month or even year for a vital change.

What the Numbers Mean

One: The Innovator

Your creative, energetic, individualistic streak may predominate in one or perhaps more than one area of your life. You can use your One times and dates to make sudden leaps, whether for mental or actual changes. Any One time or date is good for people of other name numbers to initiate a new beginning.

Two: The Integrator

Your ability to assimilate opposite trends and factors and integrate conflicting issues makes you an asset in any partnership or joint venture. You can use your Two times and dates when opposition is fierce or you need to keep two major strands of your life going. The Two times and dates can help people of other name numbers to balance diverse responsibilities or loyalties.

Three: The Achiever

Your ability to bring ideas into reality and use your talents to make things happen ensures that you are powerful in your Three role. You can use the Three times and dates to push through any major plans or to bring happiness into your life and that of others. The Three times and dates can help anyone who needs a surge of positive energy and optimism.

Four: The Realist

Your skill in making ideas and relationships work within the limitations and available resources enables you to overcome almost any difficulties. Harness your Four times and dates when you are operating in less than ideal circumstances. The Four times and dates can help to find alternatives and to compromise.

Five: The Communicator

Your ability to express yourself and your needs clearly and persuasively enables you to initiate change. Use your Five numbers and dates when you need the co-operation and approval of others. Five times can help anyone to avoid unnecessary misunderstandings.

Six: The Peacemaker

Your ability to sympathize with the feelings of others, whether in love, family matters or at work, makes you loved and valued in this facet of your personality. Use your Six times and dates for matters of the heart and for mending quarrels. Six times can give anyone the charisma to make fruitful relationships and friendships.

Seven: The Magician
This core aspect endows you with an uncanny ability to find an unconventional solution and to see beyond the immediate situation. Use your Seven times and dates when you need to trust your intuition. Seven times can offer anyone access to his or her voice and wisdom if external advice has failed or is biased.

Eight: The Entrepreneur
Your innate financial acumen and ability to bring order out of chaos puts any venture on a firm, secure footing. Use your Eight times and dates when you need to be logical, practical and to consider material security. Eight times can offer to those with different name numbers a framework in which to put one's affairs in order.

Nine: The Crusader
Your desire for justice and your courage in standing against inefficiency or corruption make you a powerful ally of those who are vulnerable. Use Nine times and dates to stand up for what you believe is right, to make changes that will benefit others as well as yourself. Anyone can use Nine times and dates to resist unfair criticism and negativity in others.

Identifying Your Number

Because we all have many facets that can be reflected in different forms of the name we use in different situations, our vibration numbers will vary. For example, in a social or personal situation, you would use the name by which friends and family call you. This may be a nickname or a shortened version of your Christian name. You would not include your surname. This will provide your Personal Number. If it is a business matter you would probably use your full and middle name to give your Work Number. If it is a core issue and you want to touch your roots, use the full name on your birth certificate to give your Identity or Core Number.

How to Calculate Your Number

There are several systems of numerology, but the simplest and most popular is called the Pythagorean system, after the Greek philosopher and mathematician who believed that all number was contained in the single digits (one to nine). The chart below shows how the numbers correspond to letters according to his system.

1	2	3	4	5	6	7	8	9
A	B	C	D	E	F	G	H	I
J	K	L	M	N	O	P	Q	R
S	T	U	V	W	X	Y	Z	

AN EXAMPLE

Patricia Mary Roberts is the name on the birth certificate of Trish, a woman in her thirties who works as a customer care manager. This is her Core Name and should be used in any calculations, such as legal and official matters or appointments with a lawyer or bank manager. The values for each letter are found and added repeatedly until they give a single digit.

PATRICIA	MARY	ROBERTS
7+1+2+9+9+3+9+1	4+1+9+7	9+6+2+5+9+2+1 = 41 21 34

41+21+34=96
9+6=15
1+5=6
Her core number is 6.

Trish's official name badge says Patricia Roberts. So her number with acquaintances and people she meets in the course of her duties would be calculated as:

PATRICIA	ROBERTS
7+1+2+9+9+3+9+1	9+6+2+5+9+2+1 = 41+34

41+34 = 75
7+5=12
1+2=3
Trish's work number is 3.

To friends and family, Trish is just Trish. So her personal number would be:

TRISH
2+9+9+1+8 = 29
2+9=11
1+1=2
Therefore her number for interactions with friends and family is 2.

Calculating the Best Times

This part is remarkably simple. All you do is to decide which number is 'you' in a particular situation and read off the number of a suitable time whose number matches your own.

YOUR DAY CHART

0015 6	0030 3	0045 9	0100 1	0115 7	0130 4	0145 1
0200 2	0215 8	0230 5	0245 2	0300 3	0315 9	0330 6
0345 3	0400 4	0415 1	0430 7	0445 4	0500 5	0515 2
0530 8	0545 5	0600 6	0615 3	0630 9	0645 6	0700 7
0715 4	0730 1	0745 7	0800 8	0815 5	0830 2	0845 8
0900 9	0915 6	0930 3	0945 9	1000 1	1015 7	1030 4
1045 1	1100 2	1115 8	1130 5	1145 2	1200 3	1215 9
1230 6	1245 3	1300 4	1315 1	1330 7	1345 4	1400 5
1415 2	1430 8	1445 5	1500 6	1515 3	1530 9	1545 6
1600 7	1615 4	1630 1	1645 7	1700 8	1715 5	1730 2
1745 8	1800 9	1815 6	1830 3	1845 9	1900 1	1915 7
1930 4	1945 1	2000 2	2015 8	2030 5	2045 2	2100 3
2115 9	2130 6	2145 3	2200 4	2215 1	2230 7	2245 4
2300 5	2315 2	2330 8	2345 5	2400 6		

TRISH'S DAY

Trish has three peak obligations: a meeting with a lawyer, a training session for her new assistant and a dinner date with a man she has just met.

The official meeting with the lawyer centres around her core number 6. 1230 and 1500 are Number 6 times when the proceedings should run smoothly.

The training session at work will operate on her professional number 3. 0930 might be a good time, as this is a 3 time, or if she took the earlier lawyer time, she could run her training session at 1515. Since 1200 is also a 3 time, Trish could take the afternoon appointment with the lawyer and run a pre-lunch training session.

As for the date, Trish's personal number is 2 and so she could meet her new boyfriend at 2000 or 2045 She also has a peak of 2 at 2315 should the evening go exceptionally well.

LUCKY YEARS

You can also work out special years, those that share your number. The emphasis of the good fortune will vary according to whether you are using your personal, social or business numbers. The number is obtained by adding up the digits of the year and reducing them by addition to a single digit.

1997 8	1998 9	1999 1	2000 2	2001 3	2002 4
2003 5	2004 6	2005 7	2006 8	2007 9	2008 1
2009 2	2010 3	2011 4	2012 5		

For each year beyond 2012 add one until you reach 9, then follow the 9 with a one.

Particular months also have resonance. For lucky months you can use the month order beginning with January as Number 1 and ending with December as 1+2=3 and Sunday as one. For individual dates, simply add the two digits where necessary; for example, 25 of the month will be number 7 and 31, number 4. Again the lucky month will vary according to whether it is a work or personal matter, or something official.

Best of all is when your number is the same as the time, day and month of an interaction. For example, if you are a 2 in your business name, 11.45 on 2 February or 2 November (also a 2 because 11 = 1+1) is a really good business time.

1 January	2 February	3 March	4 April	5 May	6 June
7 July	8 August	9 September	1 October	2 November	3 December

TRAVELLING MAGIC

MAGICAL PROTECTION

Since people first left their caves to explore the wider world, magical rituals have been performed for a safe journey and return. The perils of the modern world are very different, but no less daunting as wild animals have been replaced by the spectre of attack from human predators. Even with the best precautions, you can find yourself alone in a dark or potentially threatening place or feel anxious and under threat when travelling after dark or alone, especially in big cities. Spiritual and psychic protection can be a useful addition to earthly action both in minimizing your vulnerability and visibility to any who would do you harm and making you feel more confident of your safety while you are travelling. One of the most common forms of protection for churchgoers and non-churchgoers alike is to carry a talisman or medallion dedicated to one of the saints who guard travellers.

St Christopher, Patron Saint of Travellers

Most famous of all talismans for travel is the St Christopher medallion, worn by travellers, especially motorists and seafarers, in many parts of the world. The legends surrounding St Christopher, whose name means Christ-bearer, have endowed his medallion with magical as well as strictly religious symbolism.

St Christopher was martyred during the persecutions of Decius, at Lycia in Asia Minor in the third century. According to legend, Christopher was a giant-like man who vowed to serve only the most powerful master. Converted to Christianity, he met a hermit who told him to live a solitary life next to a deep ford and carry travellers across the fast-flowing river on his back. One day a small child asked Christopher to carry him across the river. To Christopher's surprise, the child became heavier and heavier until halfway across Christopher feared they might both be drowned. He asked the child why he was so heavy. The child revealed that he was Christ, struggling beneath the weight of the sins of the world. Immediately the burden was lightened and Christ told Christopher to plant his staff as they reached land and the next day it would bear flowers and golden leaves as a token of God's forgiveness to the world.

Before he died, St Christopher asked God to protect any place where his image was placed from pestilence, plague and other dangers. Neither should those who looked upon his image die that day. For this reason pictures of St Christopher were hung in public places and icons and Christopher carvings were erected near gateways and entrances to towns and churches. Gradually St Christopher's image on a medallion was carried by travellers to protect them on journeys and many have held the image in moments of peril.

In 1969 his feast day (25 July) was reduced to the status of a local cult because his influence had moved far beyond the Catholic Church to secular life. But 25 July is still said to be a particularly fortunate day on which to travel or begin a journey.

Julian the Hospitaller

St Julian is the patron saint of ferrymen, innkeepers, long-distance and impoverished travellers, wandering musicians and circus people. In penance for killing his parents by mistake, Julian built a hospice for the poor near a wide river which he would ferry travellers across. One night he took in a leper who was close to death and gave him his own bed. As the man died, Julian saw a vision of the departing soul who assured him that God had forgiven him. His day is 12 February which is another lucky day to travel or break a journey. Although his medallions and images are less common, he is a much loved protector, especially in the Netherlands, and you may find his talisman of use if you are undertaking a lengthy or budget-priced journey.

OTHER TALISMANS FOR TRAVELLERS

A Totaphoth

The totaphoth was a curved plate engraved with text from the Talmud worn across the forehead. Jews wore it to ensure safety on a journey and ready hospitality from those who were met in strange lands.

Protective Crystals and Minerals

You may find that wearing a crystal pendant or holding a crystal in your left hand to allay fears can help you, especially on solitary journeys, whether across the world or across your city by subway.

Dark crystals and minerals, such as bloodstones, garnets, jet and smoky quartz, are believed to lower your outer signals to any hostile forces. You will not become invisible, but you may find that you are less noticeable and blend into the background. Sceptics would say that if you have your protective talisman, you feel less anxious and so do not give off the vibes of being a victim. Whatever the 'facts', these crystals have offered protection to travellers over the centuries and continue to provide safe passage through today's urban hazards.

Amber
Bloodstone
Emerald
Garnet
Jet
Moonstone, especially if travelling at night.
Shell if travelling by water or to a sea or lake side destination.
Smoky Quartz
Turquoise

LUCKY AND UNLUCKY DAYS FOR TRAVEL

Fortunate Days

As well as 25 July and 12 February, which are under the patronage of the saints of journeying, any date with 7 or 9 in it and therefore, the months of July and September are traditionally auspicious. For travelling by land the waxing moon is favoured and for sea or air the waning, according to old lore.

Less Fortunate Days

Fridays, the thirteenth of any month and especially Friday the thirteenth are considered unlucky days to travel, although less so if falling in a lucky month or Fridays on a lucky date.

Fridays are associated with the crucifixion and 13 with the betrayal at the Last Supper and together they are seen as doubly inauspicious. Superstition seems to be borne out by statistics: a study in 1994 of accident figures on the Southern section of the M25 motorway which encircles London, England revealed that although there were fewer people using that stretch of road on six Friday 13ths, there were more injuries from accidents.

'Our data suggest the risk of a transport accident on Friday 13th may be increased by 52 per cent,' the researchers reported in the *British Medical Journal*.

The researchers, led by Dr Thomas Scanlon, Public Health Registrar for Mid Downs Health Authority, suggested that one reason for the increase in accidents might be increased anxiety about Friday 13th which would reduce concentration and contribute to accidents, something psychologists refer to as the self-fulfilling prophecy. Friday 13th is also believed to be a bad day for buying a car as it will, according to custom, spend most of its time in the hands of mechanics.

Nor is travelling by ship any guarantee of safety on these ill-omened days. Before modern timetables forced them to sail all day and every day, sailors would not put to sea on a Friday. According to popular myth, an old sailor named Friday who lived in Great Yarmouth in England, had the keel of his new boat laid on a Friday, carried out the completion ceremonies on a Friday, launched it on a Friday and named it on Friday to defy superstition.

The maiden voyage was on a Friday and the vessel returned with a large catch of herring. On the second Friday it set sail and returned not only with fish, but with valuable salvage. But the rule of 'third time lucky' failed in this instance: on the third trip it was lost with all hands.

Stories abound of journeys on Friday 13th that ended badly. On that day in June 1930, Sir Henry Segrave's speedboat crashed at 161 kph (100 mph) on Lake Windermere as he was attempting the world water speed record. Just before his attempt, a timekeeper had joked to Sir Henry: 'In view of the date, Sir, I'd better have your autograph now.' Sir Henry had laughed and signed.

Even eminent sailors respect the superstition. In November 1914, First Sea Lord Fisher overruled British dockyard authorities who wanted to put off the sailing of the *Inflexible* and *Invincible* until Friday 13th. 'Imagine being such fools as to sail on a Friday, and on a 13th,' he wrote. The order went 'Sail Wednesday'.

This tradition was defied by the British Royal Navy submarine *Osiris* which made a point of diving on the 13th hour every Friday 13th. In December 1991, its luck ran out and the dive was postponed due to technical problems.

Rituals to Ensure a Safe Journey

Throughout the world rituals and taboos have sprung up to offset any negative forces while journeying, especially on days that were considered unlucky.

Destination
It is unlucky to ask someone's destination. This lies behind the tradition of secrecy on a honeymoon and was to ensure that malevolent spirits who hovered around any celebrations would not hear and rush ahead to spoil the honeymoon (see also *Love Magic*, page 289).

Railway tunnels
It is unlucky to talk when passing under a railway bridge or in a tunnel. To avert bad luck you should touch something green. However, if you open a train window while passing through a railway tunnel and breathe in the air, it is said to cure coughs and colds.

Travel tickets
If the last number on your ticket is a seven, you will have a lucky day. If the numbers on your ticket add up to 21, you will be lucky.

Forgetting luggage
If you forget anything, you must go back into the house, sit down on a chair or the stairs and count to ten before going out again.

Boat superstitions
You should always board a boat by the right side, however inconvenient. If you whistle on board a boat, you'll summon the Devil who will send you a devilish wind. In Caithness in Scotland, no fisherman's wife would blow on her oatcakes to cool them after cooking in case she brought a hurricane down on her husband's boat.

The custom of breaking champagne over the bows of a ship when launching it is very ancient, going back to classical times when a priest with lighted torch, egg and brimstone attended. The ship was dedicated to the god whose image was carved on the prow and whose name the ship bore.

Travel sickness
In Mexico a copper penny is placed on the navel before travel to prevent travel sickness.

Protective leaves

In Japan, the leaves of the teg-a shiwa plant are used as mascots for the protection of travellers. When a family member or friend is about to depart on a journey, a meal is served to him on a teg-a shiwa leaf. The leaf is then hung over the doorway of his home to ensure a safe return.

Cleaning knives

In Oceanic and African societies, a knife belonging to an absent person was kept. As long as the blade remained bright, all would be well. Therefore the knife was cleaned regularly.

SYMPATHETIC TRAVELLING RITUALS

Sympathetic magic involves acting out something in a ritual to ensure success in the real world, as hunters would enact the killing of an animal in a dance to increase their chances of a successful mission. These rituals can be applied to travel. For example, in the Kei Islands to the South-west of New Guinea, as soon as a ship sets sail for a far-off port, the part of the beach from which it was launched was covered with palm leaves and marked as a sacred place. None might walk on it until the boat returned safely and the leaves would be renewed if any blew away or withered.

To protect the voyagers, three pure maidens remained absolutely motionless in a room while the ship was actually at sea, crouched on mats with their hands around their knees. They were not allowed to turn their heads or make any sudden movements or, it was believed, the ship would toss on the ocean. Nor were they permitted to eat any sticky substances that might slow the passage of the ship through the waves. Once it was estimated that the ship had reached land safely, the girls were able to move more freely. However, for the whole time the travellers were away, the girls were not allowed to eat fish with sharp bones and stings in case the absent voyagers injured themselves.

A Modern Ritual for a Happy Journey

Pack and prepare early, allowing plenty of time to catch any connections so that you are in a calm frame of mind (if travelling companions insist on last-minute panics, let them fret alone). When all is ready, go to a quiet place, such as a garden or a well-loved room. Into a bowl of clear water, gently drop a dark protective crystal, such as jet, smoky quartz, garnet, bloodstone or a moonstone if you will be travelling at night or a shell if travelling by sea or to a sea, river or lake side destination (see also *Water Magic*, page 472).

As the ripples spread outwards, light a yellow or blue candle (the Fire Element) for a swift, pleasurable journey. Drop a little wax into the water so that it hisses and sets on the surface, forming land (the Earth element) to represent your safe arrival. You may find the wax has made the shape of the country you will be visiting or your mode of transport.

Blow out the candle and let the smoke travel upwards, carrying you above any minor setbacks and irritations to the pleasure of at last fulfilling your dreams. Let the light from the candle precede your path, shedding doubts and anxiety.

Take your protective crystal from the water, dry it and wrap it in a silk scarf or handkerchief to travel with your in your hand luggage.

A Ritual for Creating a Safe Path when Walking Alone

Hold a dark protective crystal and visualize yourself entering it and placing a soft grey mist casting a dark-green shadow around your outline. Walk towards your destination, seeing it quite clearly just ahead, along a clear path of golden light, the kind that extends across the sea to the sun at sunset, even if it is physically out of view. Erect steep cliff walls round your path. Your footprints may seem unusually silent. That is part of the protective magical aura you are creating. Keep to the clear bright narrow passage you have made towards the wider opening of light. The rock will close behind you to deter unfriendly followers.

A Ritual to Set You Travelling

If you feel a sudden wanderlust or see the faint possibility of a trip abroad, whether in connection with your job or a holiday location, you can hurry things along and make yourself more receptive to opportunities for a temporary change of scene.

Choose a symbol for the means of transport you would use: a toy plane, boat, train, car or even a model bicycle. You can get paper or plastic flags of different countries from packs of toy soldiers for a particular country or continent you have in mind. If the place is within your own country, choose a symbol of the town or village instead of a flag. Be as inventive as you like.

Place the flag of the desired destination next to your mode of transport. Point your symbolic mode of transport in the approximate direction you will travel from your home or workplace if you are aiming for a business trip. Ring the method of transport and flag with bright crystals, beads or buttons in red, orange, yellow and white to give energy to your plans. If you have a clear crystal quartz, direct it also where you wish to travel or shine a pocket torch in that direction, all the time seeing yourself propelled on a brilliant shaft of white light towards your desired venue.

Feel the warmth of the new place, the cold snow or warm sand, whatever is an identifying feature, and look up at the sun, moon or clouds and see them in the new setting, perhaps clearer or slightly different.

Leave the crystals and the symbol pointing towards your destination for 24 hours and over the coming days do anything you can to advance your travel plans in the real world, even if it involves modifying your ideas or extending the boundaries of possibility by finding a way to raise the money or to develop your potential to make a travel offer more likely.

Collect brochure pictures or postcards and a coin of the local currency, if money is a stumbling block to your plans, and place them within the crystal ring. Each day or night at the time you first performed the ritual, direct your clear crystal or torch towards your projected destination and see the bridge of light growing more solid and real each day.

ASTROLOGICAL ASSOCIATIONS

Although everyone has a place with which there is an instant affinity, astrology makes connections for each star sign with certain cities and countries. This does not mean that these are the only places in which you will be happy, but that if you do visit any of them, especially during your birth sun sign period, the chosen place may seem especially magical and perhaps something exciting or life-enhancing will happen there for you.

An Astrological Ritual for Travel

If you do have a special destination you want to visit, see if the country or a city close to your desired destination is given below. You do not need to choose a destination within your own star sign nor even within the current star sign period. You can use a symbol of the appropriate astrological sign to bring you to one of its cities or countries. For example, if you wanted to travel to Ireland or St Louis in the United States, you would use a symbol of Taurus who rules those places.

Listed below are the sun signs with their appropriate symbols or glyphs. Write the symbol of the star sign associated with the appropriate city or country or one close to your desired destination. Draw it in spiralling patterns over and over again in pen or with a sharp tool, such as a screwdriver or chisel, on a large flat white stone or shell. Find running water and cast your astrological stone as far towards the centre as you can reach. As you do so, see it transformed into a swift boat, a bird rising from the water and ascending to the sky or a shaft of sunlight rising as shimmering water drops and turning into sunbeams.

If you can go to the sea, cast your astrological stone at tide turn for maximum power. Draw the astrological sign of your destination on a clear quartz crystal and sleep with it under your pillow. Even if you have never been to the place, you may see details in your dreams that you will confirm when you visit your chosen location. You will get there if you use the magic to galvanize your earthly efforts (see *Water Magic*, page 472).

♈ **Aries (21 March–20 April):** Birmingham (England), Florence (Italy), Kracow (Poland), Marseilles (France), Naples and Verona (Italy). Denmark, England, France and Germany.

♉ **Taurus (21 April–21 May):** Dublin (Ireland), Leipzig (Germany), Lucerne (Switzerland), Mantua, Palermo (Italy) and St Louis (United States). Cyprus, the Greek Islands, Iran, Ireland and Switzerland.

♊ **Gemini (22 May–21 June):** Bruges (Belgium), Cardiff (Wales), Cordoba (Spain), London (England), Melbourne (Australia), Plymouth (England) and San Francisco (United States). Belgium, Sardinia and the Ukraine, the United States and Wales.

♋ **Cancer (22 June–22 July):** Amsterdam (Holland), Istanbul (Turkey), Manchester (England), New York (United States) and Tokyo (Japan). Holland, New Zealand, Paraguay and Scotland.

♌ **Leo (23 July–23 August):** Bombay (India), Bristol (England), Cape Town (South Africa), Chicago (United States), Damascus (Syria), Los Angeles (United States), Madrid (Spain), Prague (Czech Republic), Philadelphia (United States) and Rome (Italy). Bosnia, Iraq, Italy, the Lebanon, Sicily and the South of France.

♍ **Virgo (24 August–22 September):** Athens (Greece), Boston (United States), Corinth (Greece), Heidelberg (Germany), Paris (France) and the State of Virginia. United States, Brazil, Crete, Greece, Turkey and the West Indies.

Libra (23 September–23 October): Copenhagen (Denmark), Frankfurt (Germany), Nottingham (England) and Vienna (Austria). Argentina, Austria, Burma, Canada, Japan, Tibet and Upper Egypt.

Scorpio (24 October–22 November): Cincinnati (United States), Halifax, Hull, Liverpool (England), Milwaukee, New Orleans (United States) and Valencia (Spain). Algeria, Morocco, Norway, Syria, the Transvaal and Uruguay.

Sagittarius (23 November–21 December): Budapest (Hungary), Cologne (Germany), Sheffield (England), Toledo (Spain), Toronto (Canada) and Washington DC (United States). Australia, the Arab Emirates, Hungary, Spain and South Africa.

Capricorn (22 December–20 January): Brussels (Belgium), Delhi (India), Ghent (Belgium), Mexico City (Mexico) and Oxford (England). Afghanistan, India, Macedonia, Mexico, the Orkney and Shetland Isles.

Aquarius (21 January–18 February): Hamburg (Germany), Moscow (Russia), Salzburg (Austria) and St Petersburg (Russia). East Africa, Poland, Russia and Sweden.

Pisces (19 February–20 March): Alexandria (Egypt), Bournemouth (England), Hollywood (United States), Jerusalem (Israel), Warsaw (Poland), Santiago de Compostela and Seville (Spain). The Gobi and Sahara Deserts, the Mediterranean Islands, Portugal and Scandinavia.

TREE MAGIC

SACRED TREES

Throughout history, the belief in magical trees with protective, healing and empowering forces has persisted. Although few people are consciously seeking to appease the tree spirits by touching wood before an important interview or when expressing a hope or wish, the action stems from relics of early tree worship.

The Tree of Life and the Tree of Knowledge

Sacred trees can be found in all cultures, although the species varied according to the country in which they grew. Early Japanese texts refer to holy sakaki trees growing on the Mountain of Heaven. Buddhists talk of the Tree of Knowledge, the Persians of the Tree of Immortality, while in the Old Testament the Hebrews' Tree of Knowledge of Good and Evil, became the Tree whose fruit lost man his immortality. In Hindu mythology, Vishnu, the preserver God, was born in the shade of the sacred banyan tree which became known as the Tree of Knowledge.

The Chinese described the Trees of Life as the peach and the date palm. The fig tree was also worshipped as the Tree of Knowledge in Middle Eastern cultures. In Norse tradition, Ygdrassil, the World Tree, was seen as a great ash, a prop to the sky, its topmost branches hung with stars, its axis the link between the worlds of Heaven, Earth and the Underworld. Odin and his brothers fashioned the first man and woman Aski from an ash tree and his wife Embla from an elm (see *Norse Magic*, page 375). In Ancient Egypt, both the cedar and sycamore were the holy trees of Osiris.

In the classical world, Zeus created the bronze race of men from the trunks of the ash trees and the Greeks believed that the ash was an image of the clouds. Ash nymphs were regarded as cloud goddesses. The laurel tree was formed after Eros shot Apollo with an arrow of gold and his lover, Daphne, daughter of the river God Peneus, with an arrow of lead. Apollo became consumed with love but Daphne was now afraid and as Apollo pursued her she prayed to the gods for help. As Apollo seized her, Daphne was turned into a laurel which henceforward became Apollo's sacred tree.

TREE SPIRITS

Tree spirits are found in many cultures. In Africa, they are held in high regard as tribal gods and benign nature spirits who control sunshine, rain and the fertility of crops and women.

Japanese mythology is rich in tree deities and spirits. Uku-No- Chi was the deity who lived in tree trunks, while Hamori protects the leaves of trees. Each tree was under the guardianship of a god, while in more popular myth, wood spirits were depicted with the heads and claws of hawks but human form.

In Ancient Arabia, the powerful jinns inhabited trees but could roam the earth in different forms. In classical tradition, dryads and hamadryads were tree nymphs, especially of oak trees. They were said to die when a tree was cut down. In Germany or Scandinavia moss-wives or wild women inhabited the trees.

TREE MAGIC

Even in the modern world, tree magic can still be seen in the custom of hanging evergreen boughs at Christmas to persuade the spring to return and the leafless trees to emulate their green sisters. On May Day, decorated maypoles form the centre of traditional earth magic dances in Europe, a custom practised in earlier times by Romans and Celts.

Druids used a form of tree divination, known as the Ogham staves, signs carved on various kinds of wood, representing the different trees. These were cast as lots (see *Celtic Magic*, page 50). The Norsemen and Anglo-Saxons made wooden runes for divination and in this, too, are reflected the names and usage of different trees (see *Norse Magic*, page 375).

ASTROLOGICAL ASSOCIATIONS

In the modern world, the most popular and accessible form of tree magic lies in the traditional associations of trees with astrology. You can identify trees that can offer you the strengths of the astrological or planetary sign with which they are associated. For example, laurel, a tree of Leo for courage, or the fig tree of Pisces if you need extra intuition at a particular time.

Holding the appropriate tree offers instant energy and healing, but you may prefer to pluck a small leafy twig or branch from the appropriate tree and place it in your bedroom, decked with your favourite jewellery or ribbons (see also *Colour Magic*, page 87, and *Metal Magic*, page 323, for a full list of associated colours and metals). You may wish to plant your birth tree or a miniature version in your garden or on open land as a focus for your own energies. You may find that, for example, in April the trees of Aries redouble your own fire and determination, whether or not Aries is your personal birth sign. I have given a list of trees throughout the world and some belong to general categories, such as the thorn-bearing trees of Aries. If you cannot find any of the trees in your region, use your intuition to match the trees to the astrological qualities. For example, a Leo tree could be large and powerful, perhaps with golden or red leaves, one that reaches outwards and upwards like sunbeams.

Trees and the Sun Signs

Trees of Aries (21 March–20 April)
These include acacia, all thorn-bearing trees, especially the hawthorn, redwood and desert trees. They strengthen the resolve to overcome any obstacles and offer determination to put plans into reality.

Trees of Taurus (21 April–21 May)
These include the cypress, apple and the vine and all trees with deep roots. They can offer strength in financial and domestic matters.

Trees of Gemini (22 May–21 June)
These include all nut-bearing trees, especially the hazel, and any bonsai trees. They can bring harmony and peace of mind to any who are troubled by the conflicts of others.

Trees of Cancer (22 June–22 July)
These include all trees rich in sap, especially the willow, and offer wisdom and insight when the way ahead seems confused.

Trees of Leo (23 July–23 August)
These include palms, orange and lemon trees and laurels or any red or golden trees. Leo trees can give courage and a certainty of success to those who may doubt their own abilities.

Trees of Virgo (24 August–23 September)
These share with Gemini all nut-bearing trees, but the special tree is the almond and all other flowering trees like magnolia. Virgo offers efficiency and order to all whose affairs are muddled.

Trees of Libra (24 September–23 October)
These include ash and poplar and all slender, tall trees and offer balance and justice to all who have been unfairly treated or face legal action.

Trees of Scorpio (24 October–22 November)
These include blackthorn and all bushy trees or those growing near salt water. They can offer protection for all matters where secrecy is essential or for bringing out hidden talents.

Trees of Sagittarius (23 November–21 December)
These include limes, mulberries, birches and oaks and can help when clear communication is necessary or you are striving for independence.

Trees of Capricorn (22 December–20 January)
These include yew, pine and elm and all trees with dark leaves. They represent fidelity, whether to a cause or person, and can help in all transitions and times of instability.

Trees of Aquarius (21 January–18 February)
These include fruit trees, especially soft fruit, grapefruit trees and the flowering cherry. They strengthen integrity and resolve when principles are at stake and are helpful in fulfilling ideals.

Trees of Pisces (19 February–20 March)
They include alder, fig and all trees growing near water, especially still water, for clear vision, intuition and psychic powers.

Trees of the Planets

Like the astrological sun sign trees, planetary Trees can be used as a focus for different energies and often overlap with the sun sign trees. They can be used to strengthen the sun sign trees and if you pick both a sun sign tree and the tree of its ruling planet, you can double the power.

For example, if you needed a sudden burst of inspiration, you would pick the twig of a walnut or olive tree for the planet tree of the sun and combine it with the birth sign ruled by the sun, fiery Leo, using an orange or laurel tree to set you on track for the stars.

You can also select planetary energies and use them with other birth sign trees of the Zodiac. For example, you might need to strengthen your resolve if others are attacking your principles. A

Mars-influenced tree, such as a juniper, combined with an Aquarian tree, such as the flowering cherry, would make you more assertive and vigorous in standing your ground.

Just as people combine flowers for different energies (see *Flower Magic*, page 221), you can collect an assortment of twigs as a focus. You can even weave them together into an amulet. Old rituals were often based on these combinations and examples are given at the end of this section. In this system we are following the principles of the old astrologers and including the sun and moon as planets.

Trees of the Sun

Trees for energy, inspiration, self-confidence and joy include almond, ash, olive, palm, walnut. The sun rules Leo.

Trees of the Moon

Trees for emotional matters, motherhood, caring for others and fertility, include the banana tree, coconut, mango tree, mountain ash, rowan and willow. The moon rules Cancer.

Trees of Mercury

Trees for clear communication, money, travel and healing, include aspen, bamboo, cedar, hazel and mulberry tree. Mercury rules Gemini and Virgo.

Trees of Venus

Trees for happy relationships, love matters, family and friendships include the apple tree, avocado, birch, coconut tree, myrtle, peach and plane tree. Venus rules Taurus and Libra.

Trees of Mars

Trees for positive action, assertiveness and the desire to fight injustice include the cashew tree, hawthorn, juniper and all gum trees. Mars rules Aries.

Trees of Jupiter

Trees for wisdom, authority, expansion of horizons and conventional success include the banyan, chestnut, fig tree, lime tree, magnolia, maple, oak and sycamore. Jupiter rules Sagittarius.

Trees of Saturn

Trees for overcoming difficulties or limitations and for patience and endurance include beech, cypress, pine, tamarind and yew. Saturn rules Capricorn.

Trees of Uranus
Trees for times of change, for developing adaptability and succeeding in exams and anything to do with the mind and learning include the jacaranda tree, the cherry, coffee tree, nutmeg, myrrh and pomegranate. Uranus rules Aquarius.

Trees of Neptune
Trees for all psychic matters, intuition, inner wisdom and water include the alder, apricot tree, all vines, marsh, swamp and pear trees. Neptune rules Pisces.

Trees of Pluto
Trees for getting rid of what is redundant, whether old guilts, destructive habits or relationships that have run their course, include blackthorn, eucalyptus, poplar and thorn apple trees. Pluto rules Scorpio.

THE MAGICAL ASSOCIATIONS OF TREES

In addition to their astrological associations, certain species of trees are seen as being especially magical. You may like to try some of the traditional rituals. For instance, you can tie a scarf, ribbon or cord around the chosen tree and as you do so, endow it with your special wishes or dreams. Hold the knot and visualize yourself in the new situation. Then release the knot and see the energies flying to the cosmos.

At this point you should take the first step towards making your dream come true. You may wish to use your own words, remain silent or adapt some words that I find useful. For example, if you wanted to be independent, you might tie your knot round an oak tree or for love use an apple tree. At the oak tree, you could in traditional fashion bind a cord or long scarf nine times round a bough and say:

Empowering Oak
Give to me
In this knot
The strength to be
Myself and me
And so
Fly free.

Untie the knot and feel yourself free from the ties that stopped you doing what you wanted. As you read the qualities of the different trees listed below, adapt the words or create your own or, as with the astrological associations, make an amulet from the twigs or keep objects made of the different woods with you as you need them. Again, adapt the magic to the trees in your own environment. For example, if there are no ash trees for healing, choose a tree that is known for its healing properties in your country.

Apple Tree: Love

This tree, sacred to Venus, can be used to attract love and for happy relationships. The apple tree is the Celtic Tree of Life and sacred also to Iduna, Norse goddess of eternal youth whose golden apples kept the deities forever young and lovely. In Native North American Indian legend it represents the Tree of Heaven. Traditionally apple wood was used for wands to cast magic circles, especially for love and fertility magic, and in Eastern Europe an apple tree is planted when a baby boy is born.

Ash: Healing

The ash is sacred to Jupiter. Ash staves used to keep away snakes and to cure diseases from farm animals. The tree was used to cure children with rickets, hernias or wounds that would not heal. An ash tree was split and the child passed through the cleft nine times. The tree was bound up and when the tree healed, according to popular belief, so would the child. A folklore remedy for toothache was to rub your gum with a new nail until it bled, then to hammer the nail into an ash or oak tree which will take away the pain.

Birch: Rebirth and New Beginnings

The birch is sacred to Venus. In Northern climes the birch symbolizes the rebirth of spring and is sacred to the Mother Goddess. It was the first tree to grow after the Ice Age retreated. A relic of this early goddess worship is found in Russia where in remote parts at Whitsun, a birch is dressed in female clothing to represent the coming of the summer.

Elder: Second Sight

The elder is sacred to Venus and is associated with seeing other dimensions. It is said that if you wear a crown of elder twigs on May eve (30 April), you will be able to see magical creatures and ghosts. Native American Indians call the elder the tree of music. So potent is the elder whistle that fairies dance to its tune.

Hawthorn: Protection

The hawthorn is sacred to Mars and also to Thor and other Northern thunder gods. It is believed to act as a shield against physical and psychic harm. In pre-Christian times it was planted around sacred boundaries and many witches traditionally surrounded their homes with hawthorns. The expression hedge witch (haw is old English for hedge) for a solitary practitioner of magic arose on both sides of the Atlantic. The hawthorn is a fairy tree and its protection is reduced at magical times, such as May Day (1 May). Midsummer eve (20 or 2 June) is the old Midsummer eve but it is now celebrated on St John's Eve, 23 May) or Hallowe'en (31 October). On these days, it is said that if you sit beneath the hawthorn you will be enchanted by the little people (see also *Fairy Magic*, page 187). A hawthorn or hazel rod is a good protective charm and if you turn it round saying, 'May no bad thing come near', you will be safe from physical and psychic attack.

Hazel: Wisdom

This tree is the traditional source for dowsing rods to discover underground streams or ley lines (see *Earth Magic*, page 153). Druids used the hazel rod as a symbol of authority and wise judgement. Viking courts were surrounded by hazel staves to mark their limits. In Wales, it is said that a cap woven from its twigs can be used to make wishes come true. Hazel nuts are also considered a symbol of fertility and old women in parts of the South-west of England and Western Europe would traditionally present brides with a bag of hazel nuts or even pelt them with the nuts. As a symbol of wisdom, hazel is associated with wise counsel and divination of all kinds.

Love Divination with Hazel Nuts

If you want to know whether you and a loved one will marry or live together, float two large unshelled hazel nuts, acorns or any well-rounded nuts in a large bowl of water. Designate one for you and one for your love. Place them together and watch their progress. If the nuts remain close, the relationship is assured of happiness. If they go in different directions, there needs to be much discussion and positive feeling to resolve any differences or to accept that you are not destined for each other.

If they float close and then away and move close again, the relationship will have periods of discontent but, given good will and patience, these can be resolved. If one seems to follow the other, the named partner who is following may have to make adjustments either emotionally or to follow the partner over distances if the relationship is to survive. If one nut sinks quickly, his or her heart is not in the relationship.

AN EXAMPLE OF HAZEL NUT LOVE DIVINATION

Sarah, a television researcher, lived in the North of England. On holiday in Arizona she had met James who ran a theatre workshop and they fell in love. She returned to England after an extended stay and they kept in touch by letter and phone calls.

Sarah's career was doing well but she felt uneasy as James had sounded very remote on their last phone call and letters were getting less frequent. She floated two large unshelled hazel nuts of similar shape and size in the centre of the bowl. The one she designated James floated off, followed by her own hazel.

The first nut paused and for a time they floated side by side, but then the pattern was repeated with James's hazel nut sailing away followed by hers. The pattern was repeated three times and Sarah realized that if the relationship had any chance of surviving she had to go to the United States to spend more time with James as he was on a contract and unable to travel to Britain.

Sarah went on holiday again and while she was there, looked for temporary work. She is now researching a programme on the Navajos for a further three weeks. However, although she and James are good friends, she is uncertain about a long-term future. Nevertheless, she feels that she was right to follow her heart and her divination and give the love match a chance.

Olive: Peace

The olive tree, sacred to the sun, was a symbol of peace and divine blessing and first grew in Ancient Egypt and Crete. Olive boughs were made into crowns and worn by Greek brides and were the highest honour in the Olympic Games for victors, after the gods on Olympus who wore olive crowns. Conquering heroes in Greece and Rome, who had brought peace with victory, were also given olive crowns. In the Old Testament, the dove returned to Noah's Ark bearing an olive branch as sign that the waters had subsided.

Pallas Athena or Minerva presented an olive branch at the naming of the city of Athens as a symbol of peace and blessing. Athena and Poseidon both wanted to name the city after themselves. The gods ordered that whoever gave the most useful gift to mankind should be the victor. Poseidon brought forth a horse from the ground with his magical trident, but Athena struck the earth and an olive tree grew. This symbol of peace was judged by the gods as the greatest gift. Its oil has been used from early times to anoint holy statues, dress candles and for sacred temple lights. For healing quarrels, the branch of an olive tree is bound with pink flowers for reconciliation. As the flowers blow away, so will the bad feelings.

The Oak: Power and Independence

The oak, the king of trees, has been revered from ancient times and is sacred to the father gods of many traditions, although in Native North American tradition it represents the Earth Mother. At Dodona, the earliest of the Grecian oracular oak groves, Zeus was worshipped in his sacred tree, Quereus. The hero Jason's ship, the *Argo*, contained a beam from Quereus which gave the Argonauts advice. The sacred oak of Jupiter was worshipped on the Capitol Hill in Rome and again was a source of wisdom from the gods. To the Druids the oak was their special tree. Druid is said to mean knowledge of the oak (from *dru* oak and *wid* knowledge). He who has knowledge of the oak is said to be able to attract the power of the elements for his own use and to control storms. The space between two oaks was said to be the doorway to unseen realms where fairies lived and gave access to other dimensions.

Divination with Oak Lots

At the sacred oak grove at Dodona, one method of interpreting the oracle was by using the oak lots that were kept at the base. It is a method that adapts well to modern decision making, especially in matters of success, money, independence, property, justice and career. If you do not have oak trees where you live, any Jupiter tree, such as the maple, or a strong broad, long-living tree will be as good.

Go to a grove or forest of oaks or 'Father Trees' at one of the sun times, dawn, midday or sunset (see also *Sun Magic*, page 410). Choose a time when the wind is rustling through the leaves. Pick up 30 sticks 15–20 cm (6–8 inches) long. Using a wooden-handled knife if possible, scratch away the bark and make a cross.

Place a light-coloured tablecloth or sheet beneath the largest oak tree and draw a circle clockwise from the North or 12 o'clock position round it on the earth with a large oak branch to mark out your place. Sitting on the due South of the cloth oak facing North (the 6 o'clock position if you do not have a compass or it is difficult to judge the sun) think of a yes/no, go/stay, act/wait question or two people or opportunities you need to choose between.

Holding your sticks in your left hand for right brain, magical inspiration, cast them all on the cloth at the same time and count the number that show the cross which I interpret as the positive side.

If there are more positives than negatives, you know that deep down that is what your inner voice is telling you. Note how close the numbers are, whether they are fairly evenly matched. If you have exactly the same number of positive and negative sticks, the issue is not clear cut. Try rephrasing the question.

If the numbers are fairly evenly divided, you might ask the trees why you have doubts. Listening to the leaves blowing, especially at the main oracle tree, was another method used at Dodona and in other sacred oak groves. Ask the question either silently or let it be carried as the breeze begins to blow. Listen to the leaves. They may answer in words, song, images or colours. Accept what you hear and see, whether externally or through your inner voice and mind's eye.

The first answer before doubts and logic set in is the correct one and will explain why your answer was 'yes but' or 'no but'. Trust these sources of wisdom to guide your actions.

Gather up your sticks and fold them in the cloth. Undo the circle with your stick anti-clockwise from the 12 o'clock and bury the stick in the grove.

When you find running water, cast your oak lots into the stream, sending forth your hopes and wishes for success and happiness. If the water passes over stones, you can use the third method of interpretation practised at Dodona and listen for wisdom in the water. Relax and listen to the sound, letting it form images in your mind. Do not try to form images but let the answer come to you.

Finally, take an acorn home and plant it in your garden or on waste land as a symbol that mighty oaks really do grow from small acorns and that any endeavour, however humble, can have results far beyond its conception.

Rowan or Mountain Ash: the Home

This tree, sacred to the moon, protects households from harm and is the tree of happy homes. Traditionally a rowan twig was removed without a knife from a tree, fastened in the shape of a cross with red twine and used as a protective device for stables, cowsheds and garages. A cross of rowan combined with birch was put over doorways at dawn on May morning for year-round protection, but had to be replaced each year. In pre-Christian times, the cross was the astrological sign for the Earth that from time immemorial has been used for good fortune, as on hot cross buns. In earlier times, milk was churned in a vessel made of rowan and a rowan twig tied to a cow's tail to prevent witches stealing the milk. Rowan is also a good dowsing tool for finding metal and lost jewellery.

A Rowan Ritual for Making a New Home Happy

When you are leaving your old home, take a rowan twig for each year you have been in your previous home and burn them one by one on a small fire. As you do so, say 'let sorrow burn and happiness return' and consign to the fire all your sad memories and regrets at leaving your old home. Place some of the ashes in a small pot, containing all the happiness from your previous home to put over your new fireplace or front downstairs window ledge.

Take some rowan twigs with you and when you arrive at your new home, bind or plait them with red ribbon and red flowers into a cross or circle and hang them inside the front door as you close it for the first time. When the flowers die, press them between paper and add them to the jar of happy memories.

If you are moving to a house, plant a myrtle tree on either side of the front door for domestic happiness. If you live in an apartment, plant sprigs of myrtle in pots beside your entrance and back window or wall if you have no door. When they grow too large, take one or two leaves for your happy jar and plant the trees on land that needs replenishment.

If rowan and myrtle do not grow in your country, choose protective trees that grow round domestic boundaries and offer protection to homes.

40

WATER MAGIC

SEA MAGIC

The most ancient and powerful form of water magic is that which flows from the sea. When man first ventured out on the sea, he realized that he was at the mercy of the waves and the weather. Hence, a whole mythology and collection of protective superstitions grew up around the sea and sailors.

Sea Deities

Sea gods were usually half-fish, half-man, bearded and grasping a trident. The Greek Poseidon (Neptune in Roman myth), the son of Kronos or Saturn and Rhea, the Earth Mother, was brother of Zeus and Hades. He was given his kingdom after the overthrow of Kronos by his sons. If angered, Poseidon could create mountainous seas and tempests and he also controlled earthquakes.

Nereus was the Greek Old Man of the Sea, an ancient ocean deity who was the father of the Nereids. The 50 Nereids were the most famous of the sea nymphs. The special province of Nereus was the Aegean Sea. Proteus was another Old Man of the Sea. According to Greek myth, he could change his shape at will but if you could cling on to him as he transformed himself into a lion, a dragon, a panther or fire, he would have to act as an oracle and answer your questions.

The reverse was the case with the Old Man of the Sea from the Arabian Nights. He posed as a harmless old man and asked to be carried a few steps on the shoulders of any traveller who landed on his island. But once his powerful legs were wrapped around his victim's neck, he made them carry him until they died. Sinbad the Sailor escaped this fate by tricking him into a drunken stupor and freeing himself. Hence any unwanted burden is called an Old Man of the Sea.

Some sea deities were regarded as malevolent unless given offerings. In the Norse tradition, Aegir, the Sea God, was said to appear above the waves to overturn ships and drag their booty to the bottom. Large waves prompted the cry: 'Beware Aegir is coming.' His sister, Ran, was equally cruel and would lurk near dangerous rocks, luring sailors with her charms and capturing them in her net, a Northern version of the Sirens. She entertained drowned sailors in her coral caves and loved gold above all else. Her golden hoard could be seen when the sun touched the waves. Therefore Norse sailors would carry some gold about them to appease her should they meet a watery end.

But the sea can also be a benign force. As the nourisher of man, it can take on a maternal form. Before the Spanish conquest, the Peruvians called the sea Mama Cocha or Mother Sea because she gave them the harvest of fish upon which they relied (see also Sedna the Sea Mother in *Eskimo (Inuit) Magic*, page 176, who could be benign or cruel unless entreated by the shaman of the people to release the sea animals into the hunting grounds).

Aphrodite was a true sea goddess, as well as Goddess of Love, since she was born from the foam. Among the Romans she was called Venus.

Why the Sea is Salt

According to Scandinavian legend, Frodi, King of Denmark, was given a magical mill that would grind anything he wished. So huge were the magical grindstones that even his mightiest warriors could not turn them. He therefore bought two giantesses as slaves, Menia and Frenia, and they ground out wealth, peace and prosperity for him.

The land prospered, peace reigned, the gold overflowed, yet still Frodi would not let the exhausted giantesses rest. Angry at their cruel treatment, they ground out an army of hostile Vikings who landed in their huge longboats and killed the Danes. But to the sorrow and fury of the giantesses, the Viking chief was not grateful to be given such a prosperous land. He refused to free them and proved an equally cruel master. He forced the exhausted giantesses to grind salt on board his ship without rest, as salt was a very valuable cargo. At last the gods took pity on the weary women and avenged the chief's cruelty. The weight of salt was so great it sank the ship and all were drowned. From that time the sea has been salt.

Why the Cliffs of Dover are White

The White Cliffs of Dover are a landmark for all who approach England across the Channel. During World War II they became the focus for returning servicemen and were immortalized by Dame Vera Lynn in the song *White Cliffs of Dover*. However, their origin is attributed to the Vikings.

The giants had a ship called *Mannigfual* that sailed the Atlantic. So big was the ship, the captain paced the deck on a horse and youths who climbed the riggings were old men by the time they came down. Once the ship went off course and the only passage home involved navigating the very narrow English Channel. It appeared the ship would not pass the straits between Calais and Dover without becoming trapped and so the captain ordered the men to soap the sides of the ship with an extra thick layer on the starboard side nearest to the dark cliffs at Dover. The ship slipped through, but the cliffs scraped off so much soap that they were henceforward white and the waves still are white and foamy around them.

THE TIDES

The tide is traditionally a powerful impetus for water magic. Ruled by the moon, the tides are at their most extreme during the weeks of the new and the full moon. During the first and last quarters, the tides tend to vary less between high and low. Because of their association with the moon, its phases can give added potency to any sea rituals.

Sea Wishes

This is a modern form of offering tributes to the sea deities. All who sailed, fished or lived close to the shore, were anxious to appease the deities of the sea and used the turning tide to offer tributes to ensure good fishing and safe journeys by sea (see also *Travelling Magic*, page 450).

Coins, part of the first catch of the season, libations of wine and flowers would be cast on to the waves at tide turn by fisherfolk in honour of the ancient sea gods long after their sway had ended in the modern world. Even today, in the Western Isles of Scotland at Hallowe'en, a fisherman wades into the sea with a cup of ale as sacrifice for the ancient sea gods.

The Turning Tide

The turning tide brings together the old and new, the rising and falling, waxing and waning energies into a crescendo of power that is released as the waves crash on the shore and are drawn back by an unseen force. Tide turn is therefore especially powerful for sea wishes. Turning tide magic is best carried out when the full moon is in the sky (see also *Moon Magic*, page 336). You can use a tide table to find out the time of high tide at a nearby shore.

Watch the waves touching the beach and feel the power of the surging water enveloping your dreams and wishes and holding it on the white crests that may be tinged with Ran's gold. You will see from the wet sand or stones when the tide is no longer rising and when the moment seems right, call: 'Tide carry my wishes to fruition.'

Choose a wave and as it reaches the shore, cast a symbol of what you desire most on to it: fruit for fertility, a coin for wealth, flowers for love, a key for a new home or a new car or the name of a desired lover carved on a stone. Let the water carry your hopes and dreams with it and with each new seventh wave breaking, throw petals or blossoms on to the water, renewing your desire and confidence in your own power to make your own dreams come true.

The Incoming Tide

The incoming tide is powerful in a different way and can be used at any change point in your life, when you are beginning a new job or enterprise, for a new relationship or when you need a fresh approach to a long-standing problem, even to put life into an ailing marriage or love affair.

This ritual is best carried out during the week of the new moon, best of all when the crescent first appears in the sky. Write or draw on a stone with another sharp pebble or a chisel a symbol or word to represent your new beginning. Throw your wish stone as far as you can to touch the most distant wave and see your innovation rising in a cascade of water like a seabird ascending over the waters.

With your writing stone, etch on the sand in large letters your name and the word or symbol of your new beginning. Place the stone in the centre of the circle and wait until the incoming tide has accepted your efforts, as symbolized by the stone, and covered your name.

The Outgoing Tide

Magic on the outgoing tide is best done during the week of the waning moon and especially during the last day when the moon can no longer be seen in the sky and we must trust it will return.

Outgoing tide magic is good for ending phases in your life that are now redundant, leaving behind any relationships that have run their course or giving up any habits that are affecting your health adversely, such as smoking, drinking too much or eating problems.

You can also cast off any old regrets, bitterness or unnecessary guilt.

Wait until the tide is receding. Pick up nine shells or pure white stones, remove your shoes, wade out into the shallows and walk in an anti-clockwise circle, kicking away the water. With each complete circle, cast a shell or stone into the water as far away as possible. As you do so, feel the weight of the Old Man of the Sea sliding from you.

When your shells are gone, face the sea and count nine waves. Reach down as the ninth wave recedes and you will find the sea has offered you a treasure as a promise of a new tomorrow. It may be a special stone with a hole through which you can see, according to tradition, past and future, a piece of quartz that when you hold it to the light reflects the sun or moon or a special shell containing the silver of the moon. Keep it as a reminder of your strength and purpose.

Before you leave the beach, find a piece of seaweed. Seaweed indoors is lucky and said to keep your home safe from fire. What is more it is said that while you have seaweed at home you will never lack friends and you may even find a special one to replace a lost love.

FRESH WATER MAGIC

Undines

Fresh water is ruled by the undines, mythical water creatures. Undine, after whom they are named, was an elemental spirit who was created without a soul. She gained one by marrying a mortal and having his child, but paid the penalties of mortality.

Jenny Green Teeth

In Scotland, Ireland, Wales and Brittany, Jenny is a lovely water maiden who appears by lonely pools. She persuades handsome young men to bathe with her. As soon as they have taken off their clothing and dived in, she turns into a hideous cackling hag with the tail of a fish. Locked in her weed-choked embrace, they are dragged to the depths of the pond, to be seen no more.

Hydromancy: Water Divination in Still Waters

Traditionally, hydromancy was practised by the side of a dark silent pool or lake. The surface was used like a crystal ball. Images cast by the psyche would appear, offering wisdom and the answer to questions in the seeker's life.

Techniques for water scrying (seeing images in water) varied in different societies but the principle remains the same. Water magic is especially effective for matters of the heart, love affairs, family concerns and any issues prone to sudden variation.

Water is a constantly changing medium, its surface varying as the sun, a candle or the moon cast light on the surface, shadows fall or the wind ripples the surface. It is especially potent for capturing a series of fast-changing images that together may give the answer or a magical insight.

In Ancient Greece, wisdom was obtained from the sound of springs bubbling over stones, for example at Zeus's sacred grove at Dodona. A mirror held just below the surface of the water was another method employed to capture the rippling impressions. Often, too, in the classical world, young boys divined the future by gazing into bowls of pure water lit by burning torches. They studied in the changes in the flickering light and invoked the gods to provide a meaning.

Hindus and Arabs used ink poured into the palm of their hand into a shallow bowl, sometimes on to water, as a focus for inspired images. In French tradition, water used for scrying came from a pure spring. Saffron was burned during divination and a bowl of water was surrounded by ash boughs, vervain or periwinkle flowers when in season. Immediately after the magical working, the water was poured away on to soil where plants grew.

Modern Divination with Water

All these methods transfer easily into modern usage, though now the insight that can be attained is not attributed to remote deities who play games with human lives, but to our own deep unconscious wisdom or as the psychologist Jung suggested, from the collective wisdom of all mankind in all places and ages.

Although seers have used plain water as a focus, it is much easier to use a contrasting thicker liquid to create images against the clear backdrop. In the section on *Domestic Magic* (page 127), I describe how women in times past would see pictures in the soap suds as they washed the clothes in tub or at the riverside and suggested a modern method using liquid detergent in cold water.

Oils and Inks

Drop dark coloured oils, oil paint from an old tube or black ink on to the surface of water. See what images appear. If you use a medicine dropper or a very thin brush, you can watch an image build up and change. You can add two or three colours and find that they form different areas of the same image.

Because the oils are quite slow-moving you may be able to capture two or three images. Experiment to find the right medium for you and change the water if it becomes stained or the oils are no longer moving freely.

Interpret the images according to your own spontaneous insights rather than relying on lists of other people's images, however expert. In the section of this book on *Tea Leaf Reading* (page 425), I have made a number of suggested interpretations, but they are just my own ideas linked with traditional associations and you should use them only if they accord with your own imagery.

Once you have a core image in the oil or ink, for example a horse or a bird, the meaning may be instantly clear. If not, do not struggle to make sense of it, as your logical conscious process will actually block the knowledge that is there just beneath the surface. Change to another activity, preferably physical, perhaps walking, digging the garden or even sorting a drawer, so that your body and consciousness are occupied, leaving your inner powers to arrange the pictures and link the watery images with your present life and dilemmas.

ALISON'S OIL DIVINATION

Alison's boyfriend Martin had asked her to invest in his new water sports business, using the small house bequeathed to her by her grandmother as security. In the three years that they had been together Martin had tried a succession of jobs and enterprises that came to nothing. This time he insisted it would be different, but Alison was worried as her house was her only asset. Martin told Alison that if she could not trust him, there was no future together and he would be forced to move abroad to find work.

Alison used a black ink that she had left for 24 hours in the sun and new moonlight. Using a dropper, she gently added it to a clear cookware bowl filled with cold water, while concentrating on her whole relationship with Martin.

The first images was quite clearly a clown, the second which formed when she added another drop of ink was a tower falling down (an image Alison knew from the Tarot). Because the water was stained, Alison washed out the bowl and used fresh water and ink for the third image. This time, it flowed as a line, a road that divided into two paths.

Alison poured away the water, washed out the bowl and planted some seeds in the garden to replace the psychic energies she believed she had taken from the cosmos during her scrying. She then went for a walk and as her feet moved automatically across a large flat field, the images swirled before her eyes and revealed their story.

The clown was Martin, great fun to be with, never serious, always producing one excuse after another when life went wrong for him. Although he brought her great joy at times, she realized that she needed security in her life. The falling tower Alison saw as the collapse of her relationship. But the collapse was freeing her from a situation she had increasingly found restrictive, supporting Martin practically as well as financially as he lurched from one crisis to another. The highs were no longer enough to support the relationship, but it could not be ended without pain. The road divided two ways and Alison realized that she must let Martin go.

Water Divination by Sun and Moonlight

This method also offers a series of cameos rather than a single images. You do not add anything to the water but allow natural sources of light to cast beams and shadows on the water.

Moonlight

Wait until a clear moonlit right. The full moon is good for magical divination as it represents the full power of any endeavour. If you scry indoors, use a pale coloured bowl or large clear dish which although small, will initially reflect your face.

Place the bowl where it catches the moonlight and if there is not sufficient light, use a pure white candle to cast its shadows and flickering light on the water. You can also sit by a quiet pool or your garden pond so that you can see the moon reflected in the water.

As this is a particularly emotive from of divination, you may not need to ask a specific question. Scrying by moonlight is especially for love issues and for questions concerning inner happiness and development.

Rather than seeing definite pictures you may be aware of impressions, like scenes through a curtained window, momentarily clear, then a blur of light and shadow, story book pages blown by the wind. They may be dream-like in their quality, fabulous beasts, fairy castles, misty islands, but if you let them speak to you, then you will see how their world is but another perspective on your own.

PAULINE'S MOONLIGHT MAGIC

Pauline, a widow for several years, was a grandmother whose world revolved entirely around her grandchildren for whom she frequently babysat. Now she had met John, a widower of the same age, of whom she had become very fond. He asked her to accompany him around Australia for three months in his motorhome. Her daughter was furious and said that her mother was entering a second childhood and that she had no right to desert her grandchildren for so long. Pauline really wanted to go but she felt guilty at leaving her family who relied on her help and who had been supportive when she was first alone.

She filled a dark cookware bowl with water and lit a pale beeswax candle behind it so that the moonlight and candle light played on the water. She sat quietly at the open window of her bungalow as the flame flickered gently in the breeze. In the water she saw the shape of Ayers Rock and two figures walking up it together and then becoming one. Pauline had never been to Ayers Rock but suddenly felt a yearning to see it with John. She then saw a tall gate and realized that she was still behind it watching and only she could open the gate back into the world. Pauline decided to go with John and to visit Ayers Rock. Her daughter was unyielding but Pauline feels that she cannot live her life solely through her grandchildren, as one day she may become a burden to them if she has no world beyond them.

Magic cannot always give easy answers, nor promise that there will be a happy ending without pain, but it can alert us to the wider world beckoning

Sunlight

Scrying with sunlight on water is especially good for decisions that affect our outer lives and achievements and for decisions involving sudden change, especially involving others.

Go to a quiet lake or pool when the sun is almost overhead so that it reflects golden ripples into the water. You can also use sunlight through a large window on to a bowl of clear water indoors. Stand or sit so that you can see yourself reflected in the water, surrounded by a halo of sunlight. Concentrate on a question or issue that is occupying your attention or a decision that must be made.

Having imposed your image on the water, move back so that you can see the afterglow in the water. With a stick or your hands, ripple the water clockwise for positive energies and wait for it to clear. Use the patterns or pictures formed by the water to trigger the vision either within the water or your mind's eye.

Let the first images form and then ripple the water for a second time to create a new cameo. Continue to do this, developing the scene in your mind's eye and listening to any words that come spontaneously. Pour the golden water on to the garden and plant some yellow flowers where it falls.

If the images seem disjointed, write or draw them on pieces of paper. Put your pieces of paper face down in a circle and use a pendulum or a symbol that has meaning for you on a cord. Hold the pendulum over each piece of paper in turn until you get a strong vibration or a yes response. That is your first image. Continue, until the pendulum has ordered your visions and the story will make sense.

This method also works for divination with a close friend or partner for a joint issue or for a past life vision.

SAM'S RIPPLED POOL SCRYING

Sam was wondering whether to buy a new racing motor bike or to put down a deposit on a small starter home in a new development as his parents were urging him. He had a good job but his passion for motor bikes took a large amount of his resources and his parents and girlfriend felt it was time for him to grow up.

Sam sat by an ornamental lake in the park near his office with the sun making ripples through the willow trees. It was hot and Sam was drowsy, an ideal state for scrying. He saw a shoal of huge golden fish leaping out of the water and forming a perfect arc. They flew faster and faster until at last they merged with the sunbeams and a sudden shower of rain and ended as individual circling rainbows.

Then he saw himself holding on to a golden sunbeam, but as he tried to follow, he saw it was tethered to a stone in the water. He called for help and one of the fish dived back, cut the ropes free and Sam was soaring higher and faster, the experience he so loved on his racing bike. Sam did not need to arrange the images or use a pendulum to make sense of his story.

He knew that he had to be free, that he was not ready to settle in a starter home with his girlfriend and that he needed to change his whole life far beyond buying a new bike. Sam handed in his notice the next day and is taking a mechanic's course so he can join a racing team. On his way back to the office, he noticed how dark the water was and that there was not a single fish in the pond.

INDEX